THE NEW CAMBRIDGE HISTORY
OF INDIA

The politics of India since Independence

THE NEW CAMBRIDGE HISTORY OF INDIA

General editor GORDON JOHNSON
Director, Centre of South Asian Studies, University of
Cambridge, and Fellow of Selwyn College

Associate editors C. A. BAYLY
Reader in Modern Indian History, University of
Cambridge, and Fellow of St Catharine's College

and JOHN F. RICHARDS
Professor of History, Duke University

Although the original *Cambridge History of India*, published between 1922 and 1937, did much to formulate a chronology for Indian history and describe the administrative structures of government in India, it has inevitably been overtaken by the mass of new research published over the last fifty years.

Designed to take full account of recent scholarship and changing conceptions of South Asia's historical development, *The New Cambridge History of India* will be published as a series of short, self-contained volumes, each dealing with a separate theme and written by a single person. Within an overall four-part structure, thirty complementary volumes in uniform format will be published during the next five years. As before, each will conclude with a substantial bibliographical essay designed to lead non-specialists further into the literature.

The four parts planned are as follows:

I The Mughals and their Contemporaries.
II Indian States and the Transition to Colonialism.
III The Indian Empire and the Beginnings of Modern Society.
IV The Evolution of Contemporary South Asia.

A list of individual titles in preparation will be found at the end of the volume.

THE NEW CAMBRIDGE HISTORY OF INDIA

IV·1

The politics of India since Independence

PAUL R. BRASS

PROFESSOR OF POLITICAL SCIENCE AND
SOUTH ASIAN STUDIES
UNIVERSITY OF WASHINGTON

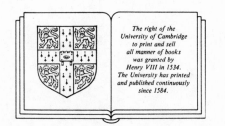

The right of the
University of Cambridge
to print and sell
all manner of books
was granted by
Henry VIII in 1534.
The University has printed
and published continuously
since 1584.

CAMBRIDGE UNIVERSITY PRESS

CAMBRIDGE

NEW YORK   PORT CHESTER

MELBOURNE   SYDNEY

Published by the Press Syndicate of the University of Cambridge
The Pitt Building, Trumpington Street, Cambridge CB2 1RP
40 West 20th Street, New York, NY 10011–4211, USA
10 Stamford Road, Oakleigh, Victoria 3166, Australia

First published 1990
Reprinted 1991

Printed in Great Britain by Redwood Press Limited, Melksham, Wiltshire

British Library cataloguing in publication data

Brass, Paul R. (Paul Richard), 1936–
The politics of India since Independence. –
(The New Cambridge history of India: IV, 1).
1. India (Republic). Politics, history.
1 Title.
320.954.

Library of Congress cataloguing in publication data

Brass, Paul R.
The politics of India since Independence / by Paul R. Brass.
p.   cm. – (The New Cambridge history of India: IV, 1).
Bibliography.
ISBN 0 521 26613 0
1. India – Politics and government – 1947–.
1. Title. II. Series.
DS436.N47 1987 pt. 4, vol. 1.
[DS480.84]
320.954–dc20   89–7350 CIP

ISBN 0 521 26613 0 (hardback)
ISBN 0 521 39651 4 (paperback)

CE

For my favorite kibbutznikim

Frances   Maida

Amir   Raan

Naava   Taal

Omri

CONTENTS

FIGURES AND TABLES

FIGURES

TABLES

PREFACE

Over the years, several friends have urged me to extend my work on Indian politics beyond my primary interest in north India and the Punjab to write a general work on *The Politics of India*. About ten years ago, I began such a book, but never completed it. The definite decision to write this book was made during my sabbatical leave at the University of Cambridge in 1983, when Gordon Johnson, John Richards, and Chris Bayly invited me to contribute to the New Cambridge History of India series.

The book builds upon my own work of the past 27 years on Indian politics, ethnicity and nationalism, and political economy, as well as that of my colleagues who have written on these subjects during the past three decades. The central theme concerns the consequences of increasing efforts by the country's national leaders to centralize power, decision making, and control of economic resources in one of the most culturally diverse and socially fragmented agrarian societies in the world. These centralizing drives, intensified in the post-Nehru era, have had increasingly contrary effects. The effectiveness of political organizations has eroded, ethnic, religious, caste, and other cultural and regional conflicts have heightened, and the ability of the central government to implement in the states and localities economic plans and programs designed in New Delhi has declined. These consequences suggest the existence of a systemic crisis in the Indian polity which will not be easily resolved. I have, however, argued that alternative paths towards such a resolution exist within Indian political and economic thought and political practices and that an alternative leadership may yet arise to seek such a resolution, basing itself on India's own traditions.

I began work on this study in 1986, but was not able to devote full time to it until my sabbatical year, 1987–1988. My debts begin in Seattle where my colleagues, David J. Olson, then Chairman of the Political Science department, and Frank Conlon, Chairman of the

South Asian Studies program in the Jackson School of International
Studies, helped secure me professional leave.

My sabbatical year and the summer of 1988 were divided among
three places, each of which offered opportunities to work on this
project as well as pleasant distractions. From October through
January, I was Associate Director of Research at the Centre
Nationale de la Recherche Scientifique in Paris, where my principal intellectual and professional connections were with the fine
group of South Asian scholars at the Centre d'Etudes de l'Inde et de
l'Asie du Sud. For the time in Paris to do what I wished, I want
especially to thank Jean Luc Domenach, director of the Centre
d'Etudes et de Recherches Internationales de la Fondation Nationale des Sciences Politiques, and Eric Meyer, director of the Centre
d'Etudes de l'Inde et de l'Asie du Sud. And for fraternity and
hospitality in Paris Jean Alphonse Bernard and Fazilé Ibrahim
Bernard, Violette and Philippe Graff, Claude and Piyali Markovits,
Alice Thorner, and Anne Vergati. I appreciated also the good
fellowship of Marc Gaborieau, Jean Claude Galey, Christiane
Hurtig, Raymond Jamous, Marie-Louise Reiniche, Henri Stern,
and Francis Zimmerman.

From February through June 1988 I was the Lester Martin Fellow
at the Truman Institute for the Advancement of Peace, Hebrew
University of Jerusalem. In Jerusalem, Shmuel and Shulamit Eisenstadt and Reuven Kahane especially provided me with a cordial
welcome and friendship. Conversations with Naomi Chazan also
were always lively and stimulating. During my five months in
Jerusalem, I was able to bring the manuscript almost to the point of
completion.

The first draft was completed in the extraordinarily fine settings
of the Rockefeller Foundation's Bellagio Study and Conference
Center, Lake Como, Italy. Here I want to thank the Cellis, Gianna
and Roberto, Susan Garfield, and the staff of the Center for their
many kindnesses and general cordiality, and for providing the
facilities to make productivity inevitable and virtually effortless.
And my thanks also to the convivial company who shared the
residency with me in August–September 1988.

Final revisions on the manuscript were done upon my return to
Seattle in the Autumn quarter, where it became all work and no

play. My revisions were aided greatly by comments from my good friends and colleagues, Bhagwan Dua, Akhil Gupta, James Manor, Myron Weiner, and John Wood. Irene Joshi, our University of Washington South Asia Librarian, provided invaluable assistance in helping me find reference sources for the final revisions, a task she has performed on countless occasions in the earlier stages of this and other projects of mine.

My debts, however, in a work of this sort which is based on my whole previous career of research and writing on Indian politics, go far beyond the persons whose names are mentioned above. Many of those debts are acknowledged in the footnotes and bibliography. Beyond specific references to the work of my colleagues in the field, however, there is much more, the sense of belonging to an international community of scholars and friends whose standards are high and among whom there is mutual respect.

Finally, once again in Jerusalem and in Israel, personal support and love came from those whose names are mentioned on the dedication page. My thanks especially to Frances and Maida and greetings to the lovely people of Kibbutz Maoz Chayim and Kibbutz Neve Eitan.

Seattle   PAUL R. BRASS
February 27, 1989

ABBREVIATIONS

AD   Akali Dal
AGP   Asom Gana Parishad
AIADMK   Anna Dravida Munnetra Kazagham
AMU   Aligarh Muslim University
BJP   Bharatiya Janata Party
BKD   Bharatiya Kranti Dal
BLD   Bharatiya Lok Dal
CLM   Commissioner for Linguistic Minorities
CPI   Communist Party of India
CPM   Communist Party of India (Marxist)
CPML   Communist Party of India (Marxist–Leninist)
CPP   Congress Parliamentary Party
CSRE   Crash Scheme for Rural Employment
DM   District Magistrate
DMK   Dravida Munnetra Kazagham
DPAP   Drought Prone Areas Program
EPW   *Economic and Political Weekly*
HYVP   High Yielding Varieties Program
IAAP   Intensive Agricultural Area Program
IADP   Intensive Agricultural District Program
IAS   Indian Administrative Service
ICS   Indian Civil Service
IPS   Indian Police Service
IRDP   Integrated Rural Development Program
JNP   Janata Party
JP   Jayaprakash Narayan
LKD   Lok Dal
M. P.   Madhya Pradesh
MFAL   Marginal Farmers and Agricultural Laborers Agency
MP   Member of Parliament
NNO   Naga Nationalist Organization
NREP   National Rural Employment Program

ABBREVIATIONS

PIREP	Pilot Intensive Rural Employment Project
PM	Prime Minister
PR	President's Rule
RLEGS	Rural Labor Employment Guarantee Scheme
RSS	Rashtriya Swayamsevak Sangh
SFDA	Small Farmers Development Agency
SP	Superintendent of Police
SSP	Samyukta Socialist Party
TDP	Telugu Desam Party
TPS	Telangana Praja Samiti
U. P.	Uttar Pradesh

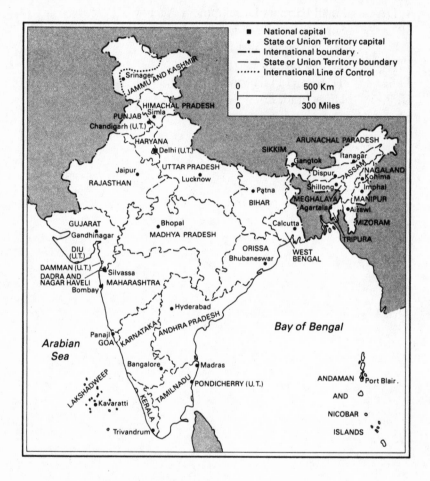

Political map of India
Based on Ashok K. Dutt and M. Margaret Geib, *Atlas of South Asia*
(Boulder, CO; Westview Press, 1987).

CHAPTER 1

INTRODUCTION: CONTINUITIES AND DISCONTINUITIES BETWEEN PRE- AND POST-INDEPENDENCE INDIA

India arrived at Independence after a long struggle and with a multiplicity of heritages and legacies which influenced its post-Independence course in complex ways. Among the legacies were the long experience of British rule itself, which extended back more than two centuries, and of the various institutions, ideas, and practices introduced by the British. Of particular importance at Independence was the Government of India Act of 1935, which was the most recent framework of rule under which the country was governed and which included a considerable measure of responsible government for Indians in the provinces. A second legacy was that provided by the shared experience of those Indians who participated in or identified with the nationalist movement and its great leaders. A third was the existing social order, the social structure and social conflicts which surrounded and influenced political movements, ideas, and practices. Finally, there was the great body of traditions and cultural practices which preceded British rule in a civilization of great depth, complexity, and diversity.

THE CONSTITUTION AND THE COLONIAL LEGACY

In some ways, it is possible to view Independence and the adoption in the early years after Independence of a new Constitution as another stage in the evolution of India towards representative government in a process that dates back to the Indian Councils Act of 1861 and continues through the Morley–Minto Reforms of 1909, the Montagu–Chelmsford Reforms of 1919, and the Government of India Act of 1935. At each of these reforms, the participation of

Indians in the central and state legislatures and in the executive councils was increased and the franchise was extended to ever larger numbers of people.

It has often been noted especially that there was a considerable degree of continuity between the Government of India Act and the Constitution of India. The features of continuity included the adoption of a federal system of government with three legislative lists of powers to be exercised exclusively by the Union, exclusively by the states, or concurrently, and a combination of a considerable degree of provincial autonomy with extensive powers left to the Center,[1] including emergency powers which made it possible to convert the federal system into a unitary one. Similarly, the Constitution of independent India is federal, but contains strong unitary features, including a strong central government which retains not only extensive emergency powers but the residuary powers of the Union as well. The states are normally supposed to function autonomously, but the Center retains the ultimate power to control, even take over the direct administration, of the states under certain conditions.

In several respects, however, the Constitution of India makes a sharp break with the British colonial past, though not with British political practices. Firstly, the Constitution adopts in total the Westminster form of parliamentary government rather than the mixed parliamentary-bureaucratic authoritarian system which actually existed in India. Secondly, fundamental rights were included in the Constitution of India, but not in the Government of India Act of 1935. Thirdly, the Constitution introduced universal adult suffrage.

The Constitution also contains some unique features that reflect a desire to depart from strict British parliamentary practices and to introduce into the charter of the country a program of social and economic reform. Most notable in this respect is the presence in the Constitution of a list of both Fundamental Rights of the People and Directive Principles, a combination of protections for the people

[1] "Center" is the most common term used to refer to the Union government in New Delhi. It carries the same sense as in the United States practice of referring to the national government in Washington, D.C. as the "federal government". However, in addition, the term is also used sometimes to allude to actions and decisions which flow from leadership circles in New Delhi as opposed to the State capitals.

against the encroachments of state authority with directives to the state to introduce specified reforms to make those rights effective. This peculiar combination, however, was later to lead to a great struggle between the government and parliament, on the one side, and the judiciary, on the other, as to which have priority, rights or directive principles.

The simultaneous presence in the Constitution of these two sets of principles and guidelines reflected some of the tensions which existed in the minds of the leaders of the country at Independence. While they respected the British–American traditions of parliamentary practice and personal liberty, some, particularly Nehru, also were influenced by the Soviet model and the Socialist traditions of Western Europe and Britain as well. They wished to extend the liberties of the people of India, but they wished also to bring about rapid social and economic change and they wanted no obstacles to stand in the way of their so doing.

There was also the idea that fundamental rights were not enough, would not be meaningful in a land where the mass of the people were extremely poor, illiterate, tied to traditions, and perceived as exploited by merchants, moneylenders, and landlords. It was feared that such rights might be used to protect the exploiters rather than the exploited. In a society based on hierarchy, caste inequality and blatant discrimination, equality of opportunity such as existed in Britain and the United States would not be enough to provide the means for enhancing the well-being of the poor. Instead, special measures would be required, such as reservations of places in representative institutions, government agencies, and public institutions for backward and disadvantaged classes and groups. There was a desire also not merely to protect the rights of the people, but to eliminate certain features of social practice, such as untouchability and *begar* or forced labor, which were explicitly abolished in the Constitution. And, finally, there was a desire to limit the role of private enterprise in India and a feeling that the protection of property provided in the Constitution might prevent the Indian state from attaining goals of economic justice, which some thought could be achieved only through the establishment of social ownership of the means of production, then identified with state ownership. So, the Constitution recognized the right to hold property as a

3

fundamental right, but also included directive principles of policy which stated that the material resources of the country must be distributed and operated in such a way as to promote the common good and avoid excessive concentration of wealth.

Those who argue that India's Independence should not be seen as marking a great break with the past also point to the preservation of such characteristic features of British autocratic rule in India as the Indian Civil Service (ICS), renamed as the Indian Administrative Service (IAS) at Independence. The small, enormously powerful, elite cadre of ICS officers was seen as the "steel frame" that had held the British Empire in India together. Authority and responsibility were concentrated in their hands in the districts, where they acted simultaneously as heads of the administration and of the judicial institutions, maintaining law and order and collecting the revenue. Yet, the leaders of independent India felt the need for maintaining that "steel frame" to help preserve order in the country, which was undergoing such turmoil at Independence. It was not long, however, before a contradiction was perceived between the predominant functions of the old ICS and the developmental goals of the independent Indian state, which required a different type of administrative structure. Since Independence, there have been numerous attempts to devise structures of local self-government, administration, and development institutions more suited for these development goals, which would also combine popular participation at the local level without undermining the older structures of state authority which the leadership of the country was unwilling to give up.

At Independence, therefore, the leaders of the country quite self-consciously maintained many features of the colonial legacy. They also adopted some new features derived from the political practices of Great Britain and the United States. However, most of the specific features of the Constitution of India and the administrative structure retained or adopted at Independence represented borrowings from abroad, which had to be adapted to the social structure, traditions, and practices of an entirely different society.

SOCIAL STRUCTURE: THE COMMUNAL AND
CASTE BASES OF INDIAN POLITICS

It was commonly argued by the British rulers of India that parliamentary democracy was unsuited to a society intensely divided into religious and other communal groupings whose social structure also was imbued with an ideology of hierarchy rather than equality. The rise of the Muslim League and the Pakistan movement, which led to the bitter catastrophe of partition of the subcontinent was seen by such persons as proof of the inherent incompatibility of Western parliamentary institutions and Indian communal realities. Indian nationalists, however, argued strongly against such ideas and insisted that Hindu–Muslim communalism itself was a British creation and that, left to themselves, Hindus and Muslims would work together in a secular political order and would divide internally on economic and class, rather than religious lines. The British, operating on a set of assumptions that treated Hindus and Muslims as distinct peoples, introduced mechanisms, notably separate electorates, which served to keep them apart. At Independence, however, the framers of the Constitution eliminated separate electorates and established only general electorates in which members of all castes, religions, and communities would vote.

It was also argued that caste Hindus and untouchable and other low castes could hardly be expected to work together as equals in a democratic political order, that the former would maintain the rigidity of traditional hierarchies and caste discriminations which would prevent the poor and disadvantaged low castes from participating effectively in politics. Congress leaders themselves were painfully aware that they had been unable before Independence to recruit successfully most low caste and disadvantaged groups. So, at Independence, though they resisted any efforts to create separate electorates for the low castes, the Constitution and government policies instituted mechanisms and procedures to ensure their full participation as equal citizens in the new order. These mechanisms and procedures included reservation of seats in the legislatures and other bodies, the mainentance of a list of low caste groups on a schedule (hence the name Scheduled Castes) entitling them to special privileges and preferential policies of all sorts, the abolition of untouchability, and the like.

The division between caste Hindus and untouchables was not the only kind of problem posed by the caste order for the effective functioning of parliamentary institutions in post-Independence India. In most villages in India, one or two large elite castes control most of the land and other resources, constituting what anthropologists call "dominant castes." After Independence, these dominant castes often were able to control and deliver the votes of their clients among the low castes, who were considered to constitute "vote banks."

Divisions among the elite and middle status land-controlling castes in large parts of India also existed at Independence. In some parts of India, particularly Tamil Nadu and Maharashtra, non-Brahman movements had been launched to displace the dominant Brahman castes in those states from their disproportionate control over jobs in the public services and other advantages in society. Backward caste leaders had argued before Independence that their place was insecure under a parliamentary system which the elite castes could turn to their advantage and that they too, like the Scheduled Castes, required special protections. Since Independence, the spread of conflict between these elite and backward caste groups has become a major source of social tension in many other states of the Union besides Tamil Nadu and Maharashtra and has precipitated considerable violence in some states such as Bihar and Gujarat.

These issues of Hindu–Muslim communal relations, of the integration of the low castes as effective participants in a democratic political order, and of caste conflict between the backward castes and the elite castes have persisted throughout the post-Independence period up the the present and have posed recurring challenges to the maintenance of an integrated society, an equalitarian politics, and non-violent mechanisms of conflict resolution.

IDEAS DERIVING FROM THE NATIONALIST MOVEMENT

Three-quarters of a century of thought and struggle over defining the Indian nation, over freeing the country from alien occupation, and over the desirable shape of the social and economic order in a future independent India had provided the nationalist leadership at Independence with a set of ideas and goals that helped to structure their responses to the problems of governing the newly independent country. At the top of all their goals, the *sine qua non* for everything else was an abiding faith in and determination to preserve the national unity and integrity of the country against all potential internal and external threats to it. The very fact that this first priority, the center of the dreams of the Congress nationalists, had to be sacrificed at Independence itself, with the partition of the country, reenforced the determination of the leaders never to make such a sacrifice again.

Since Independence, therefore, two strict rules have been followed in all dealings with dissident domestic ethnic, religious, linguistic, and cultural group demands. The first is that no secessionist movement will be entertained and that any group which takes up a secessionist stance will, while it is weak, be ignored and treated as illegitimate, but, should it develop significant strength, be smashed, with armed force if necessary. All secessionist demands in post-Independence India which acquired any significant strength have been treated in this way, especially in the northeastern part of the country and lately in the Punjab. Secessionist demands have also been headed off in such places as Tamil Nadu in the 1950s and in Kashmir from time to time by the clear understanding that force would be used against the groups who promoted such demands if they persisted.

The second rule has been a prohibition against the concession of demands for any form of political recognition of a religious community. Muslims, Sikhs, and other religious minorities are free to preserve their own personal law, to practice their religion as they see fit, to seek protection for their language and culture, but not to demand either a separate state for their community even within the Indian Union or separate electorates or any form of proportional representation in elected or appointed government bodies.

In the transformation of the Congress from a mass movement claiming to represent the entire nation into a political party engaged in free and open competition with other parties for dominance in a democratic political system, however, the Congress leaders had to

7

make a number of changes and compromises in relation to other groups whose demands were neither secessionist nor communal religious. They had to decide how to treat dissident movements and forces of all sorts. During the Independence struggle, Congress leaders had shown little tolerance for any kind of dissent which seemed in any way to threaten the unity of the movement against the British authorities. Yet, the leaders themselves knew that some groups, despite their own desires to the contrary, had been left out of the movement and that some potentially divisive problems had been put aside and now had to be dealt with. In dealing with internal and external dissident forces, the leaders of the Indian National Congress have followed hegemonic policies of absorption in relation to some groups, have deliberately set out to destroy others, and have adopted tolerant and conciliatory stances in relation to still others.

Scheduled Castes had largely been left out of the Congress during the nationalist movement and its leaders set out to rectify this situation quickly after Independence by such measures as giving Dr. Ambedkar, the great untouchable leader, a central role in the Constitution-making process, by seeking to provide other Scheduled Caste persons with positions as ministers in the central and state governments, and by pursuing a variety of preferential policies designed to improve their social standing and ameliorate their economic deprivations.

Other groups, such as the former landlords and princes, were treated quite differently. They were considered collaborators with the British, representatives of an outdated feudal order, and exploiters of the peasantry who provided the bulk of the political support for the Congress in the countryside. The Congress had, for the most part, avoided supporting direct class confrontations between the tenants and landlords in British-ruled India in order to preserve maximum unity in the fight against the British themselves. However, once Independence was achieved, the Congress governments in most states moved to expropriate the former princes and landlords through the passage of various land reform measures such as abolition of all intermediaries between the cultivator and the state and land ceilings legislation.

In relation to political opposition groups, the Congress was prepared to allow free and open competition. This did not, however, stop the Congress from adopting quite ruthless political tactics to defeat such early opposition parties as the Socialists who split from the Congress in 1948, the left wing of the Communist party in the 1960s, and, from time to time, adopting repressive measures against parties considered to be communal, both Hindu and Muslim. Moreover, in general, the Congress has sought to absorb political dissident movements it could not defeat in the electoral arena, the terms always being that any political group so absorbed must give up all vestiges of an independent political organization and its members join the party as individuals.

The Congress leaders also arrived at Independence ready to tolerate considerable internal factionalism provided no groups formed permanently with ideological goals that differed from the official Congress policy. And it was always clear before and after Independence that there was a "High Command" of Congress leaders, who exercised final authority in the country in relation to state and local factional conflicts that threatened to damage the party in any large part of the country.

The Congress had arrived at Independence largely by pursuing a non-violent path. Terrorist groups, though sometimes acknowledged as true patriots, were not condoned within the Congress. Nor did it tolerate the military style of nationalism promoted by the great Bengali political leader, Subhas Chandra Bose, who resigned from the Congress presidency in 1939 in the face of total opposition to him and his policies from Mahatma Gandhi.

On the other hand, Gandhi's tactics of non-violent resistance to untruth and injustice, which included a variety of individual and mass protest techniques, had become embedded in Congress ideology and practice. Some even argued in the Constituent Assembly that *satyagraha*[2] was a fundamental right of the people. Other Congress leaders, however, argued that now that India was independent and functioning with a competitive parliamentary system, such techniques no longer had a legitimate place. In practice, the Congress governments at the Center since Independence have followed an ambiguous policy towards such extra-

---

[2] *Satyagraha*: Gandhi's term for active, non-violent persistence in the pursuit of truth and justice in the face of the exercise of alien or unjust authority.

constitutional, non-violent forms of protest. On the one hand, they have often been allowed; on the other hand, the Constitution armed the state with several measures, most notably, preventive detention, which allowed the government of the day to deal effectively, even in advance, with any protest that threatened to become violent or was too inconvenient for the ruling party to tolerate. This exemplifies the adaptation of parliamentarism and constitutionalism in India to the particular practices of Indian society – here, in the institutionalization of a process of extra-constitutional confrontation between the state and dissident groups in which both sides use as a matter of course measures that are uncommon in Western parliamentary systems.

THE LEADING IDEAS OF THE NATIONALIST ELITE AT INDEPENDENCE

The leading ideas of the nationalist elite at Independence can be summarized under these headings: sovereignty, unity, order, a strong state, secularism, democracy and parliamentarism, economic self-sufficiency and the need for social and economic reform. The nationalist leaders at Independence were determined to declare for all the world to hear and for any internal dissidents who had a different view that India was to be a sovereign independent republic. In the Constituent Assembly, speakers denounced and ridiculed Winston Churchill who had cast doubts on the sovereign representative character of the Assembly, invited the leaders of the Muslim League to join its deliberations but insisted that if they did not the Assembly meant to speak for the nation without them, and warned the former princes that they had no divine right to rule any longer and that power in India now came from the people and its representatives in the Constituent Assembly of the country. Other speakers in the Assembly also saw India's sovereignty and independence in terms of the emergence of India not merely as an ordinary independent state but as the new leader of Asia, indeed of the world.

Unity was the second assumption of the nationalist elite. They had reluctantly accepted the partition and communal division of the country but were not reconciled to it. Many speakers in the Constituent Assembly expressed the belief that the unity of India would ultimately be restored. The partition experience also led the nationalist leaders, some of whom had previously been sympathetic to some kinds of regional cultural and linguistic demands, to reject sharply in the Constituent Assembly and in the early years after Independence any other potential division that seemed to threaten the country's unity, such as a north–south division implied in the Dravidistan slogan of the Tamil regional nationalist party, the DMK, or even the linguistic reorganization of states, which had been an implicit part of the Congress program since the 1920s.

The nationalist leaders had always feared the potential for violence and disorder in Indian society. Gandhi's non-violence was not something that simply arose out of an indigenous tradition of peace and spirituality, but rather was a tactic which acknowledged the enormous potential for violence which existed in a highly fragmented and culturally heterogeneous society. The disintegration of public order in the Punjab, in Calcutta, and in the national capital of Delhi itself, whose streets were littered with dead bodies during the riots that accompanied partition, strengthened the determination of the nationalist elite to enforce authority in independent India, to instill discipline in its people, and to maintain order at all costs. That determination was also applied to any efforts on the part of revolutionary leaders to promote violent revolution in any part of India, a major instance of that determination being the suppression of the Communist-led insurrection in the Telengana region of Andhra between 1947 and 1951.

The early nationalist leaders believed wholeheartedly in democracy and parliamentarism. They wanted the British out, but were prepared to adopt their institutions. The leaders of the Constituent Assembly studied carefully both British and American political institutions and practices and adopted the conventions of the British parliamentary system as well as some features of American political practice such as the establishment of a Supreme Court with powers of judicial review. Advocates of the development of a set of political institutions and practices derived from Indian traditions were notable for their absence in the Constituent Assembly, where Gandhian ideas of non-party government, decentralization of power and authority, and the adoption of village self-government hardly challenged the predominant consensus which favored rather the adoption and adaptation of foreign political models.

The nationalist leaders also felt strongly that political and economic independence were interrelated, that India could not retain control over its political destiny if it remained economically dependent on Britain and the other industrialized states of the West. Economic independence and self-sufficiency were associated with industrialization, which required foreign economic aid in the short term, but which would soon enable India to free itself from dependence on foreign imports and from further need for foreign aid.[3] These considerations were behind the drive which was launched especially at the beginning of the Third Five Year Plan in 1961 to create a massive industrial base in the country and to promote the policy of import substitution to eliminate India's dependence on foreign countries, particularly in the durable capital goods sector of the economy.

The nationalist elite held the view that India's social and economic progress had been retarded by centuries of British rule, that the country had been kept agrarian, its industrial potential arrested, its people kept backward, illiterate, and bound to outmoded forms of agricultural production. Consequently, it was necessary and urgent for the state itself to undertake the modernization of Indian society and to institute economic reforms that would free the country from feudalism and archaic social practices. These ideas implied centralized economic planning and direct state intervention through legislation for the removal of institutions and practices – such as landlordism, untouchability, and the giving of dowry – deemed unsuited to a modern state and society in a modern world.

Secularism was another widely-shared and deeply-felt value of the Indian nationalist elite at Independence. Secularism had negative and positive aspects. It meant that communalism and political demands of any sort based on religion would no longer be tolerated in independent India. It meant that separate electorates had to be replaced by joint electorates so that all communities could discuss issues of economic well-being and advancement on a common

[3] See especially on this point Baldev Raj Nayar, *The Modernization Imperative and Indian Planning* (Delhi: Vikas, 1972), pp. 99, 125.

ground. Positively, it meant that every cultural group in India was to be entitled to promote, preserve, and protect its cultural life, its language and script. Most important, it involved an assertion that nationalism and the nation, based on the loyalty of individuals to the state before their community, was the basis for modern politics and not religion, the deceptive slogan of the Pakistan elite.

All these leading ideas held by the nationalist elite converged to provide overwhelming justification in their minds of the need for a strong, centralized state. Once the partition decision had been reached, in the midst of deliberations in the Constituent Assembly on a federation that would be flexible enough to accommodate the Muslim-majority as well as the Hindu-majority provinces, discussions in the Assembly took an immediate about-face in which speaker after speaker emphasized the imperative necessity for India to have a "strong Centre" and a "strong State." The state was perceived as the instrument which would establish India's sovereign independent presence in the world, would preserve its unity against foreign enemies and internal secessionists, ensure authority, order, and discipline in a society perceived as always on the brink of disorder and violence, promote economic development through centralized planning which would bring India out of the backwardness of agrarian life and free it of a social order dominated by feudal institutions and practices and by religious superstitions, and make it possible for Indians also to maintain an effective parliamentary system.

INDIA'S POLITICAL CULTURE: RHETORIC VERSUS REALITY

It was commonly remarked at Independence that Indian leaders were bent upon adopting the political conventions, ideas, and practices of Western democratic societies, but that those institutions and ideas could not be separated from the societies from which they had organically evolved. India, it was argued, had an entirely different social order not suited for parliamentary institutions and egalitarian ideologies and would do better to search its own traditions for institutions more in consonance with its own culture. Those arguments were largely ignored in the Constituent Assembly, even though some of them came from Gandhi himself and his followers, mostly outside the Assembly. It became apparent very quickly after Independence, however, that fundamental trans- formations were occurring in the actual functioning of the institu- tions and practices borrowed from the West in which adjustments were made that reflected indigenous cultural and behavioral pat- terns, but without any conscious modeling on its own traditions.

Some observers attempted to encapsulate the process of contra- diction and adjustment that was going on by arguing that there were several "idioms" or "cultures" in fundamental conflict with each other – a modern or Western idiom, centred in the ideas of the nationalist elite and in the institutions in Delhi, a traditional idiom or culture, rooted in the kin, caste, and communal relations of village, locality, and province, and a "saintly" idiom characteristic- ally Indian, associated with Gandhi and his disciples involving selfless devotion to constructive work for the good of society and immune from the mimicking of foreign models or from contami- nation by the archaic superstitions and feudal practices of Indian society.[4]

These useful attempts to categorize the basic contradictions between Indian politics and society, however, left many adjust- ments, adaptations, and everyday practices not satisfactorily explained. Little attention, for example, was paid to indigenous traditions of princely rule and their effects upon contemporary political practices, demonstrated every day in the morning and evening *durbars* or audiences held by every prominent politician in the land, in the duty of prominent people to provide support and protection for their clients, in the responsibility of those political leaders who achieved power and control over public resources to distribute them lavishly to their followers, and in the practice of dynastic succession to leadership in India.

It soon became evident also that there was a massive contradiction between the rhetoric of Indian public discourse and the reality of political practice, which expressed itself in many forms. For example, although the secular ideology of the Indian National

[4] Myron Weiner, "India's Two Political Cultures," in Myron Weiner, *Political Change in South Asia* (Calcutta: Firma K. L. Mukhapadhyay, 1963), and W. H. Morris-Jones, *The Government and Politics of India* (London: Hutchinson University Library, 1964, ch. 2).

Congress became dominant politically in India after Independence and the newly independent Indian state proclaimed secularism as the official state ideology, the post-Independence Indian state leadership has nevertheless felt compelled to make official distinctions between the Hindu population and the non-Hindu populations of the country by such measures as the passage of the Hindu Code Act, which established a uniform civil code for all "Hindus" (including Sikhs) in the country, while leaving Muslims with their own system of Personal Law. It has often also been alleged that many of the politicians of the country who proclaim their adherence to secularism as a state ideology actually harbor Hindu communal sentiments. The persistence of explicitly Hindu political organizations and movements in contemporary Indian politics also has been widely noted.

One of the great, enduring games of political analysts of India has been to assert the tacit dominance and to predict the ultimate emergence of a militant Hindu nationalist political category which will overwhelm the Indian state and establish its mastery over the Indian population. Since the late nineteenth century, there have been numerous movements of "Hindu" political mobilization, which have taken a variety of forms. These include the Gaurakshini (Cow Protection) Sabhas formed in the 1890s, which have agitated for laws preventing cow slaughter in India from time to time and launched a major mass movement as recently as the 1960s; the movement to promote the development and spread of a standardized Hindi language written in the Devanagari script, rather than Urdu in the Persian–Arabic script, as the official language of education and administration in north India and ultimately as the official language of the country; and the Hindu Mahasabha which worked to create a Hindu political community and to define the Indian nation through symbols drawn exclusively from "Hindu" texts, beliefs, and practices and from non-Muslim history.

This Hindu "revivalism" or militant Hindu nationalism has persisted up to the present and has manifested itself in various political organizations and movements and politicized religious movements. Such organizations and movements include: the Rashtryiya Swayamsevak Sangh (RSS), a Hindu "cultural" organization organized into cells, whose members practice martial arts, and which promotes also an exclusively Hindu definition of the Indian nation; the Jan Sangh, originally the main political party offshoot of the RSS, but now a rump of quite extreme anti-Muslim supporters of Hindu nationalism; the Bharatiya Janata party (BJP), the more broadly-based descendant of the original Jan Sangh; and such other organizations as the Vishwa Hindu Parishad, which is currently engaged in a campaign to "liberate" alleged Hindu religious sites from their occupation by Muslim mosques built on top of them.

There is also presumed to exist a Hindu "vote" in India which can be mobilized for the sake of national unity against the secessionist or otherwise excessive demands of minorities such as Sikhs and Muslims. It has been noted that in the 1984 parliamentary elections, held in the aftermath of the assassination of Mrs. Gandhi by two of her Sikh bodyguards, the issue of national unity was communalized and made into the central issue in Rajiv Gandhi's landslide election victory.[5]

Nevertheless, there remains in India today considerable ambiguity concerning the use of the word "Hindus" to define any clearly demarcated group of people in the subcontinent and considerable doubt about the existence of a Hindu political community.[6] On the one hand, the historic problem of a split between so-called "caste" Hindus and untouchables persists in contemporary Indian politics, as do divisions among the "caste" Hindus themselves. On the other hand, there has also been an historic tendency to subsume Sikhs, Jains, and others in the "Hindu" fold. While this tendency is bitterly resented by some groups, such as most Sikhs especially, and is considered to be part of the absorptive quality of "Hinduism," it also suggests the continued indefiniteness of its religious, social, and political boundaries.

Revivalist or militant Hinduism nevertheless remains a pervasive and politically important presence in contemporary Indian politics. The tendency among militant nationalist organizations such as the

[5] Ranbir Singh, Pattern of Support Base of Congress Party in Haryana, unpublished paper, UCLA Conference on Parties & Elections, June, 1987, and Paul R. Brass, *Caste, Faction and Party in Indian Politics*, Vol. II: *Election Studies* (Delhi: Chanakya Publications, 1985), pp. 318–321.

[6] For the development of the use of the terms "Hindu" and "Hinduism" in modern India, see Robert E. Frykenberg, "The Emergence of Modern 'Hinduism' as a Concept and as an Institution: A Reappraisal with Special Reference to South India, in Gunther Sontheimer and Hermann Kuke (eds.), *Hinduism Reconsidered* (Heidelberg: South Asia Institute, 1988), pp. 1–29.

RSS and the BJP to insist that Hindu and Indian are virtually interchangeable categories has spread beyond the organizational confines of these two organizations. Even more pervasive and subtle has been the more recent tendency to secularize the meaning of the term Hindu by going back to its earlier meaning of "native of India" and identifying India as the nation of Hindus without, however, eliminating from it all the religious associations which are offensive to true Muslim, Sikh, and other believers.

A second example of a contradiction between rhetoric and reality in contemporary Indian politics concerns the disjunction between the language of planning, equality, socialism, and social justice spoken by party leaders in the country and the practices of day-to-day politics. Immediately after Independence, the leading opposition parties were the Communists and the Socialists, promoting variants of the wholly Western ideologies associated with those labels. Yet, those ideologies bore little relation to the social structure of Indian society, which lacked the class distinctions and contradictions upon which the ideologies were based. None of the political parties in India proved able to imitate the European political party traditions of disciplined behavior in the legislatures to which they were elected. Instead, Indian politicians began early to display, indeed had been practicing at the local levels since the nineteenth century, a strong penchant for opportunistic behavior in pursuit of personal ambition to achieve high office and control public resources for personal advantage and for distribution to one's followers.

The reason for this persisting disjunction between public political party discourse and actual political practice, which render meaningful comparisons between Indian and western political parties difficult, is that the issues and social forces which impinge upon party politics in India today are entirely different from those which have confronted either contemporary or nineteenth century Europe and America. There are three such sets of issues, social forces, and aspects of social structure that contribute to the distinctiveness of Indian politics: the issues of control over agrarian resources, including control over land and the work force; social fragmentation; and center–locality relationships. The primary economic, social, and political resources in India today continue to be the land and its products and the primary struggles concern access to the inputs necessary to increase productivity and control over the produce from the land. Land being inherently a local resource and rural social classes being notoriously difficult to recruit into permanent extra-local organizations, the importance of land control and issues relating to it necessarily impart a local and personal character to politics. Governments in India may pass laws abolishing landlords and inter-mediaries, establishing land ceilings, and protecting tenants, but their implementation depends upon local patterns of domination and control by land controllers over land, resources, and people.

Those who get elected to state legislatures from rural constituencies in India themselves either come from important local land controlling communities or depend for support upon them. What matters most to such people is local influence with government departments that disperse resources for agriculture, adjudicate land matters, or control the local population, particularly the police. These local politicians do not care much for party manifestoes, policy pronouncements, and development goals. They will vote as disciplined members of ruling parties in the legislatures as long as such behavior gives them access to ministers in the state government who can control local resources and the local administration and as long as there is no better alternative. When there is a better alternative, particularly one that gives them a place in a ministry where they can exercise direct control themselves over local resources, they will defect and switch to another party or coalition.

The second great feature of Indian society that imparts a distinctive character to Indian politics is the social fragmentation associated with caste. Caste too, in some of its most fundamental aspects, permeates Indian politics with local and personal features. Success in elections in rural constituencies depends primarily upon the ability to establish a base in one of the locally dominant, land controlling castes and then combining that support with an effective approach to one or more other important local caste groups or a low caste group or the local Muslim minority. Influence in the bureaucracy and in public agencies generally depends upon personal networks of kinship and caste. Legislators and politicians generally who depend upon such local support bases and are themselves part of such personal networks again are not moved or inspired by party

18

manifestoes and pronouncements, but are moved by what benefits they can get to distribute to their supporters, friends, and relations.

These two great features of Indian political economy and social structure – land control and caste – also contribute to a third political characteristic that imparts distinctiveness to Indian politics, namely, the necessity for those who wish to build power in state and national contexts to maintain direct or indirect links with those who can control local structures of power. Since government now provides or controls the greatest share of external resources of use in the local environments and since government also can threaten the hold of powerful local groups through land laws or police harassment, it is equally important for locally powerful persons to maintain connections with those who wield power in the state and national governments. These relations once again do not concern ideology, policy, and programs but concern control over resources and people, protection from harassment by the bureaucracy and the police, and the trading of political support and votes for such resources, protection, and other services. It should hardly be surprising, therefore, that the public politics of Indian political parties and legislatures, which are modeled after the British pattern and in which a language familiar to students of European politics is spoken, should in fact be dominated by faction, personal and local interest networks, struggles over patronage and distribution of resources, and political opportunism.

Indian politics have lacked the ideological underpinnings of European political traditions. In common with American political traditions, however, there is a stong moral streak in Indian commentary on politics which is displayed in constant condemnation of the corruption of the politicians and the bureaucrats and of the relentless pursuit of power. Such moralism, usually drawing inspiration from Gandhian ideals, gives force from time to time to mass mobilizations to bring down the ruling party. However, these mobilizations have not so far been as effective as the recurrent reform movements which every now and then have transformed American institutions and political practices. Nor has it been possible for most political parties in India to adhere to a consistent ideology in the manner of many European parties which formulate manifestoes, whose programs they actually implement when they achieve power. Rather, Indian politics have been characterized by an all-pervasive instrumentalism which washes away party manifestoes, rhetoric, and effective implementation of policies in an unending competition for power, status, and profit.

If American political traditions have continued to emphasize the importance of limiting the role of the state while Western Europe has adopted the model of the welfare state and the Socialist countries the model of a socially transforming state, India has adopted the model of the state which exists for its own sake. It is a good in itself and the source of all goods. It exists to provide everything that Indians need and require: sovereignty, unity, welfare, jobs for all, social justice. It is the duty of the state and the holders of its offices, moreover, to provide these goods and services directly to the people, irrespective of any ideology or any notion of a broad common good. It is there to serve everybody's interests, not just an abstract "public interest." Of course, no state can serve everybody's interests and the Indian state has not succeeded in doing so. The contradictions between the foreign models adopted, the Indian traditions which have permeated the actual practices within the Western-derived institutions, and what can actually be achieved in an agrarian society, a caste-dominated social order, and a heterogeneous civilization have been of the essence of Indian politics since Independence.

POLITICAL LEADERSHIP, MOBILIZATION AND STATECRAFT IN PRE- AND POST-INDEPENDENCE POLITICS

One of the persisting disjunctions in pre- and post-Independence Indian politics is that between mobilization and "statecraft," between the bases for mass mobilization of the people and the actual political goals of the leaders. This disjunction was introduced into Indian politics with the rise of Gandhi and his famous mass movements, beginning from 1920–21. The mass of the people who flocked to see and hear Gandhi as he toured the country and who participated in the great movements launched by him from time to time were moved more by traditional religious beliefs, including the belief that Gandhi himself was a saint or god upon earth who would bring miraculous changes in their present or future well-being and happiness, than by the specific political and economic demands made in the Congress charter of demands.[7] There was in the Congress itself a clear division between Gandhi's leadership role and the parts played by other leaders such as Sardar Patel and Jawaharlal Nehru among others. Gandhi himself kept aloof from statecraft – though not from practical politics – and left the day-to-day functioning of the Congress and later the government of the country to Patel and Nehru.

This tradition of a disjunction between mobilization and statecraft did not always imply, however, a division among the persons performing the separate tasks. Jinnah, for example, who was an early opponent of the mass mobilization techniques of Gandhi, which he saw as nothing but rabble-rousing, and who was in his early career oriented exclusively towards statecraft, at the end of his life performed both roles. In the great mobilization of the Muslim population of the subcontinent, Jinnah roused the Muslim masses behind the slogan of "Islam in danger," around a theme that implied the creation of an Islamic state, a land of the pure and the faithful when, in fact, he had no more in view than the creation of a modern, liberal, secular state in which Muslims would be in a majority.

In modern Sikh politics as well, there has been a division of roles and leadership between institutions and persons closer to the religious beliefs of the masses, on the one hand, and the politicians oriented towards party leadership and control of government in the Punjab. The secular leaders of the Sikh political party, the Akali Dal, are not equal to the task of mass mobilization and, therefore, require political alliance with a *sant*, a preacher or holy man, in order to preserve their own leadership, consolidate their control over the Akali Dal, or lead a successful political movement in pursuit of a set of political goals.

This division of roles or disjunction of political practices is, in fact, widespread in Indian politics. Even those politicians who deliberately set out to avoid the use of such techniques or even condemn it cannot escape the popular mentalities which attribute to

---

[7] See Shahid Amin, "Gandhi as Mahatma: Gorakhpur District, Eastern UP, 1921–2," in Ranajit Guha (ed.), *Subaltern Studies III: Writings on South Asian History and Society* (Delhi: Oxford University Press, 1984), pp. 1–61.

them religious or other more-than-human, charismatic qualities essential to successful leadership in contemporary Indian politics. Nehru condemned every sort of "casteism, communalism, provincialism" and parochialism in his public speeches everywhere in India and was rewarded by the devotion of the Brahmans throughout north India and the adulation of the Hindu masses who probably saw him as they saw Gandhi, as a living god on earth. We have no studies of mass perceptions of Mrs. Indira Gandhi, but it is certain that she was widely perceived in the image of the female goddess and mother of the people of India and was, in fact, often called late in life *"Mataji"* or "mother" with somewhat more reverence than that ordinarily due to an older woman and mother of children in India.

Contemporary Indian politics have also witnessed the rise of film stars to the leadership of two south Indian states, Tamil Nadu and Andhra. In both cases, these film stars were of a different sort from Ronald Reagan, for their film roles were of mythopoeic characters and their audiences identified them with the heroes and gods whom they played on the screen. In these cases, however, there has been a reunion of roles in which the mass mobilizer and the master of statecraft merge into a single demagogic type.

The irony, however, is that this type of disjunction is not the kind which Gandhi himself could have sought. It is more likely, rather, that Gandhi himself sought to maintain a distance between the exercise of moral authority, on the one hand, and political action and the practice of statecraft, on the other hand. There was an implicit assumption in Gandhi's stance that power and political responsibility in state institutions were inherently corrupting and an explicit statement that freedom from British rule was less important than self-mastery. Indeed, most of the techniques adopted by Gandhi during his mass movements involved abstention, noncooperation, and withdrawal from participation in institutions designed for India by the British. He left the definition of the means of gaining control of such institutions for the statesmen of the Congress.

This disjunction between moral and political authority has also continued to play its part in post-Independence Indian politics.[8]

[8] Partha Chatterjee, "Gandhi and the Critique of Civil Society," in Ranajit Guha (ed.), *Subaltern Studies III*, pp. 186–187.

Like the other disjunction, it has sometimes involved a division of political roles and responsibilities or of institutions, but it has often also involved the same person attempting to adopt both stances. One form it has taken has been the disavowal by the acknowledged leader of a party of any desire for public office. Rammanohar Lohia, the famous radical Socialist leader who died in 1969, adopted this form, refusing to accept any formal leadership in his party and disavowing any desire for high political office beyond his membership in Parliament. Jayaprakash Narayan adopted the different strategy of withdrawal from the political arena into constructive work in the villages, while acting at the same time as a moral critic of political authority and moral adviser to practicing politicians until his own sense of moral outrage against Mrs. Gandhi's authoritarian and perceived corrupting leadership of the country led him to take the lead as mass mobilizer in a movement to displace her from power. The third form in which this disjunction between moral and political authority has expressed itself has been in the attempt by some politicians to play crusading roles without withdrawing from politics and without renouncing political ambitions. For such politicians, their constant refrain is the need to cleanse Indian politics of its corruption and of their corrupt rivals.

In 1988, in preparation for the Ninth General Elections anticipated in 1989, a political struggle was being waged between a former Congress minister in the central government and former chief minister of Uttar Pradesh (U. P.), Vishwanath Pratap Singh and Rajiv Gandhi. The former resigned from office in 1987 in disgust over the alleged gross corruption by the holders of high office in connection with defence contracts which, it was implied, had not left the Prime Minister himself unsullied. In his initial resignation, he also stated explicitly his intention to avoid in future the acceptance of any office of state. If, in victory, he should adhere to his vow, he would conform to the role established by Gandhi and repeated by Jayaprakash Narayan after the Janata victory in the 1977 elections of remaining aloof from the actual exercise of power in order to retain the purity of moral authority.

A third legacy of Gandhi which has become even more attenuated than the other two concerns the proper role of leadership in relation to the masses. Gandhi was a mass mobilizer of unprecedented skill

23

in India who was using his skill to build a movement to expel the British from India. Yet, he distrusted the people and, by one account, even considered them at bottom a "mob," subject to immoral behavior and prone to violence.[9] Mobilization required simultaneously moral upliftment and leadership to prevent the transformation of mass political action into criminal activity and violence.

Gandhi also was clearly aware that contemporary Indian society was internally divided into castes and religious communities. Effective mobilization of the heterogeneous fragments of Hindu society required, therefore, the use of transcendent Hindu symbols to emphasize Hindu unity while at the same time making special appeals for Hindu–Muslim unity. It has often been pointed out that there was a problem of contradiction between the two goals, which Gandhi never resolved himself, though he was prepared to risk his own life for the second goal and did, in the end, become a martyr to it at the hands of a fanatical Hindu assassin.

In the post-Independence era, numerous variations on Gandhi's techniques of mass mobilization have been applied countless times in movements small and great. Increasingly, however, mass mobilization has become associated more with competitive demagogy, with the manipulation of symbols for the sole purpose of building a political following to win an election or to achieve some other purpose and with scant regard for any moral goal.

INTRA-PROVINCIAL POLITICS AND CENTER–PROVINCIAL RELATIONS BEFORE AND AFTER INDEPENDENCE

The difficulties of constructing all-India social movements and political organizations and of mobilizing the mass of the people around all-India symbols of unity or opposition arise partly out of the inherent cultural diversity of the peoples of India, partly out of the significance of local issues of land control, but also out of the dynamics of intra-provincial politics and center–provincial relations in India's multi-level political system. Those dynamics have oper-

---

[9] Chatterjee, "Gandhi and the Critique of Civil Society", p. 185.

24

ated repeatedly in similar ways, whose main patterns are the following.

Firstly, at every level of the system, factionalism, personalism, and opportunism rather than ideology, party ties, nationalism, or communalism have structured routine conflict and alliance patterns. Factional conflicts are sometimes suppressed or attenuated at the bottom and the top of the system: at the bottom, when some local leader or leaders have overwhelming power; at the top, where it is hard to maintain the links in the chain of support that lead to a leader's local structures of power. At the middle levels, particularly at the provincial levels, factionalism is generally rampant.

The second feature is the principle of interference or intrusion of politics from higher levels into lower levels. This principle has had two bases. It has operated because of the absence of any doctrine of the autonomy of local bodies or "states' rights" and the presence instead of a presumed right of higher authority to intervene to maintain order at lower levels. The second basis has lain in the need either for support at lower levels in the system to build power at higher levels or for a transcendent appeal to overcome or bypass the essentially local character of politics and structures of power in Indian politics.

The third feature of routine politics in India has been the pervasiveness in provincial and local politics of intra-communal political divisions and inter-elite cooperation across communal boundaries. The fourth feature follows from the other three and may be called the principle of division, a variation on the theme of "divide and rule." In routine politics in India, power at each level and especially across levels is attained by dividing the opposition, not by oppressing it. One offers "inducements": ministerships, patronage, non-interference in a leader's local base, cash.

The fifth feature, however, runs counter to the others to some extent. It is the principle of hierarchical loyalties, which is based on the existence in India of ascending levels of loyalty running from *jati* (the local caste group) to nation, with many intermediate stages in between, that can be called upon by leaders and movements to build support through communal unity rather than through division of the opposition. It operates at the mass level and influences popular allegiances at moments of choice, such as elections, mass movements, or communal riots. It presents itself in the form of dichotomous oppositions between caste groups, religious communities, nationalists against British rulers, and occurs whenever structures of opportunity are created to facilitate or precipitate such oppositions.

The sixth feature is the premium on charismatic or demagogic leadership that can call upon the appropriate loyalties at critical moments to transcend the features of routine politics identified above, particularly at the mass level. The strategy of dealing with local leaders then becomes one not of dividing leadership groups, but of threatening to undercut the leader's local bases of support with an appeal that will move his local supporters and break temporarily local links and allegiances. There have been several kinds of leaders in South Asian political history with this kind of capacity. One type, of which Gandhi was the preeminent example, rose to prominence through both mass leadership achieved through struggle and effective liaison with provincial leaders. He retained no local political base for himself and sought no national power for himself.

A second type, represented by the Nehru family, achieved national power through direct anointment by Gandhi, in the case of Nehru, or through their own parents, as in the cases of Mrs. Gandhi and Rajiv. Father and daughter, however, retained their powers in different ways, the father by maintaining bargaining relations with provincial leaders, the daughter by destroying them. Both, however, maintained direct popular or demagogic links with the masses. Rajiv, who has oscillated between the methods of his grandfather and his mother and lacks any distinctive leadership qualities of his own, has survived largely on the basis of divine right. The third type is exemplified by Jinnah, who built upon personal reputation rather than mass leadership, who was not really anointed by anyone but himself for the leadership role he ultimately adopted but who, at last, his own personal dispositions to the contrary notwithstanding, had to take up the same dual role that both Gandhi and the Nehrus adopted: plebiscitary or demagogic appeals directly to the masses combined with direct bargaining with political leaders.

It is a recurring feature of Indian political history that only a charismatic leader with a simple appeal can unite the subcontinent or any of its larger peoples for a political purpose. While the prevailing tendencies in normal times are towards disaggregation of power, regionalism, and opportunism, the desire to centralize power in India leads to efforts to nationalize issues, which also means their simplification and symbolization in slogans, which in turn places a high premium on charismatic or demagogic leadership. However, such mobilization is evanescent; power so aggregated soon crumbles, and defection and the scramble for places reemerges immediately the dust settles. From Gandhi's first great mass movement, the Non-cooperation/Khilafat movement of 1920–21 to the Rajiv Gandhi landslide election of 1984, Indian politics have oscillated between the sordid, everyday, patronage politics of the provincial and local politicians and the enthusiasms aroused by mass popular leaders.

PART I

POLITICAL CHANGE

INTRODUCTION

Most theoretical models of political change and development applied to the post-colonial states of Asia and Africa have emphasized the critical role of "state-building" – stabilizing, extending, and strengthening the institutions of the centralized state – as a virtual precondition for "modernization," national integration, and economic development. The central issue in these models of state-building concerns "penetration" of the institutions of the centralized state into "empty territories" or peripheral areas and into culturally and economically diverse regions which have undergone uneven economic and social development. It also involves establishing the authority of state laws and values over the traditional laws, customs, and values of autonomous religious, tribal, and other local communities. It includes as well the implementation of state goals of urban industrial development, increased agricultural production using advanced technologies, and agrarian reform in societies whose populations are overwhelmingly rural, agrarian, and dominated by peasant cultivators.[1]

One influential model of state-building has been woven around the argument that there is a basic tension between the needs for strong state authority and the increased demands for participation by populations mobilized by nationalist leaders, party politicians, and others in pursuit of a multiplicity of goals which ultimately come into conflict with each other and with the broader public interest which only an institutionalized and autonomous state can pursue effectively.[2] This view magnifies such demands for participa-

[1] Joseph LaPalombara, "Penetration: A Crisis of Governmental Capacity," in Leonard Binder et al., Crises and Sequences in Political Development (Princeton, NJ: Princeton University Press, 1971), pp. 220–227; cf. Gabriel A. Almond and G. Bingham Powell, Jr., Comparative Politics: System, Process, and Policy (2nd edn, Boston: Little, Brown, 1978), p. 22 on the importance of penetration.
[2] Samuel P. Huntington, Political Order in Changing Societies (New Haven: Yale University Press, 1968), e.g., p. 24.

tion into a developmental "crisis," threatening to state authority and civil order.[3]

All these views tend to exalt the centralized state, to assume its inevitable triumph in one way or another, and to give it an anthropomorphic shape while assigning only a secondary role to the specific actions of the wielders of state authority. It is sometimes suggested that the state may adopt federal features and may decentralize power to local institutions, but these are rarely seen as anything but measures to make more effective the capacity of the central state itself.[4] Political leaders, especially the nationalist leaders, and some of the more dynamic contemporary military leaders, have generally been seen as playing the important, but secondary role of transferring their charisma to state institutions and thereby imparting legitimacy to them. The "overloads" and crises which may lead to the collapse or functional irrelevance of "differentiated modern [state] structures" do not arise from the actions of the leaders but occur "when environmental strains become too great."[5]

The view taken here of the role of the Indian state since Independence is different in most respects from the dominant theoretical models. This study emphasizes the struggle for power among competing elites and individuals which often cuts across the functional differentiation and specialization of state institutions, bending them to the wills of the principal contenders for power. The Indian state does not mainly respond to and resolve or manage crises arising from the environment, but is, through the actions of its leaders, the principal agency directly and indirectly responsible for their occurrence in the first place. The Indian state, in common with all other states, does not merely respond to crises produced by uneven economic development and social change, but is itself the leading force providing differential advantages to regions, ethnic groups, and classes.

Although it is true that the entrance of new groups into the political process in post-Independence India has often been accom-

---

[3] See Myron Weiner, "Political Participation: Crisis of the Political Process," in Binder et al., Crises and Sequences. Weiner discusses the "participation crisis" in general, but does not share Huntington's views on it.

[4] Almond and Powell, Comparative Politics, pp. 160ff.

[5] Almond and Powell, Comparative Politics, p. 22.

panied by intensification of conflict and violence, it is of no scientific value to attribute these consequences to an objectified participation crisis. More specific explanations are required and will be provided in the three parts of this study.

It will be noted in part 1 that there have been two alternative models for political development in post-Independence India: the overwhelmingly dominant model of a strong centralized state held by virtually all Congress leaders since Independence and a much less prominent model derived from Gandhi's ideas not for a merely federal, decentralized state, but for a state built up from the village, with the latter as the central political focus and with the satisfaction of the basic needs of its people as the aim of all social and political institutions. Contrary to the role assigned to charismatic leaders in most theories of political development, Gandhi, the preeminent leader of Indian nationalism, refused to transfer his charisma to the new Indian state.

Disregarding Gandhi's views, however, India's other national leaders framed a constitution providing for a federal but highly centralized state. India's federal system, though centralized, contains so many points of potential power which must be controlled in order to remain in command in New Delhi that political competition appears to be an endless process which never reaches equilibrium.

A second general argument of part 1 is that the drives toward centralization of power in Delhi have intensified markedly since the death of Nehru and the grand succession struggle which followed. The consequences have been to produce fundamental changes in the structure and functioning of the central government, in the form and character of party political competition, and in the relationships among central, state, and local institutions of governance and of politics. Those changes, discussed in detail in chapters 2, 3, and 4 are summarized briefly here.

The struggle for power in Delhi has not only become more competitive and more ruthless but has been marked since the Emergency period from 1975 to 1977 by a tension between authoritarian and democratic political tendencies. In the process, the office of Prime Minister has emerged as the central focus of all authority and struggle in the country, with the result that most other institutions have declined in authority and effectiveness.

However, as the drive to centralize political power in New Delhi has intensified, the political support to sustain it has declined. The highly factionalized, but once mighty Congress, with its strength based in the districts and in the state capitals, was reduced by Mrs. Gandhi in many states and districts to bodies of persons oriented more towards the favor of her emissaries from New Delhi than towards local support bases and state political leaders.

Opposition forces for their part have become increasingly regionalized. In many states, the Congress no longer competes effectively against dominant regional parties or can do so only when the central Congress leadership and the Congress Prime Minister make a massive effort, using instruments of central power and patronage, to displace such parties and shore up the regional Congress organization.

Indeed, the weakening of the Congress has led to a situation in which the central government increasingly uses and abuses central instruments of control over state government and politics. As Congress support bases have disintegrated, the functioning of state institutions, notably in those states where the Congress is ostensibly in power, has come to depend upon the wishes of the central leadership in New Delhi.

In the face of these disintegrative tendencies, the Congress nevertheless remains the strongest force in the country and the only party which has been able both to win national elections and produce stable leadership. Its successes in this regard, however, have come to depend more and more on the persons and personalities of the Nehru family rather than upon the institutional strength of a functioning party organization with stable bases of support in the districts and localities of the country.

"State-building," therefore, has been leading in India not to political centralization but to regionalism and loss of effective control in large parts of the country. It has produced a systemic crisis, which arises less from failures of penetration or obstacles to it than from the subordination of goals associated with the term "penetration" to the narrow struggle for political control of the country from New Delhi. Nor are the rising demands and expectations of new groups of mobilized participants in politics responsible for the crisis. Where intense and violent conflicts between segments

34

of the population have taken place, they are usually associated either with specific types of economic or other forms of competition or with struggles for political power in which state and central government and party elites are directly involved and are not merely responding to demands for increased participation from new participants in the political process.

CHAPTER 2

POLITICAL CHANGE, POLITICAL STRUCTURE AND THE FUNCTIONING OF GOVERNMENT

PARLIAMENTARY DEMOCRACY IN INDIA

The Nehru period

Jawaharlal Nehru, the first Prime Minister of India, was not formally selected either by the Congress party organization or by the Congress party in parliament. He was simply the natural choice as the acknowledged leader of the Congress and the designated political heir of Mahatma Gandhi. However, the party organization in the early years after Independence was dominated by Sardar Patel, who was also the most powerful minister in the Cabinet after Nehru and recognized as Nehru's equal in all other respects. Numerous differences developed between Patel and Nehru in the Cabinet and a great struggle for control over the party organization culminated in a victory for Patel's candidate, Purushottamdas Tandon, as party President in 1950. However, after Patel's death in December, 1950, Nehru moved quickly to take over the party organization, forcing Tandon to resign the presidency, which Nehru then assumed himself for the next four years. After the overwhelming victory of the Congress under Nehru's leadership in the 1952 elections, there was no longer any doubt about Nehru's supremacy in the party and the government and he remained the unchallenged leader of both until his death in 1964.

Nehru's personality, attitudes, and style of leadership influenced profoundly all aspects of the functioning of the Indian political system during the period of his dominance. Nehru asserted effectively and decisively the primacy of the office of the Prime Minister against challenges from the President and from the Congress organization. He was determined also that the Indian National Congress should rule the country and achieve power not only in Delhi but in all the Indian states. In a few cases, the attainment of that goal involved considerable political manipulation and the use of

36

the power of the central government to undermine the positions of opposition parties and dissident Congress factions in states such as Punjab and Kerala. However, from the position of strength which Nehru established for the Congress, he then acted generously towards most opposition parties and their leaders, though not always so towards parties he considered to be of the extreme Right and towards the Communists. In some respects, Nehru himself was the leader of the opposition,[1] for he was constantly haranguing and berating subordinate leaders and the rank and file for not being faithful to Congress ideals and for failing to implement Congress policies.

During the Nehru period, state and central politics were largely autonomous, though the central leadership of the Congress, known as the High Command, often played arbitrating and mediating roles between competing factions in the state Congress parties. Moreover, under Nehru, a strong central government coexisted with strong states and powerful state leaders in a mutual bargaining situation in which ultimate authority existed in Delhi.

Nehru and his Cabinet also exercised firm control over both the civilian and military bureaucracies. Although the elite civil service established by the British was maintained, Nehru and his principal ministers provided clear and firm policy guidance. Similarly, the supremacy of civilian control over the military also was strongly asserted.

Finally, Nehru articulated a clear set of ideological and policy goals, which included a commitment to a non-dogmatic form of socialism, to secularism, economic development through state-directed planning, and nonalignment in international affairs. Success in achieving specific policies included under these broad goals was often limited, but they provided always a clear social and economic orientation, direction, and cohesion to state policies.

Towards the end of Nehru's life, the central party organization, with Nehru's acquiescence, reemerged as a powerful force, initially in support of Nehru's own desire to gain firmer control of both party organization and government in all the states of the Union.

[1] Ashish Nandy, "Indira Gandhi and the Culture of Indian Politics," in Ashish Nandy, *At the Edge of Psychology: Essays in Politics and Culture* (Delhi: Oxford University Press, 1980), p. 120.

Table 2.1. *Prime Ministers of India*

Jawaharlal Nehru	Congress	1947–64
Lal Bahadur Shastri	Congress	1964–66
Indira Gandhi	Congress	1966–77
Morarji Desai	Janata	1977–79
Charan Singh	Janata (S)	1979–80
Indira Gandhi	Congress	1980–84
Rajiv Gandhi	Congress	1984–

Kamaraj Nadar, former chief minister of the state of Tamil Nadu, was elected President of the Congress in 1963 and, along with four other party "bosses" from different states, took control of the party organization. Upon Nehru's death in 1964, this group, known as the Syndicate, and especially Kamaraj as party President, played the critical roles in the succession to Nehru by Lal Bahadur Shastri and of Mrs. Gandhi to Shastri two years later.

The rise of Indira Gandhi

The entire period between Nehru's death in 1964 and the consolidation of power in the country under Mrs. Gandhi's leadership in 1971–72 constituted a prolonged succession crisis and struggle for power, with the period of Lal Bahadur Shastri's prime ministership from May, 1964, to January, 1966 but a brief interregnum between Nehru and Mrs. Gandhi, the two dominant leaders of India since Independence (see table 2.1). The period is marked by five critical steps in the rise of Mrs. Gandhi and the defeat of all her potential rivals.

The first step was her own succession to power in 1966 after the sudden death of Shastri. The 1967 defeat of Morarji Desai in the Congress Parliamentary Party (CPP) was the second critical step in Mrs. Gandhi's consolidation of power, which established her preeminence against her only serious rival, despite severe losses suffered by the Congress in the 1967 elections under her leadership.

Once again an unexpected death in office, this time of the President of India, Zakir Husain (table 2.2), had the effect of speeding up a struggle that was, in any case, already in progress. The Congress split of 1969 over the Congress nominee for the presi-

Table 2.2. *Presidents of India*

Election	President
1950	Rajendra Prasad
1952	Rajendra Prasad
1957	Rajendra Prasad
1962	S. Radhakrishnan
1967	Zakir Hussain (died 1969)
1969	V. V. Giri
1974	Fakhruddin Ali Ahmed (died 1977)
1977	Neelam Sanjiva Reddy
1982	Zail Singh
1987	R. Venkataraman

dency of India was the third critical point in Mrs. Gandhi's consolidation of power. Mrs. Gandhi won the battle for the presidency with the election of her candidate, V. V. Giri, against the official Congress nominee, Sanjiva Reddy. However, in the process, she was expelled from the Congress and lost control over the party organization since most of the entrenched state party bosses remained in the Congress (O), while Mrs. Gandhi's strength was more in the CPP than in the state party organizations.

Mrs. Gandhi decided to call national parliamentary elections in March, 1971. The people of India were, in effect, asked to settle the struggle for power that had been going on since Nehru's death, to choose between Mrs. Gandhi and her opponents, between the old Congress and the new. The results of the 1971 elections were an overwhelming victory for Mrs. Gandhi, whose Congress (R) won a two-thirds majority in the Lok Sabha. Mrs. Gandhi was now unquestionably the preeminent leader of the country.

Shortly after the March, 1971, election, the civil war and secessionist movement in East Pakistan began. Mrs. Gandhi's attentions had now to be turned to this conflict, which occupied her and the country until December, 1971, when the Indian Army invaded East Pakistan, defeated the Pakistan Army in the Third Indo-Pakistan War, and became the critical factor thereby in the foundation of the new state of Bangladesh. With this triumph behind her, the Congress (R) and Mrs. Gandhi were able to go to the polls in the March,

39

1972, legislative assembly elections with confidence and gain large majorities in all the major states in the Indian Union. At this point, one can say that the first succession crisis in post-Independence India had been decisively ended in favor of Mrs. Gandhi, who now occupied a position of centrality and dominance in the Indian political system that appeared to equal or even surpass that of her father.

Mrs. Gandhi established a distinctive strategy of rulership between 1972 and 1975 that was highly personalized and centralized and that involved unprecedented assertions of executive power in the Indian political system. Within the Congress party organization also, Mrs. Gandhi established personal control, the dominance of the ministerial wing of the party over the organization, centralized direction of lower units, and authoritarian rather than democratic procedures for recruitment of party officers.[2]

Mrs. Gandhi's centralizing actions also transformed the character of center–state governmental relations in the states controlled by the Congress. Unlike her father, who preferred to deal with strong chief ministers in control of their legislative parties and state party organizations, Mrs. Gandhi set out to remove every Congress chief minister who had an independent base and to replace each of them with chief ministers personally loyal to her and without an independent base. Even so, stability could not be maintained in the states and factional manoeuvering to replace each appointed chief minister continued, the principal difference in such manoeuvering now being that the decisions could not be taken in the state capitals but only in New Delhi.

Threats to Mrs. Gandhi's dominance and the imposition of the Emergency

Threats to Mrs. Gandhi's dominance

A personalized strategy of rulership has the effect of focusing attention on the ruler, who receives the blame when things go wrong. In 1973–74, food shortages and rising prices combined with local political grievances to produce major popular demonstrations

[2] Stanley A. Kochanek, "Mrs. Gandhi's Pyramid: The New Congress," in Henry C. Hart (ed.). *Indira Gandhi's India: A Political System Reappraised.* Boulder, CO: Westview Press, 1976), pp. 95–102.

and movements that turned violent in the states of Gujarat and Bihar and that could not be handled effectively by the chief ministers appointed by Mrs. Gandhi in those states. Inside the Congress, a small group of MPs were becoming discontented with Mrs. Gandhi's economic policies.

Then, in March, 1974, a new and ominous development occurred when Jayaprakash Narayan (JP) took the leadership of the Bihar agitation and offered also to lead a countrywide movement against corruption and what he considered to be Mrs. Gandhi's increasingly authoritarian rule. JP offered a direct, personal challenge to Mrs. Gandhi's authority, legitimacy, and character from a personal position of moral authority.

In the midst of these and other developments threatening Mrs. Gandhi's dominance, the Allahabad High Court precipitated matters by finding Mrs. Gandhi's 1971 election invalid on the grounds of corrupt practices in an election petition filed by Raj Narain and decided on June 12, 1975. This event brought new hope and vigor to the opposition, which began to join forces and to plan a mass mobilization campaign to demand the resignation of Mrs. Gandhi.

The Emergency

In the early morning hours of June 26, 1975, Mrs. Gandhi moved decisively to put an end to all opposition to her continuance in office. All her principal opponents, not only in the opposition but in the CPP itself, were arrested. At her request, the President of India declared an Emergency under Article 352 of the Constitution. Parliament moved swiftly to pass new electoral laws superseding the laws under which Mrs. Gandhi was found guilty and her election voided. Within a few months, President's Rule was imposed in the two non-Congress-ruled states of Gujarat and Tamil Nadu, thereby bringing the entire country under direct dictatorial rule from Delhi. Parliamentary elections scheduled for March, 1976, were postponed and the terms of both Parliament and the state legislative assemblies extended. Mrs. Gandhi's young son, Sanjay, came forward as the principal defender of the Emergency, acquiring dictatorial powers himself because of his identification with his mother, which he exercised in an arbitrary, arrogant, and capricious manner. Tens of thousands of local-level party workers were jailed and press censorship made it difficult for other-than-local and very limited political protests to be made publicly by regime opponents who were not in jail.

It was not long, however, before considerable discontent at the mass level, though veiled, began to develop as a consequence of specific acts of the Emergency regime. The most notable set of such acts was the sterilization program of birth control introduced at the prompting of Sanjay Gandhi. Discontent also began to develop among Muslims, again as a consequence of one of Sanjay Gandhi's projects, in this case slum clearance and elimination of pavement squatters, accompanied by violent incidents, for the sake of the "beautification of Delhi." Finally, all those persons who were affected by the demands for increased discipline in the workplace, the pressures to procure sterilizations, and freezes on wage increases also became disaffected with the emergency regime.

The 1977 elections and return to normalcy

The 1977 elections

In the face of these simmering discontents, which were evidently not known to Mrs. Gandhi because of the distortions in the flow of information and communication produced by fear and sycophancy among Congressmen and government officials, Mrs. Gandhi suddenly announced in December, 1977 a call for new parliamentary elections and a relaxation of the Emergency restrictions on the press and the opposition, including the release from jail of most political prisoners. Mrs. Gandhi and Sanjay probably believed that the opposition would not have sufficient time to mobilize and gather the necessary resources to fight an effective election campaign in the few weeks available to them.

The results confounded any reasonable expectations that Mrs. Gandhi and Sanjay could have had. The Janata party achieved a great victory, winning 295 seats, a bare majority in the Lok Sabha, but the opposition as a whole secured more than two-thirds of the seats, reducing the Congress to 153 seats, only 28 percent of the seats in the House.

The return to normalcy

The Janata government that came to power with Morarji Desai as Prime Minister had promised to restore normalcy if it succeeded at the polls and it set out to do so immediately after taking office. Civil liberties of the people were fully restored, press censorship was eliminated and the independence of the press from government interference reestablished, and all remaining political prisoners were released. The Janata government restored the main features of parliamentary democracy in India and made the future imposition of an emergency somewhat more difficult.

The Indian parliamentary system, since its restoration in 1977, has survived the fall of the Janata government in 1979, the return of Mrs. Gandhi to power thereafter, the threat to Indian unity posed by the Punjab crisis and the assassination of Mrs. Gandhi in 1984, and the return of the Congress to power in 1985 under Rajiv Gandhi with an 80 percent majority in Parliament. It would be foolish to assume either that India, having weathered an authoritarian challenge to its parliamentary regime, is now secure from such a threat in future or to predict the reestablishment of authoritarianism in the future. Political practices since Independence have provided precedents for both types of regimes.

PATTERN AND STRUCTURE OF GOVERNMENT

The President

The Constitution of India formally vests virtually all the executive powers of government in the President. In fact, however, it is understood that the President's powers are to be exercised, with only rare exceptions, upon the advice of the Prime Minister and the Council of Ministers. Nevertheless, there have been persistent concerns from the time of the deliberations of the Constituent Assembly up to the prime ministership of Rajiv Gandhi that a President might misuse or abuse – in effect, actually *use* – the powers formally granted to him in the Constitution or might, under certain circumstances, be in a position to exercise discretionary powers.

The most persistent concerns have centered around the degree of freedom the President may have to select a Prime Minister in an unstable House. Because of such concerns, ever since the 1967 elections and the split in the Indian National Congress in 1969, as a consequence of which the political dominance of the Congress at the Center has not been assured and inter-party political competition for the prime ministership has become more intense, the election of the President has become a highly politicized matter.

However, it was not until Sanjiva Reddy's term of office (1977–82) that the anticipated difficulties surrounding the exercise of presidential discretion in selecting a new Prime Minister and dissolving the House and calling a new election in a divided House arose: in July, 1979, after the resignation of Morarji Desai and a month later after Charan Singh, Desai's successor, also lost his majority. In three instances, precedents were established for the exercise of discretion by the President: in rejecting Morarji Desai's request to form a new government after his initial resignation, in insisting that his successor, Charan Singh, seek a vote of confidence in the Lok Sabha by a specific date, and in his insistence, after Charan Singh's resignation with a recommendation for calling a new election, upon consulting other party leaders before making the decision himself to call a new election. Although all three actions by the President were controversial, none was inconsistent with parliamentary conventions nor did they betray a desire for the exercise of personal power by the President.[3]

Indeed, the exercise of even the limited discretionary powers available to the President has occurred so infrequently that each such exercise has occasioned extensive public comment and some controversy. In 1987, for example, Giani Zail Singh made use for the first time since Independence of the President's power to return a bill to Parliament – the Indian Post Office (amendment) Bill, authorizing the Post Office to open private mail for intelligence purposes. The employment of this power and the President's written complaints to the Prime Minister at the same time that he was not even being kept briefed on major issues precipitated a public controversy and much speculation on the President's motives and intentions, including the possibility that he might exercise his formal power to dismiss the Prime Minister. Further speculation concerning the President's intentions appeared later in 1987 when a

---

[3] For a contrary view, see Barun Sengupta, *Last Days of the Morarji Raj* (Calcutta: Ananda Publishers, 1979), ch. 10.

major government scandal involving alleged "kickbacks" to high government and party officials on weapons procurements from the Swedish arms manufacturer, Bofors, broke with the resignation from the government of former Defence and Finance Minister Vishwanath Pratap Singh. It has since become known that the President did, in fact, hold extensive consultations with Congress and opposition party leaders to consider the dismissal of the Prime Minister.[4] The latter situation notwithstanding, however, the actual constitutional reality has been that the President can function effectively only if he has the confidence of the Prime Minister and not vice versa.

There appear, therefore, to be few real grounds for concern that the President of India represents a potential political counterweight to the Prime Minister, the Cabinet, and the elected leadership of the country as long as there is a stable government in power. At the same time, future use and even misuse of the office of the President for political purposes remain real possibilities should there be an unstable government at the Center.

Prime Minister and Cabinet

The framers of the Constitution adopted the conventions of British Cabinet government as it had evolved up to that time, including the leading position given to the Prime Minister and the collective responsibility of the Cabinet.[5] During the Nehru period, from the time of the death of his chief political rival, Sardar Patel, in 1950, to 1964, the Cabinet functioned in conformity with the basic norms of "Prime Ministerial government," but one in which individual cabinet ministers were still allowed to play important political roles and of whom some were persons with substantial political followings.

Under Nehru's successor, Lal Bahadur Shastri, the Prime Minister's Secretariat emerged as an alternative source to the Cabinet of advice, influence, and power in the executive branch of government.[6] Following Shastri's example, Mrs. Gandhi used the PM's

[4] *India Today*, April 15, 1988.
[5] M. V. Pylee, *Constitutional Government in India* (New York: Asia Publishing House, 1965), pp. 345, 370–371.
[6] Michael Brecher, *Succession in India: A Study in Decision-Making* (London: Oxford University Press, 1966), pp. 115–118.

Secretariat as an independent source of advice, but she enlarged its role significantly. However, the influence of the Secretariat also declined, especially during the Emergency between 1975 and 1977, when Mrs. Gandhi came to rely heavily for both policy advice and political counsel upon her son, Sanjay.

The restoration of parliamentary government by the Janata coalition which came to power with Morarji Desai as Prime Minister in 1977 did not succeed in restoring the significance of the Cabinet as an institution. The divisions in his government were too great, the collective responsibility of the Cabinet distintegrated in open warfare, and Desai himself had to resign in July, 1979.

The pattern of prime ministerial dominance of a weak Cabinet was restored by Mrs. Gandhi after her electoral victory in 1980. After the death of her son Sanjay, in 1981, Mrs. Gandhi relied upon other relatives and former retainers of the Nehru household and turned increasingly also to her second son, Rajiv. Rajiv as Prime Minister has continued his mother's pattern of consulting his own personal circle of advisers, irrespective of their position inside or outside the cabinet.

The close advisers of the Prime Minister may come from the political sphere, business, former school associates, his immediate family, distant relatives, or family retainers. Although it is more comparable to the White House staff than to the British Cabinet, the closest parallel is to the Indian institution of the *durbar* which, in one meaning, refers to the inner circle of advisers to the ruler. Members of the inner circle are dependent upon the ruler's favor for their positions. They may receive the ruler's patronage or dispense it on his behalf, but they may also be dismissed or find themselves disregarded and have no recourse for their positions are informal, not institutionalized. Moreover, most members of the inner circle lack an independent political base. The ruler, therefore, depends upon the members of this inner circle but is not dependent upon them. He can change them at will.

The role and powers of Parliament

In principle in India, as in Britain, the Prime Minister is chosen by Parliament and he and his Cabinet are "collectively responsible" to it, that is, they must retain the confidence of a majority of the

46

members of the lower House of Parliament or resign and give way to an alternative government. On only a few occasions, however, has there actually been a contested election in the ruling parliamentary party in India. In fact, even though the CPP played an important role in maintaining support for Mrs. Gandhi in her struggles with her rivals, it is the MPs who have been in the dependent role, following a popular leader to what they have considered their best hope for power for themselves as well rather than actually selecting a leader from among alternatives.

There have, however, been two occasions in the post-Independence period when the persistence of a government in power has depended in fact upon the confidence of the House as a whole: in 1969, after the party split in the ruling Indian National Congress when Mrs. Gandhi retained a majority in Parliament and again in July-August, 1979, when the ruling Janata coalition split and Morarji Desai lost his majority in Parliament and had to resign. Individual MPs and opposition groups in the Indian Parliament also have played roles that are equivalent in importance to those played by their counterparts in Britain in the question hour, the amendment process, and debate. Equally important in India, however, have been dramatic gestures, defiance of parliamentary procedure, and other forms of demonstrative behavior designed to express total opposition to government policies.[7] Only during the Emergency was such opposition to Parliament stifled. On the other hand, some of the normal prerogatives of the legislature in India have been encroached upon by the Cabinet on numerous occasions, most notably the very frequent passage of legislation by Ordinance of the President (that is, in effect, by the Cabinet or the Prime Minister's Secretariat).

Although the Lok Sabha (House of the People) is the lower house and the supreme legislative body in India, the Rajya Sabha (Council of States) is not without importance. While the Rajya Sabha does not normally obstruct legislation passed in the Lok Sabha, it has occasionally done so, particularly on constitutional amendments which require a two-thirds majority in both houses. The second important power of the Rajya Sabha is its coequal role with the Lok Sabha as an electoral college, which includes also the state legislative

[7] Pylee, *Constitutional Government*, pp. 445–446.

47

assemblies, for the election of the President of India. The significance of these two powers taken together is that the Rajya Sabha must also be controlled before a government can consolidate its power in Delhi.

The Judiciary

The powers of the Indian Supreme Court are comparable to those of its United States counterpart, including broad original and appellate jurisdiction and the right to pass on the constitutionality of laws passed by Parliament.[8] In the exercise of its powers, however, the Court has been at the center of major controversies concerning the constitutional and political order in India. Two such controversies have been especially persistent and have had broad ramifications. One concerns the efforts by the Court to give priority to the Fundamental Rights provisions in the Constitution in cases where they have come into conflict with the Directive Principles, which specify the broad ideological and policy goals of the Indian state and to which the executive and legislature have often given priority. The second concerns the court's powers of judicial review of legislation passed by Parliament, which have on numerous occasions led to stalemates that point to a constitutional contradiction between the principle of parliamentary sovereignty and that of judicial review. Although the contradiction has not been satisfactorily resolved, with the two institutions each asserting an incompatible priority, the Court has retained an imprecisely defined power of judicial review which at its broadest, according to the judgment in the landmark 1973 case of *Keshavananda Bharati* vs. *State of Kerala*, prohibits Parliament from passing even constitutional amendments which violate "the fundamental features" or the "basic structure" of the Constitution.

During the Emergency, the Court's powers were severely eroded when both Fundamental Rights and judicial review were suspended. The Court even failed to uphold the hallowed common law right of *habeas corpus*. Although many of the Court's powers have since been restored, the executive assertion of the primacy of the Direct-

---

[8] Pylee, *Constitutional Government*, pp. 467, 500; Gerald E. Beller, "Benevolent Illusions in a Developing Society: The Assertion of Supreme Court Authority in Democratic India," *The Western Political Quarterly*, xxxvi, No. 4 (December, 1983), 516.

ive Principles has been largely sustained and the principle of judicial review has not been established as firmly in India as it has in the United States.

Nevertheless, the Court has become a centrally important institution in the Indian political system, deeply and directly implicated in the political process in ways which have rarely if ever occurred in the United States. A 1975 decision of the High Court of Allahabad (the highest court in the province of Uttar Pradesh), overturning the election of Mrs. Gandhi while she was Prime Minister, was reviewed by the Supreme Court in a judicial process that precipitated the Emergency. When the Emergency ended and the Janata government came to power, the Court passed on the constitutional validity of the following actions of the new government designed to consolidate its power in the country and to keep Mrs. Gandhi on the defensive: the dismissal of nine state governments before the end of their terms and the calling of new elections in those states (the Dissolution Case, 1977) and the appointment of Special Courts to try Mrs. Gandhi for alleged excesses and criminal acts committed by her during the emergency (the Special Courts Reference Case, 1978).

Government in the states

In India's federal parliamentary system, the structures and institutions of the central government have their counterparts at the state level. Each state has a Governor who is the official head of state, a bicameral legislature in which the directly-elected Lower House is generally called the Vidhan Sabha and the Upper House, whose members are elected under a variety of different types of franchises, is generally called the Rajya Sabha, a Chief Minister and his Council of Ministers or Cabinet, and a High Court.

These state institutions, however, have not functioned in the same way as their central models. The politics of the state legislatures have been much more fluid than politics in Parliament and there is often no clear majority in the legislature. As the agents of the central government, appointed by the President acting on the advice of the Prime Minister, it has been common since the late 1960s for the governors to intervene in such situations of instability in the states in ways which clearly indicate that they are following the explicit directives or the tacit desires of the central government rather than simply implementing their constitutional mandate to give formal approval to the decisions of the chief minister and Cabinet and to report impartially to the Center the situation in the states.

During the early post-Independence period in some states, a form of "chief ministerial" government developed, but the more common patterns were Cabinet instability and struggles for power even within the ruling Congress parties, which have always been highly factionalized, leading in many states to frequent changes in the office of the chief minister. Two factors have prevented the establishment in most states of governments dominated by the chief ministers: the fluidity of party loyalties and alignments in the legislatures and the unwillingness in the post-Nehru period of the leadership of the ruling party or coalition at the Center to permit strong chief ministers. Increasingly, therefore, many state legislatures have lost their powers to choose the chief ministers and cabinets, a function which has been taken up by the governing group at the Center. The primary activities of the state legislators consist of plotting to overthrow the government of the day and seeking patronage to distribute to followers in their constituencies.

The High Courts in the states, like the Supreme Court, have become involved in issues of fundamental rights and in matters of judicial review. Many of the constitutional issues which ultimately reached the Supreme Court were originally adjudicated in the High Courts.

In general, however, there have been marked differences in the actual practices of state and central government institutions.

LOCAL GOVERNMENT

The Constituent Assembly made only a modest concession to Gandhian ideology by establishing as a principle of state policy in the Directive Principles of the Constitution the goal of decentralizing power and participation to the subprovincial level.[9] However, the whole structure of the new Indian state ran contrary to the ideology of Gandhian decentralization, which not only was meant

[9] Granville Austin, *The Indian Constitution: Cornerstone of a Nation* (Oxford: Clarendon Press, 1966), p. 38.

to provide for direct participation by the people in planning for their own economic improvement but to minimize the role of the centralized state and its bureaucratic "agencies in the ordering of the economy."[10]

While the District Magistrate is no longer the sole focus of state administration and authority in the district and does not have the full freedom of his district ICS predecessors, he remains the central focus. At the district level, the Superintendent of Police (SP) has become nearly coequal in authority with the District Magistrate.

Alongside the pre-Independence system of administrative and police control in the districts, the post-Independence Indian state introduced a new administrative hierarchy to implement rural development plans. The community development block, whose jurisdiction comprises usually around 100 villages, is the pivotal administrative unit in the system, staffed by a multiplicity of technical administrative personnel, with the emphasis on agriculture, but also including other aspects of rural development, whose central purpose was to bring economic development and an enhanced quality of life generally to the villages.

In order to provide popular participation in development planning, a parallel system of local government in tiers from the village to the district level, called *panchayati raj*, was introduced in many states in several different forms. There were considerable differences, for example, in the extent of powers granted to *panchayati raj* institutions and in the tiers at which the powers granted were most concentrated. In some cases, these institutions were not adopted at all. In practice, morover, *panchayati raj* "institutions came to be dominated by the socially or economically privileged sections in the local community."[11]

In the face of the failure and the decline of *panchayati raj* institutions of democratic decentralization in most of the Indian states and the persisting influence of rural elites in most aspects of rural development activities, there has been a renewed call from some sources and a renewed public debate on the desirability of countering the centralizing drives of the modern Indian state with a

[10] Charan Singh, *Economic Nightmare of India: Its Cause and Cure* (New Delhi: National, 1981), p. ix.
[11] Shriram Maheshwari, *Rural Development in India: A Public Policy Approach* (New Delhi: Sage, 1985), pp. 54-55.

new dose of more effective decentralization. These issues will be discussed in chapter 4 below.

ADMINISTRATION AND DEFENCE OF THE INDIAN STATE: THE BUREAUCRACY, THE POLICE, AND CIVIL–MILITARY RELATIONS

The bureaucracy

The British ruled India through a bureaucratic system, whose primary functions were the maintenance of law and order and the collection of revenue. The fear of disorder and disintegration of the new Indian state at Independence, occasioned by the partition of the country, communal violence, and the problems involved in integrating the princely states into the Indian Union caused the leadership of independent India to rely heavily on the existing bureaucratic apparatus and to put aside any ideas of reform. At the highest levels of government in India, in fact, senior officers of the Indian Administrative Service (IAS), especially those in the Prime Minister's Secretariat created under Prime Minister Lal Bahadur Shastri, have at times become more influential than Cabinet ministers. Mrs. Gandhi especially relied upon a few senior officers in her Secretariat to carry out her political bidding as well as to provide her with policy advice. Many of the senior bureaucrats welcomed her Emergency regime. Consequently, when the Janata Government came to power, most of the senior officers closely identified with the Emergency regime were transferred to undesirable postings or suspended from service under charges of corruption. The post-Independence structure of political–bureaucratic relationships has consequently been fundamentally transformed in the direction of a patrimonial regime in which the political leadership selects officers who are personally loyal, who serve their narrow political interests, and who expect reciprocal preferments in return.[12]

The highest levels of the state administration, as well as of the central government, are staffed by IAS officers. Below the elite all-India services, there are several layers of bureaucracy in both the

---

[12] Bhagwan D. Dua has used the term patrimonialism also to apply to the selection and dismissal of chief ministers in "Federalism or Patrimonialism: The Making and Unmaking of Chief Ministers in India," *Asian Survey*, xxv, No. 8 (August, 1985), 793–804.

central and provincial governments, including the higher state civil services as well as vast armies of clerks, peons, and messengers at the lower levels. The numbers of government employees in central, state, quasi-government, and local bodies quadrupled from approximately four million in 1953 to more than sixteen million in 1983.[13] The pay and emoluments of government servants constitute a major drain on state revenues and resources to such an extent that they constitute a leading cause of the deficiency in resources needed to increase public sector capital investment in the economy.

The decision to retain the IAS system of bureaucratic control was associated also with the decision of the Constituent Assembly in favor of a predominantly centralized system of government with federal features. The proponents of an alternative, "Gandhian" tradition have succeeded from time to time in having institutional reforms enacted to introduce measures of decentralization. In fact, however, the planning process, including the articulation of goals, the allocation of resources, and the systems of bureaucratic control and accountability everywhere in India have remained highly centralized.

Below the IAS level and the level of the senior officers in other branches of administrative service in India, the bureaucracy is generally ineffective and non-cooperative in most areas of policy implementation. Although there remains some doubt about the extent to which corruption has penetrated the IAS officer cadres, there is universal agreement that bribe-taking on a small scale at the lowest levels and extensive, massive corruption at the middle and higher levels up to and including at least some IAS officers is endemic and pervasive. In order to serve the needs of the people, therefore, "middlemen," "fixers," and "brokers" have sprung up in the countryside to serve as intermediaries between villagers and bureaucracy to make actually available to the people the agricultural, medical, and other services that are supposed to be provided under myriad government programs.[14]

Thus, both at the top and the bottom, the Indian administrative system that has evolved since Independence departs significantly

[13] David C. Potter, *India's Political Administrators: 1919–1983* (Oxford: Clarendon Press, 1986), p. 159.

[14] G. Ram Reddy and G. Haragopal, "The Pyraveekar: 'The Fixer' in Rural India," *Asian Survey*, xxv, No. 11 (November, 1985), 1,149.

Table 2.3. *Indian Armed Force levels (military and para-military),*
1986

Force	Number
Armed Forces	1,260,000
Army	1,100,000
Navy	47,000
Air Force	113,000
Para-Military Forces	255,000
National Security Force	112,000
Border Security Force	90,000
Assam Rifles	37,000
Indo-Tibetan Border Police	14,000
Coastguard	2,000

Source: *The Military Balance,1986–1987* (London: The International Institute for Strategic Studies, 1986), pp. 154–155.

from "Weberian" criteria of a rational-legal system.[15] The mechanisms, ties, and attachments that make the system work are based rather on personal and social obligations to patrons and clients, kin and caste fellows, on informal connections, and on illegal fee-for-service cash payments. Although they are subordinate at the highest levels to the most powerful political leaders and at the lower levels to powerful local politicians, the higher grades of the Indian bureaucracy dominate routine decision making and, in the frequent absence of ministerial leadership, general policy making in both the central and state governments. They are no longer the elite "rulers of India" but the leading elements of a vast dominant class, whose members are the principal beneficiaries of the benefits and resources produced and distributed through the agency of the Indian state.

The police

The central government maintains several large police forces, numbering altogether above 800,000 men[16] and including, among others, the Central Bureau of Intelligence, the Central Reserve

15 Reddy and Haragopal, "The Pyraveekar," p. 1,152.
16 Henry C. Hart, "Introduction," in Hart (ed.), *Indira Gandhi's India*, p. 18.

Table 2.4. *Growth in strength of police force, 1951–81*

Year	Police strength	Percent increase	Total population (in millions)	Percent increase
1951	468,000		361	
1961	526,000	12⎱	439	22⎱
1971	707,000	34⎰ 93	547	25⎰ 89
1981	904,000	28⎰	684	25⎰

Source: Shailendra Misra, *Police Brutality: An Analysis of Police Behaviour* (New Delhi: Vikas, 1986), p. 73.

Police, the Border Security Force, the Central Industrial Security Forces (who maintain order at public sector industrial enterprises), and the Indo-Tibetan Border Police (see table 2.3). The domestic police force proper, however, is under the control of the state governments. In 1981, it comprised 904,000 men (civil and armed). The percentage increase in the police strength (table 2.4) has been slightly higher overall between 1951 and 1981 (plus 93 percent) than the percentage increase in the total population of the country (plus 89 percent), but these figures did not include a number of other special duty police forces.

The administrative structure of the Indian Police Service (IPS) is similar to that of the IAS. It is an all-India service, divided into state cadres. The IPS officers constitute an elite corps whose members fill virtually all the senior state and district police administrative positions. Officers advance from assistant superintendent of police (SP) in a district to district SP and ultimately to a deputy inspector-general or to an inspector-general position in the state capital in charge of an entire branch of state police administration. During the British period and into much of the post-Independence period, the SP was under the control of the district magistrate, but the SPs are now directly responsible for the police administration in their districts to the state inspectors-general and are no longer considered to be subordinate to the district magistrates. Below the IPS cadre is the rank of deputy SP, which is recruited by the state public service commission; below that rank are the inspectors and sub-inspectors, recruited at the district level; and at the bottom are the constables recruited by the district SP. The pay and service conditions of the IPS are comparable to those of the IAS, but those of the constables are wretched, below those of peons in civil administration.

In addition to the ordinary police establishment which carries out the routine police work and maintenance of public order on a daily basis, each state also has a substantial armed police force, known as the Provincial Armed Constabulary, which is a reserve force whose units remain in barracks most of the time, to be called out on special duty to deal with large-scale disturbances to public order.

The Indian police have become increasingly politicized in the past two decades from the local up to the national level. The more powerful district politicians want pliable and responsive SPs and Deputy SPs, who in turn require the support and patronage of the politicians. The principal sanctions which the politicians have to influence the police are the power to transfer constables to remote parts of their districts and senior officers to undesirable districts, protect corrupt police from criminal prosecution, and influence promotions. At the local level, protection from police victimization and the use of the police to harass one's rivals have become critical elements in the powers of local politicans\ Politicians in the districts of India who wish to build a stable political base for themselves, therefore, must not only be able to distribute\money and patronage, but must also be able to control the police.[17] The police in turn must have powerful political allies if they are to be effective and to advance their own careers.

Political involvement of the police in contemporary political controversies reached a peak during and after the Emergency when the police at all levels were called upon to arrest most of the important opposition leaders in the country and to keep under surveillance many others, including leading figures in the ruling Congress (I) itself. After the Emergency, the Janata government replaced senior police officers who had acted partially and, allegedly, overzealously in supporting the Emergency.

The persistence in post-Independence India of Gandhian techniques of mass mobilization and the spread of group violence in

[17] Bayley, "The Police and Political Order in India," *Asian Survey*, XXIII, No. 4 (April, 1983), 487, and Paul R. Brass, "National Power and Local Politics in India: A Twenty-Year Perspective," in Paul R. Brass, *Caste, Faction and Party in Indian Politics*, Vol. 1: *Faction and Party* (Delhi: Chanakaya, 1984), pp. 191–226.

communal riots, student agitations, and massive political demonstrations against the government of the day have increasingly involved the police in confrontations with the people. Police firings on unarmed crowds, participation of the police in brutal attacks on minorities, and provocative actions against peaceful demonstrators that provoke them to commit acts of violence have become commonplace in contemporary India.

The combination of increased group violence, decline of legitimate political authority in the countryside, politicization and criminalization of the police, and their involvement in incidents of violence has contributed to an increasingly pervasive Hobbesian state of disorder, unpredictability, and fear of violence among ordinary people in the rural areas of India. The overall contemporary performance of the police in India, therefore, can no longer be considered appropriate to a free, democratic, impartial political order. The police are not in fact maintaining order in either the urban or rural areas of India, but are themselves among the most dangerous and disorderly forces in the country.

The military and civilian–military relations[18]

India has one of the largest military forces in the world (see table 2.3) and one that has been continuously active since Independence in a wide range of actions, including the fighting of four wars, the takeover of Goa from the Portuguese in 1961, the intervention in the Sri Lankan civil war in 1987, and numerous domestic operations in support of the civil authorities.

The politicization that has so affected the bureaucracy and the police services and which has contributed to a decline in the effectiveness of their performance has not affected the functioning of the Indian military to the same degree.

The British reproduced in India the Anglo-Saxon pattern of civilian control over the military, whose officers were taught that the military must remain a politically neutral arm of the state. The values of senior Congress leaders also fostered military subordination to civilian leadership. In contrast to the pattern in many other developing countries, including neighboring Pakistan where an

[18] This section relies heavily on the works of Stephen P. Cohen. Specific references are given in the footnotes below.

alliance of the civilian and military bureaucrats developed against the politicians, in India an early alliance developed between the politicians and the civilian bureaucracy to control the military. Specific steps taken to reduce military influence and to ensure civilian control included the removal of the Commander-in-Chief from the first Cabinet in independent India, followed by the abolition of the position itself, leaving no overall commander of all the armed forces other than the civilian head of government; the subordination of all three military chiefs to the civilian Defence Minister, who has usually been either a confidant of the Prime Minister or a powerful politician; and, in recent years, the use of the more doubtful practice of appointing only politically acceptable persons as commanders of the several armed forces.[19]

There is an alternative tradition of militarization of politics and of the infusion of nationalism with military values, represented in the nationalist period by Subhas Chandra Bose, the founder of the Indian National Army which fought against the British in Asia during World War II.[20] Since Independence, political leaders have emphasized the indispensability of a strong military for the maintenance of India as a powerful and respected country and have at times introduced into Indian nationalism a military element.

Military leaders have resented the extent of civilian control over their actions, the lack of specialized military knowledge of the civilian leadership, and their own limited role in the making of military policies.[21] Internal discontents also have developed in the Indian army in recent years over pay, status, and declining opportunities for promotion. The potential for military intervention in Indian politics nevertheless remains low. There has never been an attempted *coup* in India. Even if the will to intervene were present, the obstacles to effective intervention are formidable. The military itself is too large and divided to imagine the possibility of a united leadership implementing a *coup*. The conditions which have led to

[19] Stephen P. Cohen, *The Indian Army: Its Contribution to the Development of a Nation* (Berkeley: University of California Press, 1971), p. 171, and "The Military and Indian Democracy," in Atul Kohli (ed.), *India's Democracy: An Analysis of Changing State–Society Relations* (Princeton, NJ: Princeton University Press, 1987), pp. 115–121.
[20] Stephen P. Cohen, "The Military," in Hart (ed.), *Indira Gandhi's India*, pp. 210–211.
[21] Cohen, "The Military and Indian Democracy," p. 117.

or been used as a justification for military intervention in other Asian and African countries – such as political instability, widespread corruption, absence of electoral legitimacy of the civilian politicians, politicization of the military – have either not been present in India or have not been present in the same combination or else have not progressed to the same extent. With the exception of the period just before and during the Emergency, the legitimacy of the political leadership has never been seriously questioned. A *coup* remains highly unlikely, the subordination of the military to civilian leadership remains firm, and the government in Delhi continues to be led by legitimately elected authority.[22]

The more serious problems concerning the contemporary role of the military in Indian society pertain to the increasing use of the army – on the average 40 to 50 times per year – by the political authorities in domestic disturbances of all sorts, particularly to deal with major incidents of violence.[23] Several paramilitary forces were created in the 1950s and 1960s specifically to handle situations that were beyond the capabilities of the local police. However, the army has had to be called in on several occasions to restore order within these forces themselves. In addition to its use to deal with specific disturbances, the army has also been stationed permanently or for long periods in several Indian states, continuously in Kashmir since 1947 and for long periods since 1983–84 in the troubled states of Assam and Punjab. One long-term danger to the Indian political system, therefore, is of a militarization of politics and a politicization and demoralization of the army arising from its widespread use as a mechanism of political control in a society tending towards anomie.

CENTER–STATE RELATIONS

India today is a Union of 24 states. The leadership of the Congress and the Constituent Assembly at Independence was firmly in the hands of those who believed in the necessity for a strong, centralized state in India. In the Indian federal system, therefore, there are a considerable array of central powers in relation to the states and

[22] Cohen, "The Military and Indian Democracy," pp. 138–139.
[23] Cohen, "The Military and Indian Democracy," pp. 124–127.

numerous unitary features. They include the following: 1) separate lists of legislative powers for the Center and the states, but with a concurrent list in which the Center may claim priority, with residuary powers left to the Union, and with the power held in reserve in emergencies and other situations for the Center to legislate on matters contained in the state list; 2) the power of the Center to create new states and to revise the boundaries of or even eliminate existing federal units; 3) the retention by the Center of control over the most lucrative sources of taxation and the authority to collect certain taxes on behalf of the states and to distribute the revenues among them; 4) the power of the Center to take over the administration of a state and declare President's Rule under specified conditions that have been interpreted very broadly; 5) the power to declare a national emergency that, in effect, may convert the country into a unitary state.

In practice, however, despite strong centralizing drives by Congress governments in Delhi, especially during Mrs. Gandhi's leadership, there have been recurring problems in center–state relations and long-term trends that favor regionalism, pluralism, and decentralization.[24] For one thing, the states retain sole or primary constitutional authority over several important subjects, particularly agriculture, including taxation of agriculture, education, law and order and the police, health, welfare, and local government. By action or non-action in these areas, the states may prevent the adoption of uniform policies for the country which the national leadership considers essential for the general processes of economic growth, development, and social justice. For example, the central leadership of the Congress insisted throughout the 1960s and into the 1970s that more substantial agrarian reforms through land ceilings and redistribution were important to reduce social and economic inequalities in the countryside. However, it is generally recognized that such reforms have been very limited in most states. The central policies themselves have, in consequence, been abandoned. Similarly, since the early 1960s, the Planning Commission has pleaded for increased agricultural taxation, but the state responses have often been quite in the opposite direction.

[24] Paul R. Brass, "Pluralism, Regionalism, and Decentralizing Tendencies in Contemporary Indian Politics," in A. J. Wilson and Dennis Dalton (eds.) *The States of South Asia: Problems of National Integration* (London: C. Hurst, 1982), pp. 223–264.

Moreover, even the effective use by the Government of India of central agencies such as the Finance Commission and the Planning Commission to implement national goals has often proved impossible because of the resistance of powerful state leaders. The Finance Commissions, for example, which are responsible for the distribution to the states of centrally collected taxes, have done little to rectify regional imabalances among states. The Planning Commission, which was designed to introduce a system of centralized economic planning, has never been able to ensure implementation of its goals by the states and has in general declined in influence during the past two decades. Although the Center has several times used the emergency provisions of the Constitution, especially during the 1975 to 1977 period, and has often imposed President's Rule on individual states, both of which allow it to exercise considerable direct control over the administration of the states, these measures are symptomatic of an overall weakening of effective central and state government in India rather than indications of permanent centralization.

Moreover, there have been recurring problems arising out of India's enormous cultural diversity. During Nehru's tenure in office, most linguistic, regional, and minority conflicts and controversies were ultimately resolved through pluralistic mechanisms. During Mrs. Gandhi's periods in office, however, especially in the 1980s, several issues developed into major challenges to the unity of India and to amicable relations among its major ethnic and religious communities. Some of these problems were exacerbated by the centralizing drives of and the involvement of the central leaders themselves in political manipulation in the states in contrast to the Nehru period when the central government preferred to stand back from such problems as far as possible and adopt arbitrating and mediating roles (see chapters 5–7 below).

THE ISSUE OF A PRESIDENTIAL SYSTEM FOR INDIA

India is virtually unique among contemporary post-colonial countries in having functioned since Independence, with the exception of the Emergency, with a parliamentary system modeled on the British form of government. India's parliamentary system has evolved from one in which the Cabinet and the Prime Minister were dominant and the President was a figurehead – though potentially important – into a form of Prime Ministerial government, in which both the Parliament and the Cabinet play secondary roles.

Behind the adopted form of British prime ministerial government, however, there lie two indigenous adaptations – the predominant patrimonial system of the Nehru family and the politics of personal ambition, personal conflict, and political opportunism of the Janata coalition. Each of these indigenous adaptations is inherently unstable for the one depends upon the fate of a family and on the fragilities of personal leadership in general, while the second offers the prospect of the disintegration of any central authority in the system.

India's federal system also presents some peculiarities and adaptations of a well-known form of government. Although politics in India are more regionalized than in any other federal polity in the world, reflecting the unrivaled cultural diversity of the country, the system has more unitary features than most federal systems including especially that of the United States.

In the Nehru period, there were some states which developed a sort of chief ministerial form of government comparable to the prime ministerial pattern at the Center, while other states developed more in the direction of an unstable factional and coalition politics of personal ambition, patronage, and corruption. During Mrs. Gandhi's period, most of the states in which the Congress ruled lost their autonomy and came directly under the control of the central leadership. However, underlying the overall pattern of Congress dominance in the states and increasing central control over the state governments was an alternative type of politics, involving the assertion of regional political and social forces and identities.

While the struggles for power at the Center and between regionalizing and centralizing forces have produced singular adaptations of both parliamentarism and federalism in India, they have also created tensions that have from time to time aroused a desire among some of the participants to change the system to ensure continuity and authority at the Center and the primacy of the central government in relation to the states. A current of opinion favors the adoption of a new form of government of a presidential type which would enhance still further the authority of the central leaders and the Union government to restore order in troubled areas of the country, to eliminate corruption, and to increase the pace of economic and social change.

The presidential system most widely favored is not the American type, but the French system as it functioned in the Gaullist period,with its strong executive and unitary pattern of government. The very problems which have produced a desire for stronger central authority have also produced a counter-tendency in the form of demands from several states for greater regional autonomy and in somewhat more feeble, but recurrent proposals from politicians who continue to draw inspiration from the Gandhian tradition for greater decentralization of institutions in India down to the district and village level as well.

CHAPTER 3

PARTIES AND POLITICS

Party politics in India display numerous paradoxical features, which reveal the blending of Western and modern forms of bureaucratic organization and participatory politics with indigenous practices and institutions. India's leading political party, the Indian National Congress, is one of the oldest in the world, yet it has not succeeded in providing the nucleus for an institutionalized party system which can be fitted easily into any one of the conventional categories of party systems known in the West. There has been a strong Marxist and Communist revolutionary tradition in modern Indian political history. However, unlike other such traditions in most parts of Asia, its dominant parties and movements have neither succeeded in threatening the stability of the Indian state nor been threatened with physical extinction as in Indonesia, but have instead been integrated in the form of reformist political parties within routine politics in the country. The diversities and social fragmentation of Indian society have produced a proliferation of regional and other political parties which often give to each state in the Indian Union a unique party system imperfectly integrated into the "national party system." Some characteristically Indian features pervade virtually all parties in the country – factionalism, dynastic succession to leadership, and the presence of ideological differences among the parties without ideological cleavage in the party system.

Indian politics are distinctive among contemporary developing societies in having had four decades of nearly continuous – excepting the brief Emergency period – competitive electoral politics in which also alternation in power has occurred in all the Indian states and at the Center as well. Here, also, there are numerous paradoxical features and indigenous adaptations of an essentially British electoral system. These include: varying, but often quite high turnout rates among a population still overwhelmingly agrarian and illiterate; a special form of representation for "untouchables" or Scheduled Castes; electoral arenas not yet fully dominated and controlled by organized political parties; and the critical importance of the electoral process as a mechanism for the successive introduction of groups of voters, particularly caste groups, into politics, which impart to the Indian electoral process a quality which is quite different from the classic ideal of the electoral arena as a place where the "independent intelligence of the individual voter"[1] is exercised.

A diversity of interest associations also exists in Indian politics, which give the impression that India is a pluralist society, like the United States, in which the parties "aggregate" the interests of a multiplicity of private associations into public policies and in which the groups also exercise some independent influence over policy making. The impression, however, is only partly correct for, with Indian interest groups as with the parties, there are substantial differences in the types of interests, their organizational form, and their manner of operation. These differences include, among others, the limited sectors in Indian society in which formally organized interest associations operate, the considerable importance of informal movements which arise from time to time claiming to represent large unorganized sectors of society, the existence of specifically Indian types of interest associations, including revivalist movements and caste associations, the importance also of a wholly different type of "representation" in the form of intermediaries between the people and the bureaucracy, and the far greater importance of interest groups and intermediaries in the implementation as opposed to the formation of public policy.

PARTIES AND PARTY SYSTEMS

The Indian National Congress

The Indian National Congress is formally a mass party with a dues-paying membership divided into two categories of primary and active members and with an elaborate, hierarchical organi-

---

[1] James Bryce, "Preface," in M. Ostrogorski, *Democracy and the Organization of Political Parties*, trans. by Frederick Clarke, Vol. 1 (New York: Macmillan, 1922). Bryce's statement reflects an ideal, which few would claim has been anything but imperfectly realized even in Western representative systems, but the ideal nevertheless underlies much, if not most, public discussion and scholarly analysis of the electoral process, for example especially in currently fashionable "rational choice" modeling of voting behaviour as well as other types of decision making in representative systems.

zational structure extending from local to district to state to all-India committees culminating at the top in a Working Committee, the executive committee of the national party, with an elected President as its head (figure 1). Other important structures during the Nehru period were the state and central Parliamentary Boards, which played the decisive roles in the allocation of party nominations to Congressmen to contest elections to the state legislative assemblies and to Parliament.

Although the formal structure was important in Nehru's days, more important was an informal structure of factional linkages and relationships from the local to the national level. Factions contested for control of the important committees at each level through formal elections preceded by membership drives in which competing faction leaders attempted to enroll, even if only on paper, as many member-supporters as possible. Although the factional conflicts which developed often became intense and bitter and were accompanied by frequent charges of "bogus enrollments," they also served to keep the party organization alive and to compel party leaders to build support in the districts and localities throughout the country.

Factional conflicts within the Congress ultimately culminated in struggles for control of the state governments themselves, with most states in the country divided between a ministerial wing, the faction which dominated the government and sometimes, but not always, the party organization as well and a dissident wing which struggled to gain control of the party organization in order to use it as a base to gain control of the government. Occasionally groups formed within the Congress to articulate general or particular points of view on public policy issues, but most factions – and the structure of the system as a whole – were non-ideological in nature.

Although the Congress organization, therefore, was in the 1950s and 1960s a highly factionalized, internally competitive party, ruled by personal opportunism rather than ideology, factional conflict terminated at the highest levels where, from 1950–51 onward, Nehru remained in complete mastery of policy and politics. Indeed, the national leadership of the party in those days was called the "High Command." It consisted of the trusted political confidants of Nehru who would also act as his mediators and arbitrators of factional conflicts at the state level, which threatened to get out of

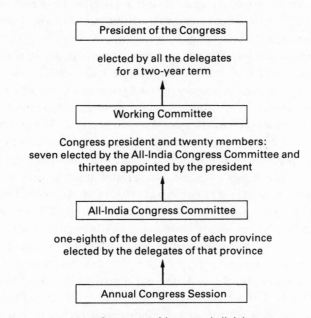

Figure 1   The national decision-making structure of the Congress
Stanley A. Kochanek, *The Congress Party of India* (Princeton, NJ:
Princeton University Press, 1968).

hand and, therefore, threatened the ability of the Congress to retain power in a state.

After the death of Nehru, and in the course of the grand succession struggle which followed between 1965 and 1972, Mrs. Gandhi emerged as the unchallenged leader of the dominant Congress party, which came to be called Congress (R) for Requisitioned – referring to a requisitioned party meeting summoned by Mrs. Gandhi during the split – but later meaning Ruling Congress. After a second split in the party in 1977, following an unsuccessful challenge to her leadership from Congressmen discontented with the effects of her leadership on the Congress during the Emergency, the Congress of Mrs. Gandhi became known as Congress (I) for Indira. The adoption of the designation Congress (I) also symbolized what had happened to the Congress organization under Mrs. Gandhi's leadership. It had become, in effect, her personal party, dependent upon her populist, sometimes demagogic leadership rather than on local party organization, to win elections. Factional conflict between ministerialist and dissident wings of the state party organizations, though they continued, were not usually allowed to run their course. Most decisions concerning the selection of the chief ministers of the states, the councils of ministers in the states, and the important leaders of the appointed PCCs were made by Mrs. Gandhi herself in consultation with a clique of personal advisers, some of whom were initially important politicians from different states in the country. Gradually, however, the party came to be controlled by personal retainers of the Nehru family and by members of the immediate family, including especially Sanjay Gandhi until his death in 1981.

The extent to which a great national movement had become converted into a Nehru family patrimony was indicated by the immediate and unquestioning acceptance of Rajiv Gandhi as Prime Minister of the country and leader of the Congress upon his mother's assassination in November, 1984. The Congress continued under his leadership to be highly centralized, with state and local leadership fragmented, and with an absence of organizational vitality.

The Congress, therefore, though it remains formally a mass party has become a cadre party with a prominent popular leader at its head and the organization at the local level dominated by notables who have maintained strong local structures of power within their caste groups or in the remnants of old landed estates, or through control of educational institutions, cooperative societies, or other government or private organizations.

In most states, particularly in north India and in Maharashtra, the Congress leaders come from the elite – or at least middle status – land-controlling, dominant castes in the countryside. In only a few states, notably Karnataka and Gujarat, have Congress leaders been recruited from the lower castes.

Popular support for the Congress, however, has been much broader than its leadership. A basic, somewhat paradoxical, coalition was put together early after Independence and strengthened under Mrs. Gandhi, consisting of strong support from the extremes of the social order, from the elite, land-controlling castes at the top, on the one hand, and from the low-castes, the poor, and disadvantaged, including many minority groups, on the other hand.

The existence of this formidable coalitional support base combined with the enormous popularity of the Nehru family leaders made the Congress the center of the party system, which scholars came to label a one-party dominant system to indicate at once the centrality of the Congress in the system and the peripherality of the opposition to the Congress in the country. In fact, however, the label has always been something of a misnomer. It was always obvious that, since the Congress itself rarely polled a majority of votes in most states and only once since Independence, in 1984, nearly did so at the Center, Congress dominance was only partly a result of its own support base. Equally important was the disunity of the opposition which, if it could be overcome, as it was in 1977, could lead to the displacement of the Congress from power at the Center. (See tables 3.1, 3.2, and 3.3.) Many opposition parties were quite serious about building counter-movements to challenge the Congress and several gradually developed strong support bases in different regions of the country. Finally, there has never really been a single, national party system but instead each region of the country has had its own distinctive party system in most of which the Congress was the dominant party, but itself had a distinctive social base and pattern of relationship with opposition parties in each state.

Table 3.1. Distribution by party of votes polled in Lok Sabha elections, 1952–84 (in percentages)

Year	INC/ INCI	NCO/ INCU/ INCJ/ INCS	CPI	CPM	SOC	PSP/ KMPP	SSP	SWA	BJS/ BJP	JNP	JNPS/ LD/ DMKP	Other parties	IND
1952	45.0	–	3.3	–	10.6	5.8	–	–	3.1	–	–	16.4	15.9
1957	47.8	–	8.9	–	–	10.4	–	–	5.9	–	–	7.6	19.4
1962	44.7	–	9.9	–	2.7	6.8	ʳ	7.9	6.4	–	–	10.4	11.1
1967	40.8	–	5.0	4.4	–	3.1	4.9	8.7	9.4	–	–	10.1	13.7
1971	43.7	10.4	4.7	5.1	–	1.0	2.4	3.1	7.4	–	–	13.8	8.4
1977	34.5	1.7	2.8	4.3	–	–	–	–	–	41.3	–	9.8	5.5
1980	42.7	5.3	2.6	6.1	–	–	–	–	–	19.0	9.4	8.5	6.4
1984	48.1	1.6	2.7	5.7	–	–	–	–	7.4	6.7	5.6	14.1	8.1

INC: Indian National Congress
INCI: Indian National Congress (Indira)
NCO: Indian National Congress (Organization)
INCU: Indian National Congress (Urs)
INCJ: Indian National Congress (Jagjivan Ram)
INCS: Indian National Congress (Socialist)
CPI: Communist Party of India
CPM: Communist Party of India (Marxist)
SOC: Socialist Party
PSP: Praja Socialist Party

KMPP: Kisan Mazdoor Praja Party
SSP: Samyukta Socialist Party
SWA: Swatantra Party
BJS: Bharatiya Jana Sangh
BJP: Bharatiya Janata Party
JNP: Janata Party
JNPS: Janata Party (Secular)
LD: Lok Dal
DMKP: Dalit Mazdoor Kisan Party
IND: Independent

Source: V. B. Singh and Shankar Bose, Elections in India: Data Handbook on Lok Sabha Elections, 1952–85, 2nd edn (New Delhi: Sage Publications, 1984), pp. 25 and 650.

Table 3.2. *Distribution by party of seats won in Lok Sabha elections, 1952–84*

Year	INC/ INCI	NCO/ INCU/ INCJ/ INCS	CPI	CPM	SOC	PSP/ KMPP	SSP	SWA	BJS/ BJP	JNP	JNPS/ LD/ DMKP	Other parties	IND	Total
1952	364	–	16	–	12	9	–	–	3	–	–	47	38	489
1957	371	–	27	–	–	19	–	–	4	–	–	31	42	494
1962	361	–	29	–	6	12	–	18	14	–	–	34	20	494
1967	283	–	23	19	–	13	23	44	35	–	–	45	35	520
1971	352	16	23	25	–	2	3	8	22	–	–	53	14	518
1977	154	3	7	22	–	–	–	–	–	295	–	52	9	542
1980	353	13	11	36	–	–	–	–	–	31	41	35	9	529
1984	415	5	6	22	–	–	–	–	2	10	3	74	5	542

Source: V. B. Singh and Shankar Bose, *Elections in India: Data Handbook on Lok Sabha Elections, 1952–8*, 2nd edn (New Delhi: Sage Publications, 1984), pp. 26–27 and 66.

Table 3.3. *Vote and seat shares for Congress in eight parliamentary elections, 1952–84*

Election	Vote (in %)	Seats Number	Seats Percentage
1952	45.0	364	74
1957	47.8	371	75
1962	44.7	361	73
1967	40.8	283	54
1971	43.7	352	68
1977	34.5	154	28
1980	42.7	353	67
1984	48.1	415	77

Source: As for tables 3.1 and 3.2

Non-Congress parties

Radical and revolutionary parties and movements[2]

Radical parties and politics have constituted a second important style of politics of differing degrees of importance in different parts of the country. The Left itself has been broadly divided since the 1930s into two main streams – Socialist and Communist.

After Independence, both broad movements split into numerous new parties, sometimes merging for a brief time only to split again. In the end, the result of the post-Independence history of splits and mergers has been the virtual disappearance of the non-Communist Left as a major political force anywhere in India and the division of the Communist movement into two chief parties, one of which, the Communist party of India (Marxist) or CPM, has achieved dominance in the state of West Bengal, was also dominant for a decade in the small adjacent state of Tripura as well, and retains considerable importance in the state of Kerala, while the other, the Communist Party of India (CPI), has important regional strength in Kerala, West Bengal, and Bihar.

[2] This section draws heavily from Paul R. Brass, "Political Parties of the Radical Left in South Asian Politics," in Paul R. Brass and Marcus F. Franda (eds.), *Radical Politics in South Asia* (Cambridge, MA: MIT Press, 1973), pp. 3–118.

Aside from the usual opportunistic reasons and leadership conflicts that have contributed to or been dominant factors in party splits among most parties in India, there has been a single principal theme which caused divisions in both the Socialist and Communist movements, namely, the stance to be taken towards the ruling Congress. Division on that issue, rather than divisions in the international Communist movement, were principally responsible for the split in the CPI in 1964, which led to the formation of the CPM, and for the splintering off from both Communist parties after 1969 of a number of romantic revolutionary and terrorist movements. The CPI, throughout most of its post-Independence history, has favored a strategy of alliance with the Congress or at least with "progressive elements" within the Congress, whereas the CPM has favored a more militant policy of opposition to the Congress. Both parties, however, have adhered to a parliamentary and reformist rather than to a violent, revolutionary path.

A similar division occurred among the non-Communist Left parties in the 1960s and constituted the principal ideological division between the more militant Socialist wing led by Dr. Rammanohar Lohia and the less militant Praja Socialist Party. However, the Socialist parties ultimately disappeared as organized entities and their various leaders ended up in several political parties which no longer bore a Socialist label.

The Communist movement also experienced two prolonged periods of debate on the question of political tactics, that is, whether to pursue parliamentarism or revolution. The first period, in which the central focus of debate was the famous Communist-led insurrection in the Telengana region of Andhra, saw the "anti-capitalist strategy" of revolutionary confrontation with state authority defeated by 1950 both in theoretical debate and in practice by the intervention of the Indian army. From 1950 to 1967, despite the split in the CPI in 1964, there was a broad consensus on the pursuit of parliamentarism and a multi-class strategy.

If the first debate was precipitated by the Telengana insurrection, the second was inspired by the split from the CPM in Bengal of a local group of party activists who were leading a violent agitation in the Naxalbari subdivision of Darjeeling district. The incidents in Naxalbari were followed by the spread of revolutionary romanticism among numerous Communist splinter groups, using terrorist tactics in widely dispersed pockets of the Indian countryside. Although the Communist parties, particularly the CPM, were initially shaken by these developments, neither of the two established parties diverged from their essentially parliamentary and reformist paths.

Revolutionary movements, represented by such formations as the Communist Party of India (Marxist-Leninist) and various fragments of it, the People's War party and numerous other small groups in Andhra Pradesh and elsewhere have not been able to mobilize large segments of the population at the national or state levels. They have failed to do so partly because of the police and military power of the Indian state and partly because of deficiencies in their ideology and tactics. Nevertheless, numerous local movements, some using violence, have continued to arise from time to time in several regions of the country.[3]

Several other ideological issues have distinguished or divided the parties of the Left from each other and from the Congress. The Socialist parties tended to favor Gandhian economic proposals for labor-intensive, small-scale industrial development and decentralization of the planning process whereas the Communists have continued to demand an even more single-minded heavy industrialization strategy than that pursued by the Congress. The Socialist parties tended to adopt distinctive positions on contemporary international issues focusing on the role of India as an independent actor in South Asia and in the world as a whole, whereas the Communist parties have been far more oriented towards the superpower struggle and towards a policy of alignment with the Socialist camp in that world struggle.

There has always been a high degree of regionalization of support for the Communist parties, whose strength was originally concentrated in Kerala, West Bengal, and Andhra. However, since the 1950s, the Communists have disintegrated organizationally in

[3] Bhabani Sen Gupta, "Communism Further Divided," in Henry C. Hart (ed.), *Indira Gandhi's India: A Political System Reappraised* (Boulder, CO: Westview Press, 1976), pp. 158–159 and 163–164, and Ghanshyam Shah, "Grass-Roots Mobilization in Indian Politics," in Atul Kohli (ed.), *India's Democracy: An Analysis of Changing State–Society Relations* (Princeton, NJ: Princeton University Press, 1988), pp. 287, 291–293, and *passim*.

Andhra, have been confronted in Kerala with a powerful Congress-led counter-coalition, and have remained strongest primarily in West Bengal. The Communist parties have been strongest in areas where Congress dominance of the nationalist movement was weakest. Their regional strength, therefore, derives more from political-historical than from economic factors.

The bastions of the Socialist movement were Bihar and U. P. where the young Socialists took the lead in the 1942 Quit India movement. Socialist strength in north India, therefore, like Communist strength elsewhere, is explained best by political-historical rather than economic factors.

The lack of clear differentiation among India's rural classes combined with the continued economic-political predominance at the local level of the elite and middle status landed castes has led most Left parties to pursue multi-class strategies rather than focusing solely on the poor peasantry and the landless. Both Communist parties have developed considerable strength among industrial workers in the major cities in India, the CPM in Kerala has considerable strength among the rural proletariat, but both the CPI and the CPM have drawn broad support from the landed peasantry as well in areas where they have been strong.

India has been distinctive among non-Communist countries in the extent to which Communist parties have actually held power at the state level. In Kerala, the CPM leads a counter-coalition against a Congress-dominated coalition, with whom it alternates in power. In West Bengal, the CPM has become the dominant party and has been in power at the head of a Left coalition in which it is overwhelmingly dominant since 1977. Compared with the Congress, the Communist parties have tended in power to be more serious about and more effective in implementing measures of agrarian reform such as land ceilings and land redistribution and programs for the poor to provide them with employment opportunities and income-producing assets.

Although the Communist parties are allowed to control state governments, there are limitations on the performance that can be expected from them in a federal system where so much power remains with the Center. Other factors limiting the ability of the Left parties to introduce more radical change have been the absence of

Left unity, the threat of political repression by the Center if the radical parties attempt to do too much too fast, and the fact that one of the leading communist parties has often been in alliance with the ruling Congress party. The prospects for further radical change in the future also are limited because the Left parties lack the necessary popular support outside of their areas of regional strength.

Right-wing, agrarian, and militant nationalist parties

The Swatantra Party. The only authentic party of the traditional Right, as that term would be understood in Europe, was the Swatantra party, a coalition of urban big business and rural aristocratic and landlord elements in which the latter were dominant. The Swatantra party, which drew together a number of regional parties such as the Ganatantra Parishad in Orissa, the Janata party of the Raja of Ramgarh in Bihar, a coalition of landed groups in Gujarat, some of the former princes in Rajasthan, and scattered discontented former landlords in other parts of the country, was formed on an all-India basis in 1959. The Swatantra party was of consequence nationally only in three general elections, in 1962, 1967, and 1972. In 1967, it succeeded in winning 44 seats in the Lok Sabha, emerging as the second largest party in the House after the Congress (see table 3.2 above). During its heyday, Swatantra was the leading secular party of the right offering a full-scale critique of the Congress policies of centralized planning, nationalization of industries, agrarian reform, and nonalignment.

Lok Dal. A second major agrarian-based party which succeeded in achieving broad support in north India after its foundation in 1969, played a central role in the Janata coalition against the Congress in 1977, and subsequently emerged as the second largest party in the Lok Sabha in 1980 was the Lok Dal. The Lok Dal began life in U. P. under the leadership of a prominent former Congressman, Charan Singh, who left the Congress to form the first non-Congress government in that state in 1967. Charan Singh drew his agrarian supporters together, most of whom came from the so-called backward or middle-status cultivating peasant proprietor castes, into a new political party called the BKD, which emerged as the second largest party after the Congress in that state in its first electoral contest in the 1969 mid-term legislative assembly elections.

In 1974, the largest section of the radical Socialists in both U. P. and Bihar, consisting primarily of those leaders whose support bases came from the backward classes in those states, joined forces with Charan Singh's BKD, which was thereafter called the BLD. In 1977, the BLD in turn merged into the Janata coalition. When that coalition itself fell apart, largely as a consequence of Charan Singh's aspirations to displace Morarji Desai and become Prime Minister himself, the old BLD reemerged as the Lok Dal.

Jan Sangh. A major political tradition in modern Indian history that carried forward into the post-Independence period has drawn its central ideas and symbols from Hindu traditions and culture. Although the Jan Sangh was considered by its detractors to be a Hindu communal, even anti-Muslim party with fascist inclinations, its members would vehemently deny such charges and would accept only that they are militant nationalists in a Hindu country which, as such, ought legitimately to draw its symbols of nationalism from the predominantly Hindu traditions of the country.

The Jan Sangh aspired to become a national party and it did succeed in winning significant representation in the Lok Sabha in several elections from 1952 onwards, reaching a peak of 35 seats in the 1967 elections, making it the third largest party in the House after Congress and Swatantra. However, the overwhelming bulk of its support always came from the north Indian Hindi-speaking states of U. P., Bihar, M. P., Rajasthan, and Haryana. The Jan Sangh was a formidable force in north India not only because of the appeal of its ideology but because it was able to call upon a disciplined body of political workers from a militant Hindu cultural organization known as the Rashtriya Swayamsevak Sangh (RSS), who always provided the most vigorous canvassers at election time.

Party manifestoes emphasized the maintenance of traditional Hindu institutions of family, caste structure, and law. They demanded the displacement of English by Hindi as the sole official language of the country. They opposed concessions to the Muslim minority on matters of language and education. On economic issues, they opposed excessive state control over the Indian economy and were in favor of more liberal policies towards business and industry.

The leadership and the principal support bases of the Jan Sangh came mainly from merchants, shopkeepers, and businessmen in the towns, from big landlords in the countryside, and from some of the middle and rich peasant groups in the countryside. Although it drew support in some areas from middle status cultivating castes, its dominant leadership generally came from elite castes, particularly Brahmans.

The rise and fall of the Janata coalition

All the leading parties of the non-Communist Left, of the Center and of the Right, with the later addition also of some defectors from the Congress, joined forces during and towards the end of the Emergency to form a new political formation called the Janata party.

The program and policies of the Janata party drew primarily from the agrarian ideas of Charan Singh for the promotion of agriculture, a self-sufficient peasantry, and labor-intensive small-scale industry. Similar ideas and an emphasis on a decentralized approach to planning also were contributed by the Socialist participants in the coalition. During the Janata period in power, a significant shift was made in the direction of increased allocations in the Sixth Five Year Plan for agriculture especially.

Structurally, the Janata party never succeeded in becoming anything other than a loosely-knit coalition of ambitious political leaders and political parties which attempted to retain their previous organizational and social support bases. A struggle for preeminence developed within the central government itself, especially between Charan Singh and Morarji Desai, with Charan Singh seeking to displace Morarji and become Prime Minister himself. In July, 1979, the coalition broke apart, Charan Singh became Prime Minister for three weeks only until his resignation and the calling of a new election, which led in 1980 to the return of Mrs. Gandhi and the Congress to power.

After the disintegration of the Janata coalition, the political parties which initially joined it either re-formed themselves with new names or disintegrated. The principal remnants of the original Janata coalition today are the Lok Dal (divided since the illness and death of Charan Singh in 1987 into two separate parties, Lok Dal [A] and Lok Dal [B]), the Janata party led by a former Congressman of

78

moderate Socialist inclinations, Mr. Chandrashekar, and the Bharatiya Janata Party, which consists primarily of former Jan Sangh leaders and members.

Regional parties

In several states in India, the largest non-Congress political parties are specific to a single state and have little or no strength outside their home state. The most important such parties are the AIADMK and the DMK in Tamil Nadu, the Telugu Desam in Andhra, the Akali Dal in Punjab, the National Conference in Jammu & Kashmir, and the Asom Gana Parishad in Assam. In fact, in all these states, the non-Congress parties won majorities in legislative assembly elections held between 1984 and 1989 (see table 3.4) and formed governments thereafter, in some cases with the support of the Congress, in most cases independently of Congress support.

These single-state parties are distinguished by their adoption of a regional nationalist perspective, by their political desire for greater regional autonomy of states in the Indian Union, for their focus on issues specific to their states, or for their base within a religious minority. Thus, the DMK and AIADMK, which trace their origins to the Dravidian movement of the nineteenth century and to the Self-Respect and Non-Brahman movements of the twentieth century stand primarily for the promotion of Tamil regional cultural identity and the Tamil language and against the intrusion of the Hindi language into Tamil Nadu. After the death of its leader, C. N. Annadurai, in 1969, the DMK split into its present two offshoots, of which the AIADMK, led by the film star, M. G. Ramachandran (MGR), emerged dominant in the 1977 elections and became the ruling party in Tamil Nadu, with MGR as its chief minister until his death in December, 1987.

The Telugu Desam in Andhra is a much more recent formation than the DMK, having been founded only in 1982. Although it does not have the long history and the deep roots in regional culture and social structure that the DMK and AIADMK have in Tamil Nadu, it appeals to similar political and social forces of regional nationalism and non-Brahmanism. It is also led, like the AIADMK under MGR, by a film star, N. T. Rao (NTR). Under NTR's leadership, the Telugu Desam swept into power in Andhra in 1983 and, in the

Table 3.4. *Number of seats won by Congress and principal
opposition party in 1984–89 State Legislative Assembly elections*

State	Congress	Principal opposition	
Andhra Pradesh	50	202	(TD)
Assam	25	64	(AGP)
Bihar	196	46	(DMKP/LKD)
Gujarat	149	14	(Janata)
Haryana	5	58	(DMKP/LKD)
Himachal Pradesh	58	7	(BJP)
Jammu & Kashmir	24	36*	(NC-F)
Karnataka	66	139	(Janata)
Kerala	33	36	(CPM)
Madhya Pradesh	250	58	(BJP)
Maharashtra	162	54	(Cong-S)
Orissa	117	21	(Janata)
Pondicherry	15	6	(AIADMK)
Punjab	32	73	(Akali Dal)
Rajasthan	113	39	(BJP)
Sikkim	1	30	(SSP)
Tamil Nadu	25	170	(DMK)
Uttar Pradesh	269	84	(DMKP/LKD)
West Bengal	40	187	(CPM)

* Congress (I) ally.
Sources: Government of India, Election Commission, *Third Annual Report,
1985* (New Delhi: Government of India Press, 1986), pp. 93 and 97; *Overseas
Hindustan Times*, January 4, 1986; *India Today*, April 15, 1987; *New York
Times*, June 23, 1987.

aftermath of some crude efforts by the Governor of the state to topple the government before the 1984 parliamentary elections, roundly defeated the Congress in the state in those elections and won a two-thirds majority in the legislative assembly elections in March, 1985.

A third major regional party is the Akali Dal in the Punjab, which arose as an offshoot of the Sikh Gurdwara Reform movement of the 1920s and has since been the principal political arm of Sikhs in the Punjab who have sought a special political status for their community in a state within the Indian Union where the Sikh religion and the Punjabi language would be especially protected and promoted. In 1966, the Akali Dal succeeded in wresting from the central government after prolonged struggle a separate, Sikh-majority province called Punjabi Suba. However, since Sikhs constitute only a bare majority of the population of the Punjab and many Sikhs have always supported the Congress, the Akali Dal has never been able to achieve the kind of dominance in Punjab gained by the AIADMK in Tamil Nadu. The Akali Dal instead has been involved in a dualistic competition with the Congress for power in the Punjab in which it has sometimes succeeded in forming the government, often in coalition with other non-Congress parties.

Jammu & Kashmir is another state in which there is an entrenched political party stronger than the Congress itself. The National Conference of Dr. Farooq Abdullah is currently the ruling party in that state, governing in 1988 with the support of the Congress, with which it developed a pre-electoral alliance. The National Conference is the descendant of the original All Jammu & Kashmir Muslim Conference founded in 1932, in which Dr. Farooq's father, Sheikh Abdullah, was the dominant force until his death in 1982 when the leadership of the party was taken over by his son. Although the loyalty of Sheikh Abdullah and his party to India has sometimes been questioned, it is more accurate to see the Abdullah family and the parties they have led as supporters of Kashmiri Muslim identity and regional political autonomy within India, but not as proponents of merger with Pakistan.

In Assam, the principal driving force behind the rise of the regional Gana Parishad as the dominant party in the state was the issue of legal and illegal migrations of outsiders into Assam, particularly from West Bengal and Bangladesh and their entry onto the electoral rolls, usually as Congress supporters. After a prolonged and often violent agitation on the part of Assamese students and politicians demanding the removal of illegal migrants from the electoral rolls and from the state and country as well, an accord was reached with the central government on these issues in August, 1985, which was followed by parliamentary and legislative assembly elections in December. In those elections, the Gana Parishad won 7 of 14 Lok Sabha seats to the Congress' 4 and also won a majority in the Assam legislative assembly and formed a government in the state thereafter.

The state units of the CPM too have become, in effect, regional parties insofar at least as their popular support is concerned. The CPM polled 81 percent of its total vote in the 1984 Lok Sabha elections in the two states of Kerala and West Bengal, 84 percent in those two states plus Tripura. In West Bengal, the CPM remained in 1989 the ruling party. In Kerala and Tripura, it was the principal opposition to the Congress.

When one considers also that in several other states, non-Congress parties are either dominant or equal rivals to the Congress in the state legislative assemblies and sometimes control their state's delegation of MPs to the Lok Sabha as well, the position of the Congress as the dominant party in the country seems much less secure than its 80 percent majority achieved in the Lok Sabha in the 1984 elections would indicate. The Congress, in fact, despite its huge majority in Parliament, was the dominant party in 1988 only in the Hindi-speaking states and the adjacent states of Gújarat, Maharashtra, and Orissa. In the northeast, in Bengal, in Kashmir, Punjab, and the entire south, non-Congress parties were dominant. In June, 1987, the Lok Dal broke the dominance of the Congress in one of the Hindi-speaking states as well, in Haryana, where it achieved a decisive majority in the legislative assembly in alliance with the BJP.

ELECTORAL POLITICS

The electoral process

As in the British parliamentary system, elections to the Lok Sabha (Lower House) of Parliament must be held within five years of the election of the previous parliament, but they may be called by the President upon the advice of the Prime Minister at any time before the expiration of the normal five-year term of the House. The actual mechanics of the election, including the delimitation of constituency boundaries, the setting of specific dates for the polling in different parts of the country, the establishment and manning of polling booths, the allocation of party symbols, the acceptance or rejection of nominations according to the electoral laws and rules, the counting of votes, the publication of the results, and the like are all supervised by the Election Commission, a semi-autonomous body whose functions are defined in the Constitution of the country.

Until 1971, when Prime Minister Gandhi called the first mid-term election for the Lok Sabha, the general practice was that a general election included the simultaneous scheduling of polling for both the Lok Sabha and the state legislative assemblies. The call by Mrs. Gandhi for a mid-term election in 1971 and the consequent "de-linking" of parliamentary and legislative assembly elections at that time included the clear design to separate the national from the state elections and thereby to capitalize upon the national appeal of Mrs. Gandhi against her rivals in the Congress organization and in state politics generally. Since 1971, the general practice has been to hold parliamentary and state legislative assembly elections separately, although they do sometimes coincide in particular states.

At present, the electoral unit, as in Britain, is a single-member constituency, in which the winning candidate is the person who succeeds in gaining a plurality of votes on the first ballot. The only distinction among constituencies concerns whether they are reserved for Scheduled Castes or Scheduled Tribes or not. In a reserved constituency, only persons from designated low caste or tribal groups may contest, but all adults are eligible to vote. The number of reserved constituencies is proportionate to the total population of Scheduled Castes or Tribes within a state. In the country as a whole, approximately 21 percent of the total Lok Sabha and state legislative assembly seats are reserved.

Most Indian constituencies are overwhelmingly rural, containing only a few small towns, in which each polling booth covers a single village or several adjacent villages. In the urban areas, there will naturally be a large number of polling booths set up in ways familiar in industrialized societies within public buildings such as schools.

Most Indians are still unable to read. Therefore, each party and independent candidate is allocated a distinctive symbol (figure 2).

Election campaigns

A campaign in a rural constituency requires a candidate who aspires to success to visit as many as possible of the 100 or so villages in an assembly constituency and at least a sample of the 500 or 600 villages of a parliamentary constituency. Such campaigning, concentrated within the statutory three-week period, is an extraordinarily grueling experience, carried out by jeep, by foot, and by bullock

INDIAN NATIONAL CONGRESS (I)

JANATA PARTY

BHARATIYA JANATA PARTY

COMMUNIST PARTY OF INDIA

COMMUNIST PARTY OF INDIA (M)

INDIAN NATIONAL CONGRESS (S)

LOK DAL

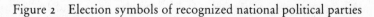

Figure 2   Election symbols of recognized national political parties

84

cart, with each candidate scheduling perhaps as many as six village visits a day. In the cities, election campaigning involves neighborhood street corner rallies, house-to-house canvassing by the candidates' workers, and parades through the city with the candidate himself riding in a jeep saluting the crowds as he drives through the town.

There are three principal means of communicating the message of a party or of independent candidates during a campaign. Each well-organized party will issue a printed manifesto in both English and the vernacular language, stating the distinctive positions of the party on the major issues of the day. The second means of communication is through public speeches by candidates and their supporters in the villages and city street corners. The third type of approach to the voters is through private and implicit appeals. Canvassers will, in this respect, depart from the printed manifestoes and public statements of their candidates and will stress ties of caste between the candidate and his brethren, his accomplishments or promises to do things for particular villages and localities, the candidate's probity and his rivals' venality, with emphasis especially on any evidence that can be found or concocted that the candidate's principal rival has had some criminal record or has had some criminal charges filed against him.

Indian voting behavior

A multiplicity of factors affect voter decisions at election time, including appeals to class, community, caste, and faction loyalty as well as the personal attractions of popular and charismatic leaders. At the local level, in the countryside, by far the most important factor in voting behavior remains caste solidarity. Large and important castes in a constituency tend to back either a respected member of their caste or a political party with whom their caste members identify. However, local factions and local-state factional alignments, which involve inter-caste coalitions also are important factors in influencing voting behavior.

Issues also matter in India and may sometimes sway many groups of voters in the same direction and create a "wave" or landslide across large parts of the country. One wave developed in 1967 against the Congress on issues of rising prices, scarcity, and the discontent of government employees and students in north India. A second occurred in 1971–72 – first in the parliamentary then the legislative assembly elections – in favor of Mrs. Gandhi in the aftermath of her struggles with the old Congress party bosses and her leadership of the country in the Third Indo-Pakistan War which brought about the Independence of Bangladesh. A third swept the Janata coalition into power in 1977 as a consequence of widespread discontent with alleged excesses committed by government during the Emergency regime. In 1984, a fourth wave arose in sympathy with Rajiv Gandhi after the assassination of his mother and in response to his appeals for national unity against forces said to threaten the unity and integrity of the country.

Parties and elections

Parties do not dominate electoral politics in India to the same extent as in Western parliamentary systems. There are many localities in India where local notables, often descendants of great landlord or princely families, and other persons with independent bases of local power and support within a caste group, for example, have sufficient independent resources either to contest elections successfully on their own or to bargain for the support of established political parties. Moreover, in contrast with Western parliamentary regimes, the notion of party loyalty is extremely weak in India. Persons from factional groups defeated in struggles to gain the party nominations for themselves or their allies and supporters in a general election rarely hesitate either to switch their loyalties to another party which offers them a nomination or to contest the election as independents.

Finally, few parties in India persist and become institutionalized. Although the Indian National Congress is one of the oldest political parties in the world and the Communist parties trace their origins to the 1920s, most other parties in India have had relatively brief existences, in some cases only for a single election, in others for two or three.

It remains possible, nevertheless, to identify in any election broad categories of voters who vote similarly in large parts of the country and to isolate general factors that influence broad groups of people. One can say, for example, that urban working classes in some of India's major cities tend to vote Communist, that the commercial classes in north Indian cities have tended to vote either for the Congress or the Jan Sangh/BJP, that the Congress gains strong support from the richer farmers and former landlords, and that the Lok Dal's strength is concentrated among the middle and rich peasantry. There is also evidence of partisan voting by segments of the electorate across several elections.[4] On the other hand, neither the candidates nor those who wish to interpret the results of Indian elections can afford to ignore the particularities of Indian voting behavior, which contribute to its volatility.[5]

Election results, 1951 to 1987

The vote for the Congress

The Congress organization clearly has been the leading political institution in post-Independence India. Since Independence, there has always been one predominant Congress organization in the country, which has always been either in power or has been the largest opposition party in Parliament and which has also always had broader support in most states of the Indian Union than any other party, even though it has never won a clear majority of the popular votes in the country (table 3.3 above).

The vote for the non-Congress parties

With the exception of the 1977 elections, no single non-Congress party has ever polled even as much as half the Congress vote in the country as a whole. The Election Commission has always made a

---

[4] For example, in West Bengal for the Communists and in Punjab for several political parties. For West Bengal, see John O. Field and Marcus F. Franda, *The Communist Parties of West Bengal*, vol. I in the series of Myron Weiner and John O. Field (eds.), *Studies in Electoral Politics in the Indian States* (Delhi: Manohar Book Service, 1974), and, for Punjab, Paul R. Brass, "Ethnic Cleavages and the Punjab Party System, 1952–1972," in vol. IV of the same series, *Party Systems and Electoral Cleavages* (Delhi: Manohar Book Service, 1975), pp. 7–69.

[5] Apparent stability in voting behavior over time is often illusory, moreover, as in the case of the Congress. William Vanderbok and Richard Sisson have remarked that "while there is relative consistency of Congress support in terms of votes aggregated on the national level . . . there have been pronounced fluctuations of Congress support in the states"; see "The Spatial Distribution of Congress Electoral Support: Trends from Four Decades of Parliamentary Elections," in Paul R. Brass and Francis Robinson, *The Indian National Congress and Indian Society: Ideology, Social Structure and Political Dominance* (Delhi: Chanakya Publications, 1987), p. 395. Similar results will be found in comparisons of votes aggregated to the state level with district voting and of district with constituency voting.

Table 3.5. *Vote shares for the Congress, "national" opposition parties, and others in parliamentary elections, 1952–84 (percent)*

Year	Congress	"National" opposition	Other parties and independents	Total
1952	45.0	22.8	32.3	100.0
1957	47.8	25.2	27.0	100.0
1962	44.7	33.7	21.5	100.0
1967	40.8	35.5	23.8	100.0
1971	43.7	34.1	22.2	100.0
1977	34.5	50.1	15.3	100.0
1980	42.7	42.4	14.9	100.0
1984	48.1	29.7	22.2	100.0

Source: As for tables 3.1 and 3.2

distinction in publishing the figures for parliamentary elections between "national" parties and other parties. For a time, there appeared to be a trend towards "nationalization" of the party system, with the vote for the "national" non-Congress parties having gone up from the 20–30 percent range in the 1950s to the 30–40 percent range between 1962 and 1971 to the 40–50 percent range in 1977 and 1980, with a corresponding decline in the relative vote shares of the category of "other parties and independents" (table 3.5). The trend, however, was partly illusory and appears especially chimerical in the face of the 1984 election results. Except for the Congress and the Communist parties, none of the other "national" parties has endured. Moreover, the second-place party has changed in every election since 1952, when the Socialist Party came in second with 10.6 percent of the vote (see table 3.1). It is also important to note that in any single parliamentary election the second-place party is likely to be different in different states. Second, many of the so-called national parties did not have a genuine national spread at all. Finally, even if there was a trend line towards nationalization of the opposition, it was demolished in the 1984 elections when the collective vote share of the "national" opposition parties was reduced to 29.7 percent, a figure lower than any in the previous five elections.

Table 3.6. *Congress and its closest competitor, by state,[a]*
parliamentary elections, 1984–85[b] (percent)

State	Congress (I)	Closest competitor	
Andhra Pradesh	41.8	44.8	(Telugu Desam)
Assam	23.6	33.4	(AGP)
Bihar	51.0	13.7	(DMKP/Lok Dal)
Gujarat	53.2	18.6	(BJP)
Haryana	55.0	19.1	(DMKP/Lok Dal)
Himachal Pradesh	67.6	23.3	(BJP)
Jammu & Kashmir	30.2	46.2	(NC-F)
Karnataka	51.6	35.1	(Janata)
Kerala	33.3	22.3	(CPM)
Madhya Pradesh	57.1	30.0	(BJP)
Maharashtra	51.2	12.1	(Congress-S)
Orissa	57.5	32.0	(Janata)
Punjab	37.6	37.2	(Akali Dal)
Rajasthan	52.7	23.7	(BJP)
Tamil Nadu	40.5	25.9	(DMK)
Uttar Pradesh	51.0	21.6	(DMKP/Lok Dal)
West Bengal	48.2	35.9	(CPM)

[a] Only the larger states of the Indian Union have been included. Excluded are Manipur, Meghalaya, Nagaland, Sikkim, and Tripura, which elect only one or two seats each to the Lok Sabha.
[b] Elections in Punjab and Assam were not held until September and December, 1985, respectively, because of disturbed conditions prevailing there at the time of the 1984 General Elections.
Source: As for tables 3.1 and 3.2, pp. 647–649.

Regional parties and state party systems

The most important reason for doubting the existence in India of anything that can be called a national party system is the fact that all the Indian states have distinctive party systems. The extent of variation in patterns of party competition and of regional variations in party strength can be seen by comparing the relative strength of the two leading parties in each state in the 1984–85 parliamentary and the subsequent legislative assembly elections (tables 3.4 and 3.6). In 17 states, the 1984–85 Lok Sabha elections produced 10 different configurations of first and second-place parties. Moreover,

Table 3.7. *Election data, Indian parliamentary elections, 1952–84*

Year	Electorate (in millions)	Polling stations	Votes polled (in millions)	Turnout (percent)
1952	173.2	132,560	80.7	46.6
1957	193.7	220,478	91.3	47.1
1962	217.7	238,355	119.9	55.1
1967	250.1	267,555	152.7	61.1
1971	274.1	342,944	151.5	55.3
1977	321.2	373,908	194.3	60.5
1980	355.6	434,442	202.3	56.9
1984	375.8	479,214	238.4	63.4

Source: Robert L. Hardgrave, Jr. and Stanley A. Kochanek, *India: Government and Politics in a Developing Nation*, 4th edn (San Diego: Harcourt Brace Jovanovich, 1986), p. 302.

it needs also to be kept in mind that, in the state legislative assembly elections, the leading non-Congress parties do much better in the smaller constituencies and in many states, as a result, they emerge as formidable opposition parties or even as the ruling parties, relegating the Congress to the opposition (table 3.4).

In short, both the attempt to nationalize parliamentary elections by delinking them from state legislative assembly elections and the overwhelming Congress dominance that is usually produced in Parliament have failed to erode significantly the distinctiveness of regional political patterns in India or to establish a truly national party system in the country.

Elections and political mobilization

Turnout has increased by nearly 17 percentage points from 46.6 percent in 1952 to 63.4 percent in 1984 (see table 3.7). Increasing turnout has also involved political mobilization of new groups of voters. In the legislative assembly elections especially, there has been a process of caste succession in the elections in which candidates both from elite caste groups which were less well represented before and from the larger backward caste groups have entered the electoral arena. Although the processes of political mobilization have affected the lower backward and the lowest castes (Scheduled Castes) as well, there is no firm evidence concerning their actual turnout rates.

The more widespread and politically significant process of political mobilization which has been occurring in many parts of the country has been the increasing mobilization of the middle status backward agricultural castes and the lower backward artisan, service, and smallholding castes. In some states, the backward castes (and some lower backward castes as well) have successfully displaced the previously dominant elite castes in leadership positions in the Congress. In other states, Tamil Nadu being the leading example, the backward castes have dominated the principal opposition to the Congress – the DMK and the AIADMK in Tamil Nadu – and have succeeded in displacing the Congress from power. In still other states, most notably the north Indian states of U. P. and Bihar, the old elite castes of Brahmans, Rajputs, and Bhumihars have remained dominant in the Congress, which itself has remained the dominant party, while the middle and lower backward castes have been mobilized by the opposition, first by the Socialists in the 1950s and 1960s, then by the Lok Dal in the 1960s and 1970s. Finally, in two other states, Kerala and West Bengal, the lower backward and even the Scheduled Castes have been mobilized by the CPM. However, electoral politics and political mobilization in most of India remain dominated by the leading land-controlling castes of elite or middle status.

INTEREST GROUPS AND INTERMEDIARIES

Interest groups

In additional to the array of political parties and revolutionary movements which have existed in India since Independence, there have also been a great number of interest groups. Like the parties, some existed before Independence, some have come into being only since Independence, some are institutionalized, others ephemeral. For analytical purposes, they can be broadly divided into the following types: organized interest groups comparable to similar formations which exist in Western industrial societies, such as trade unions, professional associations, associations of government employees, and the like: "demand groups," defined as broad

91

categories of people who have been mobilized from time to time in movements of one sort or another, such as "students" or "peasants;"[6] and influence groups, which operate in non-public arenas such as Parliament or the state legislatures or come into being at critical moments such as a succession.

In the first category of organized interest groups, most of which have apex associations and central officies, are the trade unions, business associations, professional associations, and associations of government employees of various types. In addition to these nationally organized interest associations, which organize groups and have names which are similar to those which exist in Western industrial societies, there are myriad national, state, and local associations of merchants and tradesmen whose existence is noted by journalists or scholars only when a major policy issue affects their interests and precipitates a public agitation. They include associations of food-grains traders, cloth merchants, goldsmiths, and the like.

Such organized interests operate within only a small segment of Indian society, namely, in the sectors dominated by large-scale, bureaucratic organizations: factories, urban trade associations, professional groups, and civil servants whose constituencies comprise no more than 10 percent of the population of the country.[7] These organized groups, moreover, have much less influence than their Western counterparts in the formulation of broad policies and legislation, which has been dominated since Independence by the Prime Minister, the Prime Minister's Secretariat, the Cabinet at times, and the Planning Commission. It is largely after the passage of legislation and after the formulation of rules and regulations that interest representation – as opposed to outright blockage of government legislation – matters in India and it then becomes highly individualized or localized rather than a matter of general policy formulation and implementation. It is the application of general rules to particular cases which matters most for business, for example, and the mediation of labor tribunals in local labor-

---

[6] This term comes from Lloyd I. Rudolph and Susanne H. Rudolph, *In Pursuit of Lakshmi: The Political Economy of the Indian State* (Chicago: University of Chicago Press, 1987), pp. 247 ff.

[7] Rudolph and Rudolph, *In Pursuit of Lakshmi*, p. 22.

management conflicts that matters for labor on a day-to-day basis, for another example.[8]

A further feature of the large apex organizations in India is that they are often paper organizations which cannot mobilize their memberships or they cancel each other out in such a way as to leave only the organization recognized by the state with influence or to leave none with influence at the highest levels of government. Finally, there is a general tendency at all levels within even the "organized" sectors of Indian society towards multiplication and fragmentation of organizations: in the case of labor, for example, from the national to the state to the factory level so that, at base, what one has in the factories themselves is often no effective organization at all.[9]

The second broad type of interest formation in India has been given the name "demand group" by the Rudolphs to describe the movements which arise from time to time in India to make demands on behalf of persons in the relatively less organized and bureaucratized sectors of society, such as "students" or "peasants" or whole religious or language or regional groups rather than specific functional groups.[10]

The third general type of interest association in India is the influence group with informal leaders or elites at its head who are presumed to be able to mobilize larger numbers of people for specific purposes. Examples of this type are caucuses of Muslim or Scheduled Caste MPs in Parliament, who may seek specific concessions from government or generally influence government policies on matters of concern to their constituencies simply by their evident presence or may intervene through their leaders at crisis points such as a succession.[11]

Operating across all three types of representation are two types of interest associations which are either unique to India or at least more prevalent in non-Western societies such as India than in Western industrial societies. These are revivalist movements and caste associ-

---

[8] Rudolph and Rudolph, *In Pursuit of Lakshmi*, p. 277.
[9] Rudolph and Rudolph, *In Pursuit of Lakshmi*, p. 280.
[10] Rudolph and Rudolph, *In Pursuit of Lakshmi*, pp. 252–254.
[11] See, for example, Michael Brecher, *Succession in India: A Study in Decision-Making* (London: Oxford University Press, 1966), pp. 55–56, 72–73, and S. C. Gangal, *Prime Minister and the Cabinet in India* (New Delhi: Navachetna Prakashan, 1972), pp. 37–38.

ions. Revivalist movements are formed either to protect or promote aspects of indigenous culture or practice which allegedly were destroyed or suffered severe disadvantages during the long periods of alien and colonial rule or to eliminate practices which were allegedly introduced and which were not in conformity with traditional practice. Examples of this type of movement would include such very important religious organizations as the Arya Samaj, which arose in western India in the late nineteenth century and became especially prominent in the Punjab where it continues to be a major force today. This movement flourished amid the religious controversies in the Punjab among Christian missionaries, Hindus, Muslims, and Sikhs and took as its main goals the purification of Hindu faith by going back to the original teachings in the Vedas, eliminating accretions since those days such as practices of caste discrimination and untouchability, and defending Hinduism against missionary activities of Christians or Muslims or Sikhs.[12]

A leading non-religious example has been the movement to revive, reform, and promote the teaching and practice of the Ayurvedic system of medicine throughout India. This movement, which can be traced back to the late nineteenth century, has taken modern organizational forms through various formally organized associations, publication of journals, and lobbying of prominent political leaders and the central and state governments for support.[13]

Although many revivalist movements have taken the explicit organizational form of modern, bureaucratic interest associations and are indistinguishable in these respect from their non-revivalist counterparts, revivalist movements in general are distinguished by their greater capacity to act as demand groups and to speak or claim to speak on behalf of a much wider group. So, for example, there are permanent interest associations and societies for the protection of the cow in India, which regularly publish journals and lobby state and central legislatures to prevent cow slaughter and to provide *gosthalas* or rest farms for old and non-productive cows. However, these societies, which have existed since at least the late nineteenth

[12] See esp. Kenneth W. Jones, *Arya Dharm: Hindu-Consciousness in 19th-Century Punjab* (Berkeley: University of California Press, 1976).

[13] Paul R. Brass, "The Politics of Ayurvedic Education: A Case Study of Revivalism and Modernization in India," in Susanne H. and Lloyd I. Rudolph (eds.), *Education and Politics in India* (Cambridge, MA: Harvard University Press, 1972).

century, can also sometimes launch mass movements with the participation of other organizations such as, for example, the Arya Samaj.

The second type of specialized interest association in India is the caste association. Caste associations operate both as formal interest groups in the organized sector of Indian society and as formal and informal interest groups in the small towns and rural areas of the country. The local, informal organization of a *jati* (local caste group) may be mobilized at any time for specific, local or broader political purposes such as an election campaign or a confrontation with caste rivals or with the local police.

There are also various types of more-than-local organizations of castes into caste associations or informal influence groups. Formal caste associations exist for many caste categories, that is, for castes which are not necessarily interconnected by kinship and other local ties, but which have the same name and a similar status over a broad area. Politicians from large and important castes often also act as leaders of influence groups in the state legislatures,where they may caucus across party lines or within a single dominant party, especially the Congress, to achieve ministerial office for themselves and special favors for their constituents.

With the exception of the Scheduled Castes, there are no significant caste associations at the national, all-India level. Scheduled Castes, however, constitute an officially recognized category, a grouping of the so-called untouchable castes,with a fixed number of seats reserved for their representatives in the Lok Sabha. For virtually the entire post-Independence period, Jagjivan Ram, a member of the government from Independence until his death in 1986, was treated as if he were the spokesman for this grouping of castes.[14]

Intermediaries

In discussing revivalist movements and caste associations as specifically non-Western and Indian types of interest formations, we are stretching the very meaning of the term "interest group" as it

[14] See, for example, Brecher, *Succession in India*, pp. 49 & 73, W. H. Morris-Jones, "India Elects for Change – and Stability," *Asian Survey*, XI, No. 8 (August, 1971), 725, and Gangal, *Prime Minister and the Cabinet*, p. 48.

is used for Western representative political systems. There are yet two other forms of political "representation" in India which stretch still further the concept associated with the term "interest group" and with reference to which it is preferable to use another term, "intermediaries." The term "intermediaries" will be used here to refer to informal structures and individuals who act as links between the formal institutions of the Indian political order, parties and bureaucratic agencies, and the social institutions of Indian society, caste, family, and village. Two important examples of "intermediaries" are factions and brokers.

Factions

The importance of factions as dynamic components of Indian political parties has already been discussed above, but it is necessary to specify further their linkage role in the Indian political system and their centrality to its functioning.

Although aspects of factions and factional politics found in India exist elsewhere, the combination of features which describe Indian factions are unique and consist of the following elements especially. First are personalized, leader–follower relationships modeled in part on the master–disciple relationship so that some of the followers of faction leaders are, in effect, tied to the leader in a form of political apprenticeship. Secondly, however, it is also the leader's duty to care for the material interests of his followers, failing which all but the most intensely loyal will go elsewhere. The factional relationship between leaders and followers and between different factional leaders in broader factional coalitions is, therefore, markedly transactional in character, based on an exchange of favors for support. There is, consequently, a curious and specifically Indian combination of devotion and materialism in the factional tie.

Thirdly, the central concerns of faction leaders and followers in the provinces and districts of India are different from those of the ideologically-oriented party leaders in Delhi and in some of the state capitals and center around three sets of issues and interests in particular: land control, inter-caste and inter-communal relations, and access to local resources in general. The ways in which these sets of issues and interests affect state and local politics and the relationships between local and national politics will be discussed in the next chapter. Here, however, it is important to note that these differences in orientation of national party and government leaders, on the one hand, and faction leaders, on the other hand, point to the existence of several sets of discontinuities in the functioning of the Indian political system as a whole: between ideology and practice, policy and implementation, national issues and state and local issues. Factions provide at once an indispensable set of linkages in a subcontinental federal political system in an agrarian society which remains socially fragmented and heterogeneous and a dissolvent which renders impractical most of the proclaimed goals of the national leaders of the country.

In short, factions and personal leader–follower ties have been the principal structural components of the "parties" in the Indian party or, better, the Indian factional system. Aside from the Congress, only the Communist parties in West Bengal and Kerala, perhaps the DMK in Tamil Nadu, and the Akali Dal in the Punjab, which themselves are by no means free of factions, can claim an organizational existence separate from their founding leaders.

Brokers

If factions and faction leaders act as intermediaries between political parties and the people, there is another whole class of intermediaries who act as "brokers" between the people and the administration. They are also called "middlemen" and "fixers" in English, "*dalals*" in north India and "*pyraveekars*" (persons who follow through on matters and get things done) in Andhra.[15]

It is certain that this kind of specialized brokerage has been going on in India at least since British times, especially with the introduction of the complex revenue administration.[16] However, there is little doubt that a major change and a dramatic increase in the need for brokers occurred after Independence with the extension of rural development activities and benefits to the cultivators. Moreover, the potential profitability of the broker's activities also increased sub-

---

[15] F. G. Bailey, *Politics and Social Change: Orissa in 1959* (Berkeley: University of California Press, 1963), and G. Ram Reddy and G. Haragopal, "The Pyraveekar: 'The Fixer' in Rural India," *Asian Survey*, xxv, No. 11 (November, 1985), 1,148–1,162; see also Philip Oldenburg, "Middlemen in Third-World Corruption: Implications of an Indian Case," *World Politics*, xxxix, No. 4 (July, 1987), 508–535.

[16] Ram Reddy and Haragopal, "The Pyraveekar," p. 1,151.

stantially as government began to include cash loans and subsidies in its programs for the rural cultivators.[17] A still further boost in the opportunities for money-making came with the introduction of the poverty-programs in the 1970s, which have involved the direct disbursement of cash, subsidies, animals, bullock carts, and other material benefits for designated categories of the rural poor.

The extension of rural development activities has also involved a proliferation of departments, agencies, and special programs to implement them, which are invariably poorly coordinated and often in conflict with each other. The brokers are the only persons in the local scene, aside from the seniormost district authorities, who are in a position to link the disparate activities of numerous development agencies and who have the incentive to do so.[18]

Both Bailey and Reddy have noted that, while the work of the brokers and *pyraveekars* often facilitates communication and program implementation, it also leads to the distortion of information, the diversion of development funds to persons and groups other than those for whom they are intended, and to the spread of corruption throughout the administrative system.[19] The flourishing of the brokerage system, therefore, must be seen as a reflection on the general failure of the administrative system of post-Independence India to function effectively, popularly, and honestly.

[17] Ram Reddy and Haragopal, "The Pyraveekar," p. 1,152.
[18] Ram Reddy and Haragopal, "The Pyraveekar," pp. 1,157–1,158.
[19] Ram Reddy and Haragopal, "The Pyraveekar," pp. 1,159–1,162 and Bailey, *Politics and Social Change*, pp. 60, 66, 101–102.

CHAPTER 4

STATE AND LOCAL POLITICS

Parallel trends and counter-tendencies have been at work especially in the post-Nehru period both in center–state relations and in the relations between state governments and district institutions. With regard to center–state relations, the offices and institutions of state government have increasingly been turned into instruments for implementing the will of the central government leadership. The counter-tendency, partly arising out of India's regional/cultural heterogeneity but also in response to the imposition of Delhi's direct and indirect rule over the states, has been the increasing assertion of demands for regional autonomy, revision of center–state relations, and the regionalization of state politics and party systems.

Insofar as district and local politics are concerned, similar processes have been at work. On the one hand, ruling parties in the state governments, particularly the Congress, have allowed district and local institutions of self-government to decline or have limited their powers or have even frequently superseded them altogether in order to maintain tighter control over local systems of patronage and to establish stable bases of local support. The counter-tendency has been the persistence, even the reassertion, of structures of local power which exist independently of government and party organizations and the revival of interest, especially among the non-Congress parties, in the restoration of local institutions of self-government.

STATE POLITICS

Roles of the state governor

The constitutional role provided for the state governors and the practices which have evolved in relation to the office of governor since Independence have provided the focal point of contestation over the relative balance between autonomy and central control in

99

center–state relations. The central leadership in the Constituent Assembly was concerned to maintain the strength of the Center in relation to the states and to have the recourse to intervene in cases of serious instability and political and communal unrest. At the same time, they wished to establish full parliamentary government at the state as well as the central levels, in which a governor with executive power would be inconsistent. The Constitution partly reflects this ambiguity in its specification of the appointment and powers of the state governors.

The Constitution provides that the governors are to be appointed by the President, that is, in effect by the Prime Minister.[1] By far the most difficult and controversial aspects of the governor's roles have centered around the questions of appointment and dismissal of chief ministers and the power to dissolve the legislature and recommend the imposition of President's Rule (PR) on a state.

From Independence to 1967

The major issues in this period of relative state autonomy concerned the relations between the governor and the elected state government and the functions which the governor could rightfully exercise. Former state governor Sri Prakasa, who had been governor both of Madras and U. P. at different times, complained that the governors were not being made use of nor even kept properly informed or consulted by their chief ministers.[2]

Even before 1967, however, there were occasions when the governors were in a position to exercise discretion in the appointment or dismissal of state governments and when they sometimes acted relatively impartially and independently of either the state or central government. Sri Prakasa himself refers to such a situation in his description of his actions in Madras in 1952 when it was not evident whether the Congress or the United Front of non-Congress parties was in the stronger position to form a stable government and when there was also no clear choice within the Congress of a leader with majority support in his own party. Although it does not appear that he was acting on the direction of the Congress, it is clear that his

[1] Granville Austin, *The Indian Constitution: Cornerstone of the Nation* (Oxford: Clarendon Press, 1966), p. 117.

[2] Sri Prakasa, *State Governors in India* (Meerut: Meenakshi Prakashan, 1966), pp. 11–13.

actions were helpful to the Congress in forming a stable government in the state.[3]

The most famous case involving the imposition of PR in this period was the dismissal of the Communist ministry in Kerala in 1959 after popular demonstrations engineered and exploited by the Congress under the direction of Mrs. Gandhi, then Congress President. Although the state government retained a majority in the legislature, the governor justified his dismissal of it by referring to "a tremendous shift in the minds and in the feelings of the people," that is, in "public opinion,"[4] though no election or public opinion poll was held to support his assessment of this "shift."

The position of the governor in the pre-1967 period can be summed up as follows. In normal times, when there were stable governments and strong chief ministers in the states, the governors were reduced to figureheads and were even ignored. At times of instability, which were then less common than they later became, the governors had to exercise discretion in the appointment and dismissal of government and in making recommendations for the imposition of PR. The Madras case in 1952 involved the installation of a Congress government, the Kerala case in 1959 the dismissal of a non-Congress government. In both instances and in most others during this period, the results were consistent with the interests of the Congress, which were identified with the interests of the country and defined in terms of order, stability, and Congress rule.

From 1967 to 1980

In this period, which begins with the 1967 elections and the Congress loss of power mostly to unstable non-Congress coalitions in half the Indian states, the role of the governor becomes pivotal in state politics. The tone for the whole period was set in 1967 by the actions of the governor of Rajasthan, Dr. Sampurnanand, the former Congress chief minister of U. P., who "did not invite" the leader of the non-Congress Samyukta Vidhayak Dal (United Legislature Party) to form the government, though it claimed a

[3] Sri Prakasa, *State Governors in India*, pp. 34–44.
[4] M. V. Pylee, *Constitutional Government in India* (New York: Asia Publishing House, 1965), pp. 646–647.

majority in the legislature.[5] Although a case can be made for the governor's refusal to invite the leader of the non-Congress coalition to form the government and instead to recommend the imposition of PR and the suspension of the state legislature, the significance of the Rajasthan incident is not this specific refusal but the beginning of a broader process of the use of the governor's office to further the interests of the ruling party at the Center in installing a government of its choice in a state.

The use of the governor's office to install governments of the Center's choice was not, however, routine or consistent. The Congress government at the Center might decide not to act in a situation of instability where the Congress party itself in a state legislature was not in a strong enough position to form a stable government. Another situation which often confused matters in this period was that the Congress succession crisis occurred at this time, with the consequence that the central government under Mrs. Gandhi might prefer to have a non-Congress government in power in a state than a Congress government dominated by a faction opposed to her leadership.

What is critical about this period insofar as the role of the governor is concerned, however, is that the office was used by the central government to install state governments of its choice when it did decide to act. In a choice between two uncertain alternatives, a potentially unstable non-Congress coalition and a factionalized minority Congress government, the choice would be either the latter or the imposition of PR. In the former case, the designated leader would be given ample time and the support of the central government to promote defections from the non-Congress side in order to form a "stable" government. The governors in these situations did what they were told by the Center, but did not usually play an active role in helping new chief ministers to stabilize their positions or in bringing down chief ministers opposed by the central government.

Although this period includes the years of Janata rule from 1977 to 1979, in which the Janata party directed the governors for their own purposes, its practices were defined primarily by the Congress.

[5] B. B. Misra, *Government and Bureaucracy in India, 1947–1976* (Delhi: Oxford University Press, 1986), p. 49.

If the period begins symbolically with Dr. Sampurnanand's imposition of PR to prevent the installation of a non-Congress government and to facilitate the selection of a Congress chief minister, it ends symbolically during the Emergency in 1976 with the dismissal of the government of DMK chief minister Karunanidhi in Tamil Nadu. The DMK government was dismissed on the grounds of corruption and with the charge that the state government "held out 'veiled threats' of secession" in Tamil Nadu.[6]

After 1980

A further watershed was reached near the end of Mrs. Gandhi's life in 1984 when the governors of two states, Jammu and Kashmir and Andhra, dismissed their respective non-Congress chief ministers on the alleged basis of information which they had that the chief ministers had lost their majorities in their legislative assemblies. Minority governments were installed and the newly installed Congress chief ministers were given a month to prove their majorities. Although this manoeuvre succeeded in Jammu and Kashmir, it failed in Andhra where a mass movement was launched, with participation by opposition leaders from the rest of the country, and where the press covered the events fully and in detail. As a consequence of the agitation, the governor of the state was dismissed – though it is generally believed he was acting on the instructions of the central government. When the newly appointed chief minister failed to prove his majority in the house at the conclusion of one month, requesting a postponement instead, he was dismissed by the new governor and the previous chief minister, N. T. Rama Rao, leader of the Telugu Desam, succeeded in demonstrating his majority in the Andhra Legislative Assembly.[7]

In Kashmir and Andhra, the governors were not simply following orders, but were playing direct political roles and usurping the powers of the state legislatures "in the making and unmaking of chief ministers."[8] The misuse of the governor's office in Andhra,

[6] S. R. Maheshwari, *President's Rule in India* (New Delhi: Mainstream, 1977), p. 174.
[7] P. M. Kamath, "Politics of Defection in India in the 1980s," *Asian Survey*, xxv, No. 10 (October, 1985), 1,049; Krishna K. Tummala, "Democracy Triumphant in India: The Case of Andhra Pradesh," *Asian Survey*, xxvi, No. 3 (March, 1986), 379–381, 389.
[8] Bhagwan D. Dua, "Federalism or Patrimonialism: The Making and Unmaking of Chief Ministers in India," *Asian Survey*, xxv, No. 8 (August,1985), 803.

however, precipitated a double backlash. Popular protest was so intense in both the state and in other parts of the country that the central government was compelled to resile from its actions, while denying them, and to replace the governor. Second, the governor's and the central government's actions in displacing the leader of a regional party in a southern state precipitated a predictable regional counter-response. In June, 1985, the Andhra government submitted a statement to the Sarkaria Commission on center–state relations calling for "the abolition of the position of governor and demanding constitutional equality between the states and the Center."[9]

Under Rajiv Gandhi

On the first occasion when the central government had an opportunity to continue its previous practices of using the governor's office to install a Congress government, in Karnataka in 1984, it declined to do so.[10] However, since this initial act of restraint, the central government has reverted to former practices in its use of the governor's office and has, in some respects, taken a further step in turning the office into an instrument of central control and surveillance of state governments.[11]

The reversion to past practices was most evident in the politically critical state of Tamil Nadu after the death of MGR in 1987 and the succession struggle which began immediately thereafter. The first act of the governor was to deny the request of the interim chief minister, Nedunchezhian, for a week's time to demonstrate his support in the Assembly and to recognize instead Janaki Ramachandran, the wife of former Congress ally MGR, as "the leader of the majority faction of the AIADMK" and to give "her three weeks to prepare for a vote of confidence in the Assembly."[12] However, the Congress soon became disaffected with Janaki Ramachandran because of reports that Congress (I) MLAs "were being purchased" by her group.[13] Consequently, the Home Minister of the Government of India, Buta Singh, Rajiv Gandhi's leading "troubleshooter"

[9] Tummala, "Democracy Triumphant in India," p. 394.
[10] Kamath, "Politics of Defection in India in the 1980s," p. 1,039.
[11] E.g., see *India Today*, February 29, 1988, p. 27 and March 15, 1988, pp. 23–24, on the situation in Meghalaya.
[12] *India Today*, January 31, 1988, p. 30.
[13] *India Today*, March 15, 1988, p. 37.

in the mid-1980s, personally went to Madras to persuade the governor to dismiss the Janaki Ramachandran government.

Conclusions

During the first two decades after Independence the exercise of discretion by governors and their use as instruments of the Center's will were relatively rare, although the Kerala case provided a precedent for the decisive interventions by the Center in the later periods. The Kerala precedent included a decision taken by the central Cabinet to impose PR even before the receipt of the report of the governor.[14] Since the succession struggle and the simultaneous period of unstable coalition politics in many states between 1965 and 1971, not only have the governors become entangled in state party and factional politics and intrigues at times, but they have become, as in Kerala in 1959, instruments of the central leadership's desires to control state politics.

The wide discretionary powers of the governor are, in effect, powers exercised by the central government by proxy through the governor. The more frequent use of the governor's office in these ways reflects a significant departure from the "cooperative federalism" of the Nehru era towards incessant intervention in state politics for the purpose of maintaining the ruling party, usually the Congress, in power in Delhi by controlling most of the states.

The role of the legislative assemblies

The state legislative assemblies played limited roles in the formulation and enactment of legislation, as venues of serious debate, or as watchdogs over the functioning of the government even in the Nehru period. They did, however, possess one significant power, namely, the power of selecting and replacing the government of the day.

During the non-Congress period of coalition politics, which overlapped as well with the succession struggle in the Congress and

---

[14] Even the highly biased report by the Indian Commission of Jurists, *Report of the Kerala Enquiry Committee* (New Delhi, 1960), admits as much when it says in its chronology of the events for July 29, 1959: "The Central Cabinet discussed the Kerala affairs for more than two hours. Reports from New Delhi indicated that the Central intervention in Kerala was imminent within one or two days. The Centre was waiting only for the Governor's Report, and the Report when it came clinched the issue" (p. 41).

the rise of Mrs. Gandhi, the powers of the legislatures as such in this respect declined, but those of the individual members increased. The loyalties of individual members to particular parties or coalitions were so unstable and vulnerable to purchase by the highest bidder that few chief ministers or heads of rival coalitions would be willing to risk a confidence vote in the legislature because the outcome would be unpredictable. Individual legislators remained free to sell their votes but, since few leaders wished to test the reliability of their supporters in the legislature, the curious ritual practice unique to Indian politics developed, known as the "parade" of one's supporters before the governor of the state to convince him of the majority of one side or the other. The power of choosing the chief minister then devolved upon the governor, rather than the legislative assembly.

The decline in the significance of the state legislatures was precipitous, however, after Mrs. Gandhi's consolidation of power in New Delhi in 1971–72, for the non-Congress parties lost power in most of the states and the Congress legislators lost the power to control the selection of chief ministers, which was now done directly by Mrs. Gandhi and her advisers at the Center. Intrigue and dissidence continued perpetually in every state capital, but governments could not necessarily be brought down even by a majority of state Congress legislators if the Center refused to make a change.

After the landslide victory of the Congress under Rajiv Gandhi's leadership in the 1984 Lok Sabha elections, an anti-defection amendment to the Constitution, the 52nd Amendment, was passed requiring defectors to resign their seats in the legislative assembly and recontest them. This requirement would not apply if one-third or more of party members defected for such a defection would be considered a party split. Independents remain free to offer their support to one side or another in the legislature provided they do not formally join a political party. The amendment also is not a significant deterrent to members of small legislative parties.

In effect, therefore, the ultimate power of the legislative body in a parliamentary system to provide or deny a majority to a government has been largely eroded in the Indian states. The no-confidence power of the legislators has been turned into a political resource for individual MLAs. The right to determine the choice of a new chief minister has been taken away in practice to be exercised by the Prime Minister or by the governor of the state acting at his discretion or at the direction of the central government. Often even chief ministers with a majority in the legislative assemblies are removed by the central leadership of the Congress, thereby reducing even further the sanctioning authority of the legislatures.

The powers of the legislative assemblies have declined still further under Rajiv Gandhi. During his prime ministership, chief ministers who retained majorities in the state legislatures were removed and new chief ministers installed without even the formal validation of the Congress legislature party. A chief minister who has lost support in New Delhi may be summoned to the capital and advised to resign, after which he is likely to submit his resignation to the governor without much further ado.[15]

State party systems

In the face of the centralizing and nationalizing drives of the Congress under Mrs. Gandhi's leadership, the evolution of Indian state party systems has been marked by increasing regionalization. This regionalization is manifested in two ways: by the declining significance of the Congress as the principal political actor in several states despite its still universal presence and by the increasing divergence of each state's politics from both national trends manifested in parliamentary elections and from trends in other states. The 1984 Lok Sabha and the 1985 legislative assembly elections illustrate both these points very clearly.

Despite the fact that the 1984 Lok Sabha elections produced for the Congress an even more massive landslide than 1971, there was a marked reduction in Congress performance in 8 out of 10 states in the legislative assembly constituencies when compared to the same legislative assembly segments of the parliamentary constituencies in the elections held a few months previously (see table 4.1). Moreover, in contrast to the 1971–72 election series, when the Congress left only two states in the hands of non-Congress parties, the 1985–87 assembly elections returned non-Congress parties to power in Andhra and Karnataka and left undisturbed the

[15] As in the case of the dismissal of Harideo Joshi as chief minister of Rajasthan in January, 1988; *India Today*, February 15, 1988, pp. 13–15.

Table 4.1. *Comparison of Congress (I) performance in the 1984 Lok Sabha and 1985 Legislative Assembly elections*

States	Total seats	Assembly segments won in December 1984	%	Seats won in March 1985	%
Andhra Pradesh	294	75	26	49	17
Bihar	324	262	81	193	60*
Gujarat	182	140	77	149	81
Himachal Pradesh	68	51	75	55	85
Karnataka	224	174	78	66	29
Madhya Pradesh	320	307	96	250	78
Maharashtra	288	222	77	162	56
Orissa	147	125	85	117	80
Rajasthan	200	188	94	113	57
Uttar Pradesh	425	383	90	268	63

* Percentage is based on 313 seats.
Sources: Election Commission of India, *Third Annual Report, 1985* (New Delhi: Government of India Press, 1985), p. 93, and D. Shah Khan, "Indian State Elections, 1985," *Regional Studies* 3:3 (Summer 1985), p. 160.

AIADMK already in power in Tamil Nadu and the CPM in West Bengal.

The universal presence of the Congress

Even where the Congress has been reduced to seemingly permanent minority status, however, its role cannot be ignored. Its new roles can best be seen by considering the effects on state politics of intra-party divisions in the Congress, of the delinking of parliamentary and state legislative assembly elections, and of the actions of the national Congress party in relation to ruling non-Congress regional parties.

Intra-party divisions in the Congress continued to be of great importance during Mrs. Gandhi's period of dominance, but their tenor and significance changed considerably. Nationally-induced divisions in state party politics have been of enormous import for both the whole character of center–state relations and for the regionalization of state politics. The consequences of these interventions have sometimes been to produce critical realignments in inter-party relations and in the social bases of party support which have been different in each state and which will be discussed presently below.

The delinking of parliamentary and state legislative assembly elections since 1971 has had some influence on the ability of the Congress to play the role of principal actor in state politics and on the forms its role may take. For a time, it appeared that delinking had not only freed national from state politics, but had imposed national upon state politics through the bandwagon effect. That is, once it was clear which party or party coalition was to be in power in Delhi, there was a rush by party activists to defect to the winning side and a tendency for the election campaigns in the succeeding legislative assembly elections to emphasize the desirability of strengthening the hands of the ruling leadership in Delhi by bringing its supporters to power in the state capitals as well.

On the other hand, there has also been a counter-effect at work leading to a firmer separation of national and state politics, which has contributed to the entrenchment of strong regional parties in several states. In some states, particularly Tamil Nadu, the Congress has gone to the extent of forfeiting the legislative assembly contest to the dominant regional party in exchange for the latter's concession of most parliamentary seats to the Congress. In other states, however, notably West Bengal and Andhra, the dominant regional party has succeeded in capturing most Lok Sabha seats as well as a majority of the legislative assembly seats.

Congress has used two principal strategies towards dominant or strong regional parties at different times. One is the strategy of division, of exploiting factional differences within a regional party by offering inducements to one faction to defect to the Congress or by simply providing material support to one side in its struggle with its rivals. The second is the strategy of alliance, of joining with one or more local parties to defeat another strong regional party or coalition of parties.

Regionalization of state party systems

State party systems may be divided into several types according to two criteria: the configuration of principal political parties in the state and the structure of competition among them.

One-party dominant systems

It is itself a measure of the massive changes that have occurred in state politics in India since 1967 that the only extant pure version of the once nearly universal one-party dominant system is the state of Maharashtra. In this state, the distance between the ruling Congress and its closest competitor is too great to consider the latter a serious rival for power in the electoral arena (see table 4.2). Congress dominance in Maharashtra is a mirror also of the state's social structure, which itself is dominated like its politics by a single caste category, the Marathas, who in turn control the Congress organization.

Until the Congress split in 1969, Gujarat was as much a one-party dominant system as Maharashtra, with the Congress vote share ranging between 45 and 55 percent and only one significant opposition party, Swatantra, with a considerable vote share – nearly 25 percent in 1962 – but not enough to represent a serious alternative to the Congress. In contrast to Maharashtra, however, the Congress (O) in Gujarat was a formidable rival to the Congress (R) of Mrs. Gandhi such that Congress dominance could not be restored in this state until the Congress (R) completely altered its social support base by building the "KHAM" coalition of backward castes and minorities.[16]

One-party dominant systems with institutionalized opposition

The difference between these states and Maharashtra or Gujarat is that there are opposition parties with bases which persist through time, the Congress itself is dominant more through their division and fragmentation than through its own strength, and the social structure is similarly fragmented and heterogeneous.

In three of these states, Haryana, Uttar Pradesh, and Bihar, the Lok Dal of Chaudhuri Charan Singh emerged as the principal opposition to the Congress in the late 1960s and early 1970s, displacing the former Jan Sangh and absorbing much of the leadership and support bases of the former socialist parties in the region. In three other states in this group, Himachal Pradesh, Madhya

[16] John R. Wood, "Congress Restored? The 'KHAM' Strategy and Gujarat," in John R. Wood (ed.), *State Politics in Contemporary India* (Boulder, CO: Westview Press, 1984), ch. 8.

Table 4.2. *Ratio of Congress percentage of the popular vote to that of the next largest opposition party in the 1982–89 Legislative Assembly elections*

State (year)	Congress vote[a]	Largest opposition vote	Ratio of Congress vote to largest opposition vote	Party system type
Maharashtra (1985)	43.5	17.3 (ICS)	2.5	One-party dominant
Gujarat (1985)	55.5	19.3 (JNP)	2.9	One-party dominant
Bihar (1985)	39.3	14.8 (LKD)	2.7	One-party dominant with institutionalized opposition
Uttar Pradesh (1985)	39.3	21.3 (LKD)	1.9	One-party dominant with institutionalized opposition
Haryana (1982)[b]	37.6	23.9 (LKD)	1.6	One-party dominant with institutionalized opposition
Himachal Pradesh (1985)	55.5	30.6 (BJP)	1.8	One-party dominant with institutionalized opposition
Madhya Pradesh (1985)	48.9	32.4 (BJP)	1.5	One-party dominant with institutionalized opposition
Rajasthan (1985)	43.0	18.6 (BJP)	2.3	One-party dominant with institutionalized opposition
Orissa (1985)	51.1	30.6 (JNP)	1.7	One-party dominant with institutionalized opposition
Kerala (1987)[c]	24.5	22.3 (CPM)	1.1	Competitive
West Bengal (1982)	35.7	38.5 (CPM)	0.9	Competitive
Karnataka (1985)	41.1	43.9 (JNP)	0.9	Competitive
Tamil Nadu (1989)	37.1[a]	29.5 (DMK)	1.3	Competitive
Jammu & Kashmir (1983)	30.3	47.3 (JKN)	1.6	Competitive
Punjab (1985)	37.9	38.0 (AD)	1.0	Competitive
Andhra Pradesh (1985)	37.5	46.2 (TDP)	0.8	Competitive
Assam (1985)	23.2	35.0 (AGP)	0.7	Competitive
Nagaland	32.1	32.0 (NNO)	1.0	Competitive

[a] Congress was the third party in Tamil Nadu in popular vote share in this election. The AIADMK (JL) polled a slightly higher vote share of 21.7 percent. Substituting the AIADMK (JL) vote share for that of the Congress raises the inter-party competition ratio between the two largest parties to a slightly more competitive 0.65.

[b] In the 1987 Legislative Assembly elections in Haryana, the Lok Dal, in alliance with the BJP, won a massive victory against the Congress (I) but vote share figures were not available. These election results, however, might warrant placing Haryana now in the "competitive" category.

[c] The vote share for the Congress-led United Democratic Front as a whole was 43.7 percent and that for the CPM-led Left Democratic Front was 44.91 percent giving an even more competitive ratio of 0.97.

Pradesh, and Rajasthan, the BJP has become the principal party of opposition to the Congress. In Orissa, the name of the principal opposition to the Congress has changed from the Ganatantra Parishad to Swatantra and now to Janata, but the former landlords have continued to provide the main opposition base.

These seven states may also be distinguished according to the structure of inter-party relations including the Congress. They range from dualistic systems in which the opposition is strong enough to represent a clear alternative to the Congress to fragmented multi-party systems in which only a Herculean effort of opposition unity can succeed in forging a front strong enough to displace the Congress from power.

The small state of Haryana falls into the first category. A dualistic competition has developed between the Congress and the Lok Dal, in alliance with the BJP and Congress fragments. In three other states, Madhya Pradesh, Rajasthan, and Himachal Pradesh, a persisting but unbalanced dualism between the Congress and the BJP has emerged in which the Congress is far the stronger party. A similar dualism has emerged in U. P. between the Congress and the Lok Dal. In the last state in this group, Bihar, the non-Congress parties are so fragmented that no clear pattern of opposition to the Congress has emerged, though the Lok Dal is the best institutionalized non-Congress party in the state.[17]

Competitive party systems

The competitive party systems in the Indian states can conveniently be divided into three groups.

Notes to Table 4-2 (cont.)

ICS:	Indian National Congress (S)	JKN:	Jammu and Kashmir National Conference
JNP:	Janata Party	AD:	Akali Dal
LKD:	Lok Dal	TDP:	Telugu Desam
BJP:	Bharatiya Janata Party	AGP:	Asom Gana Parishad
CPM:	Communist Party of India	ADK:	Anna DMK
	(Marxist)	NNO:	Naga Nationalist Organization
DMK:	Dravida Munnetra Kazagham		

Sources: V. B. Singh and Shankar Bose, State Elections in India: Data Handbook on Vidhan Sabha Elections 1952–85, Vols. I, II, III, IV-Pt. ii, and V (New Delhi: Sage Publications, 1987–88); Election Commission of India, Third Annual Report, 1985 (Delhi: Controller of Publications, 1985); Muslim India, No. 53 (May, 1987), p. 235.

[17] Harry W. Blair, Electoral Support and Party Institutionalization in Bihar: Congress and the Opposition, 1977–1985, unpublished paper, UCLA Conference on Parties & Elections, June, 1987.

Kerala and West Bengal. In the first group are the two states of West Bengal and Kerala, where the principal opposition to the Congress has come from the CPM, and where alternation in power is always a real possibility. In both states, each election is fought by competing alliances of parties in which the Congress is the principal partner in one and the CPM in the other. The balance in Kerala has remained close throughout most of the post-Independence period, with neither the Congress nor the CPM alone being in a position to form a one-party government. In West Bengal, on the other hand, Congress hegemony lasted until 1967 when a period of party fragmentation and government instability was replaced by the new hegemony of the CPM-led left front, which has persisted from 1977 to the present.

Karnataka. Karnataka was in the Nehru era one of the purest of the one-party dominant states. This early Congress dominance was based primarily on the support of the dominant landed communities in the state, the Lingayats and Vokkaligas. As in Gujarat, however, the Congress split of 1969 introduced serious inter-party division into Karnataka's politics for the first time and precipitated a realignment of the social support bases of the parties. The Congress in the 1970s under the leadership of Devaraj Urs shifted its appeals to the backward castes, while the Congress (O) continued to draw more heavily from the dominant landed groups of Lingayats and Vokkaligas. The Congress (O) joined the Janata coalition in the 1977 elections, since when the party system has become a competitive dualistic system with the Congress (I) and Janata constituting genuine single-party alternative governments.

The third group of competitive party systems are those in which the principal opposition to the Congress is a regionally specific party.

Tamil Nadu. After the Congress split of 1969, Mrs. Gandhi formed an alliance with the DMK in which the latter provided support to the Congress in the Lok Sabha and later conceded an agreed number of Lok Sabha seats in the 1971 elections to the Congress in exchange for the support of the Congress (R) against the Congress (O) in state politics. Since 1971, the main dynamic in Tamil Nadu politics has been provided by rivalry between the DMK and the AIADMK and, after the death of the AIADMK leader, MGR, in 1987, by the struggle for succession within the latter party.

The Congress at first sought to support the AIADMK against the DMK and to seek to find a viable alliance partner in the post-MGR succession struggle, but ultimately decided to contest the 1989 mid-term legislative assembly elections alone. In a four-way split among the Congress, the two contending factions of the AIADMK, and the DMK, the latter emerged victorious in the January 21 elections, winning 170 of 232 seats compared with only 25 for the Congress.[18]

Jammu & Kashmir. The National Conference is much the stronger of the two main parties in electoral support in Kashmir and, in 1988, was ruling the state with the support of the Congress. The principal differences between Kashmir and Tamil Nadu in relation to the two factors of the Congress presence and regionalization are that the Congress is a greater threat to the predominant regional party and that the center plays here a more active and directly interventionist role such that the National Conference, unlike the AIADMK, can never be sure that its alliance with the Congress will not be terminated and its government brought down.

Punjab. Here, when routine politics rather than civil war prevailed, the basic dynamic of politics was provided by the dualistic competition between the Congress and a specifically Sikh political party, the Akali Dal. In contrast to both Tamil Nadu and Kashmir, however, the Congress was the dominant party in Punjab and the dualism was unbalanced. The Center too has here frequently played an interventionist role, especially under Mrs. Gandhi, with disastrous consequences, which will be discussed in further detail in chapter 6.

Andhra Pradesh. In 1962, the Congress polled 47 percent of the vote and won 57 percent of the seats in the state legislative assembly. With the rise of the Congress and the decline of the CPI in the late 1950s and early 1960s, politics in Andhra revolved for a decade around the struggles of dominant castes for control of the Congress patronage system and around divisions among them.[19]

Two events occurred in the late 1960s, however, which led to a critical realignment of the Andhra Pradesh party system: the

[18] *New York Times*, January 24, 1989.
[19] F. D. Vakil, Patterns of Electoral Performance in Andhra Pradesh and Karnataka, unpublished paper, UCLA Conference on Parties & Elections, June, 1987, pp. 16–17.

national party split in the Congress and the Telengana movement for preferential treatment for residents of Telengana in government jobs and educational admissions, which burgeoned into a demand for a division of Andhra Pradesh and the creation of a separate state of Telengana (see chapter 7). Mrs. Gandhi's adroit handling of the Telengana agitation and the new coalition which arose in association with it realigned the Congress support base in relation to opposition parties, but left the Congress still the dominant party in Andhra.

A second realignment of Andhra politics occurred after the defeat of the Congress in the 1977 Lok Sabha elections, with much less felicitous results for it. The displacement of three chief ministers and five state Congress presidents between 1978 and 1983 provided to the newly-formed Telugu Desam party the basis for an electoral appeal to regional sentiment in Andhra, namely, opposition to the "imposition" of chief ministers "from New Delhi."[20]

Having been defeated in the party-electoral arena in 1983 by a regional party, the central Congress leadership decided to use the powers of the governor directly to displace the Telugu Desam from power in 1984 before the imminent parliamentary elections. This demonstration of the Center's willingness to intervene directly in Andhra politics even through extra-legal means provided a further boost to the Telugu Desam, which proceeded to win 28 of the 32 Lok Sabha seats in the 1984 parliamentary elections, in the face of the Rajiv Gandhi landslide victory nearly everywhere else in the country.

The consequence, therefore, of the Congress' interventionist strategy was the strengthening of a regional movement, whose organizational base is otherwise limited and whose life was probably extended by the very heavy-handedness of the interventions from New Delhi.[21]

Assam. Congress dominance in the state remained unchallenged through the 1970s, the Emergency, and even the 1977 Lok Sabha elections. As in Andhra, however, the bandwagon effect had its

[20] Vakil, Pattern of Electoral Performance, pp. 47–48, and Tummala, "Democracy Triumphant in India," pp. 384–385.
[21] James Manor, "Appearance and Reality in Indian Politics: The 1984 General Election in the South," in Paul R. Brass and Francis Robinson (eds.), *The Indian National Congress and Indian Society, 1885–1985: Ideology, Social Structure and Political Dominance* (Delhi: Chanakya Publications, 1987), pp. 413–419.

repercussions in Assam after the massive defeat of the Congress in the north Indian Hindi-speaking states and the Congress loss of power at the Center. The Congress split and the alliance between Assamese Hindus and Bengali Muslims collapsed on the issue of the demand from Assamese Hindus in 1979 for the expulsion of illegal immigrants from Bangladesh, mostly Muslims, whose increased numbers on the electoral rolls caused considerable alarm to many Assamese Hindus. The state came under President's Rule, but Mrs. Gandhi, determined to reestablish her hold throughout the country after her return to power in Delhi in 1980, insisted upon holding legislative assembly elections here in 1983. During those elections, boycotted by the Assamese student movement and accompanied by large-scale massacres of Bengali Muslims, the Congress "won" a Pyrrhic victory, but was unable to govern the state.

Fresh elections held in September 1985, were won handily by the Asom Gana Parishad, a party formed out of the Assamese Hindu student movement. Once again, therefore, it is evident that the desperate rush of the central Congress leadership to regain control of the states after Mrs. Gandhi's return to power in 1980 involved ill-conceived interventionist moves from New Delhi, which produced results contrary to those desired, namely, the powerful assertion of regional forces which succeeded in displacing the Congress from power in a state formerly a bastion of support for the ruling party.

The strength of regional parties and the conditions for their institutionalization

Forty years after Independence, it is evident that few political parties in India have been able to persist through time in the country as a whole or in the several states. The persisting parties are distinguished from the ephemeral formations principally in terms of whether or not they control or have privileged access to a major set of material, human, or symbolic resources.

Of the political parties with national aspirations and a wide regional or cross-regional spread, those which have been able to persist have had control of at least some of these types of resources in some parts of the country. The Jan Sangh/BJP, for example, has been able to make use of the skilled and dedicated cadres of the RSS and an ideology of militant Hindu nationalism, which has had a strong appeal to some elite castes, particularly Brahmans and Rajputs in the rural areas, and to Brahman and Vaisya castes in the cities noted for their religiosity.

Where they have succeeded in institutionalizing themselves, as in Kerala and West Bengal, the Communist parties have been staffed and led principally by non-charismatic, but skilled and dedicated full-time workers. The CPM in West Bengal, of course, has controlled the resources of the state government since 1977 and has used that control to extend its support throughout the countryside by gaining control of village *panchayats* (councils) and by implementing legislation for the protection of the rights of tenants, sharecroppers, and the landless.

The principal resources available to the Lok Dal were the popular, though not quite charismatic, leadership of Chaudhuri Charan Singh, who developed an image throughout north India as a man dedicated to the small and middle peasantry and to the cause of the backward castes.

The preeminent material and symbolic resource of the Akali Dal has been its control over the SGPC, the managing committee which controls all the Sikh *gurdwaras* (temples) and shrines in Punjab and the considerable financial and patronage resources available through it. The Akali Dal also has developed a strong and stable basis of rural support among the dominant Jat Sikh peasantry, which it has reinforced while in power by promoting the interests of this agricultural class in gaining access to the new inputs and the irrigation water necessary to sustain the green revolution in the Punjab and by avoiding the passage of legislation to reduce the size of land holdings.

The DMK and the AIADMK in Tamil Nadu have been the inheritors of two persisting dominant ideological and social elements in the history of the Tamil-speaking people from the late nineteenth century, namely, the ideology of Tamil regional nationalism and the social base of the non-Brahman movement. Second, the original DMK and the AIADMK have both been led by charismatic leaders, Annadurai of the DMK, and MGR, a film star, the leader of the AIADMK, created in a party split after the death of Annadurai in 1969. Third, the DMK and AIADMK have had a rich symbolic and material base in the huge Tamil film industry, which their leaders dominate, and which has provided these parties with a propaganda system for the spread of Tamil nationalism, ample sources of funds, and skilled leaders and workers with a natural ability to appeal to the people. Finally, first the DMK, then the AIADMK succeeded in establishing themselves as the natural governing party of the state of Tamil Nadu, which one or the other of these two parties has governed continuously – except for a break during the Emergency – since 1967.

DISTRICT AND LOCAL POLITICS

District government and administration

Gandhian desires for the dismantling of the colonial bureaucratic structure, the transformation of the Indian National Congress into an organization for constructive work in the countryside, and the creation of a decentralized form of government based on the revival and reorganization of traditional forms of local self-government (the *panchayats*) down to the village level were not taken seriously by the Constituent Assembly of India. Moreover, the entire system of British district administration, which both concentrated authority at the district level and provided for very little participation by representatives of the people, was retained virtually intact, particularly the central importance of the District Magistrate and the district courts and the police.

Community development

Although the old structure of district administration was not only retained but in some ways had its importance enhanced, new administrative hierarchies were also introduced. The Community Development program introduced a new type of administrative system based on the community development block comprising approximately 100 villages each and a network of village level workers (VLWs). Planning was from the top down, with targets sent down the hierarchy from the Planning Commission to the state governments to be implemented at the local level.

The 1957 Balwantray Mehta committee report recommended democratic decentralization of power to the sub-district level to

STATE AND LOCAL POLITICS

make possible popular participation in decision making at the local level and to "put the bureaucracy under local popular control."[22] In effect, it proposed a system of popular participation parallel to the block administrative system and, in principle, having powers of supervision and control over it.[23]

Panchayati raj (rule of village councils and other rural local bodies) was promoted by the central government as a matter of national policy from 1957 to 1963 when the state governments were pressured to adopt some form of democratic decentralization and to involve the people down to the village level directly in the planning process.[24] However, by the mid-1960s, support for panchayati raj had declined, even in its strongholds of Maharashtra and Gujarat. Most of the state political leaderships were reluctant to devolve much power to the district level and below for they feared that if such local institutions acquired real powers they would become alternative sources of political influence and patronage, which would threaten their own abilities to exercise influence in the districts and to use such influence as bases of their own power at the state level.

In practice, the introduction and withdrawal of panchayati raj institutions in particular states had more to do with calculations concerning the maintenance of power at the state level than with devolution of power to the district levels and below. For example, one of the reasons for the early adoption of panchayati raj institutions in Andhra Pradesh was the belief that they could be used "to counter the Communists in the rural areas" of the state where they then still had significant popular support.[25] On the other hand, panchayati raj institutions were suppressed or superseded by the ruling party whenever and wherever it felt threatened by a potential loss of power to other parties or when a new faction or party in power at the state level wanted to displace rival local leadership.

In 1977, 20 years after the report of the Balwantray Mehta committee, the Janata government appointed a new committee on

[22] Shriram Maheshwari, *Rural Development in India: A Public Policy Approach* (New Delhi: Sage Publications, 1985), pp. 52–53.
[23] Stanley J. Heginbotham, *Cultures in Conflict: The Four Faces of Indian Bureaucracy* (New York: Columbia University Press, 1975), pp. 68–69.
[24] Maheshwari, *Rural Development*, p. 53.
[25] Vakil, Pattern of Electoral Performance, p. 14.

Panchayati Raj Institutions, chaired by Asoka Mehta, to assess the problems faced by these institutions and to make proposals to remedy them. In the Asoka Mehta scheme, the *Zila Parishads* (District Boards) were to be given control over all the development activities in the district, although the law and order functions would remain under the control of the existing district administrative apparatus.[26] The *panchayati raj* bodies were to have two tiers (mandal and district) and, unlike most of the previously established ones, would have considerable powers of taxation.

The Janata government did not remain in power in Delhi long enough to begin a national policy process of promoting the adoption of the new scheme of *panchayati raj*. However, *panchayati raj* institutions have been revived or recast along the lines of the Asoka Mehta committee recommendations primarily in non-Congress states where they have been used as instruments for establishing alternative rural power bases for non-Congress parties. The Janata government of Karnataka, for example, adopted most of the recommendations of the Asoka Mehta committee and introduced a new system of democratic decentralization in 1983. A similar structure of *panchayati raj* was established in Andhra as well. Elections to the *zila parishads* and *mandal panchayats* were held in both states in 1987 and won by the Janata party and the Telugu Desam in their respective states.[27]

West Bengal has retained the original three-tiered system of *panchayati raj* institutions in conformity with the recommendations of the Balwantray Mehta committee report, but they were revived and politicized by the CPM government in that state in the late 1970s. Because of the penetration of the village *panchayats* by CPM cadres and party sympathizers and the displacement of the dominant landed classes by smaller landholders, teachers, and social workers, it has been possible to use the village *panchayats* for the implementation of agrarian reforms, notably registration of sharecroppers for purposes of tenancy reform and provision of loans and identification of beneficiaries for anti-poverty programs.[28]

The situation in West Bengal contrasts most sharply with that in

[26] Maheshwari, *Rural Development*, pp. 64–65.
[27] Vakil, Pattern of Electoral Performance, p. 83.
[28] Atul Kohli, "Parliamentary Communism and Agrarian Reform: The Evidence from India's Bengal," *Asian Survey*, XXIII, No. 7 (July, 1983), 801–802.

Maharashtra, where the traditional three-tiered system also has been retained, but where *panchayati raj* functions as an instrument of Maratha economic dominance and Congress political control in the countryside.[29] These institutions from top to bottom are used primarily as instruments for the differential distribution of patronage to the rural land-controlling castes, which include primarily rural development inputs and jobs, notably the appointment and transfer of teachers in schools throughout the districts, which are under the control of the *zila parishads*.

Levels and arenas of district politics

For two decades after Independence, the District Congress Committees (DCCs) were the most influential and important institutions in the district. Since the Congress split, however, the DCCs have declined in importance. Where they have persisted or been revived and have been granted extensive powers, the *zila parishads* have constituted a second or an alternative arena of power and influence at the district level. Other important institutions at the district level which local faction leaders strive to control include especially the district co-operative and land development banks.[30] The banks are a source of loans which are often distributed nepotistically and corruptly.

In addition to the *zila parishads*, the district banks, and the cooperative institutions, educational institutions constitute valuable political resources for local politicians. Many politicians have founded educational institutions either from their own resources or from resources granted by the state government. Once founded and functioning, these schools and colleges can then be used as patronage resources to hire teachers and to admit students on a preferential basis. Teachers and students so favored then become available "as political workers" during elections. In some states, such as U. P., where grants of land to educational institutions are exempt from land ceilings legislation, ex-*zamindars* (landlords and tax farmers) and ex-*talukdars* (landlords and tax farmers from the former Oudh province, with the title of *raja*) find the establishment of secondary

---

[29] Jayant Lele, *Elite Pluralism and Class Rule: Political Development in Maharashtra* (Bombay: Popular Prakashan, 1982), pp. 124–126.
[30] Lele, *Elite Pluralism and Class Rule*, pp. 116–117.

schools and colleges doubly useful as a device to avoid land ceilings legislation by establishing an endowment of land for an educational institution, which then replaces the land as a source of political influence, patronage, and profit.

One of the most impressive sources of local power and patronage anywhere in India is the network of 81 cooperative sugar factories in Maharashtra. The sugar factories in Maharashtra have become "centres of power, prestige, and patronage" such that the politics of the district "revolve around cooperative sugar factories and other cooperatives."[31]

The existence of a multiplicity of local institutions with resources to distribute provides also potential bases of power for a multiplicity of local factions. However, since the ability to exercise power and influence at higher levels in Indian politics depends upon maintaining solid control of most influence resources within a district, faction leaders struggle with each other to gain control of as many local institutions within the district as possible. Influence at the district level is most important because it provides "control over all the lower levels in a given hierarchy."[32]

Other structures and sources of local power: caste and land

Two other structures of local power exist independently of all the others and at the same time provide the underlying social bases for building institutional and political power within a district. These are caste and land control, which are often connected.

Throughout India, even where the state governments have come under the control of backward and low caste groups, local power in the countryside rests with representatives of the dominant landed castes, which are differentially distributed in regions, districts, and localities. Very often, outside of Maharashtra, there are two or more important land-controlling castes in a district, each with different sub-district regional support bases, from among whom faction leaders arise who contest for power in the various district arenas, including the factional and party political.

In general, power at the local level, including the ability to contest

[31] B. S. Baviskar, Factional Conflict and the Congress Dilemma in Rural Maharashtra (1952–1975), unpublished paper, UCLA Conference on Parties & Elections, June, 1987, p. 4.
[32] Lele, *Elite Pluralism and Class Rule*, pp. 132–134.

as a serious candidate in legislative assembly elections, depends upon the existence of a base of caste support in clusters of villages in a constituency, a *panchayat samiti* zone, or a sugar cooperative area, and is enhanced to the extent that there are many such villages in several constituences, *samitis* (councils of representatives from rural areas often comprising approximately 100 villages), or cooperative zones in a district from which a faction leader may draw strong support.

The second great independent source of local power in the countryside is, of course, land control. The very dominance of the so-called dominant castes is based on their control of the bulk of the land in the villages. Land controllers need resources which are available only or principally through cooperatives and state government agencies: access to irrigation water, to credit, seeds, fertilizers, diesel oil for pumpsets, and the like. The bigger landholders seek influence at "the higher levels in the [district] hierarchy" of institutions in order "to gain as much of a privileged access to resources as possible."[33] Despite the abolition of the zamindari system, many of the former landlords and tax farmers retain considerable illegal holdings and resources which can be used to build a base of support in a district independent of caste community, that cuts across various caste groups.

The factional bases of district politics

The characteristic form of politics in the districts of India is factional politics, especially where the Congress has been traditionally dominant or the strongest force in a district. It involves pervasive struggle to gain and retain control of the multiple political resources in a district, as discussed above: the *panchayats*, cooperatives, banks, sugar factories, and party organizations.[34]

Among the various explanations, suggestions, and hints offered over the years to explain this persistent, pervasive factionalism, four

[33] Lele, *Elite Pluralism and Class Rule*, pp. 123–124.
[34] See esp. Paul R. Brass, *Factional Politics in an Indian State: The Congress Party in Uttar Pradesh* (Berkeley: University of California Press, 1964); Lele, *Elite Pluralism and Class Rule*; Baviskar, Factional Conflict and the Congress Dilemma; Donald B. Rosenthal, *The Expansive Elite: District Politics and State Policy-Making in India* (Berkeley: University of California Press, 1977); and Dharmana Suran Naidu, Congress Party Building in Srikakulam District, Andhra Pradesh, unpublished Ph.D. dissertation, Andhra University, Waltair, 1987.

interconnected factors now seem most relevant. One must begin first with the overwhelming heterogeneity of Indian society and the distinctiveness, social separateness, and corporate character of some at least of its most important social units, particularly caste, clan, and lineage groups. On the one hand, most political leaders who come up from the localities and districts must have roots in these little societies which they cannot afford to neglect or betray, but, on the other hand, they must ally with other similarly situated persons with different roots in order to build a political coalition broad enough to capture power in the significant political arenas, which are usually more extensive than the areas in which one's own group is dominant.

The second factor is the persistence of the peasant family farm, which is often even today an extended family farm in the sense that several brothers may share land and other resources and may market their produce together. Moreover, even these peasant family farms are not entirely separate entities, for they are part of broader peasant cultivating communities of caste or clan or tribal groups whose members exchange labor, credit, resources, and marriage partners. Sons of such local peasant communities who enter politics expect the support of their communities and are expected to take care of their needs when they achieve local power and influence.

Another force favoring the persistence of local factional conflicts is the existence of large illegal land holdings on the remnants of great landed estates. To retain such a base requires political influence. To acquire political influence outside one's local area, the scion of the local estate must behave like a little raja of times past, acting as the benevolent patron and protector of his former subjects. If he does so, he will be rewarded by the loyal support of his clients, which can then provide a base for faction building, even for gaining virtually total control of a district's political resources.

The third factor which sustains pervasive factionalism in state and district politics – but not the center – is the importance of inter-level linkages from the top to the bottom of India's federal parliamentary system. The efforts of faction leaders at the state level to gain local control destabilizes local politics still further. If a factional group in the ruling party, usually the Congress, succeeds in gaining control over a state government, it will attempt to consolidate its control through applying state influence and pressure upon local leaders and local institutions, placing its own men in power everywhere. Should a non-Congress party or coalition succeed in a general election in gaining power at the state level, one of its first goals will be to gain control of local institutions in the districts.

It is evident that these three factors taken together – the social fragmentation of a heterogeneous society, the persistence of local structures of power independent of government, and the importance of inter-level linkages in Indian politics – are powerful forces for promoting instability and pervasive factionalism at both the district and state levels. How then can one explain the fact that, during the Nehru period, there were some states in which power was successfully aggregated and maintained for a decade or more by a single faction leader?

National power and local politics

Very little research has been done on the linkages between national power and local politics. During the Nehru period, it was generally assumed – probably correctly – that direct political linkages between the center and the localities were uncommon. Rather, the linkages were indirect, mediated by and through the state Congress organizations and governments. District disputes over the selection of Congress candidates to contest elections for the legislative assemblies and parliament were, it is true, ultimately decided by the Central Parliamentary Board in Delhi, especially where agreement was lacking at the local and state levels. However, the local disputes were first filtered through the State Parliamentary Boards and only then passed upward to Delhi. Where a state government and Congress organization were under the united control of a single faction leader, the effective decisions would be taken at the state and district levels.

Wherever a strong faction leader emerged in the states, whose principles were not opposed to those of the central party leadership on matters of economic development planning or secularism, he was likely to be supported wholeheartedly by the central Congress leadership. Such situations existed in West Bengal during the chief ministership of Dr. B. C. Roy, in Punjab under Pratap Singh Kairon, in Tamil Nadu under Kamaraj Nadar, in Rajasthan under

Mohan Lal Sukhadia, in Assam under B. P. Chaliha, and in several other states for fairly long periods. The existence of such stability at the state level would not eliminate district-level factionalism because social heterogeneity and local structures of power independent of government remained and the dominant faction leader might from time to time find it necessary to move against rivals or to switch allies in particular districts, but the intensity and pervasiveness of district factionalism was reduced.

The central leadership of the Congress, however, sought to stabilize the state governments by backing strong and effective leaders where possible and to mediate factional conflicts which threatened the Congress' hold on power in a state government and its electoral fortunes.

The whole pattern of linkages between national and state and national and local politics, however, changed as a consequence of the post-Nehru succession struggle, the emergence of Mrs. Gandhi as the dominant leader in the country, and the disintegration of the local Congress organizations which followed. On the one hand, direct populist appeals by the national leader to the local populations have replaced the old mediating linkages of state and district factional and caste networks. On the other hand, it has been shown in U. P. that the persistence of local structures of power independent of government and party organization has compelled the central leadership to become involved directly in relationships with influential local leaders without the mediation of the state leaders or state and local party organization.[35]

It appears, therefore, that in the face of the vast changes in leadership, party organization, and political mobilization, which political leaders have brought about in their unceasing efforts to aggregate power to the national level and maintain it, they continue to confront the necessity for mediation between themselves and the little communities and petty potentates of rural India. Neither party organization nor charismatic leadership has been able to completely bypass these persisting structures of local power.

[35] Paul R. Brass, "National Power and Local Politics in India: A Twenty-Year Perspective," in Paul R. Brass, Caste, Faction & Party in Indian Politics, Vol. 1: Faction & Party (Delhi: Chanakya Publications, 1983, ch. 6 (reprinted from Modern Asian Studies, XVIII, No. 1 [February, 1984], 89–118).

PART II

PLURALISM AND NATIONAL INTEGRATION

INTRODUCTION

India's linguistic, religious, ethnic, and cultural diversities are proverbial. So are the political mobilizations and the violent conflicts and antagonisms which have arisen from time to time among and between persons from its distinctive cultural groups. However, it is important to note that neither political mobilization nor ethnic and cultural antagonisms flow naturally out of India's diversities. The 1971 *Census of India* enumerated 33 languages with speakers of more than one million, but only 15 of them have achieved any form of significant political recognition.

The 1981 census enumerates a tribal population of more than 50 million persons divided into hundreds of distinct groups. Many political mobilizations have occurred among several of the tribal groups from the nineteenth century up to the present, of which a few have developed into bitter, violent, and secessionist movements directed against non-tribals, against particular state governments, or against the Government of India itself. On the other hand, many tribal groups have not mobilized and have not rebelled. Moreover, the forms which tribal mobilizations have taken have been diverse. Some have focused on economic grievances, have appeared to be class-based, and have drawn support from Marxist political organizations. Others have focused on political demands and have been organized and led by tribal leaders and exclusively tribal political organizations.

The whole modern history of India has been deeply affected and badly scarred by conflict betweeen separatist Muslim political leaders and organizations and the Indian National Congress and by continuing Hindu–Muslim riots and pogroms against Muslim minorities in some cities and towns. Even with respect to these conflicts and the associated violence, however, they must be contrasted against periods of Hindu–Muslim cooperation. Moreover, it must be noted and needs to be explained why such conflicts have occurred more intensely in some parts of the country and have been less intense or non-existent in others where Hindus and Muslims also live side-by-side.

In the 1980s, India has faced an extremely violent movement among militant Sikhs, some of whom have become secessionist. The Punjab, where most Sikhs live, has become virtually an embattled ground in which a violent guerrilla war is being waged between Sikh militants and the Indian police. Yet, Sikhs and Hindus have cooperated politically in the past and were never before considered to be hostile communal groups.

India has also been generally characterized as a society divided by caste and caste antagonisms. Various Indian censuses before the 1930s enumerated thousands of local castes and dozens of large caste clusters within each linguistic region. Caste mobilization and inter-caste conflict have occurred in India since the late nineteenth century among many such groups. Moreover, in the 1970s and 1980s, inter-caste conflict between so-called backward and upper caste groups became intense in several states. Once again, however, it needs to be stressed that such mobilizations and conflicts have occurred among specific groups in specific regions at particular times and not others.

Migration of persons from one linguistic region to another, particularly to the relatively less densely populated tribal regions of the country and to the northeastern state of Assam and to the major metropolitan centers such as Bombay and Delhi have also produced situations which have sometimes, but not always, led to migrant–nativist political conflicts.

Part II of this book deals with the major linguistic, tribal, religious, caste, and migrant–non-migrant mobilizations and conflicts which have occurred in India since Independence. In the discussions which follow in the specific chapters dealing with these issues, the following themes and arguments concerning the sources of ethnic and cultural political mobilizations and conflicts are stressed.

First, state recognition in both the pre- and post-Independence periods itself has been a critical factor in explaining the rise of some ethnic and cultural movements rather than others. The British gave official preference to the Bengali language in the east rather than to Assamese and Oriya and to Urdu in the north rather than Hindi.

They provided separate electorates and other political concessions to Muslims and Sikhs. They allowed migration of plains people into tribal areas in central India but forbade it in some parts of the northeast. They patronized the non-Brahman movement in south India when Brahmans were leading the Indian National Congress there.

In the post-Independence period, the government of India and the state governments sought to change the balance of recognition among some groups. Hindi was adopted as the official language of the country and of the north Indian states, definitively displacing Urdu from its remaining bastions in Punjab and U. P. Assamese was adopted as the sole official language of Assam against the wishes of the large Bengali-speaking minority and many tribal groups. Separate electorates for Muslims and Sikhs were done away with, but reservations of legislative seats and administrative and educational places for Scheduled Castes and Tribes were retained or introduced.

State recognition sometimes worked in contrary ways. On the one hand, it strengthened some of the groups so recognized and weakened others. On the other hand, in some cases, it contributed to the development of counter-movements by non-recognized groups. The best examples of this type are the numerous movements among unrecognized "backward castes" who have sought systems of reservations equivalent to those granted to Scheduled Castes and Tribes.

A second factor emphasized here, also a political one, concerns the specific policies and political strategies pursued by the central and state governments in relation to regional and sub-regional cultural entities. One general argument stressed below is that Indian state policy towards minorities has differed in the Nehru and post-Nehru periods. Under Nehru, the central government pursued pluralist policies in relation to major language and cultural movements, recognizing especially most of the large language groups among whom major mobilizations developed for the creation of separate linguistic states. At the same time, however, the Center sought to avoid direct involvement in regional conflicts among different ethnic and linguistic groups. The Center also turned a blind eye or took no action in relation to the discriminatory policies followed by dominant regional groups within the several states of the Union.

In the post-Nehru period, however, the central government has played a more directly interventionist role in regional conflicts between opposed ethnic, communal, and caste groups. It tolerated the disruptive and allegedly murderous and terrorist activities of Sant Jarnail Singh Bhindranwale in the Punjab in order to embarrass its main political rival, the Akali Dal, in that state. During the succession struggles after 1965 between Mrs. Gandhi and her rivals, the central Congress leadership in several states moved to displace upper caste leaders from state Congress organizations and replace them with backward caste persons and to mobilize the votes of the latter castes to defeat its rivals in the state Congress and in the opposition. The consequences of these interventions, some of which may justly be perceived as socially progressive, have nevertheless often had the consequence of intensifying inter-ethnic regional conflicts and of focusing some of them upon the central government itself.

A third factor influencing the mobilization of some groups and not others has been unevenness in rates of social change among different social groups leading in turn to imbalances in their relative access to jobs, educational advantages, and political power. Each region of India has a dominant language group and particular castes, usually of elite status, who have long held disproportionate shares of public employment, educational, and political opportunities. Challenges to the preponderant shares of dominant groups in various life opportunities do not usually come from those most oppressed but from persons from groups who have some resources but not others or from groups among whom processes of social change have begun such as to make elites among them acutely conscious of the disparities between the life chances of persons from their own group and persons from the dominant groups.

A related factor is the extent to which persons from different ethnic and cultural groups actually find themselves in competition for the same niches in the division of labor in society. Migrant laborers who go to areas of the country where the demand for farm or plantation labor is high may not come into conflict with local competitors, whose numbers may be much smaller than those of the

132

migrants themselves. However, it is often the case that educated persons from different religious, language, caste, and other categories compete for the most prestigious and secure jobs in public service and for the educational opportunities to gain access to them. It is not surprising, therefore, that conflict between competing educated classes in search of scarce jobs has been among the most prevalent sources of ethnic conflict not only in India but throughout the developing world.

Another factor influencing the types of conflict which occur in India concerns levels of political action and levels of ethnic loyalties. India is a society which contains both multiple levels of political arenas and hierarchies of loyalties to cultural categories. At the level of the village and its surroundings, *jati*, the local aspect of caste may provide a basis for economic action, political organization, and social conflict. In a unit as large as a district, however, correspondingly larger units of political action or political coalitions across *jati* boundaries become necessary for effective political action. The unit of loyalty and political action may then become the caste category or caste cluster or a coalition of related castes. At the state level, only the largest caste categories with wide representation throughout large parts of a state may be able to act in solidary and politically effective ways. In many cases, such actions at the state level become impossible and other kinds of loyalties to faction and party become predominant. At the national level, caste becomes virtually ineffective as a basis for sustained political mobilization for the available caste categories at this level lack appropriate social or economic content.

Alternatives to caste as an organizing principle for political conflict also exist at every level in Indian politics, particularly from the district upwards. At those levels, categories such as Hindu and Muslim become more prominent, language loyalties become critical, one's status as a migrant or a "son of the soil" may be decisive, or factional, party, and ideological bases for political division may prevail.

The three following chapters in part II deal with the major types of conflicts which have occurred in post-Independence politics in which different ethnic and cultural categorizations have been used as bases for political mobilization. Chapter 5 focuses on language conflicts, chapter 6 on conflicts involving non-Hindu minorities and between tribals and non-tribals, and chapter 7 on caste mobilization, caste conflict, and migrant–non-migrant conflicts. The central argument which links the treatment which follows of these different sets of conflicts is that India's cultural diversities do not themselves provide inherent obstacles to national unity or inevitable sources of conflict. Conflicts between language, religious, and ethnic groups tend to center around issues of jobs, educational opportunities, and local political power. The roots of these conflicts have often been quite similar in the pre- and post-Nehru periods. However, a combination of increasingly assertive centralizing drives by the Indian state and its national leadership with an intensified struggle for power in center, state, and locality have contributed to the intensification of conflicts based on such categories in the post-Nehru era.

CHAPTER 5

LANGUAGE PROBLEMS

India's national leaders had to confront several language problems in the first two decades of Independence and what appeared to some of them in the aftermath of Partition to be a real threat of the "Balkanization" of the country. These problems included the official language issue, demands for the linguistic reorganization of the provinces of India whose boundaries, during British rule, did not conform to linguistic divisions, and the status of minority languages within reorganized states. Most of the language conflicts in the Nehru period, some of which became at times bitter and violent, were ultimately resolved through pluralistic solutions. The central government and the national leadership of the Congress sought to avoid direct confrontations with the language movements and their leaders and adopted instead arbitrating and mediating roles wherever possible. In the case of the movements for linguistic reorganization of states, until mutual agreements were reached among contending language groups and their leaders, the Center attempted to ensure that the state governments were under the control of strong leaders whom it supported in efforts to maintain civil order.

In the post-Nehru period, however, several linguistic, ethnic, and regional movements have escalated to levels of bitterness and violence never experienced in the Nehru period except in the tribal regions of the northeast. It will be argued in the following chapter that the centralizing drives of the Indian state under Mrs. Gandhi's leadership and the manipulative and interventionist strategies pursued by the central government and its leaders in state politics have contributed to the intensity of such conflicts during the past two decades. Most of the problems discussed in this chapter, however, were resolved during the Nehru period and will provide a base for comparison with the unresolved problems which have persisted into the 1980s.

THE OFFICIAL LANGUAGE PROBLEM

Before Independence, the most salient language issue in Indian politics concerned the relative positions of Hindi and Urdu and of the Devanagari and Persian–Arabic scripts. The intensity of the communal polarization between Hindus and Muslims, especially during the decade preceding Independence, the position of Muslims as the single largest minority category in the population of the country as a whole, and the linking of the Hindi–Urdu issue with the communal question caused this aspect of the numerous language divisions in India to overshadow all others. The Constituent Assembly having begun its deliberations before the Partition of the subcontinent, the early debates on the language issue in the Assembly focused on this controversy. The principal issues at that stage were whether Hindi in the Devanagari script, drawing its vocabulary – especially for coining of new scientific, technological, and administrative terms – from Sanskrit should displace English as the sole official language of the country or whether Hindustani, the common spoken language of north India, written in both the Devanagari and Persian–Arabic scripts, and drawing its vocabulary from English and Urdu more than from Sanskrit, should replace English.[1]

After Partition, however, there was no question any longer of making significant concessions to Muslims on the language issue and the status of Urdu and the Persian–Arabic script became quite incidental to two other issues concerning the official language or languages of the country. The first concerned the question of whether or not and for how long English should be retained as an official language. The second concerned the relationships among the major regional languages of the country and the numerous minor languages and how their speakers would communicate across linguistic boundaries. Although the first issue involved the question of India maintaining a "window to the world," in which English was the dominant international language and the second issue involved the question of Indians communicating with each other in a country with 14 or 15 major languages and approximately 30 languages with a million speakers or more (see table 5.1), the two issues became interrelated.

[1] Granville Austin, *The Indian Constitution: Cornerstone of a Nation* (Oxford: Clarendon Press, 1966), p. 269.

Table 5.1. *Declared mother tongues – 1971 census (provisional figures): showing numerically important mother tongues at country level as of 1971 with strength of 1,000,000 and above arranged in descending order of population*

No.	Mother tongue	Persons	Status
1	Hindi	153,729,062*	Official language of India and of several north Indian states
2	Telugu	44,707,607	Official language of Andhra Pradesh
3	Bengali	44,521,533	Official language of West Bengal
4	Marathi	41,723,893	Official language of Maharashtra
5	Tamil	37,592,794	Official language of Tamil Nadu
6	Urdu	28,600,428	Listed in Eighth Schedule; official language of Jammu & Kashmir
7	Gujarati	25,656,274	Official language of Gujarat
8	Malayalam	21,917,430	Official language of Kerala
9	Kannada	21,575,019	Official language of Karnataka
10	Oriya	19,726,745	Official language of Orissa
11	Bhojpuri	14,340,564*	Minority mother tongue of Bihar and U. P.
12	Punjabi	13,900,202	Official language of Punjab
13	Assamese	8,958,977	Official language of Assam
14	Chattisgarhi	6,693,445*	Minority mother tongue of M. P.
15	Magahi/Magadhi	6,638,495*	Minority mother tongue of Bihar
16	Maithili	6,121,922*	Minority mother tongue of Bihar

Table 5.1 (*cont.*)

No.	Mother tongue	Persons	Status
17	Marwari	4,714,094*	Minority mother tongue of Rajasthan
18	Santali	3,693,558	Minority (tribal) mother tongue of Bihar and West Bengal
19	Kashmiri	2,421,760	Dominant language of Jammu & Kashmir
20	Rajasthani	2,093,557*	Name used in Rajasthan for several mother tongues
21	Gondi	1,548,070	Minority mother tongue of M. P., Maharashtra, and Orissa
22	Konkani	1,522,684	Official language of Goa, Daman and Diu
23	Dogri	1,298,855	Minority mother tongue of Jammu & Kashmir
24	Gorkhali/Nepali	1,286,824	Minority mother tongue of West Bengal & Assam
25	Garhwali	1,277,151*	Minority mother tongue of U. P.
26	Pahari	1,269,651*	Minority mother tongue of H. P., U. P., and Jammu & Kashmir
27	Bhili/Bhilodi	1,250,312	Minority mother tongue (tribal) of M. P., Maharashtra, Rajasthan, and Gujarat
28	Kurukh/Oraon	1,240,395	Minority mother tongue of Bihar, Orissa, and West Bengal
29	Kumauni	1,234,939*	Minority mother tongue of U. P.

30	Sindhi	1,204,678	Listed in Eighth Schedule; minority mother tongue of Maharashtra, Punjab, and M. P.
31	Lamani/Lambadi	1,203,338*	Minority mother tongue (tribal) of Andhra Pradesh and Maharashtra
32	Tulu	1,156,950	Minority mother tongue of Mysore and Kerala
33	Bagri	1,055,607	Minority mother tongue of Rajasthan

* In the Reports of the Commissioner for Linguistic Minorities, the 1971 returns for 46 mother tongues including these listed in the table have been grouped with Hindi, giving an "official" figure for Hindi-speakers in 1971 of 208,514,005; Government of India, Ministry of Home Affairs, *The Twenty-third Report by the Deputy Commissioner for Linguistic Minorities in India for the Period July, 1982, to June, 1983* (Delhi: Controller of Publications, 1985), pp. 292–298.
Source: R. C. Nigam, *Language Handbook on Mother Tongues in Census, Census of India, 1971* (New Delhi: Government of India Press, 1972.)

The status of English and its possible retention in India for official and other purposes raised both practical questions and an emotional question. The practical questions concerned international communication and the transmission through the educational system of modern science and technology for which none of the Indian languages were fully prepared either in vocabulary or in the availability of translated texts. Against this practical question which argued for the retention of English at least for a transition period was the emotional argument that an independent country could not be truly free until its people gave up the use of a foreign language and adopted its own at least within the borders of its own state.

If the latter argument were accepted, however, even with a transition period, the second major issue then arose concerning which one or more of the major languages of India should be adopted as the official language of the country. Only Hindi could make a claim, by virtue of its large number of speakers and extensive spread in the northern part of the country (figure 3), to recognition as the official language of India, but even Hindi fell far short of encompassing a majority of the speakers of vernacular languages and the claims by its proponents to be a link language beyond its own regions of concentration in the north could not be effectively sustained. The second great issue in the Constituent Assembly then became the status of Hindi in relation to the regional languages. Proponents of Hindi called for its recognition as the "national" language of the country, but the representatives of the non-Hindi-speaking areas insisted that their languages were equally "national" and that if Hindi were to be recognized, it could be only as the *official* language of the Union. For internal communication within their own regions, non-Hindi-speakers expected to retain the use of their own languages and the right to use English for inter-provincial communication and communication with the central government.[2] This aspect of the language controversy also had an important material component since the language recognized for official purposes would be the language in which those who aspired for employment in the public services would have to be proficient.

It is here that the two issues of English versus the vernacular or national languages and Hindi versus the other national or regional languages of the country merged as the non-Hindi-speaking representatives demanded the retention of English as the only way of blocking the elevation of Hindi, which would give a clear advantage to persons proficient in that language in the competition for scarce employment in the public sector jobs controlled by the Union government. The Constituent Assembly resolved this demand for retention of English for a transitional period by granting to Hindi the status of official language of the country, but postponing the final implementation of it for 15 years. In the meantime, English would continue to be the official language of the Union and of inter-provincial communication, the major regional languages would continue to be used permanently in their own provinces and would also be recognized as "national" languages through their incorporation into the Eighth Schedule of the Constitution. The latter provision meant in effect that speakers of the major regional

---

[2] Austin, *The Indian Constitution*, pp. 266–267.

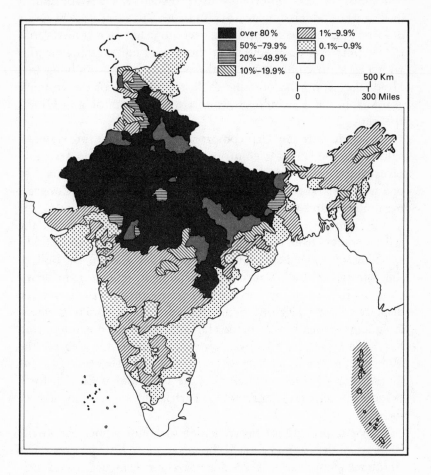

Figure 3   Percent distribution of Hindi-speakers by district
Based on Ashok K. Dutt and M. Margaret Geib, *Atlas of South Asia*
(Boulder, CO: Westview Press, 1987)

languages could continue to use their own languages in the examinations for entry into the Union public services and that they were entitled to other legal and material recognitions and benefits as well. The Constitutional compromise also provided for the establishment of language commissions in 1955 and 1960 "to survey the progress of Hindi," but these commissions were to maintain a "due regard" for the interests of people from the non-Hindi-speaking regions with regard to employment in the public services, implying that Hindi should not become the exclusive language of the entrance examinations if it would go against the interests of non-Hindi-speakers.[3]

The final vote on the compromise amendment providing a solution to the language controversy in the Constituent Assembly revealed the basic lines of division in the country on the matter. On one side were ranged most of the dominant leaders in the Congress organization and the gôvernment, with Nehru himself taking the lead in arguing strongly for a pluralist compromise solution, and the representatives from the southern states and from other non-Hindi-speaking states, including Gujarat, Bengal, and Assam. The bulk of the vote against the compromise amendment, reflecting the sentiment in the Assembly for a quick transition to Hindi and the displacement of English, came from the Hindi-speaking states, including the members from the Haryana region of Punjab and from Rajasthan.[4] Despite the heat generated during the debate, the ultimate compromise, which was carried by a large majority, was for a multi-lingual solution, including the retention of English for a 15-year interim period, after which Parliament would again take up the issue.

Efforts to prepare for the transition to Hindi as the sole official language of the country in 1965, however, made little progress. The emotional identification of speakers of regional languages with their own languages became stronger rather than weaker. Efforts to promote the spread of Hindi in the schools outside the Hindi-speaking region had little success except in states such as Maharashtra and Gujarat. An attempt to promote national integration and inter-state communication through a Three-Language Formula in

[3] Austin, *The Indian Constitution*, p. 296.
[4] Austin, *The Indian Constitution*, p. 299.

the schools also failed. The idea behind this proposal was to promote emotional integration between different language speakers and also to equalize the burdens of language learning in the North and South by requiring the schools throughout the country to teach their own regional language, a foreign language (almost always English), and either Hindi in the non-Hindi-speaking areas or a language other than Hindi in the Hindi-speaking areas. The formula failed for lack of genuine desire to implement it in most states, lack of teachers competent in the various languages willing to move outside their home states, and the recognition in north India of Sanskrit, Urdu, and the regional languages and dialects of the north as alternative third languages in the formula rather than languages of the non-Hindi-speaking regions.[5]

The Lok Sabha took up the question of India's official language once again in 1963, two years before the date designated by the Constituent Assembly for the transition to Hindi. As in the Constituent Assembly, the debates in the Lok Sabha in 1963 were heated, with Hindi proponents demanding immediate implementation of the Constitutional provision on official language and MPs from the South and from Bengal arguing strongly for the retention of English. In the event, a compromise was reached in the passage of the Official Languages Act, 1963, which came close to satisfying most representatives of the Hindi and non-Hindi-speaking regions. Under the terms of the Act, Hindi was indeed to become the sole official language of the country in 1965, but English was to be continued as an "associate additional official language." The Act also provided for a Parliamentary review committee to reconsider the situation in ten years with the power to extend the retention of English if Hindi had not made sufficient progress among the non-Hindi-speaking peoples. The remaining controversial point in the Act concerned the power of the parliamentary review committee and the extent of its discretion in recommending the retention or displacement of English. Prime Minister Nehru gave his personal assurances in Parliament that there would be no attempt to impose Hindi on the non-Hindi-speaking states, but the ambiguity remaining in the Act of 1963 left an unresolved tension that soon

[5] Paul R. Brass, *Language, Religion, and Politics in North India* (London: Cambridge University Press,1974), pp. 213–215.

exploded in the state of Tamil Nadu after the death of Nehru in 1964.

In 1964, during the tenure of Gulzarilal Nanda as Home Minister, a man known for his strong support for Hindi as the official language of the country, a directive was issued from his ministry to all other Union Ministries, in conformity with the constitutional provisions on official language and the Official Languages Act of 1963, to report on the progress made in promoting "the use of Hindi for official purposes and to indicate what steps they proposed to take to use Hindi" after the designated day of transition on January 26, 1965.[6] When news of this directive reached Tamil Nadu, there were massive student demonstrations, riots, and self-immolations, which continued for several months in late 1964 and early 1965, as a consequence of which a grand convocation of the Congress party leadership, Union ministers, and the chief ministers of all the states met in Delhi in June, 1965. At that meeting, a consensus was reached on removing the remaining ambiguities in the Official Languages Act. Under the terms of this compromise, the non-Hindi-speaking states were assured that Hindi would never be imposed upon them, that English would be retained as an associate additional official language as long as even a single non-Hindi-speaking state desired it. In addition, on the material issue of entry into the Union public services, it was agreed that all the languages listed in the Eighth Schedule of the Constitution of India, that is, all the major regional languages as well as Hindi and English, could be used as media of examination.[7]

The compromise of 1965 was introduced formally into the Official Languages Act through the Official Languages (Amendment) Act, 1967. The nature of the resolution of this longstanding controversial issue was a basically bilingual one. The Act provided for joint use of Hindi and English in Parliament, for the use of Hindi as the language of communication between the Center and the Hindi-speaking states and the use of English for communication between the Center and non-Hindi-speaking states. However, the Act and the overall compromise also contained multi-lingual elements, particularly on the matter of the languages of examination

[6] Michael Brecher, *Succession in India: A Study in Decision-Making* (London: Oxford University Press, 1966), p. 155.
[7] Brecher, *Succession in India*, pp. 164–165, 171.

for entry into the Indian Administrative Service and other Union services.

In practice, English has remained the dominant language of elite communication in the country as a whole. Within the linguistically reorganized states, the regional languages have become dominant in government, the courts, the schools, and the media. However, English is still an important language even within the various linguistic regions of the country. It is still accepted as a medium of examination for admission into the state services, alongside the official state languages, in every state and union territory in the country.[8] Hindi has not succeeded in displacing English as a lingua franca for the country. It has gained ground against English in the Hindi-speaking regions of the country but not in relation to the regional languages in the non-Hindi-speaking regions. It has remained primarily a lingua franca of north India and a regional language of the northern and central states of the Union.

Some of these relationships among the major languages of India are illustrated by the relative standing of English, Hindi, and the regional languages in newspaper concentration and circulation, shown in tables 5.2 and 5.3. It is evident from these tables that English readers continue to constitute a substantial proportion of the literate, newspaper-reading public. However, in the period from 1960 to 1983, the proportion of English-language newspapers in the country has gone down from nearly 21 percent of the total to less than 19 percent while the share of Hindi-language newspapers has increased from less than 20 percent to nearly 29 percent. Since the relative share of regional and other language newspapers (including bilingual and multilingual) has not changed much in the same period, it is evident that the increased concentration of Hindi newspapers is at the expense primarily of the English language papers and not the regional and other languages of the country. More than half the newspaper-reading public of India reads newspapers published in the predominant regional languages of the country and in other minority languages, including Urdu. However, if English language newspapers are excluded from the total, 65 percent of the total newspaper circulation in the country in 1983 was in vernacular languages other than Hindi.

[8] Government of India, Ministry of Home Affairs, *Report of the Commissioner for Linguistic Minorities*, XXIII, pp. 377–378 (hereafter referred to as *CLM* reports).

Table 5.2. *Number of newspapers by language*

Language	1983 No.	%	1980 No.	%	1970 No.	%	1960 No.	%
English	3,840	18.50	3,440	18.96	2,247	20.36	1,647	20.52
Hindi	5,936	28.60	4,946	27.27	2,694	24.41	1,532	19.09
Urdu	1,378	6.64	1,234	6.80	898	8.14	680	8.47
Regional languages	7,278	35.06	6,493	35.79	3,974	36.01	2,718	33.86
Others	2,326	11.21	2,027	11.17	1,223	11.08	1,449	18.05
Total	20,758	100.01	18,140	99.99	11,036	100.00	8,026	99.99

Source: Compiled from Government of India, Ministry of Information and Broadcasting, *Press in India, 1984* (Delhi: Controller of Publications, 1986), 21; *Press in India, 1981*, I (Delhi: Controller of Publications, 1978), 27; *Press in India, 1971*, I (Delhi: Manager of Publications, 1971), 19; *Annual Report of the Registrar of Newspapers for India 1961*, I (Delhi: Manager of Publications, 1961), 19.

Table 5.3. *Circulation of newspapers by language (× 1,000)*

Language	1983 No.	%	1980 No.	%	1970 No.	%	1960 No.	%
English	10,627	19.19	10,532	20.68	7,173	24.48	4,147	22.76
Hindi	15,458	27.91	13,709	26.92	5,852	19.97	3,583	19.67
Urdu	2,536	4.58	2,076	4.08	1,455	4.97	1,055	5.79
Regional languages	25,030	45.19	22,911	44.99	13,639	46.54	8,297	45.54
Others	1,740	3.14	1,693	3.32	1,184	4.04	1,137	6.24
Total	55,391	100.01	50,921	99.99	29,303	100.00	18,219	100.00

Source: As for table 5.2: *Press in India, 1984*, p. 31; *Press in India, 1981*, I, p. 44; *Press in India, 1971*, I, p. 44; *Annual Report of the Registrar of Newspapers for India 1961*, I, p. 43.

LINGUISTIC REORGANIZATION OF STATES

The process of lingustic reorganization of states in India was far more prolonged and divisive than the controversy over the official language of India and raised more fundamental questions of center–

state relations. The first step in the process occurred in the aftermath of a major movement in the Andhra region of the old Madras province. This led to the appointment of the States Reorganization Commission which published its *Report* in 1955.[9] Following the States Reorganization Act of 1956, the boundaries of the southern states were reorganized in closer conformity with traditional linguistic regions (cf. frontispiece and figure 4). The bifurcation of Bombay province into the present states of Gujarat and Maharashtra followed in 1960. In 1966, Punjab was reorganized and its several parts distributed among three units: the core Punjabi Suba, the new state of Haryana, and Himachal Pradesh. Several new states also have been carved out in response to tribal demands in the northeastern region of the country from time to time. All the reorganizations except those in the Punjab and in the northeastern region of the country have satisfied the grievances of the principal large language communities of India.

Moreover, in this prolonged process, the "practice" of the Indian state developed a coherent and consistent form somewhat different from the ideology proclaimed by its leaders. Many Indian leaders proclaimed their goals after Independence to be the establishment of a strong state, to which all the diverse peoples of India would transfer their primary loyalties and submerge their cultural differences in a homogeneous nationalism. Others, somewhat more attuned to the realities of India's diverse cultural differences, thought a "composite" nationalism would emerge combining aspects from the cultures of the various major religious, regional, linguistic, and tribal peoples. Virtually all, however, were fearful of accommodating too readily the demands which emerged so soon after the catastrophic partition of the country and the major struggle which occurred simultaneously with it over the integration of the princely states.

Out of the conflicts which developed between the central government leaders, with their ideology of a strong state and a homogeneous or composite nationalism to support it, and the successive demands of leaders of language movements for reorganization of the internal boundaries of the provinces, a set of rules and an overall

[9] Government of India, Home Department, *Report of the States Reorganisation Commission, 1955* (New Delhi: Government of India Press), 1955.

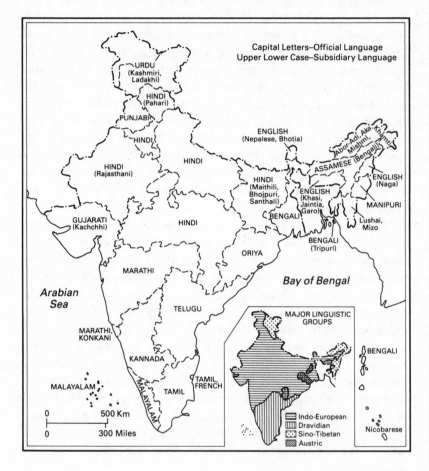

Figure 4   Official and other important languages by state and union
territory
Based on Ashok K. Dutt and M. Margaret Geib, *Atlas of South Asia*
(Boulder, CO: Westview Press, 1987), p. 111.

state strategy emerged which were more pluralist in practice than the ideology, which appeared integrationist and assimilationist. In effect, the Indian state during the Nehru period took on the form of a culturally pluralist state, in which a multiplicity of major peoples, defined primarily in terms of language, were recognized as corporate groups within the Indian Union with rights equal to all other such groups. As with any pluralist state, of course, recognition on the basis of equality did not extend to all the culturally distinctive groups or even to all the large language groups in India, but only to those language groups which were able to validate a claim to dominance within a particular region of the country. Such validation, for the most part, could be made good only by those groups whose languages had already received some official recognition under British rule and had undergone some grammatical standardization and literary development, often involving the absorption of local dialects, and had become entrenched in the government schools in their regions.

The leaders of such language groups were well placed to launch the various movements which occurred, especially during the 1950s and 1960s, for linguistic reorganization of the Indian states. It is important to recognize, however, that not all such movements succeeded but only those which were both well placed to begin with and which were able to prevail against both rival groups within the former provinces of British India and against the reluctance of central government leaders to begin and continue a process to which they saw no certain end. In the course of these struggles, the central government developed a set of four formal and informal rules, whose application led to the recognition of the dominance of some language groups and not others in major regions of the country.[10]

The first rule, which began as practice but was formalized in the Constitution itself in 1963, was that the central government would not recognize groups which made secessionist demands, but would suppress them by all means necessary, including armed force. That rule has been applied to various tribal groups in the northeastern part of the country since Independence, where the Indian Army has been engaged in more-or-less continual warfare with and suppres-

---

[10] This formulation of Government of India policies towards regional demands comes from Brass, *Language, Religion, and Politics in North India*, pp. 17–19.

sion of the secessionist demands of Nagas, Mizos, and others. It has also been applied to the Punjab since 1984 where the police have been engaged, implementing Government of India policy, in a systematic attempt to kill all alleged terrorists who are suspected to be working for the creation of a sovereign state of Khalistan. Where a linguistic group has dropped its secessionist demands, as the DMK did in Tamil Nadu in the 1960s and as several tribal leaders have done in the northeast, the government of India has been willing to make concessions and even to grant statehood to leaders of groups previously considered secessionist.

The second rule is that the government will not accommodate regional demands based upon religious differences. This rule, heritage of the bitter feelings which remain from the partition of India, was applied especially to the Punjab, the last large Indian state to be reorganized in 1966. The government of India resisted the linguistic reorganization of the Punjab more strongly than it did the reorganization of the former Madras and Bombay provinces for several reasons, but one important reason was the initial perception that the demand from the Sikhs for a Punjabi-speaking state was merely a cover for a demand for a Sikh-majority state. Only when a leadership change occurred in the Punjabi Suba movement in the early 1960s to Sant Fateh Singh, in whose sincerity the central government leaders professed to believe, was the decision made to reorganize the Punjab province and create a separate Punjabi-speaking state.

The third rule was that demands for the creation of separate linguistic states would not be conceded capriciously nor on the merely "objective" grounds that a distinctive language was the predominant spoken language in a particular region. This rule developed out of the general reluctance of the central leadership to divide the existing provinces rather than out of any clear principle. In practice, it meant that politicians who set out to demand the reorganization of a province had to mobilize large numbers of people from the concerned region in sustained agitations to persuade the central government that the demand had popular support and was not merely a device for the politicians themselves to acquire power in a new and smaller political unit. Thus, a demand from politicians from western Uttar Pradesh in 1954, supported by 97 members out of 100 in the Legislative Assembly of that province, for the creation of a new province out of western Uttar Pradesh and the then Haryana region of Punjab, but which had no significant popular basis, was never taken seriously by the central government. That "objective" language differences also would not suffice for a demand for reorganization to succeed was also demonstrated in the northern part of Bihar province, where a cultural and literary elite demanded the creation of a separate province for speakers of Maithili, a language distinct from both its neighboring communities of Hindi- and Bengali-speakers. This demand, which in any case never succeeded in establishing a strong base of popular support, also has been ignored.

The fourth rule was that the central government would not agree to reorganization of a province if the demand was made by only one of the important language groups concerned. The reorganization of the southern province of Madras was taken up first in the process of linguistic reorganization partly because it had strong support from both the Telugu- and Tamil-speaking peoples. However, the reorganization of the former Bombay province was postponed for several years because the demand came primarily from the Marathi-speaking region and was opposed in Gujarat, where for a time it was felt that the loss of Bombay City was too high a price to pay for a separate Gujarati-speaking state. In Punjab also, the reorganization was delayed even longer and has not yet been completed because of the opposition of both Hindi-speaking Hindus from the Haryana region and Punjabi-speaking Hindus within the Punjab region.

During the Nehru period, the reorganization of the southern states and of the Bombay province was carried out successfully through the application of these rules. The way the process was carried out also led to a particular kind of balance in center–state relations, in which the center avoided placing itself in a position of confrontation with powerful regional groups but instead adopted a posture of mediation and arbitration between contending linguistic–cultural forces. Although the central leadership often played very strong background roles in these disputes, Prime Minister Nehru himself and his Cabinet members always avoided the appearance of being opposed to any popular movement which did not violate the four rules. The Center would emerge forcefully and publicly through either a decision to reorganize or the appointment of a commission to decide the matter only when all conditions for a reorganization had been satisfied.

The completion of the prolonged process of linguistic reorganization of states has left unresolved problems in two regions of the country and within the reorganized states themselves. The two regions where reorganization has not satisfied the demands of all groups are the Punjab and the northeast. Within the reorganized states themselves, there have also been recurring problems concerning the status of minority languages. Insofar as the Punjab and the northeast are concerned, it is important to consider whether the prolongation of inter-ethnic conflicts in these regions arises out of inherent differences in the nature of the issues in comparison with those handled successfully in the south and in the former Bombay province or out of differences in the ways these issues have been treated in the post-Nehru era, in which Indira Gandhi was the dominant leader. The special problems of these two regions will be taken up in the next chapter. The problems of linguistic minorities in the reorganized states have been less explosive than the unresolved problems in Punjab and the northeast, but they too must be considered for a more complete understanding of the process of political integration in post-Independence India.

PERSISTING LINGUISTIC MINORITIES IN THE STATES

The third important linguistic problem in post-Independence India has concerned the status of minority languages within the reorganized states, each of which contains smaller or larger numbers of speakers of languages other than the predominant regional language (see table 5.4). In contrast to the pluralist policies pursued by the government of India, many of the States have pursued discriminatory policies towards their linguistic (and other) minorities within their boundaries. Moreover, the Center has been unable to protect such minorities effectively against the opposition of the state governments concerned. Among the casualties, for example, have been Urdu in the north Indian states and the various so-called "mother tongues" or "dialects" of Hindi and other larger languages,

Table 5.4. *Official and dominant state languages (1971)*

State	Official language(s) (dominant languages)[a]	Percent speaking dominant language[b]
Kerala	Malayalam & English	96.01
Gujarat	Gujarati & Hindi	90.00
Rajasthan	Hindi	91.40
Himachal Pradesh	Hindi	88.87
Uttar Pradesh	Hindi	88.50
Haryana	Hindi	88.00
West Bengal	Bengali	86.00
Andhra[c]	Telugu	85.40
Tamil Nadu	Tamil	84.50
Orissa	Oriya & English	84.12
Madhya Pradesh	Hindi	83.00
Bihar	Hindi	79.70[b]
Punjab	Punjabi	79.60
Meghalaya	English (Khasi & Garo)	77.65
Maharashtra	Marathi	76.70
Mizoram	Mizo & English	75.00
Tripura	Bengali	69.00
Karnataka	Kannada	66.00
Manipur	English (Manipuri)	63.24
Assam[c]	Assamese	60.80
Jammu & Kashmir[a]	Urdu (Kashmiri)	55.50
Sikkim	Nepali	64.00
Nagaland	English (Ao, Konyak, Angami, Sema)	53.90
Arunachal Pradesh	English (Nissi/Dafla)	24.40

[a] In some cases, the official and dominant regional languages do not coincide.
[b] The figures for the dominant languages often include regional languages, dialects, and mother tongues some of which are quite distinct. The figures for M. P. and Bihar are especially inflated by such inclusions. The 1961 figures for Hindi in M. P. were 67.00 and for Bihar 44.30 percent. See Myron Weiner, *Sons of the Soil: Migration and Ethnic Conflict in India* (Princeton, NJ: Princeton University Press, 1978), p. 50 and, for Bihar, Paul R. Brass, *Language, Religion, and Politics in North India* (New York: Cambridge University Press, 1974), p. 65.
[c] Bengali in Assam, Nepali in West Bengal, and Urdu in Andhra and West Bengal have the status of additional official languages in selected districts.
Source: Government of India, Ministry of Home Affairs, *The Twenty-Third Report by the Deputy Commissioner for Linguistic Minorities in India for the Period July, 1982, to June, 1983* (Delhi: Controller of Publications, 1985), pp. 11–12, 372–373.

which have not been granted official recognition by either the central or state governments. Some of these "dialects" – for example, the Maithili language of north Bihar state – are, in fact, separate languages in all but official recognition. To avoid the controversial issue of distinguishing between "languages" and "dialects," however, it is best to follow the practice of the Indian census authorities and use the term mother tongue to encompass both terms.

The languages and mother tongues of India are, in effect, arranged in a hierarchy of official status. At the top are the two languages, Hindi and English, recognized as official languages of the Union. At the next level are the regional languages recognized as official languages in the linguistically reorganized states, all of which are also listed in the Eighth Schedule. At a third level are those languages listed in the Eighth Schedule which have no official status in any province, namely, Sanskrit and Sindhi, the language of the province of Sindh now in Pakistan.

A listing on the Eighth Schedule carries symbolic and material advantages: a presumptive right to recognition as a minority language in states where other languages are dominant, including a presumptive right to recognition as medium of instruction in both primary and secondary school classes in such states, a right to the protection of the President of India (i.e. the central government) on the advice of the Commissioner for Linguistic Minorities against discrimination in use of the language, and representation on language development committees appointed by the central government. Spokesmen for languages such as Maithili, which have not been able to develop strong enough movements to achieve a separate linguistic state, strive to gain recognition in the Eighth Schedule. Since, however, all languages listed in that schedule except Sanskrit and Sindhi have also been recognized as the official language of one or more states, the government of India has opposed such demands, partly because such recognition to a geographically compact language group would provide a basis for making a further claim thereafter for the creation of a new linguistic state.[11] Moreover, the government of India also anticipates that listing of further languages in the Eighth Schedule would "lead to an unending demand for

[11] Brass, *Language, Religion, and Politics in North India*, pp. 105–6, 198, 214.

154

LANGUAGE PROBLEMS

addition of more and more languages therein" from among the "more than 3,000 mother tongues . . . recorded during the 1971 Census."[12]

At the lowest level are those mother tongues of the people which are not recognized either as official languages of India or of any state and are not listed in the Eighth Schedule. Such mother tongues (along with the officially recognized languages) were recorded fully for the first time in the 1961 census of India, where some 1,652 were listed, many of them spurious in the sense that they are names declared by census respondents who do not know the "proper" name of the mother tongue they speak. Among these mother tongues in 1971, however, were 33 (including the 14 modern languages listed in the Eighth Schedule) with recorded speakers of more than a million (see table 5.1).

There are four Articles in the Constitution of India which protect the rights of linguistic minorities, only one of which, however, specifically refers to mother tongues. Article 350A obliges every state and local authority "to provide adequate facilities for instruction in the mother-tongue at the primary stage of education to children belonging to linguistic minority groups." Articles 20, 30, and 350, which refer to "languages," confer broader rights upon linguistic minorities to preserve their "distinct language, script or culture" (Article 20), "to establish and administer educational institutions of their choice" (Article 30), and to submit representations for redress of grievances to any central or state authority in any language (Article 350). The struggles of spokesmen for the rights of mother tongues, therefore, have taken two forms: demands for enforcement of Article 350A and demands to be recognized, as for example in the Eighth Schedule, as a "language," not just a mother tongue. In both respects, such spokesmen have faced strong resistance from state governments which wish to avoid the administrative costs of implementing mother tongue instruction for a multiplicity of minority languages and, even more important, from

[12] The Government of India and the CLM have also resisted demands for inclusion of other languages on the Eighth Schedule on the grounds that there is no legal-constitutional difference between listed and unlisted languages, a specious argument which ignores practical realities. The CLM himself notes, for example, in the case of Bihar that "languages other than those included in the Eighth Schedule of the Constitution are not being used as media of instruction" at the secondary stage. *CLM*, XXIII, p. 49.

those in and out of government who wish to secure the dominance of the major regional languages in their states and seek to assimilate the speakers of such mother tongues to the dominant language.[13]

The status of the Urdu language

The largest minority mother tongue is Urdu, which claimed sixth place in the country as a whole in the 1971 census, with nearly 29 million speakers, most of whom are concentrated in the north Indian states. At the spoken level, Urdu is but the name used by Muslims for the Hindi language, but the script preferred by Muslims is the Persian–Arabic, whereas that used by nearly all Hindus is the Devanagari. The literary forms of the two languages also diverge, with Hindi writers drawing from Sanskrit and Urdu writers drawing from Persian–Arabic sources in vocabulary and style.

It has been noted above how the case for recognition of Urdu as an official language of the Union was disregarded in the Constituent Assembly after the partition of the country in 1947. Urdu, which had been recognized up to Independence as an official language along with Hindi in U. P., also lost its place in that state in the Uttar Pradesh Official Language Act, 1951 in which Hindi was declared the sole official language of the state.[14] Although Urdu is listed in the Eighth Schedule of the Constitution, it is an official state language only in the small state of Jammu and Kashmir. However, it is the single largest minority language in U. P., where 11.6 million speakers were recorded in the 1971 census, comprising 10.5 percent of the total population of the state. More than 6 million speakers (or 8.8 percent of the total population) were recorded in Bihar. It is a significant minority language in several other states as well, notably Andhra (7.5 percent), Karnataka (9.0 percent), and Maharashtra (7.2 percent).[15]

Despite the large number of declared Urdu-speakers in the country as a whole and in north India in particular, the demands of Muslim spokesmen made through various organizations and movements launched in the 1960s and 1970s for recognition of Urdu as the second official language of the states of U. P. and Bihar was

---

[13] *CLM*, xxiii, p. 201.   [14] *CLM*, xxiii, p. 198.
[15] *CLM*, xxiii, pp. 156, 170, 213.

resisted in both states. Only in the 1980s was Urdu granted the status of a second language – by ordinance rather than formal legislation – for official purposes in 15 districts of Bihar and in the western districts of U. P., but the U. P. ordinance later lapsed.[16] Moreover, in practice the state governments of both U. P. and Bihar have followed discriminatory policies towards Urdu, which have limited its use as a medium of instruction in the schools and contributed to a severe decline in its use as a medium of communication in north India.

For example, in U. P., with a 1981 Muslim population percentage of 15.93 percent and a declared population of 10.50 percent Urdu-speakers, only 3.68 percent of students enrolled at the primary stage were receiving instruction in Urdu and only 3.79 percent at the secondary stage in 1979–80. The absolute number of students receiving instruction in Urdu at the primary stage was 352,022. By contrast, the figures for Karnataka were 360,009 and for Maharashtra 438,353, both states with much smaller Muslim and Urdu-speaking populations than U. P.[17] Bihar has supplied no figures to the Commissioner for Linguistic Minorities on educational facilities provided for speakers of minority languages since 1972–73. At that time, the situation was more favorable than in U. P. for Urdu-speakers at the primary stage where Urdu enrollment was 6.62 percent, but it was only 2.14 percent at the secondary stage in a state where 14.13 percent of the population is Muslim and 8.8 percent are declared Urdu-speakers.[18] The consequences of such discrimination could only be a decline in the use of Urdu, reflected for example in the publication of Urdu newspapers and periodicals, which declined from 268 in U. P. before Independence to only 114 in 1970. The number of Urdu newspapers had risen once again to 264 in 1983, but kept far behind the rise in the number and circulation of Hindi newspapers.[19]

Attempts to persuade the central government to intervene decisively on behalf of Urdu with the relevant state governments also

---

[16] *Muslim India*, 54 (June, 1987), 257, and *CLM*, XXIII, pp. 55, 372–373.

[17] *CLM*, XXIII, pp. 342–351.

[18] *CLM*, XVII, pp. 237, 253.

[19] Brass, *Language, Religion, and Politics in North India*, p. 159, and Government of India, Ministry of Information and Broadcasting, *Press in India, 1984* (Delhi: Controller of Publications, 1986), p. 199.

have had limited success. A Committee on Promotion of Urdu (Gujral Committee), appointed by the central government in 1972, presented its report to government in 1975 during the Emergency. The committee recommended, among other measures, the establishment of Urdu medium primary schools wherever the population of Urdu speakers, in a single village or urban ward, exceeded 10 percent, the enforcement in the Hindi-speaking states of a three-language formula for the schools, which would include Urdu compulsorily along with Hindi and English, and the arrangement of facilities for the use of Urdu by the public for communication with officials at the local level.[20]

However, because of opposition from within the cabinet by its seniormost member, Jagjivan Ram, no action was taken on the report. The Janata government, with its former Jan Sangh component as well as others opposed to concessions to Muslims and Urdu-speakers, also sought to ignore the report. It was, however, released by the Janata party President, Chandrashekhar, on his own authority, which compelled the government to present it to Parliament. Nevertheless, no action was taken on the report during the Janata regime. In 1984, the central government once again took up the Gujral Committee report, but merely appointed a new committee "to review the report and make recommendations for implementation to the Union and State governments." Little effective action has since been taken in the north Indian states.[21] Only in the southern states, such as Andhra and especially Karnataka, where Hindu–Muslim relations have historically been much less hostile than in the north, have effective measures been taken to implement the recommendations of the Gujral Committee concerning the provision of facilities for instruction through the medium of Urdu at the elementary stage and for provision of instruction in the Urdu language at more advanced stages.[22]

The long-standing demand for the declaration of Urdu as the second official language of those states where Urdu-speakers constitute a substantial minority of the population, especially in U. P. and Bihar, however, remains unfulfilled. Urdu is recognized only as an

[20] *Muslim India*, 54 (June, 1987), 257–258.
[21] *Muslim India*, 54 (June, 1987), 257.
[22] *Muslim India*, 57 (September, 1987), 417.

additional official language in specified districts of Andhra and Bihar and for specified purposes in U. P. Moreover, this type of official declaration has acquired such symbolic significance among militant Hindu political spokesmen that the Gujral Committee itself and most organizations for the promotion of the Urdu language have downplayed this demand and have sought instead the implementation of specific recommendations for the use of the Urdu language for administrative and educational purposes.[23]

Hindi and the mother tongues of North India

The struggle for dominance between Hindi and Urdu in north India, which goes back to the late nineteenth century, is part of a broader process which has an equally long history by which spokesmen for the Hindi language have attempted to establish Hindi as the regional standard language for the entire region from Punjab to Bengal and Assam in north India, including as well the present states of Rajasthan and Madhya Pradesh. As a practical matter, the struggle has taken the form of achieving official recognition for Hindi as the language of each of the states in this region and excluding other rivals. In the great struggle between Hindi and Urdu, the claims of other north Indian vernaculars were ignored until after Independence. Even after Independence, few sustained demands for formal recognition have been made on behalf of mother tongues other than Hindi and even fewer have been made effectively.

Leaving aside the question of tribal languages for the moment, Grierson's massive *Linguistic Survey of India* identified two great branches of the Hindi language area, which he labeled Western and Eastern Hindi,[24] in each of which were included numerous mother tongues, some of which also had experienced considerable literary development. On the borders of the Hindi language areas, Grierson also identified three groupings of mother tongues so distinctive from Hindi that he gave them separate classifications, to wit, Rajasthani, Bihari, and Pahari in each of which also were included

---

[23] *Muslim India*, 54 (June, 1987), 257.
[24] G. A. Grierson, Linguistic Survey of India, vol. I, pt. i: Introductory; vol. v, *Indo-Aryan Family, Eastern Group*, pt. ii: *Specimens of the Bihari and Oriya Languages*; vol. IX, *Indo-Aryan Family, Central Group*, pt. i: *Specimens of Western Hindi and Panjabi* (Delhi: Motilal Banarsidass, 1967–68).

numerous mother tongues. The ambitions of the promoters of Hindi as the regional standard language of north India have included the absorption of all these mother tongues and of others as well, including Punjabi. With the sole exception of Punjabi, those ambitions have been largely successful so far.

The first great success for the spread of Hindi occurred in Bihar in 1881 when Hindi displaced Urdu as the sole official language of that province. In this struggle between the two competing regional standards, the potential claims of the three large mother tongues which Grierson included in the "Bihari" group – Maithili, Magahi, and Bhojpuri – were ignored. After Independence, Hindi was again given the status of sole official language of the state in the Bihar Official Language Act, 1950. Yet, in the mother tongue census of 1961, only 44.30 percent of the population of the state declared Hindi to be their mother tongue while 35.39 percent declared the several mother tongues included under the designation "Bihari." Within this group, the largest category was Bhojpuri, with nearly 8 million declared speakers, followed by Maithili with nearly 5 million, and Magahi with nearly 3 million.[25] For the most part, however, the educated speakers of Bhojpuri and Magahi and their political representatives have accepted the inclusion of these two mother tongues as "dialects" of Hindi. Spokesmen for Maithili, however, have always insisted that Maithili is an entirely distinct language from Hindi and went so far as to make a claim for a separate linguistic state in the 1950s and 1960s. Even among Maithili-speakers, however, this claim has been largely restricted to an upper caste elite, while many, if not most, middle and lower caste groups in the Maithili-speaking districts of north Bihar have accepted Hindi as their language.

Although the claims of Maithili-speakers have not been ignored entirely, success in gaining recognition for the language in Bihar has been limited. Maithili was recognized by the Bihar government officially as a mother tongue in 1949, which meant that Maithili-speaking children had the right to have their children educated through the medium of Maithili, but the Bihar government never provided enough teachers or textbooks in the language and has refused since 1961 to provide figures showing the numbers of

[25] Brass, *Language, Religion, and Politics in North India*, p. 65.

children actually receiving instruction through the medium of Maithili. Other demands, for the teaching of Maithili at the secondary stage and for recognition of Maithili as an official language of administration in districts in the Maithili-speaking region have been resisted.

In contrast to Bihar, the struggle between Hindus and Muslims over the status of Hindi and Urdu as the dominant regional language of U. P. was so prolonged and divisive that the overwhelming majority of the people of this state declared their mother tongue as either Hindi or Urdu in the 1961 mother tongue census. For example, although there are probably as many or more native speakers of Bhojpuri on the U. P. side as on the Bihar side of the Bhojpuri-speaking region, only 120,119 Bhojpuri speakers were recorded in U. P. in 1961 compared to nearly 8 million in Bihar. However, in the northwestern hill districts of U.P., whose languages Grierson included in "Pahari," nearly 796,880 speakers of Garhwali were recorded in the 1961 census as well as 248,089 speakers of "Pahari-unspecified." In the 1971 mother tongue census, Garhwali and Pahari were ranked twenty-fifth and twenty-sixth in the country as a whole (see table 5.1), each with more than a million speakers, though neither mother tongue has achieved more than token recognition as a medium of instruction in the primary schools.

Several other large mother tongues of north India have received no more than nominal recognition at the primary stage in two other states of north India where the sole official language is Hindi, namely, Madhya Pradesh and Rajasthan. These mother tongues include Chattisgarhi, with nearly 7 million speakers (1971 census) in Madhya Pradesh and Rajasthani with more than 2 million speakers (1971) in Rajasthan. Even speakers of tribal languages which have no connection whatsoever to the Hindi language or even to the Indo–Aryan language family have received little formal recognition in the north Indian states. For example, the 1971 census recorded 3.6 million speakers of Santali, a tribal language in the Munda language family of whom more than half live in the Santal Parganas district of Bihar, most of the rest across the border in Bengal. However, the Deputy CLM reported in 1982–83 that "facilities for instruction through the Santhali language are almost non-existent due to lack of an agreed script for Santhali."[26] Even where tribal languages have had for some time or have recently accepted agreed scripts, the situation is no better outside of the northeastern region of the country.[27]

Moreover, recognition of a mother tongue by a state government is no guarantee that facilities will actually be provided for students in government schools to receive instruction through the medium of their mother tongue. State government rules and regulations generally require that the parents of the children who wish such instruction formally request it and that a certain number of children in each school and classroom must do so in order to receive such instruction. Even then, competent teachers and textbooks in the language may not be available.

Spokesmen for several other tribal languages in both the predominantly Hindi-speaking states and in other states with large tribal minorities have demanded instruction for their children in their mother tongue, but the Scheduled Areas and Scheduled Tribes Commission appointed by the Government of India in 1960 reported that, "in actual fact some of the states have taken this matter very casually."[28] Moreover, the state governments in general have tended to ignore the requests of the Commissioners for Linguistic Minorities and for Scheduled Castes and Tribes even for information on the extent to which speakers of tribal minority mother tongues have acually been provided with facilities for instruction in their mother tongues. For example, the government of Bihar claims to have provided facilities for instruction through the medium of Oraon, Ho, Santali, and Mundari but has not provided any figures to support its claims since 1975–76.[29]

The only language in north India which has succeeded in establishing its separateness from Hindi to the extent of official recognition both in the Eighth Schedule and as the official language of a state is Punjabi. This success, however, was achieved only after prolonged struggle. In Punjab, in contrast to the rest of north India

---

[26] *CLM*, xxiii, p. 253. [27] *CLM*, xxiii, p. 249.
[28] *Report of the Scheduled Areas and Scheduled Tribes Commission*, Vol. I, 1960–61 (New Delhi: Government of India Press), p. 226, cited in Pradip Kumar Bose, The Congress and the Tribal Communities in India, unpublished paper prepared for UCLA Conference on Parties & Elections, June, 1987, p. 15.
[29] *CLM*, xxiii, p. 47.

before Independence, promoters of Hindi failed to gain official recognition for the language in that province where English and Urdu remained the official languages until Independence. During the late nineteenth and twentieth centuries, however, there was extensive promotion of the two main vernacular languages of the province, Hindi and Punjabi, by private efforts, particularly of the Hindu reform movement, the Arya Samaj, and by the Singh Sabhas among the Punjabi-speaking Sikhs. In this period, the principal political struggle over language recognition was between Hindus and Muslims over the status of Hindi and Urdu. In this competition, Hindus whose mother tongue was Punjabi began the practice of declaring Hindi as their mother tongue in the censuses in order to gain a numerical advantage over Muslims and Urdu. Most Muslims, for their part, actually spoke the various Punjabi dialects, though their political leaders fought to maintain official standing for Urdu.

After Independence, which involved the partition of the Punjab, the emigration of the entire Muslim population to Pakistan, and the immigration of the entire Sikh population from west Punjab to the Indian Punjab, the struggle for recognition now became one between Hindi and Punjabi. In the Haryana region of the Indian Punjab, Hindus were the predominant population and Hindi their language. In the rest of the Indian Punjab, Sikhs were in a small majority compared with Hindus, but both were primarily Punjabi-speaking. The issue of language recognition, however, became tied to the simultaneous demand of the Sikh political party, the Akali Dal, for the creation of a separate province of Punjab, excluding Haryana, in which the Sikhs would be in a majority and Punjabi would be the sole official language of the province. The Punjabi-speaking Hindus, however, did not wish to see such a Sikh-majority province created. So, in an effort to defeat the Punjabi Suba movement, Punjabi-speaking Hindus continued to follow the advice of Arya Samaj leaders and declare their language as Hindi. This device enraged Sikh political leaders in the Akali Dal and contributed rather to an intensification of the Punjabi Suba demand, which was ultimately conceded in 1966.

The Punjabi Suba movement and the development of the Punjab crisis of the 1980s will be discussed in further detail in the next chapter. It is relevant to the discussion here concerning minority languages in reorganized states and the related question of the absorption by Hindi in north India of numerous mother tongues from the following points of view. First, it brings out sharply the intensity of the effort of north Indian Hindu organizations such as the Arya Samaj to promote the Hindi language even to the extent of shifting their mother tongue identification. Second, it also demonstrates that only language groups which derive their support from other-than-linguistic issues can achieve success against the assimilationist drive of the Hindi movement. In the case of Punjabi, as in the case of Urdu, the underlying support for linguistic differentiation from Hindi came from separate religious groups. Third, it also suggests the importance of a distinctive script in achieving separate status for a language in the north Indian context, for both Urdu and Punjabi have scripts of their own, Persian–Arabic and Gurmukhi, respectively.

The status of minority languages in the non-Hindi-speaking states

It is not, however, only the Hindi-speaking areas where processes of linguistic assimilation and differentiation have been occurring. For example, Bengali-speakers and the Bengali language in the course of its modern development and standardization during British rule in the late nineteenth and early twentieth centuries came into conflict with Oriya-speakers and the Oriya language in Orissa, with Assamese in Assam, and with speakers of tribal languages in Tripura. Even today, in Assam, conflicts persist between Bengalis (18.0 percent of the population of the state) and Assamese and between the Bengali-speaking population and the tribals in Tripura.

Assam provides an example of a region outside the Hindi-speaking area where a struggle between spokesmen for two languages has occurred, in which the speakers of one, Bengali, have attempted to deny the separateness of the other, Assamese. When the struggle for self-assertion was won by the Assamese, however, they then sought to establish the dominance of their own language and to displace Bengali as an official language and a medium of instruction in the schools. Before 1974, when it became "a separate chief commissioner's province," Assam was part of the province of Bengal, in which English and Bengali were the official languages.

Assamese was recognized as a separate language and a medium of instruction in the primary and secondary schools and as a court language only in 1871. Assam was reincorporated for a brief period into west Bengal during the Partition, between 1905 and 1912, after which it reverted to its former status as a chief commissioner's province, but with the inclusion in it of two Bengali-speaking districts, Cachar and Sylhet. Even after the separation of Assam from Bengal, the educated classes came primarily from Bengal and from Bengali-speakers in the Assam region, who dominated the administrative services and the modern professions, including the teaching profession. The predominance of Bengali-speakers in Assam continued even until after Independence. According to the 1971 census, Bengali-speakers still outnumbered Assamese-speakers in the urban areas of the state.[30]

After Independence, however, when Assamese took control of the state government, they wished to provide greater employment opportunities for Assamese by giving them "preference in appointments to the state administrative services"[31] and by establishing Assamese as the sole official language of the state and the medium of instruction in the schools, which would serve the same purpose of giving an advantage in public employment opportunities to Assamese. Bengali-speakers, of course, argued for the retention of both Bengali and Assamese as official state languages. Ultimately, amid rioting and violence between Bengali- and Assamese-speakers, Assamese was adopted in 1960 as the sole official language of the state.[32] Bitter conflicts between Assamese- and Bengali-speakers in the state continued, however, and became violent at times, as in 1972 when a struggle developed over the medium of instruction and the language of examination in the colleges of Gauhati University to which the colleges of the predominantly Bengali-speaking district of Cachar were affiliated. In that clash, the proponents of Assamese

[30] The figures were 516,320 (40.0 percent) Bengali-speakers and 499,066 (38.7 percent) Assamese-speakers. An additional 15.6 percent of the urban population was recorded as Hindi-speakers; Census of India,1971, Assam, Series 3, Pt. I-A: General Population, by K. S. Dey (Delhi: Controller of Publications, 1979) and Pt. II-C(ii): Social and Cultural Tables (Delhi: Controller of Publications, 1981).
[31] Myron Weiner, Sons of the Soil: Migration and Ethnic Conflict in India (Princeton, NJ: Princeton University Press, 1978), p. 111.
[32] Weiner, Sons of the Soil, p. 117. Bengali was given the status of "additional official language" in Cachar district; CLM, XXIII, p. 131.

succeeded in completely displacing Bengali from all the affiliated colleges of Gauhati University.[33]

Within the state of West Bengal itself, a militant movement developed in the 1980s among the Gorkhas in the hills of Darjeeling district, whose mother tongue is Gorkhali (Nepali), the official language of the bordering sovereign state of Nepal. Nepali, which is part of the Pahari language group, including also Garhwali, was the declared mother tongue of 1.3 million people in the 1971 census, most of them living in Darjeeling district.[34] The demands of the movement included citizenship status for all Nepali-speaking immigrants from Nepal, the inclusion of Nepali in the Eighth Schedule of the Constitution, and the creation of a separate state of Gorkhaland within the Indian Union.[35] The latter demand was resisted vigorously by the CPM-led government of West Bengal. In a pattern which has become increasingly common in South Asia in the past decade, this movement engendered considerable violence amounting in early 1988 to a virtual state of civil war in the district between Gorkha activist insurgents and the civil authorities and the police.[36] For a time, it appeared that a lack of coordination between the central government and the state government in responding to the Gorkha National Liberation Front (GNLF) demands was encouraging the latter's militant tactics, as in other similar movements in the Punjab and in the northeast. However, the central and state government leaders ultimately resisted the temptation to take advantage of the situation to further their separate political interests and worked together to reach an accord in August, 1988, with the GNLF whose principal element was the creation of a Gorkha Hill Council within the state of West Bengal. None of the other major demands of the GNLF were conceded in the accord.[37]

The unexpected rise of the Gorkhaland movement suggests that there remains considerable potential in the array of diverse ethno-

[33] Myron Weiner and Mary F. Katzenstein, *India's Preferential Policies: Migrants, the Middle Classes, and Ethnic Equality* (Chicago: University of Chicago Press, 1981), p. 98.
[34] The percentage of Nepali-speakers in West Bengal in 1971 was given as 1.38. Based on the 1981 population figures, the total number of Nepali-speakers in the state, of which the vast majority live in Darjeeling district, is approximately 750,000; *CLM*, XXIII, p. 68.
[35] *Asian Recorder*, February 26–March 4, 1987, p. 19,338.
[36] *India Today*, January 15, 1988.
[37] *Asian Recorder*, September 30–October 6, 1988, pp. 20,227–20,230.

linguistic groups in India for the development of political movements among at least some of them from time to time. It is not to be expected, however, that each and every one of even the largest unrecognized mother tongues will provide the source for political movements. On the contrary, Hindi and the other regional languages listed in the Eighth Schedule of the Constitution continue to extend their dominance within their own regions and to assimilate to the prevailing regional standard speakers of a multiplicity of local languages, dialects, and mother tongues. Linguistic minorities which have the best chance of maintaining their languages and gaining recognition for them as mother tongues entitled to be used as media of instruction in the primary schools are those listed in the Eighth Schedule living in other states, for example Bengali speakers in Assam or Telugu speakers in Tamil Nadu.[38] Even speakers of these and other Eighth Schedule languages, however, confront difficulties outside their home regions. The governments of Punjab and Haryana, for example, insist that there are no linguistic minorities and accord no facilities to minority language speakers in their states, though it is apparent that there are substantial minorities whose mother tongues are Punjabi in Haryana and Hindi in the Punjab.[39]

It is, at the same time, also to be expected that where there are other factors reinforcing linguistic differences, such as religion or job competition for specific places in the economic division of labor in a region or other economic grievances which affect especially the speakers of a distinct language, ethnolinguistic movements will develop, among both Eighth Schedule language speakers living outside their home regions and among speakers of unrecognized mother tongues within their home regions. The importance in the

[38] Consider the situation in Madhya Pradesh in 1981–82, as reported by the CLM. The largest mother tongue, Chattisgarhi, with a 1971 census population of 6.7 million, is not recognized for any purpose, being considered a dialect of Hindi. The main acknowledged minority languages are the two tribal mother tongues, Bhilli (3.1 percent) and Gondi (2.8 percent), Marathi (2.4 percent), and Urdu (2.3 percent). However, no facilities for instruction through the medium of the tribal languages are provided in the state, while such facilities are provided not only for Marathi and Urdu, but for Bengali, Gujarati, Oriya, Sindhi, and Telugu, all Eighth Schedule languages. *CLM*, xxiii, pp. 29–31.

[39] *CLM*, xxiii, pp. 261–262. According to the 1971 census, the percentage of Punjabi-speakers in Haryana was 8.4 and of Hindi-speakers in Punjab was 19.9; *CLM*, xxiii, pp. 78, 91.

development of these movements of the presence of such other factors is well illustrated by the history of ethnic conflict in the Punjab and Assam. The Punjab and Assam problems are discussed in detail in the next chapter.

CHAPTER 6

NON-HINDU AND TRIBAL MINORITIES

From the point of view of the centralized Indian state, the post-Independence leadership has had considerable success in confronting and resolving the major language issues which arose especially during the first two decades after Independence. Linguistic federalism has proven to be a satisfactory means of maintaining the unity of the country and the loyalty of the citizens of the principal language regions of the country. No territorial solution to ethnic problems, however, can by itself satisfy the claims of all minority groups. We have seen that many minority language speakers have remained within the linguistically reorganized states and that several political movements have arisen among them claiming discrimination against their language by the speakers of the dominant regional language in a state.

Moreover, the political leaders of India have not been able to resolve as satisfactorily as in the case of the major language groups the political demands and the political status of non-Hindu and tribal minority groups. States reorganization has either failed or been a far more prolonged and violent process before satisfying the political aspirations of the Sikhs in the Punjab and the tribal peoples in the northeastern region. Even outside the northeastern zone, the Indian state has come into violent conflict repeatedly with various tribal groups in widely scattered parts of the country. Finally, 40 years after partition, Indian state leaders have failed to resolve satisfactorily the persistence of Hindu–Muslim communal division, which continues to find expression in vicious killings in cities and towns in many parts of the country.

The question naturally arises, therefore, whether the Indian state is pluralist only in relation to cultural groups which remain within the broadly defined Hindu fold but discriminates against non-Hindu minorities and groups such as some tribals whose Hindu identity is marginal. Such a presumption would seem to imply that India has departed from its proclaimed secularism and has become a

169

state based implicitly on a Hindu definition of nationality. It will be argued here, on the contrary, that it is the secular ideology itself together with the persistent centralizing drives of Indian state leaders and the unending struggle for power in New Delhi, intensified during Mrs. Gandhi's leadership of the country, which have been more responsible for the failures to resolve the political problems of non-Hindu minorities.

FAILURES AND PROBLEMS IN STATES REORGANIZATION: THE PUNJAB AND THE NORTHEAST

The Punjab crisis and the unity of India[1]

In contrast to the South and Bombay, where language differences were more important than religious differences, religious differences and communal organizations on religious lines were more important in the Punjab in the nineteenth century and up to the partition of the country in 1947, in which the Punjab was in fact the center of the storm. The Punjab in the late nineteenth and early twentieth centuries saw the rise – partly at first in response to Christian missionary activities – of Muslim revivalist movements and of corresponding movements among Hindus and Sikhs. The Sikh *gurdwara* reform movement of the 1920s brought a critical change in the institutional vitality and political organization of the Sikhs as a community, for it brought into being two organizations which continue to this day to be the central religious and political institutions of the Sikhs. These are the Shiromani Gurdwara Prabhandak Committee (SGPC), a central managing committee for the Punjab *gurdwaras*, which controls the Sikh shrines and its vast resources, and the Akali Dal, the political movement which led the *gurdwara* reform movement and became the principal political organization of Sikhs in the Punjab before and after Independence.

Another special feature of the Punjab situation was the effect of partition itself, which was a great crisis for the Sikh community. The Sikh leaders thought that they had been promised a special status in

[1] This section draws heavily on a more extended analysis by Paul R. Brass, "The Punjab Crisis and the Unity of India," in Atul Kohli (ed.), *India's Democracy: An Analysis of Changing State-Society Relations* (Princeton, NJ: Princeton University Press, 1988), pp. 169–213.

independent India, in a compact region of their own, though no specific terms were ever drawn up in any document. Not only was the Sikh community not granted a special status in post-Independence India, but the demands of the Akali Dal leaders for the inclusion of the Sikhs in the general process of reorganization of states in the 1950s and early 1960s were denied. Only in March, 1966, after a change in the leadership of the Akali Dal and after the Indo–Pakistan War of 1965, in which Sikh soldiers and the Sikh population of Punjab played critical roles, was the demand for a Punjabi Suba finally conceded by Prime Minister Indira Gandhi.

In this Punjabi Suba, however, Sikhs have a bare political majority without the political dominance sought by the Akali Dal. The Akali Dal, whose support has been confined primarily to rural Jat Sikhs, has been a minority party in the Punjab, forced to seek alliance with other parties in order to provide an alternative to the Congress.

A further feature of the Punjab situation which distinguishes it from earlier linguistic reorganizations is that it has never been completed. In particular, there have been three outstanding issues which have not been resolved in the two decades since the reorganization: the status of the capital city of Chandigarh, which remains still the joint capital of Punjab and Haryana; the status of some mixed Hindi- and Punjabi-speaking territory in which Hindus are the predominant population; and the division, for irrigation purposes, of river waters which run through the territories of both states.

The unresolved issues of the Punjab reorganization do not, however, provide a sufficient explanation for the violent turn taken in Punjab politics in the 1980s, the rise of terrorist groups, and the adoption by some militant Sikh groups of a secessionist demand for the creation of a sovereign state of Khalistan. The turn to violence, civil war, and the long-term presence of the Indian army in the Punjab has developed principally because of two independent developments, which merged in the 1980s. The first, arising out of the historic drive within the Sikh community to maintain internal cohesion and orthodoxy and the separateness of the Sikhs from Hindus, was the development of a bitter and extremely violent confrontation between militant orthodox Sikh groups and a heterodox Hindu–Sikh sect, the Nirankaris. Out of this conflict emerged the figure of Sant Jarnail Singh Bhindranwale, an important Sikh preacher who saw as his mission the consolidation of the Sikh community, the purification of its practices through enforcement of the elements of the traditional Sikh discipline, and the reclamation of apostate Sikhs.

The second development was a fundamental transformation in the context of center–state relations under Mrs. Gandhi's leadership and the consequent adoption by the central government of an entirely different role in Punjab politics – and in the politics of other states as well – from that adopted by the central government under Prime Minister Nehru in the 1960s. Most important, state politics themselves no longer mattered in their own right as the issue everywhere became the effects of state politics on power in Delhi. The great fear in Delhi since the Punjab reorganization has been that the granting of concessions to the Punjab, which might be considered too one-sided, would create a backlash in Haryana, which would then spread to the major north Indian Hindi-speaking states and cause a loss of support for the central government sufficient to bring it down in the next election.

These differences in center–state relations and in the consequent political calculations made by the central leadership in dealing with politics in Punjab in particular are reflected clearly in the different methods used in the 1960s and in the 1980s to deal with the demands of the Akali Dal. During the Punjabi Suba movement in the 1960s, Prime Minister Nehru was secure in his power in New Delhi and gave his full support in the Punjab to Chief Minister Pratap Singh Kairon, who was the dominant figure in that state's politics for a decade until his assassination in 1964. Second, the Congress followed a strategy of dividing the Akali Dal through a variety of methods designed to displace the more extremist Akali leaders and aid more moderate leaders to come to power.

In the 1980s, in contrast, Mrs. Gandhi and the central Congress leadership were never willing to repose confidence in a single leader in the Punjab Congress and followed instead a strategy of balancing between opposing groups. The unity of action between the central and state governments, therefore, so important in the 1960s, was absent in the 1980s.

Second, in contrast again to the 1960s, when the Congress

successfully exploited divisions in the Akali Dal to displace Master Tara Singh from power and aid the rise to power of the more moderate Sant Fateh Singh, in the 1980s the Congress supported the extremist Sant Bhindranwale to undermine the moderate leadership of the Akali Dal.

These differences in tactics in the 1980s were demonstrated especially in three major series of protracted negotiations between the Congress and the moderate leadership of the Akali Dal held between September, 1982, and June, 1983. During these negotiations, the central government not only was unwilling to make significant concessions to the moderate Akalis, which would reinforce their credibility in relation to more extremist groups, but its leaders refused to take action against Bhindranwale and terrorist groups whose members had begun to assassinate Hindu opponents and even innocent Hindus as well.

Ultimately, in June, 1984, the central government felt compelled, after a series of assassinations of innocent Hindus in the Punjab and with a general election due by the end of the year, to launch an assault on the Golden Temple in Amritsar, in whose precincts Sant Bhindranwale and his followers had taken sanctuary. The assault, which cost thousands of lives of Sikhs in the Temple and on the side of the Indian army as well, was most costly of all in terms of the embitterment of virtually the entire Sikh population, moderates and extremists alike. Mrs. Gandhi was herself assassinated by two Sikh bodyguards in November, 1984. A massacre of thousands of innocent, mostly poor Sikhs, in Delhi, Kanpur, and Begusarai followed with the complicity or malign neglect of the authorities, the police, and the Congress leaders.

Although the new Prime Minister, Rajiv Gandhi, reached an Accord with the Akali Dal leadership in September, 1985, to resolve all the outstanding issues, most of its provisions have to this date not been implemented.

In elections held in the Punjab in September, 1985, in the aftermath of the Accord, the Akali Dal won a majority of seats in the Punjab legislature. The failure of the Punjab government to end terrorist actions and the killing of innocent Hindus in the Punjab, however, led the central government to place the Punjab under President's Rule in May, 1987. The central government itself, meanwhile, increasingly frustrated by the failures of its own police, paramilitary, and military forces to impose order in the Punjab, has, with the aid of the 59th Constitution Amendment Bill, 1988, imposed an emergency in the state of Punjab which effectively eliminates the civil liberties of the people of the state.

Although Rajiv Gandhi's policies seemed at first to involve a silent rejection of his mother's policies and a return to the pluralist policies of his grandfather, the failure to implement most of the provisions of the Accord with the Akali Dal continues to stand in the way of a settlement of the conflict in the Punjab and a return of civil order. While Rajiv has, therefore, moved in principle more in the direction of the pluralist policies of Nehru, in practice he has not been able to restore the old balance in center–state relations either in the Punjab or elsewhere in India.

The reorganization of Assam

If Punjab represents a case where linguistic reorganization was delayed primarily because of the association of the demand there with a religious group, some of whose political spokesmen were considered to have secessionist inclinations, and because of the opposition to it of the large Hindu minority, Assam and the northeast represents a case where the central government faced explicit secessionist demands. It provides the clearest examples of central government responses to secessionist threats and of the different policies pursued by the central government to such threats during the Nehru period and after.

Three sets of ethnic confrontations intersect in Assam: conflict between linguistic groups, particularly between Assamese- and Bengali-speakers, between plains peoples and tribal hill peoples, and between the indigenous population and a large migrant population. Here, the discussion will focus in detail only on the specific problems of states reorganization, which have centered around the demands of the tribal peoples, though it will be necessary to note how the several sets of ethnic issues at times have overlapped and influenced each other.

Within the chief commissioner's province of Assam during British rule, the numerous tribal populations who inhabited the hilly regions of the state had a separate administrative status. The

Naga hills especially were classed as "Excluded Areas,"[2] where direct British administration was prohibited because it was considered that the culture and economy of the tribal populations were fragile and would be overwhelmed by both direct alien rule and penetration by Hindus from the plains.

There were a multiplicity of tribal groups in Assam, speaking a wide variety of mother tongues. However, most were grouped into a smaller number of confederacies, among which the Nagas and the Mizos have become the best known.

Although the languages of the tribal peoples are entirely distinct from Assamese and although Christianity spread to many of them, language and religion were secondary issues in the demands of the spokesmen of the tribal peoples for separation from the province of Assam and secession from India. The post-Independence moves to establish Assamese as the sole official language of the state added a further dimension to the tribal demands for separation from Assam. However, the main impetus for separation and secession came from the argument that tribal peoples were simply not Indians at all.

The reorganization of Assam and the border region, formerly called the Northeast Frontier Agency (NEFA), has taken place in stages and has led to the formation of four new predominantly tribal states: Nagaland, granted statehood in 1963; Meghalaya formed as a separate state in 1972 for the Garo, Khasi, and Jaintia tribes; Arunachal Pradesh, the name given to NEFA, created as a Union Territory in 1948, upon its conversion to full statehood in 1987; and Mizoram, formed into a Union Territory in 1971 and granted the status of a separate state in 1987.[3] Of these several tribal movements, the two which have attracted the most attention because of their widespread popular support, explicitly secessionist goals, and prolonged insurrectionary activities were those of the Nagas and the Mizos.

The Naga demand for secession was made by the famous Naga leader, Angami Zapu Phizo, at the time of Independence when the Assam government violated an agreement with the Naga National

---

[2] Bhagwan D. Dua, India: Federal Leadership and the Secessionist Movements on the Periphery, unpublished paper, UCLA Conference on Parties & Elections, 1987, p. 8.

[3] Myron Weiner and Mary F. Katzenstein, India's Preferential Policies: Migrants, the Middle Classes, and Ethnic Equality (Chicago: University of Chicago Press, 1981), p. 115.

Council to recognize it as "the principal political and administrative force in the Naga Hill district" and proceeded to extend "its administration to the Naga area." Throughout the entire Nehru period, after the failure of an initial meeting between Nehru and Phizo in 1952 to reach any agreement, the central government refused to have anything to do with the Naga secessionist leaders.[4] When the Naga movement turned into a violent insurrection, the central government adopted a policy of suppression by military means, which at times involved an entire Indian Army division and various other paramilitary and police forces, the complete suspension of civil liberties in the hills, and other drastic measures such as the regrouping of entire villages to separate them from the guerrillas.[5]

At the same time, as in the Punjab, the central government demonstrated its willingness to negotiate with moderate non-secessionist leaders. In fact, the non-violent, non-secessionist leadership of the Nagas was "patronized by the Assam administration" and encouraged by the positive signals coming from Delhi. "After prolonged negotiations," the central government agreed to the formation of Nagaland as the sixteenth state of the Indian Union in March, 1960.[6] The state of Nagaland was established officially in 1963. In the meantime, the Indian army continued its military operations against the Naga rebels, which persisted until 1978, despite the arrangement of cease-fire agreements in 1964 and 1975.[7]

Throughout the Nehru period, the central government's policy towards Naga political demands and organizations was clear. It refused to have anything to do with secessionist leaders and groups, but encouraged the formation of non-secessionist groups among the Nagas, negotiated with their leaders, and even granted a separate Naga state to them. Under Mrs. Gandhi, however, the methods changed considerably. In 1966–67, she negotiated directly in New Delhi with secessionist leaders, thereby undermining the position of the non-secessionist chief minister of the newly formed state of

[4] Dua, India: Federal Leadership, p. 10.
[5] Pradip Kumar Bose, The Congress and the Tribal Communities in India, unpublished paper, UCLA Conference on Parties & Elections, 1987, pp. 40–42.
[6] Dua, India: Federal Leadership, pp. 10–11.
[7] Dua, India: Federal Leadership, p. 12, and Bose, The Congress and the Tribal Communities, pp. 42.–44.

Nagaland.[8] In fact, during both her tenures as Prime Minister, in Nagaland as in all other states in the Indian Union, Mrs. Gandhi and the central government played a direct interventionist role in the politics of the state, in which the interests of maintaining a Congress government under a chief minister personally loyal to the Prime Minister overrode the previous policy of supporting non-secessionist Naga political organizations and refusing to deal with secessionists. On the contrary, Mrs. Gandhi dealt directly with secessionist groups even when such intervention weakened her own Congress government in the state and sought to prevent any agreement between non-Congress governments and the rebel underground leaders.

The Mizo insurrection began later than that of the Nagas, in 1959, after a famine during which the Assam government allegedly failed to provide adequate relief to the people. During the famine, a Mizo National Famine Front was formed, whose members crossed into Burma to secure food from tribal peoples living across the border. After the famine ended, the Mizo National Famine Front was converted into a political organization with the name Mizo National Front (MNF), led by L. C. Laldenga.[9]

In March, 1966, "the MNF declared Independence for Mizoram"[10] and Mizo forces launched an insurrection. As in the case of Nagaland earlier, the Indian Army was sent to suppress the revolt. After the suppression of the revolt, the central government took the conciliatory step of "separating the Mizo Hills district from Assam," which was converted into a Union Territory called Mizoram. However, some insurgent activities still persisted.[11]

After the 1972 elections, the Congress succeeded in forming a government which, though it managed to remain in power until 1977, faced strong opposition from the People's Conference led by T. Sailo. Sailo, who allied with the Janata party in the elections of 1977, formed a government in Mizoram thereafter, which remained in power until 1982. Following the same pattern as in Nagaland, Mrs. Gandhi sought to find a more effective counterforce to the

[8] Dua, India: Federal Leadership, pp. 12–13.
[9] Dua, India: Federal Leadership, pp. 13–14.
[10] Dua, India: Federal Leadership, p. 14.
[11] Bose, The Congress and the Tribal Communities, pp. 45–47; see also Dua, India: Federal Leadership, pp. 14–15.

Congress opposition by making a deal with the leader of the insurgency, Laldenga, who was allowed to fly to New Delhi to negotiate directly with Mrs. Gandhi in 1982. The Congress won the 1984 elections to the Mizoram Legislative Assembly by emphasizing its new relationship with Laldenga, whose own interest also lay in defeating the more moderate opposition to the Congress, which had been in power between 1977 and 1982.[12]

In 1986, Rajiv Gandhi and Laldenga signed an accord granting full statehood to Mizoram after which the incumbent Congress chief minister was removed and replaced by Laldenga.[13] Once again, therefore, in Mizoram as in Nagaland and in the Punjab, both Mrs. Gandhi and her son departed from the consistent policies of the Nehru period of refusing to have any dealings with secessionist leaders and preferred instead to make alliances with any local and regional forces that would secure or regain power for the Congress itself.[14]

The one consistent principle, however, that emerges strongly in both the Nehru and the post-Nehru periods is that no secessionist movement will be allowed to prevail and that massive force will be used to suppress insurrectionary activity. From this point of view, it can be argued that the new policies of the central government in dealing with secessionist forces directly are meant only to "domesticate" them, not to encourage them.[15] The dangers in such a policy, however, include not only the distortion of the old balance in center–state relations, but that the weakening of the independent bases of local moderate leaders places the center, particularly the Congress party, in the position either of permanent involvement in regional politics or of dependence upon local militant leaders in order to maintain its own base in a region.

---

[12] Dua, India: Federal Leadership, pp. 16–17.

[13] Dua, India: Federal Leadership, p. 21.

[14] Dua, India: Federal Leadership, pp. 18–19, 26; see also Bose, The Congress and the Tribal Communities, p. 53, fn.

[15] It has also been noted that Laldenga was hardly bargaining from a position of strength, but was taking "a pragmatic step, bowing to the inevitable, the enormous military superiority of the Indian armed forces," and thereby avoiding the fate of the Naga leader, Phizo, namely, permanent exile; Bose, The Congress and the Tribal Communities, pp. 47–48.

INDIAN STATE POLICIES AND THE POLITICS OF
TRIBAL PEOPLES

The militant, secessionist movements of the Naga and Mizo peoples have attracted disproportionate attention, considering that they constitute only a tiny fraction, less than 2 percent, of the tribal population of the country as a whole. According to the 1981 census, there were 52 million tribal people out of a total population of 665 million or about 8 percent of the total population of the country (see table 6.1).

In the early post-Independence years, the Congress and the central and state governments adopted a medley of policies designed to promote tribal development while protecting the tribal peoples. These included: reservation of seats in the legislatures and positions in administrative services for Scheduled Tribes, as for the Scheduled Castes, and provision of other special benefits such as educational scholarships; the establishment of development blocks specifically for tribal peoples emphasizing the establishment of "cottage and village industries," and the settlement on permanent plots of land of tribals who were still "practising shifting cultivation";[16] the enactment or enforcement of existing legislation to protect tribal peoples from exorbitant interest rate charges by moneylenders and from loss of their lands to non-tribal peoples; and the enforcement of Article 350A of the Constitution by ensuring that tribal peoples were instructed through the medium of their own mother tongue in the primary schools.

The practice, however, as in so many Government of India policy areas, has been far removed from the goals. The emphasis of all policies introduced since Independence has in fact been on economic development in the tribal areas rather than preservation of tribal cultures. Although funding for tribal development, as for other minority and disadvantaged groups, increased significantly in the 1970s after Mrs. Gandhi's *garibi hatao* ("get rid of poverty") election campaign, it was associated also with increased centralization of the planning process, which left the tribal peoples out of the decisions taken for their own "benefit."

Numerous examples exist in the literature on tribal economic development of government practices and their consequences for

---

[16] Bose, The Congress and the Tribal Communities, pp. 13–14.

Table 6.1. *Number and percentage of Scheduled Tribes to total population by state, 1981 census*

State[a]	Population	Percentage
Mizoram	461,907	93.55
Nagaland	650,885	83.99
Meghalaya	1,076,345	80.58
Arunachal Pradesh	441,167	69.82
Tripura	583,920	28.44
Manipur	387,977	27.30
Sikkim	73,623	23.27
Madhya Pradesh	11,987,031	22.97
Orissa	5,915,067	22.43
Gujarat	4,848,586	14.22
Rajasthan	4,183,124	12.21
Maharashtra	5,772,038	9.19
Bihar	5,810,867	8.31
Andhra Pradesh	3,176,001	5.93
West Bengal	3,070,672	5.63
Karnataka[b]	1,825,203	4.91
Himachal Pradesh	197,263	4.61
Tamil Nadu	520,226	1.07
Kerala	261,475	1.03
Uttar Pradesh	232,705	0.21
Haryana	None	0.00
Jammu & Kashmir	None	0.00
Punjab	None	0.00
Total[c]	51,628,638	7.76

[a] Assam, excluded from the 1981 census operations in 1981 because of the unsettled conditions "prevailing there at the time," had a Scheduled Tribe population of 1,101,648 according to the 1971 census, comprising 10.99 percent of the total population of the state.

[b] The census table notes that the figure for Karnataka is higher than it should be because of the inclusion of non-Scheduled Tribe persons in the lists from communities with names "similar to those included in the list of scheduled tribes."

[c] The total figure is for the country as a whole including union territories not shown in this table. It excludes Assam for reasons stated in note a and is somewhat high because of the inflated figures for Karnataka as indicated in note b. Although the figure is, therefore, not exact, it is approximately correct because the Assam and Karnataka figures nearly balance out.

Source: *Census of India, 1981*, Series 1: *India*, Pt. II–B (iii), *Primary Census Abstract: Scheduled Tribes*, by P. Padmanabha (Delhi: Controller of Publications, 1983).

the tribals. Access to the forests and its resources is denied to the tribals ostensibly for conservation purposes, but the actual practice is deforestation through the corrupt distribution of timbered tracts to contractors. Tribal lands are acquired to build steel plants and· dams to provide employment and irrigation in tribal areas, but the more evident results have been that the tribals end up in slums near the work sites "working as casual labourers for private construction companies." Similarly, where there are valuable minerals on traditional tribal lands, mining operation leases are granted through the favor of Congress politicians to "unscrupulous mining operators" who then "evict the tribals from their land and make them slog for [a] pittance."[17]

A well-documented case of this type comes from the remote, heavily forested, predominantly tribal district of Bastar in Madhya Pradesh.[18] Penetration and exploitation of the forests and peoples began in the latter half of the nineteenth century and were intensified after Independence. In the process, tribal rights to use the forest and its products were increasingly curtailed. After Independence, new forest acts and regulations became a means for harassing the local populations in order to provide corrupt local officials with a considerable income derived from differential application of fines and penalties on the tribals for making use of their traditional rights to the forest and its products.

In 1966, a movement developed centering around the role and person of the god-king Maharaja of Bastar, which led to confrontations with the local administration and police in a series of demonstrations, and culminated in the massacre of the king and a number of tribals.

In the 1970s, the Government of India entered this complex, corrupted, and disordered society with a World Bank-sponsored Bastar Forestry Project. The forests were nationalized and a project developed to clear-cut and replant the Bastar forests with trees suitable for industrial exploitation. While the rhetoric of the planners envisioned an improvement in employment opportunities and

[17] Bose, The Congress and the Tribal Communities, pp. 24–25.
[18] Robert Anderson and Walter Huber, *The Hour of the Fox: Tropical Forests, the World Bank, and Indigenous People in Central India* (Seattle: University of Washington Press, 1988).

the quality of life of the tribals, in fact the only roles assigned to them were the lowest forms of menial labor.

Increasing criticism of the project was made by biologists and ecologists. Ultimately, the Government of India decided to shelve the project. The authors of the Bastar study argue that the project failed because of inadequate respect for historic tribal uses of the forest, poor understanding of their dependence upon the forest economically and ritually, and a lack of appreciation of the knowledge that the tribal peoples have of the forest.[19]

As of 1985, when one of the authors of the Bastar study returned to the district, the forestry project remained abandoned. However, a process of "sacrificial development"[20] of the area and of exploitation of its people through dolomite mining, dam construction, coal mining, and smuggling continues.

Bose argues that, aside from the specific harmful consequences to tribal cultures, way-of-life, and well-being noted above, there have been two broad general consequences of Congress policies. One has been to intensify existing stratification patterns within tribal communities – as has occurred elsewhere in the development process in India – with local tribal elites getting most of the benefits, economic and political, that accrue to the tribal peoples.[21] The second, arising out of the destructive consequences of Congress policies for the mass of the tribal peoples, has been the proliferation of tribal protest movements among them.[22]

Congress strategies towards tribal peoples and protest movements

Since Independence, the Congress has followed three different types of political strategies in order to gain tribal support and to deal with tribal protest movements when they arise in opposition to its policies and their implementation. The first has been what Bose calls a strategy of accommodation of tribal elites through the electoral process and distribution of patronage. This strategy began immedi-

[19] Anderson and Huber, *The Hour of the Fox*, ch. 8.
[20] Anderson and Huber, *The Hour of the Fox*, p. 132. Protest also continues. Anderson and Huber report that, for example, the dolomite mine project was suspended in 1985 after a tribal demonstration against it (p. 133).
[21] Bose, The Congress and the Tribal Communities, pp. 27–28.
[22] Bose, The Congress and the Tribal Communities, pp. 28–29.

ately after Independence with reservations of seats in the legislatures, posts in the administrative services, and places in educational institutions, sometimes with scholarships, for Scheduled Tribes and with the tribal development projects.

The strategy was sometimes used in dramatic ways to stem tribal discontent and the loss of tribal support in particular areas. For example, a tribal movement arose in the 1970s among the Bodo people, whose mother tongue was listed in the 1971 census with more than half a million speakers, many of them concentrated in the Goalpara district of Assam. The Congress responded to the movement's economic demands by locating an oil refinery in the district. It also followed the successful political strategy of nominating a Bodo candidate in elections in the district.[23]

The second Congress political strategy for dealing with tribal protest movements has been "appropriation," that is, dividing the movement, coopting its leadership, and satisfying elite demands for power and patronage. This strategy was followed with great success in dealing with the famous Jharkhand movement in the Chota Nagpur region of southern Bihar, in which the central demand was for the creation of a tribal state, to be called Jharkhand ("Land of the Forests") out of six districts of southern Bihar, Madhya Pradesh, and Orissa.

Development of the region's extensive mineral resources began during the British period with coal mining in Dhanbad and mineral exploitation throughout the territory. After Independence, the pace of development in the region increased and widened.[24] However, most of this "development" not only did not benefit the indigenous tribal population of the area, but was harmful to their well-being. Tribals found few jobs in the new industries, the lands of many were alienated "by outsiders," the government bureaucracy was run by non-tribals, and few tribals attended the new colleges established in the region.[25]

One of the greatest ironies of the "development" of the Chota

[23] K. N. Deka, "Assam: The Challenge of Political Integration and Congress Leadership," in Iqbal Narain (ed.), *State Politics in India* (Meerut: Meenakshi Prakashan, 1976), p. 43.
[24] Myron Weiner, *Sons of the Soil: Migration and Ethnic Conflict in India* (Princeton, NJ: Princeton University Press, 1978). p. 147.
[25] Weiner, *Sons of the Soil*, pp. 148–149.

Nagpur area was that while it was taking place, hundreds of thousands of the tribal peoples were emigrating to work elsewhere, especially in the tea plantations of Assam while the new opportunities to acquire land and exploit the region's resources brought many immigrants to the area. In 1971, the tribals had been reduced to less than a third (32.2 percent) of the region's population.[26]

One major set of cultural consequences for the tribal peoples of Chota Nagpur of centuries of incorporation has been the loss of many of the distinctive characteristics of traditional tribal peoples. Two-thirds of the tribals in the region declare themselves Hindu in the censuses. Most tribals also now practice sedentary agriculture.[27]

The tribal populations of Chota Nagpur are themselves ethnically diverse, consisting of several distinct tribes, particularly the Santal, Ho, Oraon, and Munda. Penetration of the region during British rule also included the arrival of numerous Christian missions, as a result of which 14.3 percent of the tribal population, mostly Oraon and Munda, are today classified as Christian.[28]

As a result of the long history of incorporation, penetration, and exploitation of Chota Nagpur, its resources, and its peoples, the tribals have developed a very considerable sense of grievance, particularly over land alienation and the lack of employment opportunities for them in the region they consider their own. Weiner reported in 1978 that land loss remained the main complaint of the tribal peoples up to that time.[29]

Despite massive emigration and the conversion of large amounts of forest lands to tribal cultivation, there has been a continuing decline in available cultivable land per capita among the tribals. Moreover, the absence of irrigation in this region and the consequent failure of the green revolution to spread here has kept agricultural productivity low.[30] Even many of those who own some land, therefore, remain dependent for subsistence on outside employment by them or their children, for whom mostly only low-level manual and heavy labor are available.[31] Those landless who remain in Chota Nagpur as agricultural laborers are paid poorly, with the result that most able-bodied men seek work in the towns.[32]

[26] Weiner, Sons of the Soil, p. 149.　　[27] Weiner, Sons of the Soil, pp. 155–156.
[28] Weiner, Sons of the Soil, p. 186.　　[29] Weiner, Sons of the Soil, pp. 160–161.
[30] Weiner, Sons of the Soil, p. 173.　　[31] Weiner, Sons of the Soil, p. 174.
[32] Weiner, Sons of the Soil, p. 169.

Since Independence, some tribals have sent their children to the new secondary schools in the region and a few to the colleges as well. However, the number of jobs suitable for secondary school and college graduates in Chota Nagpur is very small and tribals have tended to lose out in job competition with non-tribals. Demands made by tribal political leaders for preferential treatment for the indigenous population in public and private sector employment have had little effect

Tribal grievances over agrarian exploitation and land loss provided the principal motive force behind several nineteenth-century protest movements among tribals in the region, of which the most famous was the Birsa Munda rebellion of 1899. Another movement, known as the Tana Bhagat movement, spread among the Oraons from 1915 into the 1920s and involved refusal to pay rents to the landlords.

The most important movement among the tribals of Chota Nagpur in the twentieth century, however, was that led by the Jharkhand party which rose in the 1930s after the decline of emigration left the remaining population with fewer opportunities outside the region. The Jharkand movement traces its origins to the formation of an *Adivasi Mahasabha* (Tribal Association)[33] in 1937 under the leadership of the Oxford-educated tribal leader Jaipal Singh. In 1949, the *Mahasabha* was terminated and replaced by the Jharkhand party, still under the leadership of Jaipal Singh, with its goal of the creation of a separate state.[34] Although the Jharkhand party succeeded in becoming a major party in Chota Nagpur, winning 33 seats there in the 1951 elections, its demand for a separate state was rejected by the States Reorganization Commission.

The caste Hindu populations residing in these districts were unalterably opposed to the creation of a Jharkhand state. The strength of the Jharkhand movement, however, meant that the Congress had to devise another strategy to deal with its demands.

Although the Jharkhand party repeated its electoral success in 1957, winning 32 seats this time, the rejection of the demand for separate statehood meant that the party was doomed to permanent

[33] The term *adivasi* means "original inhabitant" of the land.
[34] Bose, The Congress and the Tribal Communities, p. 35.

ıority political status and ·consequent ineffectiveness in state politics. Consequently, sentiment began to grow among Jharkhand party members to join the Congress and thereby at least "get a share in power." As a consequence of defections to the Congress and division in the movement, therefore, the party was reduced to only 20 seats in the 1962 elections, after which Jaipal Singh himself decided that the wisest course was to merge with the Congress. A remnant of Jharkhand refused to join the Congress and remained in opposition, but it then split into numerous factions. By 1984, the Congress had become "the main force in the tribal region."[35]

The Congress success in appropriating the base of tribal political protest and fragmenting its principal movement was largely due to its ability to exploit divisions among the tribal peoples of the region, particularly the division between Christian and non-Christian tribals. Although the Jharkhand was formed by Christian tribals, it once had majority support among the tribal peoples of Chota Nagpur generally.[36] The Christian leadership was widely accepted by the tribals until the rise of educated non-Christian tribal leaders.[37] The Congress naturally supported the developing non-Christian tribal leaders as a challenge to the traditional Christian tribal leadership.[38]

The Jharkhand party drew its main inspiration from the historic grievances of the tribal peoples of Chota Nagpur concerning their loss of land to immigrants to the region and sought to rectify their situation by obtaining a state of their own in which the people of the region would determine their own future and the tribals would somehow be dominant. In contemporary times, tribal movements in Chota Nagpur have developed in new directions with different emphases. Of these more recent tribal formations, the Birsa Seva Dal has been one of the most radical. Its leadership and activists have been mostly educated youth from the "urban areas" of Chota Nagpur. Although it launched "antilandlord movements" and made the traditional demand for a separate state,[39] it was strongly oriented to gaining preferential access to jobs for tribal peoples,[40] that is, for

[35] Bose, The Congress and the Tribal Communities, pp. 35–36.
[36] Weiner, Sons of the Soil, p. 188.
[37] Weiner, Sons of the Soil, pp. 191–192.
[38] Weiner, Sons of the Soil, p. 193.
[39] Weiner, Sons of the Soil, pp. 177–178.
[40] Weiner, Sons of the Soil, p. 182.

educated tribal youths in the towns seeking government employment primarily.

The third Congress strategy for dealing with tribal protest
movements has been "repression."[41] This strategy has been applied
to two types of tribal movements: secessionist movements, discussed above, and local tribal revolts against economic exploitation
and discrimination. Congress policies towards tribal peasant rebellions will be discussed here.

A very considerable proportion of local radical protest in India
since Independence has either involved heavy tribal participation or
has been exclusively tribal in composition (see also chapter 9). In
Chota Nagpur also, there have been tribal revolts focusing specifically on economic grievances. For example, in Dhanbad district,
where the Santals are the predominant tribal group in the rural areas,
centuries of migration of Hindus to the area have taken place,
leading to control by the latter of "trade and money-lending."
According to an account by Das, the Hindu traders and moneylenders "subjected the tribals to ruthless exploitation and set in motion
the process of land alienation."[42]

Within Dhanbad, the Community Development Block of Tundi
is more than 50 percent tribal. A movement among the Santals
developed in the 1970s in Dhanbad and in neighboring districts of
Chota Nagpur and was particularly strong in Tundi Block. At the
end of 1972, the Jharkhand Mukti Morcha was formed with the
following program: restoration of tribal lands, reclamation of waste
lands, and development of the local economy in general, especially
irrigation, so that High Yielding Varieties (HYVs) of foodgrains
could be adopted.

The Jharkhand Mukti Morcha raised also the traditional slogan of
creating "an autonomous state of Jharkhand comprising parts of
Bihar, Madhya Pradesh, Orissa and West Bengal."[43] The major
focus of the movement, however, initially was on "the restoration of
illegally alienated lands," which began with a peaceful procession in
February, 1973, followed later by forcible crop-cutting, which led in
one village to an armed confrontation between landlords and tribals

[41] Bose, The Congress and the Tribal Communities, p. 29.
[42] Arvind N. Das, *Agrarian Unrest and Socio-Economic Change in Bihar, 1900–1980*
(New Delhi: Manohar, 1983), p. 257.
[43] Das, *Agrarian Unrest*, pp. 271–272.

in which two landlords were killed. This incident was in turn followed by "police repression" of the movements, including the arrest of the principal leaders.[44]

A second well-known example of a predominantly tribal revolt developed among the extremely deprived "girijans" (hill people) in the late 1960s in Srikakulam district of Andhra Pradesh. Girijan poverty arose from several factors common to tribal areas in post-Independence India already noted above, including: loss of lands "to non-tribal outsiders and widespread indebtedness," leading to bonded labor,[45] restrictions imposed by government regulations and "corrupt local officials on tribal access to forest land for the collection of forest products and for cultivation," and even at times outright displacement of tribals from their homes. Restrictions on tribal access to and displacement of tribals from forest lands were imposed for the ostensible purposes of promoting reforestation.[46]

Under a "Maoist" Communist leadership, incidents of violence occurred in 1969 between tribals and police, which were followed by a spread of terrorist actions from the side of the tribals against landlords and by an increasing scale of police repression, which ultimately led to the suppression of the movement by the mid-1970s.

The stated policy goals of the Government of India towards tribals are pluralist in intent, as with other minority groups. However, it is evident that government in India applies a variety of flexible policies towards tribal as towards other minorities and that it has developed a variety of responses to tribal protest movements. It is also evident that there are boundaries which minorities cross only at their peril. One such boundary is secessionism, another is violent insurrectionary activity. The Government of India since Independence has demonstrated its resoluteness and its ability to suppress both secessionist and revolutionary movements among minorities and its willingness to apply whatever force is necessary to do so.

---

[44] Das, *Agrarian Unrest*, pp. 275–276.
[45] Leslie J. Calman, *Protest in Democratic India: Authority's Response to Challenge* (Boulder, CO: Westview, 1985), pp. 26–27.
[46] Calman, *Protest in Democratic India*, p. 29.

THE PERSISTENCE OF HINDU-MUSLIM
COMMUNAL DIVISION

According to the 1981 census, Muslims constitute 11.4 percent of the total population of the country. More than half of the Muslim population lives in the three states of U. P., Bihar, and West Bengal (See table 6.2 and figure 5).

There is both a high degree of internal regional–cultural differentiation *among* Muslims in different parts of the country as well as considerable assimilation of Muslims into different regional non-Muslim languages and cultures, including forms of local popular

Table 6.2. *Number and percentage of Muslims to the total population of the major Indian states, 1981 census*

State[a]	Number	Percent
1 Jammu & Kashmir	3,843,451	64.19
2 West Bengal	11,743,259	21.51
3 Kerala	5,409,687	21.25
4 Uttar Pradesh	17,657,735	15.93
5 Bihar	9,874,993	14.13
6 Karnataka	4,104,616	11.05
7 Maharashtra	5,805,785	9.25
8 Gujarat	2,907,744	8.53
9 Andhra Pradesh	4,533,700	8.47
10 Rajasthan	2,492,145	7.28
11 Tamil Nadu	2,519,947	5.21
12 Madhya Pradesh	2,501,919	4.80
13 Orissa	422,266	1.60
14 Punjab	168,094	1.00
Total[b]	75,512,439	11.35

[a] Assam, excluded from the 1981 census of religion, had a population of 3,590,000 Muslims according to the 1971 census, comprising 24.0 percent of the total.
[b] Figures do not add to total, which includes all states and union territories.
Source: *Census of India, 1981*, Series-1: *India*, Paper 3 of 1984: *Household Population by Religion of Head of Household*, by V. S. Verma (Delhi: Controller of Publications, 1985).

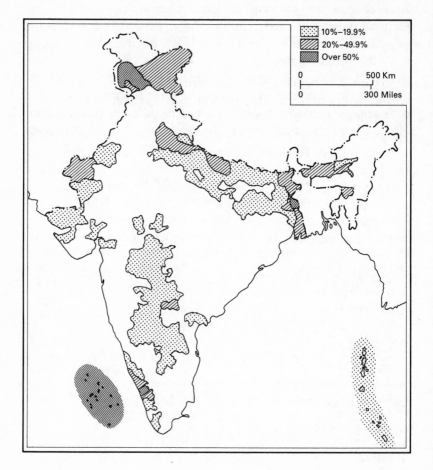

Figure 5   Distribution of Muslims, 1971, to total population by district
Based on Ashok K. Dutt and M. Margaret Geib, *Atlas of South Asia*
(Boulder, CO: Westview Press, 1987)

worship.[47] Although many, even most, Muslims can from time to time be mobilized on a broad basis, using symbols of Islam and Muslim communal identification, such mobilization has in general been ephemeral, including the great mobilization that was the Pakistan movement in its final phases.[48]

Congress policy towards Muslims

The Congress, since before Independence, has had a political alliance with orthodox Muslims, and specifically with those associated with the Jamiyyat-ul-Ulama, an organization of Muslim clerics associated with the famous orthodox Islamic university at Deoband in western U. P. The Jamiyyat's cooperation with the Congress has involved a political bargain in which the ulama have given their support on the assumption that the Muslim Personal Law (shariat) would be maintained, as would endowments, mosques, and other institutions and aspects of Muslim culture.[49]

The apparent liberality and secular approach of the Congress leadership towards the Muslims under Nehru and later under Mrs. Gandhi drew to the Congress the most secular, liberal, and often Marxist Muslim politicians as well.

Muslim grievances in north India

In addition to the issue of the status of Urdu discussed in the previous chapter, in the years since Independence Muslim political spokesmen have raised several other issues concerning the protection of the Muslim minority, its culture and institutions.

The status of the Muslim Personal Law (shariat)

The absence of a uniform civil code for all Indians and the status of the Muslim Personal Law were dramatized most recently in the

[47] Gail Minault, "Some Reflections on Islamic Revivalism vs. Assimilation Among Muslims in India," *Contributions to Indian Sociology*, XVIII, No. 2 (1984), 301–302.

[48] Robinson's view is different; see Francis Robinson, "Islam and Muslim Society in South Asia: A Reply to Das and Minault," *Contributions to Indian Sociology*, xx, No. 1 (January–June, 1986), 97–104 and cf. Minault, "Some Reflections on Islamic Revivalism vs. Assimilation," p. 302.

[49] Yohannan Friedmann, "The Attitude of the *JAM'IYYAT-'ULAMA' – HIND* to the Indian National Movement and the Establishment of Pakistan," *Asian and African Studies*, VII (1971), 173–174.

Shah Bano case of 1987 in which the civil courts awarded alimony to a divorced Muslim woman contrary to the provisions of the *shariat*. When agitation against the Shah Bano case decision among orthodox and conservative Muslims developed, intensified, and appeared to gain mass support, Prime Minister Rajiv Gandhi capitulated to conservative Muslim opinion to the extent of passing the Muslim Women (Protection of Rights on Divorce) Bill. The latter, passed on May 6, 1987, literally adopted the provisions of the *shariat* into secular law.

The question of the status of the Aligarh Muslim University

A third issue has concerned the status of the Aligarh Muslim University (AMU), which has had central symbolic importance as the preeminent educational institution for Muslims in India for nearly a century. The AMU functioned from the passage of the Aligarh Muslim University Act of 1920 until its amendment in 1951 under a special charter, which contained three controversial features: a provision for compulsory religious education of the students, its residential charter, and its administration by Muslims.

The 1951 amendment modified the original charter in all three respects. A further amendment in 1965, which threatened the autonomy of the University, precipitated an agitation to restore the 1920 AMU Act. The agitations gathered considerable force among Muslims in north India before the 1967 elections. Despite promises made by Mrs. Gandhi thereafter, the Aligarh Muslim University (Amendment) Act, 1972 failed to respond to the most important Muslim demands, causing on the contrary further resentments. Only after the Janata government reopened the issue in 1978, and the Congress responded with new promises to Muslims in the 1979 election campaign, was a new Amendment Act passed in 1981 which satisfied most Muslim opinion by recognizing explicity the minority character of AMU.[50]

---

[50] Paul R. Brass, *Language, Religion, and Politics in North India* (London: Cambridge University Press, 1974), pp. 223–227, and Violette Graff, "The Muslim Vote in the Indian General Election of December, 1984," in Paul R. Brass and Francis Robinson (eds.), *The Indian National Congress and Indian Society, 1885–1985: Ideology, Social Structure and Political Dominance* (Delhi: Chanakya Publications, 1987), p. 465.

Muslims in the political parties and in government service

Muslims have generally been underrepresented in the national and state legislatures[51] and, with some exceptions,[52] in the central and state government services. In the 1970s and 1980s, however, Muslim representation in government service and in the legislatures was affected positively, though not always permanently, in several states by the new Congress strategy of appealing to backward classes by reserving places for them. For example, in Karnataka, the Urs government included Muslims among the backward categories[53] even though they were already better represented in government service there than in most other states.[54]

Although the extent of political and public service representation for Muslims has varied and has occasionally been equal to or above its population percentage in some states and government departments, Muslims in general in India constitute a disadvantaged and underrepresented minority in this respect. Among the current demands, therefore, of Muslim political organizations such as the Majlis-e-Mushawarat, is the extension of "reservations for the Muslim community as a Backward Class in public services and higher education."[55]

The demand for "liberation" of Hindu places of worship occupied by Muslim mosques

In 1986, a local controversy in the ancient Hindu town of Ayodhya in Faizabad district (U. P.) erupted into a major national issue dividing Hindus and Muslims. The controversy, which had recurred

[51] Brass, *Language, Religion, and Politics in North India*, pp. 228–230; Ghanshyam Shah, Strategies of Social Engineering: Reservation and Mobility of Backward Communities in Gujarat, unpublished paper, UCLA Conference on Parties & Elections, 1987, p. 40–a; G. Thimmaiah and Abdul Aziz, "The Political Economy of Land Reforms in Karnataka, a South Indian State," *Asian Survey*, XXIII, No. 7 (July, 1983), 816; Graff, "The Muslim Vote," p. 458.
[52] Such as Mysore/Karnataka; Thimmaiah & Aziz, "The Political Economy of Land Reforms," p. 823.
[53] Amal Ray and Jayalakshmi Kumpatla, "Zilla Parishad Presidents in Karnataka: Their Social Background and Implications for Development," *Economic and Political Weekly* [hereafter *EPW*], XXII, Nos. 42 & 43 (October 17–24, 1987), 1829.
[54] See esp. the detailed figures on Muslim representation in all public services and institutions in Karnataka as of 1984, taken from the report of a commission of the Government of Karnataka, cited in *Muslim India*, Nos. 52, 53, 54, 55, 57, & 58 (April, May, June, July, September, and October, 1987).
[55] *Muslim India*, No. 55 (July, 1987), 297.

since the mid nineteenth century, arose again in 1986 when, in response to a Hindu demand for restoration of a disputed mosque site for Hindu worship, the district judge removed the padlock placed there 36 years before after a previous court decision and acceded to the Hindu demand.

The district judge's decision, which was completely inconsistent with all previous judicial decisions concerning this issue, became an occasion for the eruption of communal violence in places remote from Faizabad and also for the creation of a Babari Masjid (Babur's Mosque) Coordination Committee to mobilize Muslims throughout the country for the restoration of the mosque as a place of worship for Muslims and for the protection of other mosques threatened by Hindu takeovers elsewhere in the country.[56] Militant Hindu groups such as the Vishwa Hindu Parishad ("World Hindu Society"), the RSS, and the BJP, for their part, have prepared lists of mosques in various places in the country which were built atop Hindu temples and other sites sacred to Hindus and have demanded their restoration to their original purposes.

Contemporary Muslim politics and political organization

Muslims as an influence group within the Congress

Although usually underrepresented proportionate to their population in Parliament, a sufficient number of Muslims have generally been elected on the Congress ticket for them to play a role as an influence group at critical times. For example, Muslim MPs played a pivotal role after the Congress split in 1969 and were mobilized on behalf of Mrs. Gandhi by two Muslim ministers in her Cabinet: Fakhruddin Ali Ahmed and Yunus Salim.[57]

Muslim political parties, interest associations and leadership

Kashmir is the only state in India where the Muslims are in a majority and where the dominant party, the National Conference, is led by Muslims. In Kerala, because of the concentration of Muslim

---

[56] The issue has been followed closely in the pages of *Muslim India*, which itself plays an important role in mobilizing educated Muslim opinion for the restoration of the mosque; see below.

[57] S. C. Gangal, *Prime Minister and the Cabinet in India* (New Delhi: Navachetna Prakashan, 1972), p. 38.

numbers in Malabar, the Muslim League has been able to play a balancing role between the Congress- and Communist-led coalitions which have alternated in power there for the past two decades.[58] As a result, the League was a member of every government in the 1960s and 1970s, was able to protect Muslim interests effectively, and succeeded to the extent of compelling the state government to create a Muslim-majority administrative district. In the 1987 legislative assembly elections in Kerala, the League was once again a partner in the Congress-led United Democratic Front, to which it contributed 15 of the 60 seats won by the coalition.

In north India, no Muslim political organization can hope to succeed in having a significant effect as an exclusively Muslim political party. Consequently, the strategies pursued have alternated between loyalty to the dominant party, the Congress, during the first fifteen years after Independence, on the one hand, to attempts to use the Muslim vote as a balance in inter-party conflicts and thereby hope to persuade some parties and candidates of various secular political parties to be more sympathetic to Muslim causes.

The latter strategy was tried notably by the All-India Muslim Majlis-e-Mushawarat (MMM), formed in August, 1964, during a meeting of Muslim leaders in Lucknow.[59] In 1967, it published a *People's Manifesto* and bargained with political parties and candidates to support it. The non-Congress coalitions which came to power in the two north Indian states after 1967, however, failed to satisfy Muslim demands. When the time came for implementation of party promises, the opposition of the Jan Sangh and internal divisions in other parties prevented the achievement of the goals of the MMM. The MMM declined in significance for more than a decade thereafter.

In recent years, however, the MMM has revived and become a more vital and dynamic organization under the leadership of the controversial Syed Shahabuddin. The MMM publishes a monthly journal, *Muslim India*, in English and Urdu, which keeps track of the status of all issues and controversies of concern to Muslims. It also acts as an umbrella organization for many other Muslim interest

[58] Graff, "The Muslim Vote," p. 437.
[59] Brass, *Language, Religion, and Politics in North India*, p. 248.

associations and political parties throughout India by bringing them together for conferences and in political action committees on specific issues before the Muslim community in India such as, for example, the Babari Masjid issue.

Other parties, associations, and leaders

Outside of Kashmir, north India, and the deep south, there are a few other Muslim political organizations and leaders who have played continuous roles in local and national politics. These include the Majlis-i-Ittehad-i-Muslimeen of Hyderabad city, a communal party which has been in existence for several decades,[60] as well as interest groups of several types. Such organizations include, among others, the Jamiyyat-ul-Ulama-e-Hind, whose primary political purpose has been to defend the Muslim Personal Law and oppose "any attempts by the state to change or interfere with it through either specific laws or through the enactment of a uniform civil code"[61] and the Jamiyyat-e-Islami (JUI), fundamentalist, revivalist, and missionary in orientation, rather than orthodox, though it shares with the Jamiyyat-ul-Ulama the goal of preserving the *shariat* for Muslims in India.[62] They include also non-economic interest associations such as the Anjuman Taraqqi-e-Urdu (Hind), which has been the leading organization in India, and especially in U. P. and Bihar, "supporting the cause of Urdu"[63] and occupational and class associations among the handloom weavers, especially in Bihar where the Momin Ansars are a predominantly rural Muslim backward class constituting more than 20 percent of the Muslim population of the state.[64]

Syed Abdullah Bukhari, the Imam of the Jama Masjid in Delhi, has played a personal role in national politics since 1977 when he spoke out against Mrs. Gandhi and the Emergency and campaigned

[60] Graff, "The Muslim Vote," p. 439. The Majlis won the largest number of seats in the last municipal elections in Hyderabad, 38 out of 100 compared to 24 each for the Congress (I) and the Telugu Desam and was thereby able to elect its candidate as mayor; Jaya Kamalakar, "Ethnic Politics in Municipal Corporations," *EPW*, XXIII, No. 19 (May 7, 1988), 945–946.

[61] Brass, *Language, Religion, and Politics in North India*, p. 238.

[62] Violette Graff, "La Jamaat-i-Islami en Inde," in Olivier Carré and Paul Dumont (eds.), *Radicalismes Islamiques*, vol. II (Paris: L'Harmattan, 1986), pp. 62–63.

[63] Brass, *Language, Religion, and Politics in North India*, p. 242.

[64] Brass, *Language, Religion, and Politics in North India*, pp. 245–246.

against the Congress and for Janata in the Lok Sabha elections. In 1980, the Imam, disaffected with the Janata regime, supported the Congress, but he again moved to oppose the Congress in 1984.

Muslim voting behavior

General pattern of Muslim voting behavior since Independence

All observers agree that Muslims voted predominantly for the Congress until 1962, but that there was a withdrawal of Muslim support from the Congress in the 1967 general elections in the aftermath of the rising Muslim discontent over the issues of Urdu, the status of the Aligarh Muslim University, and the increased level of communal violence (see table 6.3) especially in the north.

In 1972, Muslims not only returned to the Congress but were said to have "voted to an unprecedented degree" solidly for Mrs. Gandhi, who presented a strong secular image.[65] There is wide-spread – though not universal – agreement that the Muslims, especially in north India, shifted their voting behavior once again in 1977 away from the Congress to the Janata coalition.[66] Hostility among Muslims to the demolition scheme to remove squatter settlements and shops from congested urban areas was said to have especially influenced Muslims.[67] On the other hand, the Muslim desertion even in north India does not seem to have been universal, for Blair reports that Muslims in Bihar stayed with the Congress.[68]

Internal division within the Janata coalition in which the Lok Dal leaders themselves charged that the Jan Sangh and the RSS were responsible for an increase in incidents of communal violence led Muslims "who had supported Janata in 1977" to shift away from its

[65] W. H. Morris-Jones, "India Elects for Change – and Stability," *Asian Survey*, XI, No. 8 (August, 1971), 722–723, 728.

[66] Myron Weiner, *India at the Polls, 1980: A Study of the Parliamentary Elections* (Washington, D.C.: American Enterprise Institute, 1983), p. 38; Barnett R. Rubin, "The Civil Liberties Movement in India: New Approaches to the State and Social Change," *Asian Survey*, XXVII, No. 3 (March 1987), 375; Graff, "The Muslim Vote," p. 430.

[67] Weiner, *India at the Polls*, p. 40. Among the shops and stalls demolished at the time were those surrounding the Jama Masjid, which were owned by the Imam himself, Syed Abdullah Bukhari.

[68] Harry W. Blair, Electoral Support and Party Institutionalization in Bihar: Congress and the Opposition, 1977–1985, unpublished paper, UCLA Conference on Parties & Elections, June, 1987, pp. 8–9.

Table 6.3. *Incidents of communal violence and numbers of persons killed by community, 1954–82*

Year	Incidents	Killed			
		Hindus	Muslims	Others/police	Total
1954	83	N.A.	N.A.	N.A.	N.A.
1955	72	N.A.	N.A.	N.A.	N.A.
1956	74	N.A.	N.A.	N.A.	N.A.
1957	55	N.A.	N.A.	N.A.	N.A.
1958	41	N.A.	N.A.	N.A.	N.A.
1959	42	N.A.	N.A.	N.A.	N.A.
1960	26	N.A.	N.A.	N.A.	N.A.
1961	92	N.A.	N.A.	N.A.	N.A.
1962	60	N.A.	N.A.	N.A.	N.A.
1963	61	N.A.	N.A.	N.A.	N.A.
1964	1,070	N.A.	N.A.	N.A.	N.A.
1965	173 (676)[a]	N.A.	N.A.	N.A.	N.A.
1966	133 (132)[a]	N.A.	N.A.	N.A.	N.A.
1967	209 (220)[a]	N.A.	N.A.	N.A.	N.A.
1968	346	24	99	10	133
1969	519	66	558	49	674
1970	521	68	176	54	298
1971	321	38	65	0	103
1972	240	21	45	3	70
1973	242	26	45	1	72
1974	248	26	61	0	87
1975	205	11	22	0	33
1976	169	20	19	0	39
1977	188	12	24	0	36
1978	219 (230)[b]	51	56	1	108 (110)[b]
1979	304	80	50	31	261
1980	427	87	278	10	375
1981	319	N.A.	N.A.	N.A.	196
1982	474	N.A.	N.A.	N.A.	238
Total	6,933	530	1,498	159	2,723

[a] Source (1).
[b] Sources (1) and (4).

remnants in the 1980 election and to return to voting for the congress in larger numbers.[69] Although there are some differences of detail concerning the interpretation of Muslim voting behavior in 1980,[70] the consensus is that Congress was helped by a return of some Muslim voters to it, but that the distribution of Muslim voting overall was not significantly different from that of the general population and that it conformed to regional as well as national trends.

In the 1984 election, far from minority demands providing either a threat to or a support for either the ruling party or the opposition, it was the Hindu majority which was mobilized on this occasion in an atmosphere of hostility to minority demands and behavior. The Congress itself appealed to Hindu nationalism and communalism in this election. The upshot was that Muslim voting behavior was similar to 1980. The general consensus is that approximately half the Muslim electorate voted for the Congress, as did the rest of the country, and that there were considerable regional variations in the Muslim vote.[71] The natural diversity of Muslims in India is now reflected in the diversification – regionalization and localization – of Muslim voting behavior.

Notes to Table 6.3 (cont.)

Sources: (1) 1954–1968: Centre for Research in Rural and Industrial Development, Communal Violence and its Impact on Development and National Integration (no publication details), citing Ministry of Home Affairs, Bulletin for the National Integration Council, 16 May, 1969, p. 8 and Ratna Naidu, The Communal Edge to Plural Societies: India and Malaysia (Ghaziabad: Vikas, 1980). (2) 1965–1967: Government of India, Ministry of Home Affairs, Report, 1966–67, p. 51 and Report, 1967–68, p. 40 and (3) 1968–1980: Communal Riots and Minorities, unpublished, undated, mimeo report, p. 1. (4) 1981–1982: Government of India, Ministry of Home Affairs, Report, 1982–83 (New Delhi: Government of India Press, 1983), p. 3.

[69] Weiner, India at the Polls, pp. 19–20.
[70] Cf. Graff, "The Muslim Vote," pp. 430–431 and Lloyd I. Rudolph and Susanne H. Rudolph, In Pursuit of Lakshmi: The Political Economy of the Indian State (Chicago: University of Chicago Press, 1987), p. 194.
[71] Graff, "The Muslim Vote," pp. 443, 460; also Rudolph & Rudolph, In Pursuit of Lakshmi, p. 194; and Robert L. Hardgrave, Jr., "India in 1984: Confrontation, Assassination, and Succession," Asian Survey, xxv, No. 2 (February, 1985), 142–143.

Hindu–Muslim communal violence

The numbers of communal incidents and of persons killed in them have increased significantly since the mid-1960s, as indicated in table 6.3. It is evident from the figures that, with rare exceptions, the numbers of Muslims killed are usually much higher than the numbers of Hindus. Moreover, in most major riots police firings are directed disproportionately at Muslim mobs and many of the Muslims killed in these riots are killed in the police firings themselves, rather than by Hindu rioters.[72]

The most notorious police force in India is the Provincial Armed Constabulary, particularly that in U. P., which has become infamous among Muslims for its murderous behavior against them in several riots and which, despite increasing recognition that the charges against the force "are not unjustified,"[73] has been called out repeatedly to "restore order" in situations of communal violence, particularly in western U. P.

There have been major riots during the past 25 years in Jamshedpur (Bihar) in 1964, Ranchi (Bihar) in 1967, Ahmedabad (Gujarat) in 1969 and in 1985, Bombay in 1984, Delhi in 1987, Meerut (U. P.) in 1982 and 1987, and many other cities and towns mostly in the northern and western states of the country.

Conclusion

Many alternative explanations for the resurgence of regional and communal conflicts in the past fifteen years have been offered, including the persistence of immutable primordial cleavages in Indian society, their underlying basis in economic or class differences, and specific policies and political tactics pursued by the central and state governments. The analysis here has given primacy to the latter. However, it is also true that the problems in the Punjab and in the northeastern region have been complicated by the presence of other factors which were not present in the linguistic reorganizations of states which took place during the Nehru period. In the Punjab case, the most important difference is the fact that the Sikhs are a separate religious as well as linguistic group. In the

[72] Communal Riots and Minorities, unpublished official government of India paper, no further publication details.
[73] Communal Riots and Minorities, p. 12.

northeast, the issues have been tangled by the presence there of several tribal minorities, whose demands have been secessionist, by the migration of large numbers of people from other provinces of India, particularly West Bengal, to the northeastern states of Assam and Tripura especially, by illegal migrations from Bangladesh as well, and by the presence of large numbers of both Hindus and Muslims among the migrant and local populations.

The problems in the tribal regions of the country have been especially severe because of the profound cultural and economic differences between the tribal peoples and the peoples of the plains. Moreover, the Indian state has used its powers to penetrate ever more forcefully into tribal territories and has, in the process, become identified with those who have long been engaged in appropriating the traditional lands and rights of the indigenous populations of these areas.

The persistence of Hindu–Muslim conflicts reflects yet another set of tensions both in Indian society and in the functioning of the Indian state. Muslim political behavior, especially voting behavior, suggests a high degree of integration into the Indian political order. On the other hand, this integration has been taking place in the face of increased Hindu hostility and communal violence directed against Muslims.

Increasing evidence has been accumulating in recent studies of communal riots in several towns in western U. P. and Maharashtra of a connection between these riots and local economic and political struggles.[74] Considerable changes have taken place in Muslim social structure during the past two decades, especially the rise of new business classes competing with Hindu businessmen in industries over which the latter previously had dominant or monopolistic control. It is alleged that behind many local riots which begin with a focus on traditional inflammatory features such as "music before mosques" or an elopement of a Hindu girl with a Muslim boy is such Hindu–Muslim economic competition in which Hindu businessmen help to precipitate or take advantage of a developing

[74] See esp. Ashgar Ali Engineer, "The Causes of Communal Riots in the Post-Partition Period in India," in Ashgar Ali Engineer (ed.), *Communal Riots in Post-Independence India* (Hyderabad: Sangam Books, 1984), pp. 33–41; also Centre for Research in Rural and Industrial Development and National Integration, "Communal Violence and its Impact on Development and National Integration," unpublished paper, no further publication details.

riot situation to destroy the property and threaten the lives of economic rivals. The local politicians in turn enter the fray and seek to exploit such situations by inciting communal elements further or by standing forth as "protectors" of one or the other community. The connections between local Hindu and Muslim businessmen and politicians need to be further explored since it is evident that local political control over licenses, permits, taxes, and the like may aid or hinder businessmen in pursuing their economic activities. Such local riots, whose origins lie in specific, local circumstances are then contextualized by situating them in an alleged broader pattern of deteriorating Hindu–Muslim relations, which draws upon the bitter history of Hindu–Muslim relations before Independence and on emotions tied to the three wars between India and Pakistan since Independence. Such broader contextualization provides further stimulus to local communal politicians who then see themselves as involved in a broader national cause for the preservation of the unity of the country or the defence of the Muslim minority threatened by an oppressive Hindu majority.

It is necessary, however, to seek the sources of broader anti-Muslim hostility not only among Hindu communal ideologies and organizations, but in the secular ideology which, since Independence, has exalted the state and its unity as the highest political value. This exaltation of the state was tempered in the Nehru period by pluralist political practices in relation to minorities and by Nehru's personal condemnation on countless occasions of the evils of "casteism, communalism, and provincialism."

Mrs. Gandhi's exaltation of the Indian state went far beyond that of her father and was manifested, as just noted, in increasing attempts to centralize power and policy-making in Delhi. Moreover, she tended to *use* Muslim discontent to appeal to Muslims for support by implying that their own safety against Hindu communalists could be ensured only by remaining loyal to the Congress. Further, both the Congress under her leadership and the opposition also began to *use* incidents of communal violence as sticks with which to beat each other.

It needs to be recognized, therefore, that the flourishing of local communal violence has been enhanced since Nehru's death by the political uses to which it has been put in competitive politics at the national and state levels and by the entrenchment of an ideology of the secular state which, in its tolerant face, justifies pluralist practices but can also be used to condemn minority demands as a danger to national unity and the integrity of the Indian state.

CHAPTER 7

VARIETIES OF ETHNIC CONFLICT

Caste and migrant–non-migrant relations have provided two further bases for ethnic conflict in post-Independence India, which have at times turned violent and murderous. These two types of conflicts have some distinctive features and some which they share with the others dealt with in the previous two chapters. State recognition has been a major factor in the issues of caste conflict discussed in this chapter. The central and state governments have pursued policies of "protective discrimination" for the lowest castes and Scheduled Tribes, but not for the middle status castes. The recognition by the state of caste status as a legitimate basis for political mobilization has, however, provided the potential for backward caste groups in several states to demand protective treatment for members of their castes as well. The drive of the Congress leadership in the 1970s to provide alternative support bases for some state parties in its conflicts with local Congress and non-Congress rivals was a second major factor in the rise of inter-caste conflicts at the provincial level. Unevenness in the rates of social change among different castes and job competition among their members have provided the social bases for such caste mobilization.

The situation with regard to migrant–non-migrant relations has been somewhat different on the matter of state recognition and state policies. The central government has resisted attempts to establish categories which discriminate among or even distinguish between migrants and non-migrants, though ultimately it has made such concessions. State governments have, however, been quite willing to impose restrictions on opportunities available to migrants whenever the latter have been in competition with vocal "sons of the soil." As in the case of inter-caste conflicts, migrant–non-migrant conflicts have arisen especially around issues of job competition, but also around issues of local political dominance.

It is not to be assumed, however, that conflict and violence are inherent either in the caste system or in migrant–non–migrant relations. On the contrary, the normal modes in both cases are non-conflictual. Conflict and violence between castes or between migrants and non-migrants have occurred rather when combined with particular economic conditions and when political elites seek short-term advantage from potential conflicts.

One of the principal underlying bases for both caste and migrant–non-migrant conflicts has been job competition among educated middle class youth from different ethnic categories. Indeed, behind such conflicts, there is often a clear politics of privilege, a struggle among already advantaged segments of the population to gain or maintain privileged access to the most secure and prestigious jobs in the public sector. Language, regional, and caste loyalties are often but the symbolic covers for such struggle.

Issues of political control at both the local level and between the center and the states also affect the course of ethnic conflicts. It is commonly assumed that the politicians are confronted with ethnic cleavages and hostilities which determine their political actions and alignments. The evidence from post-Independence Indian politics, however, is that the politicians have followed different political strategies at different times with different results in relation to similar types of conflicts.

There is, in particular, in the cases discussed here, as in the previous issues of language and majority–minority conflicts, a considerable difference in political strategies followed by the national leadership in the Nehru and post-Nehru periods. These differences arise primarily from two interrelated causes: the succession struggle which occurred after the post-Emergency elections of 1977, on the one hand, and the efforts of the Congress (I) under Mrs. Gandhi's leadership to mobilize new segments of the electorate in order to defeat her rivals in particular states.

Caste and migrant–non-migrant conflicts, therefore, have been closely related in the post-Nehru period to both local struggles for political control and to the struggles among the national leaders of the country to maintain central control over the states. It will be shown below how shifting political alignments at the local level and the national level have interpenetrated and profoundly affected the formation and disintegration of ethnic coalitions and the course of ethnic conflicts in the states and localities of the country.

CASTE CONFLICT AND PREFERENTIAL POLICIES

Caste and caste conflict in post-Independence politics

The Nehru period

The leadership of the nationalist movement and of the Indian National Congress in virtually the entire subcontinent was in the hands primarily of men from the elite Hindu castes, especially Brahmans in most regions, Kayasthas in north India, Banias in many regions, and other regional high caste groups in other parts of the country. In between the elite and lowest castes in India are a huge number of both agricultural and artisan castes, of middle status, some of whom are land controlling castes, others of whom are economically nearly as disadvantaged as the low castes. The more disadvantaged castes among this broad spectrum of Indian society are generally called "backward castes" or "backward classes." At the bottom of the hierarchy of status, well-being, and political power before and after Independence were the Scheduled Castes and Scheduled Tribes.

Among both the elite and middle status castes, a process of caste succession had begun before Independence and was intensified after it with the adoption of adult franchise by which, in election after election, new leaders from previously unrepresented or underrepresented castes began to emerge and the castes themselves to be mobilized. In some states, the newly mobilized castes were integrated into the Congress system, while in others they provided a support base for opposition parties. In general, the linguistic reorganization of states assisted the processes of caste mobilization in two ways: indirectly by eliminating language as an alternative source of political mobilization and conflict and directly by reducing the size of the states, thereby enhancing the political potential of regional caste groups which, for the most part, are specific to linguistic regions.[1]

Many other, more specific factors have contributed to the rise of inter-caste conflicts in several states and localities in the post-Independence period. The intermediate castes acquired increased

---

[1] I am indebted to John Wood for stimulating this observation. Cf. also Selig S. Harrison, who anticipated these results in *India: The Most Dangerous Decades* (Princeton, NJ: Princeton University Press, 1960), p. 105 and ch. 4 *passim*.

voting power through adult suffrage and increased economic power through *zamindari* abolition. Their leaders naturally resented the fact that the central government, most state governments, and the Congress organizations were dominated by upper caste leaders in the early years after Independence. Intermediate castes with economic resources sought not only political power but educational benefits and urban jobs for their children. As they acquired such opportunities, they came increasingly into conflict with persons from upper caste groups represented in far greater proportionate and often absolute numbers in educational and political institutions. Conflicts between persons from different caste groups have tended to become most intense when resource opportunities have been denied or have been perceived as going to one group, region, or locality rather than another in which one's own group would benefit more. At the local level, traditional patron–client ties which had often bound the lower to the middle and upper land controlling castes have weakened considerably as a consequence of land pressures, the movement of lower caste persons to the cities and to more prosperous agricultural areas in search of work, and the increasing importance of cash rather than traditional, annual payments in kind to laborers.

Although caste conflict and competition at the state level began to acquire importance in the Nehru period, it did not structure completely political competition either within the Congress or between Congress and opposition parties. In general, however, the importance of conflict structured along caste lines increases as one goes down to the local level. Caste factors are of marginal importance in national politics and caste has never structured political competition at the central level. Institutional structures and relationships such as marriage and kinship ties, caste *panchayats*, and other forms of corporate organization rarely cross language borders and almost never do so effectively. At the state level, those caste clusters which have large numbers as well as significant geographical dispersion have been sometimes able to act in relatively solidary ways and caste competition among such large groups has partially structured political competition in a few states, notably Bihar.[2] Caste becomes the

[2] Harry W. Blair, Caste, Politics and Democracy in Bihar State, India: The Elections of 1967, unpublished Ph.D. dissertation, Duke University, 1969.

primary, though not the exclusive, basis for building political support at the district level and below.[3] In the districts and villages throughout the subcontinent, the land controlling agricultural castes have tended gradually to take control of most local political parties, government institutions, and cooperatives.

The post-Nehru period

During the grand succession struggle which developed after Nehru's death, especially after the split in the Congress in 1969 and during and after the 1971 elections, the Congress led by Mrs. Gandhi intensified its appeal to the disadvantaged groups in order to counter the power of the state party bosses, which rested mostly on the upper and landed castes. Electoral support from these disadvantaged groups was of critical importance in Mrs. Gandhi's triumph in the 1971 elections.[4] The loss of support from the Scheduled Castes and other disadvantaged groups was a major factor in the heavy defeat of the Congress in the post-Emergency 1977 elections. In the 1980 elections, Congress again drew heavy support from the Scheduled Castes and Scheduled Tribes.[5]

Reservations and the political roles of disadvantaged and backward castes and classes

The mechanism of reservation of seats in the legislatures ensures the election of a fixed proportion of Scheduled Caste and Scheduled Tribe representatives to Parliament and the state legislatures. Jagjivan Ram, the famous Scheduled Caste leader from Bihar and a minister in the central government throughout most of both the Nehru and post-Nehru periods, was always thought to be able to control 40 to 60 votes in Parliament and was deferred to in the

[3] Harold A. Gould, "A Sociological Perspective on the Eighth General Election in India," *Asian Survey*, XXVI, No. 6 (June, 1986), 651–652; Paul R. Brass, *Caste, Faction and Party in Indian Politics*, Vol. II: *Election Studies* (Delhi: Chanakya Publications, 1985), esp. chs. 1 & 6; Ian Duncan, Party Politics and the North Indian Peasantry: The Rise of the Bharatiya Kranti Dal in Uttar Pradesh, unpublished paper, School of African and Asian Studies, University of Sussex, [1987].

[4] W. H. Morris-Jones, "India Elects for Change – and Stability," *Asian Survey*, XI, No. 8 (August, 1971), 722–723.

[5] Myron Weiner, "Congress Restored: Continuities and Discontinuities in Indian Politics," *Asian Survey*, XXII, No. 4 (April, 1982), 340, and *India at the Polls, 1980: A Study of the Parliamentary Elections* (Washington, DC: American Enterprise Institute, 1983), pp. 19–20.

Congress for that reason. He also played a swing role at several critical points in the post-Nehru period: when he threw his support to Mrs. Gandhi in the second (1966) succession, when he stayed with Mrs. Gandhi when the Congress split in 1969,[6] and when he deserted Mrs. Gandhi and joined forces with the Janata in 1977.

Although the lowest castes and tribes have provided a critical support base for the Congress and a few leaders like Jagjivan Ram have been coopted into positions of power at the national and state levels, for the most part politicians from these groups have remained outside the inner circles of party and government power and have been dependent upon more powerful upper caste leaders. Village politics continue to be primarily factional, with the leaders of opposing factions coming from the elite and dominant castes, but with lower castes recruited into the factions.

In contrast, however, during the post-Nehru period, a shift in both the leadership and the support bases of the Congress parties to the non-dominant or "lower" backward castes did occur in some states, notably in Karnataka and Gujarat. In other states, particularly north India, where the elite castes of Brahmans, Rajputs, and Bhumihars have been more numerous and well entrenched both economically and politically, there has been an intensification of conflict between them and several of the backward castes.

The issue of class versus caste conflict

Political analysts of caste and caste conflict in post-Independence India have been divided between those who treat caste interest, solidarity, and competition as independent forces, with their own realities, and Marxist scholars who see class interest behind caste conflicts. This issue will be taken up in chapter 9. The focus here is exclusively on issues which have raised the question and precipitated action on the bases of caste solidarities, without implying that other bases of action do or do not occur in contemporary Indian politics. Most especially, in the remainder of this discussion of caste conflict in contemporary India, the focus will be on the issue of reservation of jobs and scholarships for both the Scheduled Castes and Tribes and the backward castes, especially the latter, which one observer

[6] S. C. Gangal, *Prime Minister and the Cabinet in India* (New Delhi: Navachetna Prakashan, 1972), p. 38.

has characterized as "the new frontier of Indian politics in the 1980s."[7]

Central government policies

Since Independence, the central government has provided a variety of benefits, protections, and programs for the Scheduled Castes and Scheduled Tribes. The central government has not, however, followed the same policies in relation to the backward castes. The Constitution refers vaguely to a third category of persons, besides the Scheduled Castes and Scheduled Tribes, who are entitled to special protections against discrimination and to special benefits for their advancement. The adoption of "preferential treatment for backward class peoples" was specifically sanctioned in Articles 15(4) and 16(4).[8]

However, the issues both of extending special benefits to the backward castes and of designating the specific castes to be included in any measures enacted for their benefit have been far more controversial than the issues surrounding the specification of Scheduled Castes and Scheduled Tribes and the extension of benefits to them. A consensus had already been reached among the national leadership before Independence both on the desirability of extending special benefits to these groups and, for the most part, on the specific castes and tribes to be included. The designated castes were already listed on a schedule by the Government of India (Scheduled Castes) Order, 1936.[9] A similar list of Scheduled Tribes had been prepared in 1935.[10]

However, no such consensus existed with regard to the backward castes. Although there was some ambiguity concerning the status of many of the Scheduled Castes, there was at least a common referent around the idea of including castes which, as groups, had been subject historically to numerous discriminations at the hands of the caste Hindus summarized by the term "untouchability." With

[7] Subrata Mitra, "The Perils of Promoting Equality: The Latent Significance of the Anti-Reservation Movement in India," *Journal of Commonwealth and Comparative Politics*, xxv, No. 3 (November, 1987), 309.

[8] John R. Wood, Reservations in Doubt: The Backlash Against Affirmative Action in Gujarat, India, unpublished paper, UCLA Conference on Parties & Elections, 1987, p. 7.

[9] Marc Galanter, *Competing Equalities: Law and the Backward Classes in India* (Delhi: Oxford University Press, p. 130).

[10] Galanter, *Competing Equalities*, p. 149.

regard to the backward castes, however, there is no such single criterion which could be easily applied throughout the country, for the status and economic well-being of the numerous intermediate castes between the "untouchable" group and the elite (or "twice-born" castes) vary greatly from region to region.[11]

The first Backward Classes Commission was set up by the central government in 1953. It reported in 1955. Although the Commission expressed doubts about adopting "caste as the basis for identifying backward classes,"[12] it nevertheless "identified 2,399 castes as socially and educationally backward." The central government, however, "did not accept the recommendation of the Commission on the ground that it had not applied any objective tests for identifying Backward Classes."[13]

It was not until 1978, when the Janata coalition displaced the Congress from power at the Center, with considerable support in north India from Backward Caste groups, that the central government again took up the issue of preferential treatment for the backward castes by appointing the Second Backward Classes Commission. The second commission, unlike the first, explicitly recommended the adoption of "caste as a criterion"[14] and identified "3,248 castes or communities comprising 52.4 percent of the population of India, roughly 350 million people."[15] By the time the Commission submitted its report, however, the Congress had returned to power. The central government did not present the report to Parliament until April, 1982, and the Congress government took no decision on it.[16]

State government policies and problems
The south

The AIADMK and its principal rival in Tamil Nadu politics, the DMK, both trace their origins to the Dravidian movement of the

[11] Galanter, Competing Equalities, ch. 6.
[12] Mitra, "The Perils of Promoting Equality," p. 296; Wood, Reservations in Doubt, p. 7.
[13] Ghanshyam Shah, Strategies of Social Engineering: Reservation and Mobility of Backward Communities in Gujarat, unpublished paper, UCLA Conference on Parties & Elections, 1987, p. 14.
[14] Mitra, "The Perils of Promoting Equality," p. 298; also Wood, Reservations in Doubt, p. 13.
[15] Wood, Reservations in Doubt, p. 9.
[16] Shah, Strategies of Social Engineering, pp. 16–17.

late nineteenth century and to the Justice Party and the Self-Respect Movement of the 1920s and 1930s, all of which drew heavily upon non-Brahman castes and sought to displace the Brahmans from their preeminent positions of leadership in public life and government service in the province. Party competition for the support of the backward castes in Tamil Nadu has led to a generous policy of reservations for them. Thirty-one percent of government jobs have been reserved for 105 categories of backward castes and communities in the state since 1972.

A Backward Classes Commission was not appointed in Andhra until after the Congress split, in 1970, when the Congress (I) was seeking to broaden its popular base here and elsewhere among the Scheduled Castes, backward castes, and minorities.[17] Since 1975, the state government has provided reservations for 92 categories of "backward" castes and communities.

In 1986, the Telugu Desam government of N. T. Rama Rao (NTR) decided "to raise the quota of reservations for backward classes from 25 percent to 44 percent."[18] When the courts declared that the new reservations policy was unconstitutional, the chief minister withdrew the additional reservations and was then confronted with an agitation by "backward-caste associations," which "launched a statewide protest, setting buses on fire, demonstrating and clashing with the forward castes and with the police."[19]

In Karnataka, the Congress leadership and popular base in the 1950s came predominantly from Lingayats and Vokkaligas.[20] Although these two communities are the dominant land controlling groups in Karnataka, they both received recognition as backward castes entitled to preferential treatment.

Under the Congress regime of Devaraj Urs in the 1970s, a Backward Classes Commission (the Havnoor Commission) advocated "special concessions to the Backward classes" and "recom-

---

[17] F. D. Vakil, Patterns of Electoral Performance in Andhra Pradesh and Karnataka, unpublished paper, UCLA Conference on Parties & Elections, June, 1987, pp. 5, 29–32.
[18] Mitra, "The Perils of Promoting Equality," p. 309, fn. 4.
[19] Myron Weiner, "Rajiv Gandhi: A Mid-Term Assessment," in Marshall M. Bouton (ed.), India Briefing, 1987 (Boulder: Westview Press, 1987), p. 11.
[20] Vakil, Patterns of Electoral Performance, p. 23.

mended a reclassification of the backward castes." Urs' adoption of the Havnoor Report led to a split in the Congress.[21]

The Congress continued under Urs' leadership to broaden its base among the backward castes by selecting a large number of candidates from among them to contest the 1978 elections.[22] Since 1979, a policy of 40 percent reservations for 297 categories has been in effect.[23] Under the new reservations policies of the Urs regime, however, recognition of the Lingayats as a backward community was withdrawn, but not that of the Vokkaligas.[24]

After the defeat of the Congress by Janata in the 1977 parliamentary elections, differences developed between Mrs. Gandhi and Devaraj Urs leading to his displacement as leader of the Congress (I) and a split in the party. After the split, the Congress reduced its dependence upon the non-dominant backward classes and increased the representation of the dominant Lingayat and Vokkaliga communities.[25]

The Janata party of Ramakrishna Hegde succeeded in defeating the Congress in two legislative assembly elections in 1983 and 1985. Its base also is primarily among the two dominant landed castes.[26]

In 1986, the Second Backward Classes Commission (Venkataswamy Commission), appointed in 1983, presented its report. The Commission recommended the exclusion of the Vokkaligas from the list of backward classes because its criteria had demonstrated that they were in fact a highly advanced community. Instead, Hedge issued an ordinance bringing "almost all the castes in the state within the ambit of the backward classes," but with the "Vokkaligas and Lingayats . . . classified under separate groups of backwardness."[27]

[21] Vakil, Patterns of Electoral Performance, pp. 36–37.
[22] Vakil, Patterns of Electoral Performance, pp. 38–39.
[23] Wood, Reservations in Doubt, p. 30.
[24] Amal Ray and Jayalaksmi Kumpatla, "Zilla Parishad Presidents in Karnataka: Their Social Background and Implications for Development," *EPW*, xxii, Nos. 42 & 43 (October 17–24, 1987), 1,829.
[25] Vakil, Patterns of Electoral Performance, pp. 52–53.
[26] Ray & Kumpatla, "Zilla Parishad Presidents," p. 1,826.
[27] Vakil, Patterns of Electoral Performance, pp. 79–80; Wood, Reservations in Doubt, p. 41, fn. 41; Mitra, "The Perils of Promoting Equality," p. 309, fn. 4.

The north

The situation in the northern states has been entirely different. In these states, the elite castes of Brahmans, Rajputs and Bhumihars are major land controlling castes. During the 1960s and 1970s, several political parties in the north, particularly the Samyukta Socialist Party (SSP) under the leadership of Dr. Rammanohar Lohia and the BKD/Lok Dal of Chaudhuri Charan Singh developed strength among the backward castes and advocated policies of preferential treatment for them.

In 1978, during the Janata period in Bihar, chief minister Karpuri Thakur, formerly of the SSP and himself from the lower backward caste of Nais (barbers) announced a policy of reserving 26 percent of jobs in state government service for the backward classes.[28] The issue precipitated a crisis in April, 1979, when the former Congress (O) and Jan Sangh ministers resigned from the Cabinet. At the same time, the followers of Jagjivan Ram in the Cabinet also resigned. As a consequence of these resignations, the Karpuri Thakur government was brought down and Ram Sunder Das, a Scheduled Caste man, became the new chief minister.[29] In this coalition against the policy of backward caste reservations, there was revealed a characteristic feature of north Indian politics, namely, the joining together of the elite and lowest castes in an alliance against the backward castes.

In Uttar Pradesh, the most important land controlling groups of castes were the Brahmans and the various Rajput castes and clans. Brahmans were at Independence already in predominant positions in the Congress organization at both the state and district levels. Rajputs also soon became prominent in most of the district party organizations of the Congress and to a somewhat lesser extent at the state level.

In U. P., the important backward castes are the Ahirs (Yadavs), Kurmis, and, in western U. P., the Jats. During the 1960s in eastern U.P., the SSP built a broad base of support among the backward castes. After Charan Singh, the Jat leader from western U. P., left

---

[28] Myron Weiner and Mary F. Katzenstein, *India's Preferential Policies: Migrants, the Middle Classes, and Ethnic Quality* (Chicago: University of Chicago Press, 1981), p. 133.
[29] Barun Sengupta, *Last Days of the Morarji Raj* (Calcutta: Ananda Publishers, 1979), pp. 50–51.

the Congress in 1967 to become the first non-Congress chief minister of the state, he drew support especially from his own caste of Jats, but also from the more widely distributed Yadav caste category. During this period, "16 percent of state government jobs [were] reserved for the backward classes."[30] The Congress, for its part, since its return to power in 1973 has been dominated more than ever by Brahmans and Rajputs and has had no interest, therefore, in adopting policies of preferential treatment for the backward castes. The Janata governments which came to power in the post-Emergency period between 1977 and 1980 also did not adopt a broad new reservations policy.

Maharashtra

Maharashtra, like Tamil Nadu, experienced an early non-Brahman movement, which led ultimately to the gradual displacement of Brahmans by the predominant rural land controlling caste of Marathas from the 1930s onwards. Their dominance has been so well established that no reservations policy beyond that for the Scheduled Castes and Tribes has been adopted.

The problem of Gujarat

Political background. Upper caste Brahmans and Banias dominated the Congress organization before Independence and the state government and party organization after Independence through the 1960s.[31] The Patidars and Kunbis, the largest and most prosperous middle peasant castes, were also important in the district organizations since the days of Sardar Patel – himself a Patidar – from the 1920s, but the bigger land owners among them, who resented the continued dominance of the upper castes and opposed Congress land reforms, joined the newly-formed Swatantra party during the 1960s.

Left out of the Congress or hostile to it throughout the nationalist movement and the early post-Independence years were two important groupings of castes, both taking the label of Kshatriyas: one upper caste grouping of ex-princes and large landlords and the other a heterogeneous collection of backward castes, of which the Kolis

---

[30] Weiner and Katzenstein, *India's Preferential Policies*, p. 133.
[31] Shah, *Strategies of Social Engineering*, p. 22.

were the largest and claimed Kshatriya status. When the Swatantra party was formed in 1959, the Kshatriyas flocked to it and 19 of them were given party tickets to contest the 1962 elections.[32] Swatantra did not defeat the Congress in 1962, but did well enough, especially in Kheda district, to cause the Congress to take measures to coopt some of the Kshatriya leaders into the party by giving them positions in the district party organizations and by awarding 15 tickets to Kshatriyas in the 1967 elections compared to only 7 in 1962.

After the Congress split in 1969, most of the Kshatriya leaders joined the Congress (O), but some joined Congress (I) and the two parties fielded the same number – three – of Kshatriyas as party candidates in the 1971 Lok Sabha elections.[33]

The 1972 legislative assembly elections mark the beginning of a decisive change in Gujarat politics when the Congress absorbed the bulk of the backward caste leaders and voters. Madhavsinh Solanki, a backward Kshatriya leader, who had been elected to the legislative assembly on the Congress ticket in 1962 and in 1967, emerged as one of the strongest state leaders of the Gujarat Congress. The Congress won 140 out of 168 seats in the Assembly in the 1972 elections.

It was not until 1976, however, during the Emergency, that the first Congress (I) government under the leadership of Madhavsinh Solanki was formed. Solanki distributed the majority of portfolios in his government to persons from backward castes, especially Kshatriyas, and adopted the "KHAM" strategy of alliance among Kshatriyas, Harijans, Adivasis, and Muslims in the 1977 elections. The Congress, however, was defeated in the post-Emergency 1977 elections.

Then, in 1980, the Congress (I), now with Solanki as the chief minister designate, pursued the KHAM strategy even more vigorously.[34] Of the 140 successful Congress candidates, 96 came from one of the groups in the KHAM coalition. Solanki became chief

[32] Shah, Strategies of Social Engineering, p. 32.
[33] Shah, Strategies of Social Engineering, pp. 35–36.
[34] Shah, Strategies of Social Engineering, p. 38; John R. Wood, "Congress Restored? The 'Kham' Strategy and Congress (I) Recruitment in Gujarat," in John R. Wood (ed.), State Politics in Contemporary India: Crisis or Continuity? (Boulder: Westview Press, 1984), pp. 210–214.

minister, and more than two-thirds of the Cabinet members were drawn from these four disadvantaged groups in the coalition.[35]

The split in the Congress in 1969, therefore, led to a fundamental transformation in the social basis of the dominant Congress led by Mrs. Gandhi. The upper castes went with Congress (O) and later to Janata. Mrs. Gandhi, however, ultimately adopted Solanki as the Congress leader in Gujarat, who proceeded from 1977 onwards to base the party on the support of the Kshatriyas and other disadvantaged groups and minorities, using the KHAM strategy.[36] Under Solanki's leadership between 1980 and 1985, the Congress base among the KHAM categories, particularly the Kshatriyas, was consolidated.

Since the Congress split in 1969, the strength of the Kshatriyas alone in the Legislative Assembly has doubled and they have become the most powerful force in the state government, displacing the previously dominant elite and middle agricultural castes.

Backward classes commissions in Gujarat. The first Backward Classes Commission (called the Bakshi Commission) was appointed in 1972 and presented its report in 1976. It identified 82 castes and communities as backward and recommended reservations of 10 percent of places in government service and educational institutions for them.[37] The Congress took no decision on the report, but its recommendations were later accepted by the Janata government in 1978, which reserved 10 percent "of lower level and 5 percent of higher level government posts" for the designated backward categories.[38]

After the Congress government returned to power in 1980 under Solanki's leadership, it appointed another Backward Classes Commission (the Rane Commission), which submitted its report in October, 1983. This Commission "rejected caste" as the basis for identifying backward categories and adopted instead economic criteria, with an emphasis on occupation, identifying 63 such

[35] Wood, "Reservations in Doubt," pp. 17–18.
[36] Mitra, "The Perils of Promoting Equality," pp. 301–302; Howard Spodek, From Gandhi to Violence: Ahmedabad's 1985 Riots in Historical Perspective, unpublished paper, 1987, p. 4.
[37] Shah, Strategies of Social Engineering, p. 16; also Wood, "Reservations in Doubt," p. 16.
[38] Wood, "Reservations in Doubt," p. 21.

occupations as backward and recommending 28 percent reservations for persons coming from the designated occupational groups.[39]

Background and development of the anti-reservation movement. In Gujarat, the initial introduction of "systematic reservations in post-graduate medical courses" in 1975 precipitated an immediate protest reaction from upper caste students and "student strikes lasting about twenty days."[40] A second, more serious set of incidents occurred between January and March, 1981, leading to extensive rioting in "Ahmedabad and its surrounding villages" in which more than "fifty people, mostly Scheduled Castes, were killed."[41]

These medical course-related incidents, however, pale by comparison with the violence of 1985, which began as a direct reaction to the broader reservations policies of the Congress state governments under the leadership of Chief Minister Solanki. After the Rane Commission report and just before the 1985 elections, on January 10, the Solanki government announced a major increase in the percentage of reservations for "other backward classes" from 10 to 28 percent.[42]

The anti-reservation agitation began in the medical and engineering colleges, but soon spread to colleges and secondary schools throughout Ahmedabad, leading to their closure by the authorities.[43] It soon turned also into uncontrolled rioting, fusing "caste, class, communal and police-citizen conflict[s]" which had nothing to do with the reservations policy.[44] On April 22, 1985, the police themselves "went on a rampage" of "looting, killing, and burning," in which "they terrorized the city and gutted the office of the *Gujarat Samachar*," a newspaper which had criticized the police during the rioting.[45] With the police out of control, the army had to be called in, but even the army could not restore order fully.

The Solanki government was ultimately forced to resign in July,

[39] Shah, Strategies of Social Engineering, pp. 15–16; Wood, "Reservations in Doubt," pp. 21–22; Spodek, From Gandhi to Violence, pp. 5–6.
[40] Mitra, "The Perils of Promoting Equality," p. 302.
[41] Wood, "Reservations in Doubt," p. 20.
[42] Mitra, "The Perils of Promoting Equality," p. 303.
[43] Spodek, From Gandhi to Violence, p. 5.
[44] Wood, "Reservations in Doubt," p. 2.
[45] Wood, "Reservations in Doubt," p. 2; Spodek, From Gandhi to Violence, p. 10.

1985, and the new government cancelled "the proposed increase in reservations."[46] By the end of the long months of violence, 275 people had been killed and 12,000 people displaced and put in relief camps.[47]

The new chief minister, Amarsinh Chaudhury, is a tribal and a "pro-reservationist" and the Congress in Gujarat continues to be dominated by backward castes, Scheduled Castes, and Scheduled Tribes. The "politicization" of the disadvantaged groups in Gujarat is a permanent aspect of Gujarat politics which was further "enhanced" by "the events of 1985." On the other hand, the 1985 riots also demonstrated the impossibility of ignoring the opposition and resentments of the upper and middle castes, who remain powerful and numerous, in implementing an expanded reservations policy.[48]

The issue of caste versus economic criteria in reservations policies

Clearly, caste rather than economic criteria have been used in all the states.[49] Moreover, both the use of caste criteria and the inclusion and exclusion of specific castes from the lists of backward castes have less to do with relative disadvantage than with the processes of competitive caste mobilization by political parties.

While the reservation system, like the affirmative action policies in the United States, favors elites within the disadvantaged groups, it at least provides new opportunities for persons from such groups and provides an example of the possibilities available to "less advanced members" of such groups.[50] On the other hand, the policy of reservations has had distinct limitations in practice. First, except in the case of political representation, the reserved quotas are often not filled. When serious efforts are made to fill them, as in Gujarat in the 1980s, upper caste antagonism becomes intense and may lead to a strong and violent counter-reaction. Second, as already mentioned, reservation of government jobs benefits primarily the better-

[46] Mitra, "The Perils of Promoting Equality," pp. 302–303; Spodek, From Gandhi to Violence, pp. 13–15.
[47] Wood, "Reservations in Doubt," p. 24; Spodek, From Gandhi to Violence, p. 1.
[48] Wood, "Reservations in Doubt," pp. 27–28.
[49] Wood, "Reservations in Doubt," pp. 7–8.
[50] Mitra, "The Perils of Promoting Equality," p. 304.

off segments, principally "the propertied class from the backward castes."[51] Finally, there remains an incongruity in policies which provide for reservations for categories of people who represent more than half the population of the country. Protective discrimination then becomes a discriminatory set of policies against upper caste minorities, not all of whose members are privileged, on behalf of a backward and lower caste majority, not all of whose members are underprivileged.[52]

Conclusions

It has been argued that the difficulties in implementing consistent and acceptable preferential policies for other backward castes/ classes in the several states have revealed the need for a "national political consensus" comparable to that achieved "on the treatment of the 'untouchables' during the decades immediately preceding Independence."[53] Why then has the central government not undertaken this task?

First, there are serious and quite genuine difficulties in deciding on a listing of the most disadvantaged castes in a society where 40 to 50 percent of the total population of the country lives below the official "poverty line." Second, the extension of policies of preferential treatment to the backward castes, using "objective" criteria, never offered clear political advantages to the Congress. Therefore, the adoption of preferential treatment for backward castes and the assignment of castes to categories entitling them to such treatment has arisen out of two processes: 1) demands from particular backward caste groups left out of the system of political distribution of patronage and 2) processes of competitive political mobilization by political parties in elections.

Two major factors preventing the adoption of a consistent, "objective" national policy towards the backward castes have been the resistance of the upper castes to further extensions of the reservations system in general and of the dominant middle castes to any system of reservations which would leave them out. The upper castes were hardly threatened by reservations for Scheduled Castes

---

[51] Shah, Strategies of Social Engineering, pp. 47–48.
[52] See also Wood, "Reservations in Doubt," p. 29.
[53] Mitra, "The Perils of Promoting Equality," p. 309.

since the quotas reserved for them could not be filled in any case and there was a massive overall increase in government employment opportunities after Independence. Reservations for other backward castes, however, are seen as more threatening because of the far larger numbers of such castes and the fact that some of them are relatively better off economically and are, therefore, in a stronger position to take advantage of any preferences that might be established. It is not clear, therefore, that over all, a national policy could be constructed that would gain more votes for the party or coalition that introduced them than it would lose.

Finally, the central leadership of the Congress believes it already has policies for the poorest in India, which are in their best interests. All the programs for the poor – whatever the defects in implementation – adopted by the central government since Mrs. Gandhi's *garibi hatao* election mainly benefit the Scheduled Castes, Scheduled Tribes, and the poorest from among the lower backward castes.

The course of the Gujarat anti-reservation riots of 1985 also raises questions of center–state relations and political control in India, which have arisen as well in the discussions above of language problems and the demands of minority groups in Punjab and the northeast. In Gujarat, as in nearly all other states in India since Mrs. Gandhi's rise to power, the chief minister was an appointee of the central government.

During the pre-Independence era and up to the death of Sardar Patel in 1950, the lines of political power and authority in Gujarat were clear. They were in the hands of Sardar Patel and his followers, who had the sanction of Gandhi and the support of the central government of which Sardar Patel himself was the most powerful minister after Nehru. After Sardar Patel's death, authority and political control in Gujarat passed into the hands of Morarji Desai who, like Patel, also was ultimately brought into the central government.

Although Solanki was not undermined by the center until the end and although it provided army contingents to aid the civil authorities, the central government did not act quickly enough or decisively enough to support the state government in containing and controlling the rioting. That such rioting even in the 1980s can be successfully contained and controlled was demonstrated the very next year, in 1986, when the Armarsinh Chaudhury government faced a vicious outbreak of Hindu–Muslim communal rioting. This time, however, the Union minister in charge of internal security "flew to Ahmedabad," coordinated his actions with the chief minister, called up immediately 54 companies of paramilitary forces, and gained control of the situation within 24 hours.[54] In 1985, however, the center did not act decisively for four months.

Solanki, like Mrs. Gandhi and Rajiv Gandhi himself, was a populist leader, without an effective political organization to sustain him despite his ability to win massive electoral majorities for the Congress in Gujarat. The huge majorities which such leaders win, therefore, reflect the absence of real power and authority in the system and of genuine local organization, the fragility of the coalitions which provide their support bases, and their vulnerability in the face of shifting coalitions and anomic violence.[55]

MIGRANTS *VERSUS* "SONS OF THE SOIL"[56]

A second variety of ethnic conflict which has, like urban inter-caste conflict, occurred in different parts of India and raised similar issues has been that concerning the relationships between migrants and the local populations.

Table 7.1 shows the percent of migrants in the total population of the larger states and union territories. These figures themselves, however, do not provide a guide to the places where migrant–non-migrant conflicts have been important. They have been unimportant, for example, in Delhi, which has the largest migrant population (45.35 percent) among the states and union territories in the country and quite important in Andhra and Bihar, which are among the states with the smallest proportion of migrants to the total population of the state. In the latter two cases, however, migrant–non-migrant conflicts have occurred primarily between residents of the same state.

There have been two characteristic types of situations involving migrants and "sons of the soil," which have led to political

[54] Spodek, From Gandhi to Violence, pp. 17–19.
[55] Spodek, From Gandhi to Violence, pp. 39–40.
[56] This section draws primarily and heavily from the works of Myron Weiner and Mary Katzenstein on the subject: specific references are given below.

Table 7.1. *Migrants by state of residence (1981)*

State	Number	Percent of state population
Tripura	499,631	24.34
Arunachal Pradesh	260,686	19.81
Sikkim	58,844	18.60
Haryana	1,625,609	12.58
Nagaland	81,506	10.52
Punjab	1,740,039	10.36
West Bengal	5,584,307	10.23
Meghalaya	123,755	9.26
Maharashtra	4,677,535	7.45
Mizoram	35,538	7.17
Himachal Pradesh	231,256	5.40
Madhya Pradesh	2,361,681	4.53
Karnataka	1,664,945	4.48
Rajasthan	1,471,517	4.29
Gujarat	1,299,040	3.81
Orissa	791,772	3.00
Tamil Nadu	1,207,846	2.50
Manipur	33,463	2.35
Jammu & Kashmir	123,085	2.06
Bihar	1,330,921	1.90
Uttar Pradesh	1,966,623	1.77
Andhra Pradesh	899,945	1.68
Kerala	360,437	1.42
India[a]	32,135,007	4.83

[a] Figure includes union territories as well, but excludes Assam where census operations could not be carried out in 1981. The percentage of migrant population in Assam, according to the 1971 census, was 10.18; B. Datta Ray, *The Pattern & Problems of Population in North-East India* (New Delhi: Uppal, 1986), p. 36.
Source: Compiled from *Census of India, 1981*, Series 1: *India*, Pt. V, A & B (i): *Migration Tables* by P. Padamanabha (Delhi: Controller of Publications, 1988), table D–1. The figures in all cases are for migrants from other states/ union territories in India and from abroad.

mobilization of ethnic categories and often to violence. The first has been the migration of populations into areas where either employment, land or other new resources are available, such as tea plantations or forests or mines. The type of migrant–non-migrant conflict which arises in this situation has been most common and bitter in the tribal areas of the northeast, discussed in the previous chapter, but it has affected non-tribal areas as well, such as the Assam plains and Telangana in Andhra, to be discussed below. The second has been migration into the major urban areas of the country, including both the industrial–commercial cities and the administrative capitals.

Commonly, the migrants are middle class professionals or business managers or entrepreneurs or contractors, who come to a new region, exploit its resources and often its local population, and ultimately meet local resistance as well. In other cases, poor laborers or cultivators leave an overpopulated, land-short region for another area where there are jobs or even land.

Several types of issues also may provide the catalyst for political mobilization and migrant-local conflicts. These include job and other resource competition, language conflicts – which are usually closely related to job competition – and conflicts for political control of the local territory.

Migration and the Indian constitutional order

Constitutional duality and ambiguity

Several of the legal and constitutional issues raised by migrant–non-migrant political conflict are similar to those already discussed in connection with the issue of preferential policies for backward castes, but the Constitution is even more ambiguous concerning the status of preferential policies for local residents than it is for backward castes. The Constitution guarantees free movement of the peoples of India from one state to another, the right of settlement of Indian citizens wherever they choose in the country, and the right to have their children instructed through the medium of their mother tongue in the primary schools even in states where the official language is different from their own. On the other hand, the Constitution also permits Parliament to enact laws providing preferences on the basis of local residence "within a State or Union territory."[57]

Many of the states, however, have acted on their own without reference to Parliament and "have issued directives or exhortations to employers to prefer local persons . . . at all levels of employment."[58] States and localities also have followed numerous other informal practices which are designed to ensure that local persons are given preference for admission into educational institutions and for employment in state and local government.[59] The cumulative effect of these state policies and practices and the fact that many of them appear to contradict constitutional principles and national policy guidelines has been to lead to the development of dual citizenship in India, in which the full rights of national citizenship are not automatically transferable from one part of the country to another.[60]

This departure from constitutional legality in India, which recognizes in principle only one citizenship for all Indians no matter where they are born, reflects deeper feelings of dual nationalism among large segments of the country's population. Many Assamese, Bengalis, Sikhs, and Tamils identify both as members of a linguistic or religious or cultural "nationality" and as members of an Indian "nation" as well. However, feelings of regional nationalism, of identification of a language or cultural group with a part of the territory of India to the extent of insisting that the territory in question "belongs" properly to that group, may justify in local eyes the treatment of migrants from other parts of the country as "foreigners" and the consequent imposition of restrictions upon the exercise of their full constitutional rights as citizens of India.

Three types of nativist movements have been analyzed by Weiner and Katzenstein.[61] Nativism in Assam has occurred among a numerically dominant ethnic group within a linguistic state confronting linguistically distinct minorities who are perceived as competitors for middle class jobs and for local political control. The

---

[57] Weiner and Katzenstein, *India's Preferential Policies*, pp. 22–23.
[58] Weiner and Katzenstein, *India's Preferential Policies*, p. 26.
[59] Weiner and Katzenstein, *India's Preferential Policies*, p. 41.
[60] Myron Weiner, *Sons of the Soil: Migration and Ethnic Conflict in India* (Princeton, NJ: Princeton University Press, 1978), pp. 344–348.
[61] See fns. 28 and 60.

nativist movement among Marathi-speakers in Bombay is similar to that aspect of the conflict in Assam which has centered around job competition except that it occurs in an urban setting. The third is the situation of a regional minority within a larger state, which is illustrated by the Telangana movement in Andhra. The special problems arising out of migration of plains peoples into tribal areas have already been discussed in the preceding chapter.

Assam

History of migration

Since the beginning of the present century, some "six and a half million migrants and their descendants have settled in Assam."[62] These new migrants in their different ways monopolized or dominated virtually all new opportunities for resource exploitation or for jobs in the modern sectors of the economy and in government service. Laborers from central India took the jobs in the new tea plantations, Bengali Hindus took most of the middle class jobs in the private sector and in government service and even became the dominant population in the cities and towns of the province, Bengali Muslims occupied previously uncultivated virgin lands, and Marwaris dominated business, commerce, and banking.[63]

The migrations have been so large as to threaten to transform the indigenous Assamese Hindu population into a minority.[64] However, it is not a simple matter now to separate for purposes of estimation the indigenous from the migrant populations.[65] If one looks at language figures alone, which give a highly simplified but nevertheless important view of a major aspect of ethnic diversity in Assam, Assamese speakers constitute a majority in the countryside, but a minority of 39 percent in the total urban population, where

[62] Weiner, *Sons of the Soil*, pp. 80–81.
[63] Weiner, *Sons of the Soil*, pp. 96, 103–104; B. P. Singh, "North-East India: Demography, Culture and Identity Crisis," *Modern Asian Studies*, XII, No. 2 (1987), 265.
[64] Sanjib Baruah, "Immigration, Ethnic Conflict, and Political Turmoil – Assam, 1979–1985," *Asian Survey*, XXVI, No. 11 (November, 1986), 1,188.
[65] Baruah, "Immigration, Ethnic Conflict, and Political Turmoil," pp. 1,189–1,190; Atul Goswami and Jayanta K. Gogoi, "Migration and Demographic Transformation of Assam: 1901–1971," in B. L. Abbi (ed.), *Northeast Region: Problems and Prospects of Development* (Chandigarh: Centre for Research in Rural and Industrial Development, 1984), p. 61.

they are outnumbered by Bengali-speakers (40 percent) and where Hindi-speakers constitute another 16 percent of the total.[66]

Assamese- and Bengali-speakers in Assam

Although the Assamese-speaking Hindus constitute the dominant indigenous plains population and the "rural hinterland" in Deutsch's famous model of nationality conflict,[67] their majority status in the country has been made doubtful and their majority position even in several rural districts has been modified by the vast migrations of East Bengali Muslim peasants. Although the language of these migrants originally – and of the majority even today – is Bengali, most have chosen for reasons of political expediency to declare Assamese as their mother tongue. In fact, it is only through the inclusion of these Muslim Bengalis into the category of "Assamese-speakers" that the latter category, which constituted only 36 percent of the population in the present boundaries of Assam in the 1931 census, today comprises 63 percent of the population.[68]

Job competition

Under the British, Assam was initially integrated into the Bengal presidency and the Assamese nobility were displaced by Bengalis in the new administrative services.[69] The use of Bengali as the principal medium of instruction in the schools further enhanced the advantage of Bengali-speakers in obtaining employment in the state, with the result that Bengalis came to dominate up through the post-Independence period to the present in high-paying public and private sector jobs and "in middle-class occupations" generally.[70] After Independence, however, the state government gave preference to Assamese in public employment[71] and also asked private sector

[66] Census of India, 1971, Assam, Series 3, Pt. 1-A: General Population by K. S. Dey (Delhi: Controller of Publications, 1979) and Pt. 11-C (ii), Social and Cultural Tables (Delhi: Controller of Publications, 1981).
[67] Karl W. Deutsch, Nationalism and Social Communication (Cambridge, MA: MIT Press, 1953).
[68] Baruah, "Immigration, Ethnic Conflict, and Political Turmoil," p. 1,189 and Census of India, 1971, Assam.
[69] Weiner, Sons of the Soil, pp. 91–92.   [70] Weiner, Sons of the Soil, pp. 94–95.
[71] Weiner, Sons of the Soil, p. 111.

companies to give preferences to " 'local' people for jobs paying a salary of up to Rs. 500."[72]

The language issue

It was in this context that the language issue emerged as the focus of conflict between Assamese and Bengali Hindus in the post-Independence period, with the former pushing for Assamese as the sole official language of state administration and as the medium of education in the schools and the Bengalis demanding a dual language policy. The passage of an act making Assamese the sole official language of the state led to riots in 1960.[73]

Political protest: Assamese Hindus and Bengali Muslims

The second great controversy between migrants and non-migrants in Assam in the post-Independence period took the form of a directly political conflict between the indigenous Assamese Hindus and tribal populations, on the one side, and the mostly rural Bengali Muslims, on the other side. The years between 1979 and 1985 were marked by "governmental instability, sustained civil disobedience campaigns, and some of the worst ethnic violence in the history of post-independence India, including the killing of 3,000 people during the February 1983 elections."[74]

The demographic background to this latest phase of migrant–non-migrant conflict in Assam developed during the Pakistan civil war from March, 1971 onward, when there was a considerable "influx" of both Hindu and Muslim Bengalis into the state. The issue first arose in 1979 in a by-election in a constituency containing a large number of East Bengali immigrants, which "drew public attention to a rapid expansion of the number of voters since the previous elections two [years] earlier."[75] At this point, Assamese Hindus, who had seen themselves before primarily in competition with Bengali Hindus for middle class jobs, now also articulated the broader fear of being overwhelmed "numerically, politically, and

---

[72] Weiner, *Sons of the Soil*, pp. 126–127 and Weiner and Katzenstein, *India's Preferential Policies*, pp. 106–107.
[73] Weiner, *Sons of the Soil*, p. 117.
[74] Baruah, "Immigration, Ethnic Conflict, and Political Turmoil," p. 1,184.
[75] Baruah, "Immigration, Ethnic Conflict, and Political Turmoil." pp. 1,191–1,192.

culturally" by a "massive migration influx."[76] In the absence of agreement between the leaders of the protest movement and the government, governmental stability in the state was weakened and routine electoral politics could not be carried on. Elections for parliament were held in only 2 of the 14 constituencies in the state in 1980.[77] The state assembly elections were held in 1983, providing an occasion for mass murder.[78]

Political alignments

The policies of the state government towards migrants in Assam have depended upon which ethnic groups and political coalitions have been in power and have shifted as political coalitions and their underlying ethnic bases have shifted. With the extension of representative institutions to Assam, which in turn was associated with the increasing polarization of conflict in eastern India between Hindus and Muslims, Bengali Muslims gained control over the state government in the 1930s and 1940s.

After Independence and Partition, which involved the transfer of the Muslim majority district of Sylhet to Pakistan, Assamese Hindus came to power in Assam for the first time. In contrast to the situation in Punjab after Partition, millions of Muslims remained in eastern India, including Assam, where many had no legal status.

In order to protect themselves from expulsion, therefore, Bengali Muslims allied with the Assamese within the dominant Congress.[79] They "declared their mother tongue was Assamese, accepted the establishment of primary and secondary schools in Assamese for their children, supported the government against the Bengali Hindus on the issue of an official language for the state and the university, and cast their votes for the Congress party."[80] Thus, whereas before Independence the predominant political cleavage was between Bengali Muslims and Assamese, after Partition the

---

[76] Weiner and Katzenstein, *India's Preferential Policies*, p. 90.

[77] The cancellation of the parliamentary elections in Assam is discussed in relation to the political crisis in the state at the time in Myron Weiner, *India at the Polls, 1980: A Study of the Parliamentary Elections* (Washington: American Enterprise Institute, 1980), pp. 94–100.

[78] Baruah, "Immigration, Ethnic Conflict, and Political Turmoil," pp. 1,192–1,193.

[79] Weiner, *Sons of the Soil*, p. 124.

[80] Weiner and Katzenstein, *India's Preferential Policies*, pp. 102 and 115–116.

Assamese allied with Muslims politically in the Congress against the Bengali Hindus.[81]

The factors which led to the break up of this alliance were political and were connected as much with national as with local political realignments. The split in the Congress after the Emergency and the 1977 elections had a profound impact in Assam where the party divided "into pro- and anti-Indira Gandhi factions" and where the two Congress parties combined could win only 34 seats out of 126 in the legislative assembly elections of March, 1978.

The split in the Congress also "ended the post Independence coalition of Assamese Hindus and Bengali Muslims."[82] Assamese Hindus, determined to retain their political dominance in the state, became much more aware of their previous dependence upon Bengali Muslims, who were now perceived also as a threat in a situation of shifting political coalitions. In this context, therefore, of the break-up of old political and ethnic coalitions and the absence of stable government in Assam, the Assamese movement was launched demanding the expulsion of illegal migrants,[83] most of whom were Bengali Muslims.

When the Congress returned to power in the state in 1980, it formed a government headed by an Assamese Muslim, which lasted only six months. President's Rule was imposed after which another Congress government was formed in January, 1982, this time headed by an Assamese of the Ahom caste. This government in turn lasted only two months, after which the 1983 legislative assembly elections were called in the face of the continuing Assam movement, the failure of negotiations between the movement leaders and the central government, and the call by movement leaders for a boycott of the elections. The Congress won this election and installed the same Ahom chief minister thereafter.[84]

The next phase in the political and ethnic realignment of Assam politics occurred with the accession to power of Rajiv Gandhi as Prime Minister and the signing of an accord between the central government and the Assam movement leaders. The 1985 elections brought the Asom Gana Parishad (AGP) to power, a party based on

---

[81] Weiner, *Sons of the Soil*, p. 110.
[82] Weiner and Katzenstein, *India's Preferential Policies*, pp. 116–117.
[83] Weiner and Katzenstein, *India's Preferential Policies*, p. 119.
[84] Baruah, "Immigration, Ethnic Conflict, and Political Turmoil," p. 1,200.

the Assamese movement, dominated by Assamese Hindus in coalition with plains tribals, tea plantation workers, and Assamese Muslims.[85]

Center–state relations and the role of the central government

Although the problem arising out of large-scale migration of Bengali Muslims to Assam has a long history and was a major political issue before Independence and Partition, it was kept out of political controversy between 1947 and 1979 for two reasons primarily. First, the language issue and the competition for jobs between Assamese and Bengali Hindus were the dominant ethnic issues in this period. Second, there was a local alliance between Assamese Hindus and Bengali Muslims, which also served New Delhi's interests, for it provided political stability at the governmental level in a border state which was undergoing repeated inter-ethnic conflicts and secessionist movements. The local absorption of Muslims into the Congress organization also fitted well with national Congress strategy of maintaining a strong popular base among India's minorities, especially the Muslims. The rise of the Assam movement in 1979, therefore, and the demand of its leaders for the expulsion of "all immigrants from foreign countries"[86] who had not been granted citizenship status raised difficult questions for the central Congress leadership.[87]

Despite the considerable difficulties involved in arriving at a reasonable solution acceptable to all parties, progress was made between 1980 and 1982 in negotiations between the central government and the Assamese movement leaders on a number of points. Most important, agreement was reached on the granting of citizenship status to immigrants who had come between 1951 and 1961, on the one hand, and the denial of citizenship and the expulsion of those who came after 1971.[88] Under the terms of the Assam Accord of 1985, illegal immigrants who entered the country between 1961 and 1971 will be disfranchised for ten years.[89]

[85] Baruah, "Immigration, Ethnic Conflict, and Political Turmoil," pp. 1,204–1,205 and Singh, "North-East India," p. 281.
[86] Baruah, "Immigration, Ethnic Conflict, and Political Turmoil," p. 1,189.
[87] Baruah, "Immigration, Ethnic Conflict, and Political Turmoil," p. 1,192 fn.
[88] Baruah, "Immigration, Ethnic Conflict, and Political Turmoil," p. 1,192.
[89] Baruah, "Immigration, Ethnic Conflict, and Political Turmoil," p. 1,204.

During the Nehru period, strong state governments formed long-lasting political coalitions which endured with the backing of the central government. During the first period of Mrs. Gandhi's dominance, from 1965 to 1977, the old pattern of center–state relations was retained except that the chief ministers of Assam, as elsewhere in India, were appointed by the central Congress leaders in New Delhi. After 1977, however, when Congress power in Assam was shattered and especially after 1980 when Mrs. Gandhi returned to power in New Delhi and sought to consolidate her power in the country once again, the compulsions involved in maintaining power in Delhi prevented the success of negotiations to restore the peace of Assam. Denial of citizenship to immigrants and their expulsion to the extent demanded by the Assamese movement leaders would have deprived the Congress of a large segment of its electoral support and threatened the party's loss of power in the state. In the post-Nehru era of center–state relations, such losses were considered too risky to accept, for the loss of any state was seen as a danger to Congress dominance of the Center. Without a solution to Assam's ethnic problems and without a credible leadership, the Congress chose to attempt to regain control of the state in 1983 by holding the elections in an atmosphere in which the political process had lost legitimacy to the majority of the dominant Assamese ethnic group and its tribal allies.

The strategy pursued by Rajiv Gandhi has been the adoption of the policy of non-enforceable accords. It involves giving the opposition its head, handing over the administration of a state with apparently irresolvable problems to the non-Congress movement leaders and allowing them to govern and to resolve their problems without central government interference and even with central government support. Such a strategy, while less opportunistic than that pursued by Mrs. Gandhi, has built-in difficulties which make long-term success unlikely.

The central government cannot enforce the expulsion of Bengali Muslim migrants from Assam, which would cause serious international problems with Bangladesh and, even more important, would cause serious problems with the Muslim minority in the rest of the country who would be placed in the position of observing a necessarily prolonged process of enforced deportation of Muslims from India.[90] On the other hand, the Congress, with its increased sensitivity in the 1980s to militant Hindu opinion in north India, must also be concerned not only about the loss of support from Hindus in Assam but from Hindus in the whole of north India, where the BJP is conjuring up the threat of the country being inundated with a "massive influx of Muslim infiltrators from Bangladesh, particularly in the northeastern states and in West Bengal and Bihar as well, and from Pakistan in the western states."[91]

While there are no easy solutions to problems such as those which exist in Punjab and Assam, it is evident that the only strategy which has succeeded in the past has been one based on strong leadership in New Delhi supporting strong leadership in the states in pursuit of a consistent policy for dealing with inter-ethnic conflicts and minority problems. Under Mrs. Gandhi and Rajiv, in contrast, the center has become directly involved in confrontations with local movements, has lacked a credible intermediary state leadership, and has failed to pursue consistent policies.

Andhra Pradesh

History of migration and the establishment of a policy of preferences for natives (mulkis)

The origins of the migrant–non-migrant conflict in Andhra Pradesh lie in the history of the former princely state of Hyderabad in the Telangana region of the present state. Local protest against the influx of foreigners and against the resultant alleged control of the state "by a clique of north Indians"[92] led as early as 1868 to adoption of measures to give preference to natives (known as *mulkis*) and to limit stringently the hiring of persons from outside the region in the Hyderabad state service.[93] The imminent merger of Telangana, the central region of the old Hyderabad province, into the new linguistic, Telugu-speaking state of Andhra Pradesh in 1956, however,

[90] The alleged harassment of Muslims, their improper removal from the electoral roll, forcible removal of Muslims and other minorities from their lands in Assam, and the politics of the AGP movement in that state in general are followed in the Muslim press in north India. For example, see *Muslim India*, Nos. 52, 53, & 58 (April, May, and October, 1987).

[91] *Muslim India*, No. 51 (March, 1987), 114–119; citation from p. 114.

[92] Weiner and Katzenstein, *India's Preferential Policies*, p. 61.

[93] Weiner and Katzenstein, *India's Preferential Policies*, p. 66.

brought the *mulki–non-mulki* issue once again to the fore for it clearly would involve the transfer of government officials from Andhra to the new state capital of Hyderabad. In order to allay the fears of the *mulkis* of Hyderabad and to smooth the integration of the two regions, the Gentlemen's Agreement of 1956 provided for the retention of the *mulki* rules, the assurance of a fixed number of places in the state ministry to politicians from Telangana, and preferences for students from Telangana for admission into educational institutions in the region, including the prestigious Osmania University, among other protections.[94]

Job competition and other grievances of people of Telangana

Job competition in Hyderabad became particularly "acute after 1965–66, when the suspension of the third five-year plan" and the consequent reduction in public investment "brought the tempo of development to a standstill" and reduced employment opportunities. At the same time, there had been considerable educational expansion in Hyderabad with the result that there were many more graduates of the secondary schools and colleges "than the number of jobs that became available."[95] The number of state government jobs available dropped from 15,700 in 1966 to 10,200 in 1967 to 8,800 in 1968. Thus, "when the student movement commenced in early 1969, it was at a time when the number of new jobs available had reached a low point, and a time when the number of secondary school and college graduates was increasing."[96]

It was also felt that the state government and administration were "dominated by people from the Andhra region."[97] It was claimed that, as a consequence, "more money and attention was given by the state government to the Andhra region than to the backward Telangana region."[98] It was more convenient to blame the "growing unemployment" in Hyderabad and Telangana on "the neglect of their region by the government, and . . . the domination of political elites from coastal Andhra"[99] than on the general contraction in development expenditures for the state as a whole.

[94] Weiner, *Sons of the Soil*, pp.222–224.   [95] Weiner, *Sons of the Soil*, p. 229.
[96] Weiner, *Sons of the Soil*, pp. 245–246.
[97] Weiner and Katzenstein, *India's Preferential Policies*, p. 81; also Weiner, *Sons of the Soil*, p. 228.
[98] Weiner, *Sons of the Soil*, p. 228.   [99] Weiner, *Sons of the Soil*, pp. 245–246.

Political protest: the Telangana movement

The precipitating factor initiating the Telangana movement was a 1969 court decision invalidating a decision by the state government to accommodate the demands of "the Telangana nongazetted officers union" by extending "the domicile rule to cover appointments to the state electricity board in the Telangana area."[100] The movement was begun by students, but "nongazetted officers soon joined." The movement soon "became transformed into a violent mass struggle for a separate Telangana state."[101] An accord was reached between the state government and the movement leaders on January 19 under which the government agreed to appeal the January 3 court judgment. Two further court rulings, however, in February and March invalidated the application of state residency requirements to a region within a state, namely, Telangana, which led to intensification of the agitation.[102]

In the midst of these and other contradictory court decisions, the Telangana movement acquired sufficient momentum to form a political party, the Telangana Praja Samiti (TPS), which contested the 1971 Lok Sabha elections "on the sole plank of a separate Telangana state"[103] in which "jobs for domiciles" would be reserved.[104] The new party won 10 of 14 Lok Sabha seats and 48 percent of the vote, against 37 percent for the Congress of Mrs. Gandhi, which otherwise won a landslide victory in most of the rest of the country. An agreement was reached on continuation of the *mulki* rules, and the TPS itself merged with the Congress in September, 1971.[105]

Class, region, and ethnicity in the Telangana movement

The success of the Telangana movement reveals much about the conditions for rapid and effective political mobilization in contemporary Indian politics. It shows especially the relatively greater ease with which large masses of people can be mobilized around

[100] Weiner and Katzenstein, *India's Preferential Policies*, pp. 82–83.

[101] Weiner and Katzenstein, *India's Preferential Policies*, p. 82; also Weiner, *Sons of the Soil*, pp. 217–218.

[102] Weinzer and Katzenstein, *India's Preferential Policies*, pp. 82–83; Weiner, *Sons of the Soil*, p. 248.

[103] Weiner and Katzenstein, *India's Preferential Policies*, p. 84.

[104] Weiner, *Sons of the Soil*, pp. 217–218.

[105] Weiner and Katzenstein, *India's Preferential Policies*, p. 84.

appeals to a separate cultural/regional identity than around appeals to class. The movement originated within a privileged class in India, among those already employed by government and those who had acquired or were about to acquire the educational "ticket" to such employment.

The leaders broadened their movement by arguing that not only the middle classes, but the people of Telangana generally were being treated badly by a government dominated by "Andhras." To give added force to the regional argument, they went to the extent of attempting to fabricate out of rather limited elements of cultural distinctiveness a positive regional identity separate from that of the people of the rest of Andhra.[106] However, the movement was dominated by Telugu-speaking Hindus who were rather closer culturally to their Telugu-speaking Hindu brethren in Andhra than to the Urdu-speaking Muslim cultural minority of Hyderabad.

Center–state relations and the role of central government

The formation of the Andhra province was the first post-Independence concession made by Nehru and the central government to the burgeoning demands for the reorganization of states. In this process, as noted earlier, the central government always sought to keep one step removed from regional conflicts and to enter only in the last stages as an impartial mediator.

The Government of India's involvement in the issue of the *mulki* rules was consistent with this general strategy. Its initial role in this matter was to act as the arbiter of an agreement called the Gentlemen's Agreement, worked out between the politicians in Telangana and Andhra. This stance was consistent with national policy to go slowly on demands for reorganization and to seek compromises within existing provincial boundaries on the basis of mutual agreement of opposed regional forces wherever possible.

There were similarities and differences as well between the handling of the Telangana movement between 1969 and 1973 and the policies pursued by the central government in Andhra politics in Nehru's day. The similarities consist in the positive, arbitrating role played by the central government in relation to the demands for preservation of the *mulki* rules in the face of a mass of contradictory

[106] Weiner, *Sons of the Soil*, pp. 236–240.

court rulings. The arbitrating role of the central government culminated in the September, 1973, Six-Point Formula to resolve the dispute which "outlined a strategy for development, a method of recruitment, and a policy for admission to educational institutions in different regions of the state."[107]

As in the earlier period also, the central government agreed to pass a constitutional amendment, the 32nd, to implement the formula. Although the old *mulki*–non-*mulki* rules and distinctions were done away with, the central government in effect made possible the extension of local preferences within the state of Andhra to all localities (districts or regions within the state) however the state government chose to define them.[108]

Weiner and Katzenstein argue that the aim of the central government in playing a mediating role in the Telangana–Andhra dispute was "to find a formula that would keep the [Andhra] state intact, for it feared that the bifurcation of Andhra would stimulate demands for the break-up of other states."[109]

Mrs. Gandhi's primary political interest during the entire period of the Telangana and Andhra movements from 1969 to 1973 was to displace the previously dominant Andhra leadership associated with her Syndicate rivals in the succession struggle and to replace them with leaders of her choice and to establish her direct control over Andhra politics. In order to achieve this goal, the central leadership adopted a dual strategy of undermining the dominant Andhra leadership by supporting the Telangana movement demands for employment and other preferences, though not the demand for a separate state, on the one hand, and on the other by supporting an alternative coalition of backward and lower caste groups led by hand-picked men of her choice in the Andhra region.

There are three primary reasons why the intervention of the central government in Andhra was more successful here than elsewhere in the long as well as the short run. The first is that the Telangana movement lacked a solid ethnic/cultural basis for a self-sustaining regional movement. Second, it succeeded in achieving its aims of maintaining the privileges of the educated classes of

---

[107] Weiner and Katzenstein, *India's Preferential Policies*, p. 86.
[108] Weiner, *Sons of the Soil*, pp. 253–255.
[109] Weiner and Katzenstein, *India's Preferential Policies*, p. 89.

the region, whose goals did not extend beyond securing their privileges. Third, the arbitration formula advanced by the central government did in fact provide a solution acceptable to all sides in the conflict. The resolution of the Telangana–Andhra controversy, therefore, must be recognized as one of the few long-term successes of the new political strategy of the central government under Mrs. Gandhi and of the new pattern of center–state relations, in which the arbitrating policies of the Nehru period were combined with the divide, rebuild, and rule politics of the Indira Gandhi period.

Bombay

Marathi-speakers constitute the largest language group in Bombay, with a plurality of 43 percent of the city's population, followed by Gujarati-speakers with 19 percent. The third principal language of Bombay is Hindi, the language especially of the mill workers and other manual and unskilled laborers who have mostly migrated from north India. Speakers of the several south Indian languages constitute another 8 percent of the population.

Although Marathi-speakers constitute by far the largest ethnic/ linguistic group in the population of Bombay, many of the educated middle class have perceived themselves to be at a disadvantage in the competition for jobs "in the modern sector of Bombay's economy," where south Indians in particular are seen to have a disproportionate share of the most desired "office jobs."[110]

The political formation which has articulated the demands of the Marathi-speaking middle classes has been an organization called the Shiv Sena (Army of Shivaji), formed in 1966 under the leadership of Bal Thackeray, a Bombay journalist. The Shiv Sena early established itself as a major force in the city's politics by contesting municipal elections in 1967 and winning 42 out of 140 seats, nearly all of them in constituencies where the Maharashtrian population was above 50 percent.[111] Its principal political objectives became the "extension of preferences in all job categories, in both the public and the private sectors, to those who are Maharashtrian by the definition of mother tongue."[112] The Maharashtra state government responded posi-

[110] Weiner and Katzenstein, *India's Preferential Policies*, pp. 44–45.
[111] Weiner and Katzenstein, *India's Preferential Policies*, p. 43 and Jaya Kamalakar, "Ethnic Politics in Municipal Corporations," *EPW*, XXIII, No. 19 (May 7, 1988), 945.
[112] Weiner and Katzenstein, *India's Preferential Policies*, pp. 45–46.

tively to the demands of the Shiv Sena by issuing circulars and directives in 1968 and 1973 establishing systems of preferences and quotas for the employment of "native Marathi speakers" for both lower-level and managerial positions.[113] In the 1985 municipal elections in Bombay, the Shiv Sena won the largest number of seats, 76 out of 170, compared to only 37 for the Congress (I).[114]

The Shiv Sena has combined its economic orientation on jobs for Maharashtrians with an explicitly Hindu revivalist and militant Hindu nationalist ideology as well. In a press conference which he called in March, 1988, Bal Thackeray issued "a one-month ultimatum" to the Sikh leaders of Bombay demanding that "they should send a delegation to Amritsar instructing the high priests to issue a hukum-nama [written order] against the extremists," failing which he would institute an economic boycott of their numerous business enterprises in the city.[115] He accused the Sikh community of Bombay of having provided funds for terrorists and of supporting the Khalistan demand.

In recent years, the Shiv Sena has sought to establish itself as a broad regional party of Hindu Maharashtrians and has extended its attacks on both the Sikh and Muslim minorities in the state.[116] However, in previous general elections, it has not been able to break out of its narrow urban support base in ethnically homogeneous Maharashtrian constituencies.[117]

The three nativist movements discussed above, despite differences in their regional, linguistic, and urban/rural contexts, share with each other and with the caste movements discussed in the earlier part of this chapter origins in the discontents arising from frustrated aspirations or perceived limited life chances among groups whose members seek desirable positions in the modern, middle class sectors of the economy. Adult franchise and competitive party politics, in a political context in which advocates on behalf of ethnic categories are permitted to struggle for the prize of official state recognition, make possible the effective political mobilization of such groups around caste and regional solidarities and nativist ideologies.

[113] Weiner and Katzenstein, *India's Preferential Policies*, pp. 46–47.
[114] Kamalakar, "Ethnic Politics," p. 945.
[115] *India Today*, April 15, 1988, p. 31.
[116] See *Muslim India*, Nos. 49 & 56 (January and August, 1987).
[117] Kamalakar, "Ethnic Politics," p. 946.

The articulation in such movements of a wider nativist ideology by spokesmen for "sons of the soil" may arise either as a means of political mobilization to achieve economic demands or after their achievement as a means of building upon their successes to gain political power. Such an ideology may be necessary to provide a mass base sufficient to threaten the power of the authorities or even to gain control of a state government. Thus, the *mulki* movement in Andhra sought to develop a wider Telangana regional identity around the movement for a separate state in order to achieve its demands. In Assam, the student movement leaders actually succeeded in gaining control of the state government through the formation of a political party, the Asom Gana Parishad. The Shiv Sena case, however, is one in which the articulation of a wider nativist ideology has persisted beyond the achievement of its economic goals to be used as a basis for building on its achievements in order to remain a major political force or to capture local power.

CONCLUSIONS

Many alternative explanations have been offered for the resurgence of regional and communal and the rise of caste and other varieties of ethnic conflicts in the past 15 years, including the persistence of immutable primordial cleavages in Indian society, their underlying basis in economic or class differences, and specific policies and political tactics pursued by the central and state governments. It has been argued throughout part II that the cultural cleavages in Indian society are far from immutable. On the contrary, group definitions and boundaries, their political mobilization, and the content of their demands all have been influenced by state policies and by processes of competition between political parties. It has also been argued that, although specific forms of economic competition have provided the social bases for political mobilization of various ethnic categories in Indian politics, they cannot be considered to reflect some underlying and more "objective" class differences. Rather, such conflicts have been most intense among persons and groups from within the same or aspiring to the same class position in Indian society who perceive themselves at a disadvantage in relation to others from a different ethnic or cultural category.

240

In explaining the intensification and the increased variety of ethnic conflicts in India in the 1970s, emphasis has been placed on the role of state recognition of particular categories and on the competitive mobilization of regional and ethnic minorities in both state political conflicts and, in the post-Nehru era, in center–state political divisions. The close connection in the 1970s and 1980s between problems in center–state relations and the conflicts among various ethnic groups in several states have highlighted a major structural problem in the Indian political system. That problem arises from the tensions created by the centralizing drives of the Indian state in a society where the predominant long-term social, economic, and political tendencies are towards pluralism, regionalism, and decentralization. Although the same tensions existed in the Nehru years, central government policies then favored pluralist solutions, non-intervention in state politics except in a conciliatory role or as a last resort, and preservation of a separation between central and state politics, allowing considerable autonomy for the latter. From the early 1970s, however, during Mrs. Gandhi's political dominance, the central leaders have intervened incessantly in state politics to preserve their dominance at the Center, the boundaries between central and state politics have disappeared in the critical north Indian states especially and have been challenged elsewhere as well, and pluralist policies, though not discarded, were often subordinated to short-range calculations of mutual benefit.

PART III

POLITICAL ECONOMY

INTRODUCTION

Some observers of Indian politics, economic development, and social change since Independence argue that it is not state policies, the complexities of building political power in India, or the centralizing drives of Mrs. Gandhi which are principally responsible for the political disintegration and economic failures of the past 15 years. These are all rather reflections of deeper economic forces and of the dominance of particular social classes over Indian society and economy. According to one view, the countryside has come under the increasing political and economic dominance of the landed castes. The commercialization of Indian agriculture in the post-Green Revolution period has let loose forces which have undermined traditional social relations in the countryside and have promoted class polarization and class conflict. The latter are in turn largely responsible for increased political instability and violence in the countryside.[1]

Another view is that there are structural forces in Indian society, entrenched social classes, whose actions constrain the political elites from implementing policies against the former's interests. State policies increasingly have come to reflect the interests of the dominant classes – the rich farmers who benefit from government price support and input subsidy programs, industrial capitalists who have profited from the import substitution policies and have learned to turn to their advantage the industrial licensing system, and the professional bureaucrats who have gained considerable corrupt income from their administration of programs for the benefit of the farmers and their control

[1] See esp. Francine R. Frankel, *India's Political Economy, 1947–1977: The Gradual Revolution* (Princeton, NJ: Princeton University Press, 1978) and, for two critiques of it, Atul Kohli, "Democracy, Economic Growth, and Inequality in India's Development," *World Politics*, XXXII, No. 4 (July, 1980), 623–638, and Paul R. Brass, "Class, Ethnic Group, and Party in Indian Politics," *World Politics*, XXXIII, No. 3 (April, 1981), 454–457.

over the investment decisions of the industrialists and the business classes.[2]

These structural class and economic explanations agree that "accommodative politics"[3] have failed and cannot succeed in the face of growing class antagonisms in the countryside and the increasing dominance of India's "proprietary classes." Their prognosis, in the event of the continuation of the present regime and its policies, is for the intensification of violent class conflict in the countryside. To avert it, they propose the displacement of the dominant rural classes through more thoroughgoing agrarian reform, the strengthening of the Indian state and of its autonomy from the now dominant social classes, and a return to a more rigorous implementation of policies of state-directed, centralized economic planning and heavy public investment in an economy dominated by the public sector.

The arguments to be developed in part III are rather different. The existence of dominant castes at the local level is recognized and their constraining effects on many types of policies are acknowledged. At the same time, the view taken here is that the policies of heavy industrialization through centralized economic planning have been ill-adapted to India's economic resources, to the basic needs of its peoples, to its social order, and to the political values of its educated classes. Moreover, many of the policies adopted for the agricultural sector have been self-contradictory or have not been implemented. Land reforms were introduced after Independence to promote a system of peasant proprietorship in which inequalities in land ownership would be reduced, all cultivators would own their lands, and their holdings would be economically viable. These reforms, however, were only partly implemented while more radical reforms such as cooperative farming were proposed.

Poverty, hunger, and malnutrition have persisted in the rural areas less because of the oppressions and exactions of the landed castes in the countryside than because government policies have not encouraged the development of alternative forms of employment. Meanwhile, as is to be expected, the locally dominant classes and

2 See Pranab Bardhan, *The Political Economy of Development in India* (Oxford: Basil Blackwell, 1984) and the critique by Myron Weiner, "The Political Economy of Industrial Growth in India," *World Politics*, xxxviii, No. 4 (July, 1986), 596–610.
3 Frankel, *India's Political Economy*, p. 27.

bureaucrats take advantage of the ameliorative anti-poverty programs which have been introduced in the 1970s and 1980s and extract benefits and profits for themselves from them.

In the face of the distortions in resource allocations for economic development in India since Independence and the contradictory policies often pursued, one of the more impressive, though still limited, economic achievements has been the adoption in parts of the country and for some crops, notably wheat, of the package of practices which have promoted the increase in agricultural production that goes by the name of the Green Revolution. The successes of the Green Revolution were in turn criticized for promoting commercialization of agriculture, the creation of a *kulak*[4] class, and the inevitable development of class polarization and class conflict in the countryside. The argument in chapter 9, however, is that the focus on the so-called new *kulak* class distorts the realities of the Indian countryside, in which the vast majority of peasants are small and medium cultivators in need of policies and subsidies that would help to make them viable farmers. Moreover, despite the persistence in contemporary India of local protests by the poor and landless in scattered areas of the Indian subcontinent, there is no evidence of either a general class polarization or an impending class war in the countryside.

---

[4] The term *kulak* in the Leninist literature refers to rich peasants and farmers who employ and exploit farm labor to whom they are also generally antagonistic.

CHAPTER 8

POLITICS, ECONOMIC DEVELOPMENT, AND SOCIAL CHANGE

POLITICS AND POLICIES: MAJOR ISSUES OF ECONOMIC DEVELOPMENT AND SOCIAL CHANGE

Two discontinuities have marked the debates on politics and policies concerning major issues of economic development and social change in India since Independence and have marred the effective implementation of most of the policies adopted. One is a discontinuity of discourse between adherents of foreign models for economic development and social change, many of them Marxists, and proponents of alternative strategies that are usually called "Gandhian" and derive inspiration and seek legitimacy from Gandhi's writings and speeches. Though the models for economic development were foreign, the motives of the Indian leadership in adopting them were authentically nationalist, arising out of the belief that rapid heavy industrialization was required to ensure India's independence in every sense and to achieve great power status.[1]

The second discontinuity is between levels in the Indian polity, between the goals set at the Planning Commission and in the inner circles of policy making in the central government in Delhi, on the one hand, and the realities of regional and local structures of power and decision making in the provincial capitals and in the districts, on the other hand, which prevent effective implementation of policies formulated at higher levels and, in recent years, even penetrate upwards to influence decision making in Delhi itself. The con-

[1] Nayar describes the adherence to the heavy industrialization strategy that came to dominate Indian economic development policy as arising out of a "modernization imperative" which dictated the strategy to be adopted if the above goals were to be achieved. Baldev Raj Nayar, *The Modernisation Imperative and Indian Planning* (Delhi: Vikas, 1972). In a similar vein, John Toye characterizes the nationalism and the economic development strategy associated with it as "mimetic," though no less authentic for that; *Public Expenditure and Indian Development Policy, 1960–1970* (Cambridge: Cambridge University Press, 1981), pp. 21–27.

sequences of these discontinuities for policy making and implementation in India can be demonstrated in relation to the major issues and themes that have recurred in the formulation of the goals and evaluation of the results of India's five year plans.

Public sector and private sector

The first issue has been the debate over the relative roles of the public and private sectors in economic development planning. The basic outlines and strategy of Indian economic development planning in the post-Independence era were set during the Second Five Year Plan from 1956 to 1961 (see table 8.1), whose principal architect was P. C. Mahalanobis. The central core of that plan was a move toward capital intensive, fast-paced heavy industrialization, led by the public sector, which would build the key industries and control the commanding heights of a new modern industrial economy for India, leaving the private sector "to play a complementary role in the mixed economy."[2] Although the strategy knowingly implied heavy dependence on imports, foreign exchange, and foreign aid in the short term, it was justified in the long term through the import-substitution aspect of the strategy, which promised ultimate self-sufficiency by making it possible for India to produce machines that produce other machines.

The Mahalanobis–Nehru strategy did not draw its principal inspiration from a reasoned analysis and assessment of the political economy of India: of its resources, social structure, and the immediate needs of its people. Instead, it drew upon a model of what a modern industrial society and a big military power looked like in the twentieth century and upon the methods used in the past by the big industrial military powers to achieve their current status, and drew up the requirements for India to achieve a similar status irrespective of its own resources, social structure, and the needs of its people. Although the model was based largely on the achievements of the Soviet Union, leavened by social democratic values, it implied heavy dependence on foreign aid from the capitalist countries for success. It also meant the sacrifice or postponement of virtually all other ideal goals to which Nehru and the planners paid lip service: the

[2] Isher Judge Ahluwalia, *Industrial Growth in India: Stagnation Since the Mid-Sixties* (Delhi: Oxford University Press, 1985), p. 147.

Table 8.1. *Sectoral allocation of expenditure in the Five-Year Plans (in percentages)*

Sector	First Plan 1951–56	Second Plan 1956–61	Third Plan 1961–66	Annual Plans 1966–69	Fourth Plan 1969–74	Fifth Plan 1974–79	Sixth Plan 1980–85	Seventh Plan 1985–90
Agriculture and allied sectors	14.8	11.7	12.7	16.7	14.7	12.3	12.8	12.6
Irrigation and flood control	22.2	9.2	7.8	7.1	8.6	9.5	12.5	9.4
Power[a]	7.6	9.7	14.6	18.3	18.6	18.8	19.8	19.1
Village and small industries	2.0	4.0	2.8	1.9	1.5	1.3	1.8	1.5
Industry and minerals[a]	2.8	20.0	20.1	22.8	18.2	24.1	21.0	22.4
Transportation and communications	26.5	22.0	24.6	18.5	19.5	17.8	15.9	16.4
Others	24.0	23.4	17.4	14.7	19.0	16.6	16.2	18.6
Total	100.0	100.0	100.0	100.0	100.0	100.0	100.0	100.0
Total plan expenditure (Rs. billion)	19.6	46.7	85.8	66.3	158.8	286.5	975.0	1,800.0

[a] Power alone comprised 16.9 percent of total Sixth Plan expenditures and 19.0 per cent of the Seventh. Evidently, items previously included under the heading of "industry and minerals" have been grouped with "power" under the broader category of "energy".
Sources: V. N. Balasubramanyam, *The Economy of India* (London: Weidenfeld and Nicolson, 1984), p. 80; Sixth and Seventh Plan figures calculated from Government of India, Ministry of Finance (Economic Division), *Economic Survey, 1985–86* (Delhi: Controller of Publications, 1986), pp. 137–139.

development of agriculture, the creation of employment opportunities, balanced regional development, and improvement in the well-being and quality of life of the rural poor.

The heyday of the strategy was the decade between 1955–56 and 1965–66, when India was able to draw vast foreign aid resources from both the capitalist and socialist countries and to build the heavy industrial base in steel, chemicals, machine tools, cement, and the like that the country has today. However, a major crisis for the public sector, capital intensive, heavy industrialization strategy arose during the discussions surrounding the formulation of the Fourth Five Year Plan as a consequence of a decline in foreign aid, problems of internal resource mobilization, and the heavy dependence of India on the U.S. for food aid occasioned by the neglect of agriculture in the plans. During these discussions, which involved a three-year hiatus between the end of the Third and the adoption of the Fourth plan, the coherence of the planning process itself, achieved by focusing on the public sector heavy industrialization strategy, was lost and the planning process became more and more open to the conflicting pulls of competing strategies and competing demands for resources, and to political manipulation. A further consequence of the loss of momentum in the mid-1960s was an increasingly evident deceleration in the rate of growth of the economy, traceable primarily to a decline in the rate of industrial growth. This decline has been attributed to, among other causes, the slowdown in public investment since the end of the Third Plan, the inefficiency of public sector enterprises, and the restrictions placed on private enterprise by bureaucratically imposed import control procedures designed to ensure priority to the public sector and to import substituting enterprises.

In the face of the crumbling of the entire structure of public investment and government regulation of private investment, the old ideological debate between public and private sector adherents emerged once again with the rise to power of Rajiv Gandhi and the formulation of the Seventh Five Year Plan. Rajiv Gandhi's government resisted demands for a reinstatement of the pre-Fourth Plan public investment strategy and instead shifted the balance in the planning process in favor of private investment while taking several modest measures to "liberalize" the licensing, import control, and foreign trade regimes which have been criticized for restricting private enterprise and for distorting and corrupting the entire development process.

Industry and agriculture

A second recurring issue in public discussion of the planning process in India, closely related to the first, concerns the relative attention paid to and the resource allocations for industry and agriculture in the plans. The controversy on this broad theme has, over the years, matured into competing, alternative models for economic development and alternative growth strategies. The leading alternative approach to Indian economic development, identified with former Prime Minister Charan Singh and other Gandhian-inspired political leaders, takes as its premises that capital and land are in short supply, while labor is abundant and under-employed. India's needs, therefore, are to conserve capital and maximize the use of labor by promoting labor-intensive, employment-generating industries and land-augmenting strategies to increase the product from the land.[3]

Although the momentum of heavy industrialization strategy was considerably slowed during the Fourth Plan that followed the 1965–67 food crisis, there was no major change in the overall allocations between industry and agriculture. Instead, this time, the fortuitous arrival on the scene in 1965 of Norman Borlaug, with his dwarf wheat seeds, introduced the potential for the "green revolution" in India. The Government of India quickly saw the possibilities of the new seeds and adopted the so-called New Agricultural Strategy for India based on the adoption of the high yielding seed varieties (HYVs). Although the New Agricultural Strategy was in principle a central component of the Fourth Plan, the actual increases in the relative allocations for agriculture were marginal (see table 8.1). The first and only major challenge to the entire public sector heavy industry strategy came with the Janata government that captured power in 1977 in the midst of the Fifth Plan and during discussions for the Sixth. The Janata government period produced discussion of an entire alternative strategy based on agriculture,

[3] Charan Singh, *Joint-Farming X-Rayed: The Problem and its Solution* (Bombay: Bharatiya Vidya Bhavan, 1959).

rural development, creation of employment opportunities for the rural poor through the establishment of small-scale industries in the countryside, and the diversion of significantly increased resources from the public sector heavy industry projects to the new programs. The Sixth Plan, however, though it did take some significant steps in the new directions, did not succeed in displacing completely the old strategy and replacing it with a new one. As with the public sector–private sector controversy, so with the related industry–agriculture debate, there has been no resolution, nor firm reestablishment of the old course nor any dramatic setting out upon a new one. Instead, planning has become a process of competition and struggle over resources, goals, strategies, and patronage without an overall design, a piece of patchwork rather than a coherent structure.

Agrarian reform

A third issue has concerned the place of agrarian reform and reorganization within the overall economic development strategy. Beyond the virtually unanimous sentiment after Independence for abolition of intermediaries and other exploiters of the peasantry, there was division among Congressmen concerning more drastic forms of agrarian reform and reorganization. There was a broad consensus among the central leaders that inequalities in the countryside were inconsistent with the democratic and socialist goals of the Congress and that, therefore, land ceilings should be imposed and the surplus land made available be distributed amongst the poorer farmers and the landless. However, agriculture being a state subject the central leadership could only set guidelines and attempt to persuade state leaders to institute land ceilings and implement redistribution. The state leadership of the Congress virtually everywhere had no interest in such proposals, which could only antagonize the party's predominant rural supporters, the principal land controlling castes in the countryside. Virtually everywhere, therefore, land ceilings legislation was a farce and land redistribution practically non-existent or cruel to those who "benefited" from it by receiving barren, unproductive, or alkaline soil to farm without resources to make use of it.

Agricultural development policies

The fourth issue concerns the methods to be used to bring about rural change and increased agricultural productivity within the existing allocations for agricultural development. The basic pattern of rural development emphasized in the first two Five Year Plans was extensive and integrated rural development, with programs that were to be spread evenly across the country for the benefit of all and that would include overall improvements in the quality of rural life generally, not simply improvements in agricultural techniques. In the 1960s, however, as a consequence of perceived failures in the earlier approach, the emphasis shifted to *intensive* development of favored districts through the Intensive Agricultural District Programme (IADP) and to technical changes in agriculture through the development of an elaborate research and extension system radiating out from new agricultural universities modeled on the American land grant system.

The new approach was consistent with the overall design of the planning process instituted by Nehru and Mahalanobis since it did not call for drawing significant resources away from the heavy industry strategy. The New Agricultural Strategy was to follow up and reinforce the change in policy already introduced in favor of intensive agricultural development with the emphasis on new technologies and adoption of the new high yielding varieties rather than on overall rural development. The High Yielding Varieties Program (HYVP) also, like the IADP before it, could be integrated into the plans without affecting the priority commitments to urban, capital-intensive industrialization.

There have been no major shifts in the basic strategy towards agriculture since the adoption of the HYVP, but there have been two tendencies at work, one to modify, another to reinforce it. The modification has come in the form of an attempt to extend the benefits of the new seeds to the small farmers. Then, in the late 1970s, further efforts were made to intensify the agricultural extension system through the World Bank-sponsored Training and Visit System, which reinforces strongly the exclusive emphasis on agricultural technology rather than on Community Development, while seeking to extend that technology to the small farmers as well. In effect, therefore, the currently favored resolution of the issue of extensive versus intensive, community development versus agri-culture-oriented rural programs is in favor of agriculture-oriented, but extensive development designed to reach all farmers who can possibly benefit from new seeds and improved methods.

Mobilization of resources and center–state relations

The adoption of the Nehru–Mahalanobis strategy made Indian economic development foreign exchange-dependent and required vastly increased domestic savings and revenue mobilization. In the early 1960s, in conformity with Third Plan resource requirements, pressures were put upon the state governments, which have consti-tutional authority over land revenue and agricultural taxation, to raise resources from the rural areas through such devices as bet-terment levies, agricultural income taxes, and surcharges on the existing land revenue.

The efforts to mobilize resources to support an urban-biased, capital-intensive industrialization strategy precipitated a counter-challenge, mostly political, but with some intellectual and ideo-logical support already noted above, in favor of an alternative development strategy that would shift the allocation of resources from industry to agriculture and from the center to the states. The overall political movement in the Indian states generally since the 1960s has been away from centralized planning and urban industrial development to demands for more resources from the center for agriculture and rural development in the states.

Assessing the growth performance of the Indian economy

There are several ways by which the overall growth performance of the Indian economy since Independence have been measured. These include: 1) comparisons with pre-independence performance; 2) comparisons of economic growth rates with population growth rates; 3) comparisons of achievements in relation to targeted goals; 4) comparisons with other developing countries; 5) overall assess-ments of India's changing status in the world economy. These five possible ways of assessing India's economic growth performance lead to quite different results, with the first producing the most favorable, the last the least favorable.

The overall growth rate of the Indian economy as a whole

between 1950 and 1980 is generally taken to be approximately 3.5 percent per year. This figure compares very favorably with most estimates of pre-Independence growth rates of "no more than 1 percent per annum for the first half of the twentieth century."[4] However, by the measure of comparison with population growth rates, that is, in terms of per capita income growth, India's rate of growth goes down to a very modest 1.3 percent per year, after deducting the 2.2 percent annual rate of population increase.[5] Moreover, even using the 3.5 percent growth rate unadjusted for population growth as a basis for comparison with other countries, India's growth performance compares unfavorably with the most dynamic economies in the developing world and even that of China. Its level of performance is roughly comparable to the mediocre- and low-performing developing countries "such as Pakistan, Kenya, Sri Lanka, Egypt and Indonesia."[6]

If one attempts to assess India's growth performance in relation to the central goals of the Five Year Plans from the Second Plan forward, which were to establish India as a modern, self-sufficient industrial military power, the results on the face of things appear more favorable. India's achievements in these respects, however, have been questioned by Surendra Patel who argues that India's growth performance has been so poor, in fact, that there has been an overall decline in India's position in the world economy that bodes ill for its future influence in world affairs. Patel has shown that by virtually every measure of economic achievement India has done worse than nearly all other countries in the world and that, as a result, there has been a "regression" in India's position in the world economy. India's share of world trade declined from 2 percent in 1950 to 0.5 percent in 1980, with the result that India had become "practically a marginal trading partner among the Third World countries."[7] India's share in world industrial output has declined from 1.2 to 0.7 percent in the world as a whole, from 12 to 4.6 percent among developing countries. This "regression," however,

---

[4] V. N. Balasubramanyam, *The Economy of India* (London: Weidenfeld and Nicolson, 1984), p. 43.
[5] Balasubramanyam, *The Economy of India*, pp. 30–31.
[6] Balasubramanyam, *The Economy of India*, p. 43.
[7] Surendra J. Patel, "India's Regression in the World Economy," *EPW*, xx, No. 39 (September 28, 1985), 1,652.

needs to be balanced against India's other achievements and assessed in relation to its own goals. Since India's early development goals emphasized import substitution rather than export promotion, its relatively poor performance in world trade is understandable. Moreover, the dramatic industrialization of small countries such as Hong Kong, Singapore, Taiwan, and South Korea accounts for much of India's apparent "regression" in manufacturing among the developing countries generally. Finally, India's avoidance of the massive debt burdens of countries such as Mexico and Brazil is certainly a measure of national strength which affects favorably its international standing.

However, if one accepts that Indian development policy in the 1950s set out deliberately to sacrifice or postpone the achievement of all other goals (such as the welfare of the people, employment, increased agricultural production, removal of poverty, illiteracy, and disease, and the like) in order to establish India as an increasingly self-reliant, modern industrial military power and one judges the growth performance of the Indian economy in that respect alone, it would appear that the regional and world status and image India has achieved is not consistent with its economic accomplishments.

The persistence of regional imbalances

It is well known that the consequences of British rule were manifested unevenly in the different regions and provinces of India and that there were considerable differences as well between areas ruled directly by the British and most of the princely states. Most of the amenities of modern life, such as higher education and hospitals, were concentrated in the urban areas, though in many provinces there was a spreading out of such facilities to the district head-quarters towns as well.

At Independence, therefore, there were substantial regional differences in India between the provinces that had experienced greater urban, industrial growth and higher educational expansion, such as Bombay, Madras, and West Bengal, and the rest of the country; between urban enclaves such as Kanpur and Ahmedabad within otherwise overwhelmingly rural states; between agriculturally better off areas such as the canal-irrigated areas of Punjab and parts of other regions, and the rest of the country.

Table 8.2. *Estimates of per capita state domestic product (state-wise) for different years (in rupees), states ranked in descending order on last column*

State	1962–3	1967–8	1970–1	1973–4	1975–6	1982–3
1 Punjab	421	880	1,067	1,484	1,688	3,418
2 Haryana	381	786	932	1,276	1,514	2,873
3 Maharashtra	429	664	811	1,157	1,455	2,634
4 Gujarat	413	675	845	1,116	1,236	2,400
5 Himachal Pradesh	345	543	676	953	1,165	1,967
6 West Bengal	420	659	729	920	1,100	1,771
7 Andhra Pradesh	338	531	586	868	897	1,713
8 Jammu & Kashmir	267	414	557	720	825	1,705
9 Kerala	303	519	636	876	1,000	1,689
10 Karnataka	327	514	675	992	1,038	1,679
11 Tamil Nadu	365	525	616	865	997	1,626
12 Rajasthan	289	502	629	826	873	1,622
13 Assam	349	607	570	676	848	1,596
14 Uttar Pradesh	258	490	493	677	727	1,501
15 Manipur	172	449	408	792	904	1,498
16 Madhya Pradesh	280	467	489	714	790	1,423
17 Orissa	261	458	541	765	834	1,339
18 Meghalaya	*	*	644	729	899	1,308
19 Bihar	232	419	418	559	669	1,120
20 Sikkim	N.A.	N.A.	N.A.	N.A.	N.A.	1,079
21 Nagaland	N.A.	395	508	683	949	N.A.
22 Tripura	297	555	569	729	872	N.A.

* Included in Assam.

Source: Grace Majumdar, "Trends in Inter-State Inequalities in Income and Expenditure in India," in L. S. Bhat *et al. Regional Inequalities in India: An Inter-State and Intra-State Analysis*, Papers presented at an all-India conference on Centre-State Relations and Regional Disparities in India at New Delhi in August, 1980 (New Delhi: Society for the Study of Regional Disparities, 1982), p. 33, and *Asian Recorder*, August 20–26, 1986, p. 19045.

On the whole, most indexes designed to measure the relative standing of the several states do not show much change since Independence. The more urbanized states and the states that benefited from intensive irrigation development ranked high in per capita income and net domestic product at Independence and they continue to rank high today (see table 8.2). Those states that experienced little of either urban or rural development before Independence ranked low in per capita income and net domestic product then and continue to do so today.

The fact that the relative position of most states has remained approximately the same since Independence does not at all mean that there have been no significant changes in the poorer states or that most benefits of planned development have accrued to the better-off-states and been denied to the more backward ones. Since public and private investment have continued in the better-off regions as well, it is simply that such investments have not altered the relative positions of the various regions of the country.

Balanced regional development has been a repeatedly declared goal of the central government and of its two principal agencies that can influence the process, namely, the Planning Commission and the Finance Commission. It has been the policy of the several Finance Commissions to use the mechanism of resource transfers as a device for inter-state equalization or, in other words, "as a means of redressing regional imbalances."[8] In fact, however, such redistributive transfers have been resisted effectively, for the most part, by the better-off states in the controversies that have surrounded the deliberations of the successive Finance Commissions.

Similar issues have occurred concerning the deliberations of the Planning Commission, which also has repeatedly declared balanced regional development to be one of its major goals in allocating central assistance to the states. However, the equalizing impact of the Planning Commission's distribution of central resources also has been very limited.[9]

Whatever the reasons, there is virtual unanimity among scholars who have analyzed inter-regional disparities in India on two points: the disparities have increased and central policies on resource transfers have not only been unable to prevent the increasing gap between the rich and poor states, but may have contributed to accentuating the disparities. In consequence, therefore, it can only be concluded with respect to the repeatedly reaffirmed goals of the Five Year Plans to achieve "balanced regional development" and

[8] Government of India, *Report of the Finance Commission, 1973* (Delhi: Controller of Publications, 1973), p. 8.
[9] B. S. Grewal, *Centre–State Financial Relations in India* (Patiala: Punjabi University, 1975), pp. 55–61, and H. K. Paranjpe, "Centre–State Relations in Planning," in S. N. Jain *et al.*, *The Union and the States* (Delhi: National, 1972), p. 218.

reduction of inter-state disparities that "the results of planned development" have not been "in consonance with this national objective."[10]

THE PERSISTING PROBLEMS OF POVERTY, HUNGER, AND MALNUTRITION

The persistence of widespread, extreme, and endemic poverty in India 40 years after Independence raises fundamental issues concerning the appropriateness of the economic development strategy adopted by the Indian state and its ability to provide an environment in which the basic, minimal needs of its population can be satisfied. The commitment in the early 1970s by the Government of India to new approaches to abolish poverty and the failures of most of the programs adopted since then to achieve that goal reveal some of the basic limitations of the Indian political system and the constraints imposed by the dominant classes in the Indian state and in the countryside upon successful formulation and implementation of policy innovations on behalf of the poor.

The commitment to abolish poverty was connected with major political changes in the functioning of Indian politics introduced by Mrs. Gandhi in the early 1970s. The recognition at the time of the persistence of widespread poverty implied either a major failure in the previous economic development strategy or at least pointed to its association with consequences that were no longer considered tolerable. The commitment to abolish poverty raised once again very sharply the question of whether or not it was feasible or realistic to envision the elimination of extreme poverty and inequality in India without major structural changes in society to sustain such an ambitious program.

The Indian "war on poverty" provides an example of the problems involved in formulating and implementing policies in India's multi-level political system. The weaknesses of most of the programs adopted arise in large part out of the difficulties involved in formulating policies in New Delhi to be implemented at the state and local levels with the existing bureaucratic apparatus. Many of

[10] M. M. Ansari, "Financing of the States' Plans: A Perspective for Regional Development," *EPW*, xviii, No. 49 (December 3, 1983), 2,077.

the problems encountered in the implementation of anti-poverty programs also reveal the extent to which locally dominant classes are able to absorb and even profit from programs meant for the poor.

The pervasiveness of poverty

When scholars and planners talk about poverty and the poor in India, they are not usually referring to a small, disadvantaged segment of the population, but to virtually half the population of the country, with the incidence varying from state to state in a range from less than a quarter of the rural population in Punjab and Haryana to two-thirds of the population in West Bengal.[11] These rural poor, who are mostly of intermediate and low caste status, come from the landless agricultural laborers and the small peasantry with "tiny plots"[12] of land or with holdings that are inadequate to provide a subsistence for the household population dependent on their produce.

In most of rural India the bulk of the land, usually above half the cultivated area, is controlled by an elite of peasantry with economic holdings between 5 and 25 acres, comprising usually less than 20 percent of the rural population, and coming primarily from the dominant rural classes and castes of intermediate and upper caste status. Members of this class or group of castes are generally in controlling positions in local political and development institutions and take a keen interest in all rural development activities, including programs for the poor and for poverty alleviation.

The nationalist leaders who took power at Independence were aware both of the pervasiveness and depth of poverty in India, along with associated problems of unemployment and under-employment, and of the inequalities in resources and income among the rural population. However, as has been noted above, that leadership chose not to attack these problems directly. Their first priority was heavy industrialization. The problems of the poor were to be alleviated in the short term by land reforms, community

[11] Montek S. Ahluwalia, "Rural Poverty in India: 1956/57 to 1973/74," in Montek S. Ahluwalia et al., *India: Occasional Papers*, World Bank Staff Working Paper No. 279 (Washington, D.C.: World Bank, 1978), p. 17.
[12] D. N. Dhanagare, "Agrarian Reforms and Rural Development in India: Some Observations," offprint from *Research in Social Movements, Conflict and Change*, Vol. 7 (JAI Press, 1984), p. 196.

development, food procurement, price control, and rationing in times of scarcity. In the long term, however, the solution to poverty was to come through the "trickling down" to the mass of the poor population of the economic benefits that would arise from a dynamic, industrializing economy.

The incidence of poverty in India and its measurement

Most measures of the incidence of poverty in India establish a "poverty line" based on the amount of income required for a person to purchase a given caloric norm of food per day.[13] In 1971, Dandekar and Rath published in the *Economic and Political Weekly* a benchmark study on poverty in India, giving precise estimates of the numbers, consumption expenditures, and calorie intake of the poor in 1960–61 and of the changes that had occurred in all three during the decade of the 1960s.[14] Defining the poor as those persons required to live on less than 50 paise[15] per day in the rural areas and 75 paise per day in the cities, 38 percent of the rural population and nearly 50 percent of the urban lived below this level of virtual destitution, which implied an inadequate calorie intake as well.

During the decade of the 1960s, covering the Third Five Year Plan and the Annual Plan years between it and the Fourth Plan, the main benefits of increased income and expenditure accrued to the upper middle and richer sections of the population. The bottom 40 percent, that is, virtually all the poor, did not benefit at all from the economic changes that occurred during the decade. Moreover, the per capita expenditure of most of the rural and urban poor actually declined, significantly so (15 to 20 percent) in the case of the poorest of the poor, the bottom 10 percent of the population. Dandekar and Rath argued that the results till then had shown that the process of economic development would not improve the position of the

[13] Ahluwalia, "Rural Poverty in India," p. 7. Another index that is often used side-by-side with others is Sen's poverty index, which measures the intensity of poverty in an index that combines a measure of the distance between the poverty line and "the mean consumption of the poor, as well as the extent of inequality amongst the poor"; Ahluwalia, "Rural Poverty in India," p. 5, and A. K. Sen, "Poverty, Inequality, Unemployment: Some Conceptual Issues in Measurement," *EPW*, VIII, Special Number (August, 1973).
[14] V. M. Dandekar and N. Rath. "Poverty in India: Dimensions and Trends," *EPW*, VI, No. 1 (January 2, 1971), 25–48, and No. 2 (January 9, 1971), 106–46.
[15] There are one hundred paise to the rupee.

poorest in India in the foreseeable future unless specific policies and programs were adopted for their benefit.

The Dandekar and Rath report on poverty in India came at approximately the same time as the beginning of Mrs. Gandhi's *garibi hatao* campaign and the poverty programs that followed it. Their report, therefore, has provided a benchmark since then for assessing the direction of change, if any, in the numbers and condition of the poor, the relative successes and failures of the various poverty programs introduced since 1971, the extent to which there is any correlation between the performance of the economy and the general condition of the poor and whether or not an entirely different overall strategy for solving the problem of poverty in India is required.

Trends and fluctuations in the incidence of poverty

In an important World Bank-sponsored study published in 1978, Ahluwalia established on the basis of the available survey and statistical data that there had been no discernible long-term trend in the incidence of poverty in the country as a whole between 1960–61 and 1973–74. The incidence of poverty had neither increased nor decreased during this period, although there had been considerable fluctuations up and down in the interim.[16]

On the whole, the all-India findings did not differ significantly from state to state. For most states, the absence of a long-term trend and "the pattern of fluctuation" was similar to that "for India as a whole."[17] Detailed case studies at the local level have also confirmed a persisting high incidence of poverty.[18]

Poverty and agricultural performance

There is a curious agreement among some scholars and politicians concerning the relationship between poverty and agricultural production and development. Those who favor greater emphasis on agriculture in resource allocation and less on capital-intensive industrialization argue that the best way to eliminate poverty in an

[16] Ahluwalia, "Rural Poverty in India."
[17] Ahluwalia, "Rural Poverty in India," p. 16.
[18] Indira Hirway, "Direct Attacks on Rural Poverty," review of *Direct Attack on Rural Poverty: Policy, Programmes and Implementation* by Prabhu Ghate (New Delhi: Concept Publishing Company, 1984), *EPW*, XXI, No. 1 (January 4, 1986), 22.

agrarian society with abundant labor and limited land per person is to focus on increasing production per acre with available manual and animal power rather than by introducing capital-intensive machinery, thereby increasing employment opportunities on the land and the available supply of food.[19] On the other hand, some who have favored continued emphasis on the heavy industrialization strategy have argued that the new agricultural technology makes it possible to avoid major resource reallocations by increasing agricultural productivity and employment through the adoption of the HYVs. The New Agricultural Strategy was adopted with just that hope in mind, namely, that a small increased allocation of funds for agricultural development would lead to a large increase in production and a reduction in poverty through the "trickle down" effect, making it possible to retain the public sector-led heavy industrialization strategy.

The absence of a trend in the incidence of poverty parallels the absence of any long-term trend in "the growth of agricultural output" from 1956–57 to 1973–74, which "just about kept pace with the growth of the rural population."[20] However, the fluctuations in the incidence of poverty also paralleled fluctuations in agricultural performance in India as a whole and in half the states (Andhra Pradesh, Bihar, Karnataka, Madhya Pradesh, Maharashtra, Tamil Nadu, and Uttar Pradesh). Ahluwalia found a definite association between improved agricultural performance and "reductions in the incidence of poverty,"[21] which supported the view that there had been "some trickling down of benefits from increases in agricultural production."[22] The results suggested that the "trickle down" effects of increased agricultural output were more limited in states where land reforms had been least effective or where other factors such as more rapid population growth were at work as well. These latter associations were, however, less clear than the general association between fluctuations in the incidence of poverty and in agricultural output per head, with the former declining when the latter increased in India as a whole, in half the Indian states, and in most of the other

---

[19] Charan Singh, *Economic Nightmare of India: Its Cause and Cure* (New Delhi: National, 1981), p. 112.
[20] Ahluwalia, "Rural Poverty in India," p. 25.
[21] Ahluwalia, "Rural Poverty in India," p. 25.
[22] Ahluwalia, "Rural Poverty in India," p. 28.

states as well when the influence of other adverse factors was accounted for.

A reanalysis by Prasad of Ahluwalia's figures appears to resolve the doubts about the association between poverty and agricultural growth. After breaking down Ahluwalia's figures into two periods, pre- and post-Green Revolution, he found a clear "trend of decline" in the incidence of rural poverty in all the major states after 1967–68, a negative correlation between "the poverty percentage" and "per capita agricultural production," and an association between the decline in the poverty percentage over time and increased "per capita foodgrain production." Although the decline in the incidence of rural poverty "has been low," Prasad argues, it is because the rate of growth in agriculture also has been slow.[23]

The linkage established by both Ahluwalia and Prasad between poverty reduction and agricultural growth supports the following conclusions. 1) "Trickle down" effects benefiting the poor do occur with increased agricultural output. 2) Since, however, the incidence of rural poverty by all accounts has remained very high and the per capita rate of growth in agriculture slow, there is a need for further, more rapid and more widespread extension of the HYV-technology. 3) It is unlikely, however, that a sufficiently high, sustained rate of increase in agricultural productivity will occur even with the spread of HYV technology to obviate the need for further measures to help the poor directly. 4) There is indirect evidence that the persistence of "semi-feudal"[24] relations in agriculture and of exploitative tenancy and sharecropping arrangements act to increase poverty and to offset the positive effects of agricultural growth in reducing poverty. 5) There is, therefore, a case on this evidence to reinforce other justifications for at least bringing tenancy and sharecropping arrangements in the states of the eastern region, where such arrangements are most unfavorable to the cultivators and agricultural performance also is below most other states, in line with the basic pattern of peasant self-cultivation in the more prosperous agricultural regions of the country. 6) In the absence of a major structural reorganization of agrarian society and economy,

[23] Pradhan H. Prasad, "Poverty and Agricultural Development," *EPW*, xx, No. 50 (December 14, 1985), 2,221–2,224.
[24] The term is Prasad's, "Poverty and Agricultural Development."

special programs for the poor are required to eliminate or reduce poverty significantly.

Poverty programs: origin and types

The initiation of large-scale anti-poverty programs as increasingly important and integral components of the planning process occurred after the 1971 parliamentary elections in which Mrs. Gandhi's central election slogan was "garibi hatao" (abolish poverty). The adoption of this slogan and of the programs that followed it were part of Mrs. Gandhi's political strategy of building an independent national support base that would free her from political dependence upon the party bosses in the states, whose own support bases were primarily among the dominant rural proprietary castes and the urban commercial classes. Although the 40 to 50 percent rural and urban poor lacked political weight, they represented a potential national vote bank that was far larger than any alternative sources of votes for her rivals.

The programs that followed involved further centralization of the planning process in relation to programs that were to be implemented throughout the country, in the rural areas, and at the local level. Although implementation had to be carried out through the existing bureaucratic apparatus and local political institutions, the development of the schemes and proposals was done primarily in New Delhi. These programs also provided the central political leadership with new and vast patronage resources to be disbursed to states and districts throughout the country.

The new anti-poverty programs were launched in the early 1970s simultaneously with a centrally-sponsored move to institute a second stage in reducing and enforcing more effectively land ceilings that had been adopted earlier in most states. There was, therefore, an overall central design at this time to eliminate poverty, reduce inequalities in the countryside, and erode the traditional dominance of the rural landed castes. The state governments, however, continued to depend upon the dominant rural classes for political support in the countryside.

The anti-poverty programs themselves fell into two broad types. One was designed to actually lift beneficiaries above the poverty line by providing them either "with productive assets" or skills or both "so that they can employ themselves usefully to earn greater incomes."[25] Under this heading of "beneficiary-oriented" programs were the Small Farmer Development Agency (SFDA), the Marginal Farmer and Agricultural Labor (MFAL) program, and most recently the Integrated Rural Development Program (IRDP). The IRDP, introduced in 1978–80 under the Janata regime, consolidated the existing programs such as the SFDA and MFAL, and also introduced the *antayodaya* principle of beginning with the poorest.[26]

The second type of program was designed to be ameliorative only, to provide temporary wage employment for the poor and landless in seasons when employment opportunities are reduced and in areas such as dry and drought prone districts where they are less available than in more favored districts even in the best of times. These programs have had names such as the Crash Scheme for Rural Employment (CSRE), the Drought Prone Areas Program (DPAP), the Pilot Intensive Rural Employment Project (PIREP), the National Rural Employment Programme (NREP), and the like.[27]

The most important of the anti-poverty programs in terms of resource allocations have been the beneficiary-oriented IRD programs. In the Sixth Plan, nearly three times as much funding (Rs. 4,500 crores[28]) was provided for the IRDP, compared to Rs. 1,600 crores for the NREP.[29] In the Seventh Plan, however, somewhat more funds were allocated for employment programs (Rs. 2,487 crores for the NREP and Rs. 1,744 crores for the Rural Landless Employment Guarantee Programme [RLEGS]) than for the IRDP (Rs. 3,474 crores).[30]

Altogether, however, the funds allocated for the three main

[25] Nilakantha Rath, " 'Garibi Hatao': Can IRDP Do It?" *EPW*, xx, No. 6 (February 9, 1985), 238.
[26] *Antayodaya* means "uplift of the poorest." Under this principle, the selection of initial beneficiaries is to be done from among the poorest persons and families in each village in a community development block, who are to be provided with productive assets sufficient for them to lift themselves above the poverty line.
[27] John W. Mellor, *The New Economics of Growth: A Strategy for India and the Developing World* (Ithaca: Cornell University Press, 1976), pp. 101–102 and Rath, p. 245.
[28] One crore is 10 million.
[29] Rath, " 'Garibi Hatao': Can IRDP Do It?", p. 245.
[30] Government of India, Planning Commission, *The Seventh Five-Year Plan, 1985–90*, Vol. II: *Sectoral Programmes of Development* (Delhi: Controller of Publications, 1985), p. 70.

anti-poverty programs in the Seventh Plan – IRDP, NREP, and RLEGS – constitute only 4 percent of the total plan allocations.[31] In effect, therefore, the anti-poverty programs remain a supplement in a broader economic development strategy, which continues to avoid radical institutional solutions to poverty and inequality and to rely upon the long-run hope that the benefits of growth and development will ultimately "trickle down" to the poor.[32]

Poverty programs: performance and implementation

The principal justification for the beneficiary-oriented programs as opposed to the employment-oriented poverty programs is that the former are designed to solve the problem of poverty by providing income-generating assets to the poor whereas the latter merely provide a subsistence income at state expense and do not offer a solution. While the IRDP idea makes sense in principle and has the added appeal that it threatens no one, in practice evidence has been accumulating that the IRD programs have not had the desired effects. Moreover, it has provided large new sources of patronage and corrupt income for local politicians, bureaucrats, and locally influential persons.

The IRD asset creation programs involve a wide range of persons and institutions in their implementation, thereby making its workings incomprehensible to the poor, requiring intermediaries between the poor and the agencies and persons who are supposed to help them, and multiplying the opportunities for the non-poor to make quick and large profits from them. Raj Krishna, Rath, Paul, and other observers have pointed to numerous deficiencies in implementation of the IRDP and have argued that only a small percentage of the total beneficiaries have actually received productive assets of sufficient quality to generate the income to keep them permanently above the poverty line.[33]

The poor performance of the poverty programs notwithstanding,

---

[31] Calculated from Government of India, Planning Commission, *The Seventh Five-Year Plan*, Vol. I: *Perspectives, Objectives, Resources*, p. 28.

[32] B. M., "Policy-Frame for Seventh Plan," *EPW*, xx, No. 28 (July, 1985), 1,165.

[33] Raj Krishna, "Growth, Investment and Poverty in Mid-Term Appraisal of Sixth Plan," *EPW*, xvii, No. 47 (November 19, 1983), 1972–1977; Samuel Paul, "Mid-Term Appraisal of the Sixth Plan: Why Poverty Alleviation Lags Behind," *EPW*, xix, No. 18 (May 5, 1984), 760–766; and Rath, " 'Garibi Hatao': Can IRDP Do It?"

the most recent available estimates of the rural population in poverty, for 1983–84, indicated a decline from 39 percent in 1977–78 to 31 percent in 1983–84.[34] Although the planners have claimed credit for this decline as a consequence of their anti-poverty programs, the more likely explanation is the persistence of a modest upward trend in the growth rate of foodgrains production combined with the fact that 1977–78 was a very bad drought year and 1983–84 a favorable year. Hardly any professional economists outside the Planning Commission credit the results to the anti-poverty programs of the Sixth Plan, whose performance generally fell below the standard of other plan programs.[35]

It is a vulgar Marxism that attributes the adoption of the anti-poverty programs to the machinations of the dominant "rural oligarchy" in cahoots with a corrupt and cynical bureaucracy with world imperialism in the background encouraging the policy shift towards these programs. The alleged purpose of this alliance is to defeat the Indian development strategy of capital accumulation by the state by drawing resources away from productive capital investments.[36] There is no doubt, however, that such programs are adopted in the first instance, in preference to more radical solutions, because they do not threaten the dominant rural castes and classes and that they are sustained in large part because they benefit those same castes and classes and provide vast new sources of corrupt income to an underpaid, demoralized, inefficient, and cynical bureaucracy.

DOMINANT CLASSES AND INEQUALITY

There are three broad alternative explanations for the persistence of a system that has so far fallen short of achieving any of its principal economic goals. These explanations all naturally assume that, ideologically and/or materially, identifiable classes and groups are benefiting from the system and sustaining it. They are also more

[34] Montek S. Ahluwalia, "Rural Poverty, Agricultural Production, and Prices: A Reexamination," in John W. Mellor and Gunvant M. Desai (eds.), *Agricultural Change and Rural Poverty: Variations on a Theme by Dharm Narain* (Delhi: Oxford University Press, 1986), p. 60, and Prasad, "Poverty and Agricultural Development," p. 2,223.

[35] Paul, "Mid-Term Appraisal," p. 763.

[36] Prasad, "Poverty and Agricultural Development," p. 2,221.

complementary than conflicting, though they differ in identifying the particular forces which sustain the system.

One explanation assumes the autonomy or relative autonomy of the state and its leaders, their ability to make free choices concerning the main directions of economic development policy for India, and the nationalist underpinnings of the choices they made. All these factors made it possible for the predominant Congress leadership to embark upon the economic development strategy they preferred, namely, the capital-intensive, public sector-led, heavy industrialization strategy.

In this explanation, the predominant leadership at Independence is seen as not the creature of any dominant class, but as acting relatively independently, from a powerful state and political base, in the service of deeply felt nationalist and ideological goals. It was able to adopt an economic development strategy that, in the short and intermediate run at least, would clearly not be in the interests of many classes and groups in Indian society not only because of the strength of the state and the party, but because of the weakness of the potential opposition and because some of its policy measures did benefit important classes and groups. Much room was left for the private sector and indigenous industrial entrepreneurs who were now protected from competitive British colonial enterprises as well as from any new threats from modern multi-national corporations as a result of the import-substitution policy and measures associated with it that gave protected monopolies to domestic industries. The former zamindars and princes who had been collaborators with the British Raj were in no position to contest the power of the state and the Congress organization.

More important, however, was that the Congress, by 1947, had developed a very strong rural support base among the upper tenantry, the petty landlords, and the owner-cultivators or peasant proprietors who controlled the Congress organizations in the districts. Although the national Congress leaders talked about agrarian reforms, even including joint cooperative farming (or collectivization), which were not at all in the interests of the locally dominant rural classes, it gradually became evident to most of them that no serious structural reforms and redistribution were planned and that even the moderate land ceilings measures introduced in most states could be frustrated quietly. In effect, therefore, the national Congress leadership was able to pursue an economic strategy that neglected agriculture and favored urban industrial development for three reasons: 1) it eliminated or reduced significantly the power of the former landlord class and empowered the new class of independent rural landowning proprietors; 2) it provided sufficient rural development patronage to its main rural supporters among this new class; 3) it took no really effective measures to threaten the interests of the new class.

The idea of the relative autonomy of the Indian state and its top leadership can be applied also to Mrs. Gandhi's long period of dominance to explain both the persistence of the overall strategy and the new emphases in economic policy that were introduced from 1971 onwards. Early in the period of Mrs. Gandhi's dominance, the weaknesses of the Nehru strategy had become increasingly evident in industrial stagnation, in the failure of the agricultural sector to increase productivity, in the persistence of mass poverty, unemployment and under-employment, in urban decay, and in increasing inflation.

In the midst of these considerable economic difficulties, Mrs. Gandhi waged a major political struggle against the party bosses who had dominated state politics in her father's days and emerged victorious and in complete control of the central and state governments. She sought to remedy some of the major economic problems that had become evident by the end of her father's life, most notably through the New Agricultural Strategy and the anti-poverty programs introduced after the 1971 election campaign. With her power consolidated in the country in the mid-1970s, she sought once again, as her father had done, to compel the state leaderships to introduce serious land ceilings legislation and to redistribute surplus land to the poor.

We have seen, however, that none of these measures proved effective. The New Agricultural Strategy helped to promote the Green Revolution which, however, has been a very partial revolution, as will be shown in the next chapter. Anti-poverty programs have followed upon one another in rapid succession, but have not had a major impact upon the incidence of poverty and malnutrition, which have declined somewhat in recent years for other reasons

271

indicated above. The second round of land ceilings legislation proved to be as much of a farce as the first.

This explanation of policy failures under both Nehru and Mrs. Gandhi focuses on leadership, on political and organizational factors, and on the structure of center–state relations.[37]

A sophisticated Marxist variation on the argument presented above has been elaborated by Pranab Bardhan.[38] In his view, while there is no dominant class in India that controls state policy and while, therefore, the state in India is relatively autonomous in relation to social classes, there are three dominant or "proprietary" classes whose common interests and conflicts of interests have influenced Indian economic development policy from the beginning. These three classes, whose members come from the upper 20 percent of the population in income, are the urban industrial and professional classes and "the rural hegemonic class of rich farmers."[39]

The deficiencies in Indian economic development planning and implementation in this view arise out of the conflicts of interest among these dominant classes, none of whom "is individually strong enough to dominate the process of resource allocation," which leads, therefore, to "the proliferation of subsidies and grants to placate all of them, with the consequent reduction in available surplus for public capital formation." These subsidies include high support prices and subsidized inputs for the rich farmers; low food prices for urban consumers and hence lower wage costs for industrialists; and low-priced materials and services as well as protection from competition for the industrialists.[40]

In this view, the Congress in the Nehru period did not so much provide an economic direction and a base of political support to sustain the policy initiatives of its leadership, but rather it acted more as "a subtle and resilient mechanism for conflict management and transactional negotiations among the proprietary classes."[41] For

[37] This explanation is a composite one, derived from the predominant political science literature on Indian politics since Independence, including my own.
[38] Pranab Bardhan, *The Political Economy of Development in India* (Delhi: Oxford University Press, 1984).
[39] Bardhan, *The Political Economy*, p. 54.
[40] Bardhan, *The Political Economy*, p. 61.
[41] Bardhan, *The Political Economy*, pp. 77–78.

the most part, the system operated in such a way as to preserve liberal democracy in India as the most suitable political form for bargaining and distribution of spoils. However, in the 1970s and 1980s, the system began to fall apart. Corruption, waste, and mismanagement fostered by such a system of bargaining and patronage dispensation led to "fiscal and managerial crisis." The dominance of the three "proprietary classes over the subordinate classes" began to weaken.[42] Internal divisions among the three proprietary classes also began to sharpen, in such a way as to divide the rural rich farmers increasingly from the urban industrial and professional classes.

Bardhan's view of the economic and political results produced by the Congress system and the Five Year Plans differs from the first only in the importance it attaches to the three so-called proprietary classes.

There is no doubt that the top business and industrial leaders have, since before Independence, favored a policy of government-supported rapid industrialization, including encouragement by government for development of new industries and protection for indigenous industries. They have also accepted the necessity for state ownership and control of some large enterprises. The big industrial houses have been able to manipulate successfully the import and other licensing regulations managed by the government bureaucracy.

However, most Indian businessmen surely would prefer, and have lobbied consistently for, an increased role for the private sector, a liberalized import–export regime, and a general reduction in the role of the public sector and of government controls over the economy. Most would surely also prefer to pay a reduced rate of taxes to government than a higher rate divided between government and corrupt tax collectors. I believe, therefore, that it makes more sense to see most Indian businessmen and industrialists as victims in a system which they do not so much control, but which many twist to their own advantage and which they grease with money in order to protect themselves from government harassment and to advance their business interests. In other words, businessmen as a class have relatively little influence over the direction of economic policy, but

[42] Bardhan, *The Political Economy*, p. 79

273

individual businessmen and business houses may nevertheless prosper in India's "mixed economy" by influencing the implementation of government regulations.[43]

It is hardly surprising, therefore, that business response to the Seventh Five Year Plan under Rajiv Gandhi, with its emphasis on the private sector, on a liberalized import–export regime, and on a reduced rate of taxation has been favorable. On the other hand, business groups opposed the efforts of Rajiv Gandhi's former Finance Minister, V. P. Singh, to ensure through "tax raids" on individual businessmen that the latter actually conformed to the new system by paying their taxes.[44] It can be concluded, therefore, that the business community as a whole certainly has supported the rapid development of industry in the country in preference to a rural-led strategy, they have acquiesced in policies that have created a large public sector but have disliked it, many have worked the system successfully and many more have operated within the black, parallel, or underground economy based on tax evasion, smuggling, and other illicit operations, but it is certain that most businessmen are unhappy with the system and would prefer to see most of the structure of bureaucratic controls and regulations dismantled and the bulk of the public sector enterprises turned over to private hands.

Bardhan's second dominant proprietary class, that of the professionals and urban intellectuals, is a misnomer that mistakes a part for the whole, for it is only a segment of this class that wields effective power in India, namely, the professional bureaucrats. When Bardhan talks about the professionals as a proprietary class, he refers primarily to the upper levels of the administrative service and the "battalions of bureaucrats [who] wield the weapons of monopoly control, foreign exchange regulation, industrial licensing and credit and input rationing to keep the industrialists on the defensive and to increase their own political leverage and corrupt income."[45]

The broader professional and urban classes constitute a "ruling

[43] Stanley A. Kochanek, *Business and Politics in India* (Berkeley: University of California Press, 1974), ch. 15.

[44] Jean A. Bernard, "A Maturation Crisis in India: The V. P. Singh Experiment," *Asian Survey*, XXVII, No. 4 (April, 1987), 425.

[45] Bardhan, *The Political Economy*, p. 58.

class" in Mosca's sense of the term rather than Marx's in that they constitute the source for recruitment of the administrative groups. Moreover, through their education and personal relationship with the bureaucratic personnel, the more successful and politically astute among them may gain preferential access to the privileges of education, housing, foreign travel, scarce consumer goods, and good jobs for themselves and their children.

A considerable segment of the intellectual classes in most industrializing and industrialized countries, particularly those who depend on government jobs in administration or education or who are employees of private organizations on fixed salaries with limited opportunities for upward career mobility, such as journalists, naturally tend to support state expansion rather than to take their chances on the market. They overwhelmingly prefer urban to rural life and, in India, the development of the kinds of urban amenities that exist in more advanced industrial countries.

Bardhan's third proprietary class, the so-called rich farmers, is perceived as a class increasingly in conflict with the other two in the dominating coalition, which serves its interests by restraining and constraining state policies supported by the others while also grabbing subsidies, price supports, and other benefits for themselves. Bardhan sees this class as comprising the upper segments of the broader class of self-sufficient small and middle peasantry over whom it exercises hegemony. It can exercise hegemony over the middle peasantry because the latter gain as well, if not as much as the rich farmers, "from lower irrigation and power rates, higher prices for farm products and subsidized credit and inputs like fertilizers" which the state provides to secure the support of the rich farmers.[46] Although they continue to be divided by "deep political, cultural and economic divisions that make consistent class action virtually impossible even in a localized area," the rich farmers unite "on matters of state policies affecting [their] common class interests" such as "agitating for higher farm product prices or in frustrating land ceilings legislation."[47]

Bardhan's analysis of the class hegemony of the rural rich farmers is somewhat oversimplified, as will be pointed out in the following

---

[46] Bardhan, *The Political Economy*, pp. 47–48.
[47] Bardhan, *The Political Economy*, p. 50.

chapter. It is, however, broadly correct, and it became evident as early as the early 1960s, that the class of middle and upper peasantry had become dominant in most state governments, that they were in a position to frustrate all attempts at serious land ceilings legislation or rural resource mobilization, and that their common interests often cut across party divisions. It seems strange, however, to include as members of a dominant ruling coalition in the country as a whole a class that acts primarily as a constraining, restraining, and frustrating force against the implementation of Government of India policies at the state level. The policies of the Indian state continue overwhelmingly to favor public – and private – investment in industry and power, rather than in research and extension to promote agricultural productivity. Rich farmers, in other words, like big industrialists and businessmen, operate effectively within and gain benefits and privileges from a system they do not like and which does *not* serve their class interests, but which is sufficiently corrupt, incoherent, and flexible that privileged segments in the rural areas may twist it to their advantage.

A third explanation for the failures and inconsistencies in Indian planning focuses especially on the persistence of widespread rural poverty and argues that it is produced by "urban bias." State and private investment allocations are channeled principally to the cities in factories, roads, five-star hotels, and sports stadia for the Asian Games while the rural areas, especially the rural poor, receive pitifully small allocations for investment in the land, in cheap agricultural implements, in drinking water, or in agricultural research and extension.[48] The rich farmers also benefit from a policy process that favors the urban areas because "they sell their extra output to the cities," get easy credit and input subsidies, and use their profits for urban investments.[49]

The origins of policies that lead to "urban bias" in developing countries are in the strategy of rapid industrialization and the supporting economic theories that argue that such industrialization can be brought about only by extracting a surplus from the countryside. At first, the rich farmers do not benefit. They are

---

[48] Michael Lipton, *Why Poor People Stay Poor: A Study of Urban Bias in World Development* (New Delhi: Heritage, 1980), p. 13.
[49] Lipton, *Why Poor People Stay Poor*, p. 17.

"squeezed," through taxation or collectivization, or are even physically eliminated, as in the case of the Russian *kulaks*.

In the second stage of rural policy making, failures in producing and extracting the necessary agricultural surplus precipitate a change in direction. The aim of extracting a surplus from the countryside remains foremost, but now the rich farmers, instead of being squeezed to produce it, are provided incentives to do so.

This idea of "urban bias" in economic development in developing countries has increasingly become part of the political polemic in India, where it was presented most emphatically by Charan Singh and his allies and supporters in the BKD, the Janata coalition, and the Lok Dal. In their view, which in its most recent formulations incorporated Lipton's arguments though it precedes his statement of it,[50] India's leaders set out to copy the Soviet Union and the West through policies of heavy industrialization that neglected agriculture. Agriculture, in consequence, was starved of capital, the farmer was exploited, and the village deprived of the basic amenities of life.

This critique of Indian economic development policy has been widely shared and has led to proposals from foreign economists, Gandhian and other non-Marxist economists and intellectuals in India, and the leaders of agrarian-based parties in India such as Charan Singh, for major changes in Indian economic development strategy. The types of changes envisioned by such critics would involve massive shifts of resources for extensive agricultural development for the benefit of *all* the viable peasantry, for vastly increased funds for rural development generally, including provision of basic amenities of life for the villages of India, and for a labor-intensive strategy of promoting local, small-scale industries.

Such a policy shift, however, remains remote because the Indian state and its policies continue to be dominated by a political class which adheres ideologically to the drive for industrial and technological modernity through state-directed economic development planning. The main beneficiaries of those policies continue to be the politicians themselves and their corrupt allies and dependants in the bureaucracy, business entrepreneurs who manipulate the system

---

[50] Charan Singh cites Lipton approvingly in his *Economic Nightmare of India: Its Cause and Cure* (New Delhi: National, 1981).

effectively or thrive in the black economy, and the urban classes who obtain growing access to indigenously produced or smuggled foreign luxury products and the amenities of urban life. Although a few rich farmers in the countryside also benefit, the bulk of even the landowning cultivating classes retain mainly the power to prevent their own destruction through radical agrarian reform, but not the ability to extract major resources for the development of a dynamic, increasingly productive agricultural sector that would improve the quality of life and the well-being of both the cultivating and the laboring rural classes who continue to comprise the overwhelming majority of the population of the country.

CHAPTER 9

POLITICAL ASPECTS OF AGRICULTURAL CHANGE

AGRARIAN ISSUES IN INDIAN POLITICS

The year 1966 was a major turning-point in the history of Indian agricultural development policy. In that year, three significant sets of events occurred that profoundly affected the determination of Government of India policy makers to intensify measures to increase agricultural production as rapidly as possible in order to make India self-sufficient in foodgrains. The first was the great drought/famine of 1966–67 in north India, which followed upon a previous bad year for Indian agriculture and which occurred simultaneously with scarcity conditions in other areas of the country. The second was the initial harvesting of the new HYVs of wheat brought to India in the winter of 1965–66 by Norman Borlaug and his associates and planted in several locations in north India and elsewhere during the *rabi* (winter) season of 1966. The third was a combination of domestic and international factors affecting U.S. government foreign policy-making, including the Vietnam war, U.S. balance of payments problems, and the potential use of U.S. food exports for hard currency payments to alleviate those problems.

Although these three sets of events constituted a turning-point, the solutions adopted to deal with the crisis events of 1966–67, namely, the drought and shifts in U.S. attitudes toward India, were entirely consistent with previous Indian government policies for economic development, agricultural development, and agrarian reform. Those policies, which focused on the rapid adoption of the HYVs and the associated technology, ignored the long-standing issues of agrarian reform and were designed to be acceptable to the dominant political and economic elites in the provincial capitals and in the Indian countryside. They fed into and reinforced historic regional and social imbalances in economic development in India. They ignored the problems of the small cultivators in vast regions of

the country, most notably in the great rainfed paddy-growing areas
of India stretching from eastern U.P. to Bengal and including as well
large parts of Madhya Pradesh, Orissa, and Assam. They also failed
to solve, only postponed facing the hard solutions to, the basic
production problems of Indian agriculture in those areas of the
country that comprise the bulk of its territory and population and
that depend upon the monsoon or lack either adequate irrigation or
dependable rainfall.

The eastern U.P. and Bihar famine of 1966–67: incidence, implications, and consequences

The great drought/famine of 1966–67 in north India might have
conveyed three clear messages to Indian agricultural policy makers.
First, it pointed to a persistent problem rather than merely a sudden,
unanticipatible crisis, namely the historically low and unstable
yields of rice, the main food crop in the main cropping season in a
vast area of the country. Second, it indicated clearly that some areas
of the country were in a better position than others to withstand
drought, notably the canal and tubewell-irrigated areas. Third, it
suggested what had already been pointed out in a Planning Commission report on the Eastern Districts of U.P., published in
January, 1964,[1] that there were severe environmental constraints
and a great dearth of capital resources, both of which made it
difficult to envisage major changes in the development of agriculture
in the eastern region of the country unless considerable external
resources were provided to alter agricultural practices there.

These were not, however, the lessons that were drawn by
Government of India policy makers. Although they perceived that
the crisis of 1965–67 reflected underlying structural problems in
Indian agriculture, they generalized the problem to Indian agriculture as a whole rather than emphasizing the particular problems
of rainfed agriculture in northern and eastern India. Second, they
perceived the problem as one requiring primarily an urgent, dramatic increase in the aggregate production of foodgrains in the country
as a whole in order to satisfy the consumption needs of the

[1] Government of India, Planning Commission, *Report of Joint Study Team, Uttar
Pradesh (Eastern Districts): Ghazipur, Azamgarh, Deoria, Jaunpur* (Delhi: Government
of India Press, 1964).

population as a whole. Finally, Government of India policy makers, while recognizing the special needs of the "backward" areas of the country, such as eastern U.P. and Bihar, and while calling for policies to rectify existing regional imbalances and disparities in development and in income, adopted a New Strategy for Agriculture that led to the concentration of resources and technology in the already more advanced regions of the country and among the "progressive farmers" who were in a position to adopt them.

The new strategy for agriculture

The new strategy for agriculture was less a strategy than a hope, less a major shift in direction than a modest intensification of resource allocations for agriculture to existing areas and programs, fortified by the promise of the new HYVs to increase production quickly and dramatically. The plan outlay for agriculture was increased somewhat and new programs for particular areas and crops were established. The Intensive Agricultural District Programme (IADP) was maintained and new resources were provided for the districts involved in the program. The main orientation of the HYVs was to the bigger farmers with the knowledge, resources, and local influence to be in a position to adopt the new HYVs and purchase the necessary inputs. These bigger farmers were given the euphemistic label of "progressive farmers" and their "emergence" was heralded as "a notable development in 1966–67"[2] that augured well for the future of the new strategy.

Nor did the new strategy involve any dramatic shifts in the relative share of total resources devoted specifically to programs designed to increase agricultural production. Overall allocations for agriculture, irrigation, and flood control increased only marginally from 20.5 percent of the total Third Plan expenditure to 23.8 and 23.3 percent, respectively, in the Annual Plans from 1966–69 and in the Fourth Plan (see table 8.1). It was hoped that the new HYVs would be so successful that it would not be necessary to alter the broader goals of economic development for India, which continued to emphasize industrial development and power generation.

[2] *Economic Survey of Indian Agriculture, 1966–67*, p. viii.

Policies towards the agricultural sector

The various drives to increase agricultural production in post-Independence India, of which the new strategy was the most important, were carried out within a broader framework of policies towards agriculture and the agricultural sector of the population. Those policies can conveniently be classified under four headings: land reforms and measures to protect specific categories of the rural population; policies relating to the pricing, procurement and distribution of foodgrains and cash crops; policies concerning the selection of particular areas of the country for intensive agricultural development; and policies relating to technology transfer.

Land reforms and special programs for disadvantaged sectors

The principal land reforms in post-independence India were the various measures that eliminated the zamindari system and other types of intermediary rights to the land and the land revenue. Such measures were passed ultimately in all the Indian states, with varying degrees of effectiveness in design and execution.

The second stage of land reform in all the states of India was the passage of land ceilings laws designed to limit the size of landholdings to a relatively small multiple of an economic holding and to redistribute surplus lands in the hands of former landlords among the poorer peasants and the landless. These laws were much less effectively designed and implemented in all states than the laws eliminating intermediaries, which at least ultimately suceeded in their principal purpose.

It has long been apparent to informed observers of the "progress" of land refoms in most of the Indian states that there has been no serious intention to link the issue of agricultural production with that of agrarian reorganization through either land ceilings and land redistribution or through the establishment of cooperative farms. Rather, the state governments in India have been content to establish in the countryside a system of land ownership or land tenure that eliminates revenue intermediaries between the cultivator and the state, that gives title to the actual operator-manager-cultivator of the land, but that also permits extensive sharecropping. The cumulative result of the legislation to abolish intermediaries and to limit the size of landholdings has been to curtail significantly the political and economic control over the land of the former big *zamindars* and *talukdars*, to perpetuate the local political and economic influence of the major elite proprietary castes such as the Brahmans, Rajputs, Jats, and Bhumihars in north India, and to enhance the independence and economic power of the major cultivating castes of middle status, particularly the Ahirs (Yadavs) and Kurmis in north India, the Jats of western U. P., Haryana, and Punjab, the Marathas in Maharashtra, the Kammas and Reddis in Andhra, and the like.

Price, procurement, and distribution policies

If the Indian government's agricultural production programs were designed to leave the prevailing patterns of rural control and dominance in the countryside intact and to avoid precipitating rural class conflict, its price, procurement, and distribution policies were designed to provide incentives to cultivators to increase agricultural production without diverting significant resources from plans for rapid industrialization of the country and without causing prices of foodgrains to rise in the cities that would precipitate urban political protest and urban–rural conflict. The devices used to further these goals were: 1) price support policies that were meant to provide producers sufficient incentives to increase foodgrain production and production of selected crops but that would not push prices so high as to cause inflation; 2) the establishment of a system of ration and fair price shops for public distribution of foodgrains to the poor and lower middle classes, sometimes at below-market prices; 3) procurement policies to acquire grain at fixed prices from both traders and farmers to ensure an adequate supply of food for both the cities and deficit rural areas; 4) a policy of single-state food zones that prohibited the transport and sale of grain across state boundaries in order to contain food deficits to areas where crop failures actually occurred and to prevent price fluctuations from occurring in non-deficit states through the operations of the free market; and 5) import policies that allowed for the purchase under the U.S. Public Law 480 program of vast quantities of foodgrains that served to keep consumer prices down and to supply foodgrains to deficit areas. The import of U.S. foodgrains under the P.L. 480 program relieved the pressure upon government in India to procure sufficient food by its own efforts to feed the population of the country and made it unnecessary to face up to redistributive pressures that might otherwise have mounted.[3]

These policies were internally self-contradictory and often ineffectively implemented. Procurement targets were rarely achieved except in states like Punjab and Haryana, which produced foodgrains far beyond the needs of their populations. The desire to keep consumer prices low conflicted with the desire to ensure adequate prices for producers. Food imports became a substitute for internal procurement efforts and also depressed producer prices.

The occurrence of the Bihar and east U. P. famines in 1966–67 after a previous year of crop failures in other parts of the country and at a time when the supply of food from the U.S. had become politically conditioned[4] threatened to bring the whole structure down. Had U.S. food imports not again saved the day, the state and national governments would have had to face very starkly issues of "inter-regional and inter-personal equity in distribution"[5] that would have placed the severest strains on center–state relations, urban–rural relations, and relations among class and caste groups in the countryside. In these respects, therefore, as in others, the hopes placed on the new strategy and its HYV Program were very great, for the failure of the program would threaten the political stability of the country and the peace of the countryside.

The intensive area approach

Problems of increasing agricultural production have been viewed by Indian policy makers since Independence primarily in aggregate terms and in terms of consumer needs rather than in terms of the needs and goals of the farmers themselves. The peasantry of India have been often looked upon either as obstacles to progress and increased production because of their alleged backwardness, lethargy, or poverty, or as potential instruments for solving the con-

---

[3] For a useful review of these developments, see R. N. Chopra, *Evolution of Food Policy in India* (Delhi: Macmillan, 1981).

[4] See James Bjorkman, "Public Law 480 and the Policies of Self-Help and Short-Tether: Indo-American Relations, 1965–68," in Lloyd I. Rudolph and Susanne H. Rudolph *et al.*, *The Regional Imperative* (Atlantic Highlands, NJ: Humanities Press, 1980), pp. 201–262.

[5] *Congress Bulletin* (January–March, 1966), p. 490.

sumption needs of the country could they only be brought out of their deplorable condition and induced to produce more. A basic distrust of or lack of faith in the capacity of the Indian peasantry as a whole and an orientation toward maximizing production to solve aggregate consumption needs dictated a policy of focusing on those areas of the country where conditions seemed to favor rapid production increases.

The hope that a selective concentration of resources in the agricultural sector would solve India's production–consumption problems was clearly tied into the increased emphasis on allocation of the major new resources for the Second Plan to heavy industry and a consequent reduction in the proportionate allocation of resources for agriculture. The policy was adopted most explicitly in the Third Plan, with its definitive shift toward the goal of rapid industrialization of India and its simultaneous adoption of the Intensive Agricultural District Programme (IADP) "which envisioned concentration of resources and efforts in specially endowed areas to achieve a quick breakthrough in production."[6]

The approach adopted in the Third Plan called for concentration of resources in selected districts, for the identification within those districts of "progressive farmers" best able to adopt intensive methods of agriculture, and for an emphasis on "profitability at the farm level."[7] In other words, the thrust of the program was to create in selected districts in India a profitable sector of commercial agriculture. When the new strategy and the HYVs were adopted in 1966–67, they were grafted on to the IADP and IAAP. Although the HYVP was not confined to the latter districts, the IADP districts were assured of the provision of the necessary inputs to sustain the HYVs, whereas other districts were not.

Technology transfer

Technology transfer was an integral and inseparable part of the new strategy, which was based on the beliefs that new technologies were available from the international crop centers for the two major food

---

[6] Government of India, Ministry of Agriculture and Irrigation, *Report of the National Commission on Agriculture, 1976*, Pt. 1: *Review and Progress* (Delhi: Controller of Publications, 1976), p. 149.

[7] *Report of the National Commission on Agriculture, 1976*, Pt. 1: *Review and Progress*, p. 149.

crops of wheat and rice, that the technologies were transferable to India, and that the institutions and values associated with agricultural development in other parts of the world also were applicable to India. The basic elements in the package of practices, concepts, and institutions that the Government of India eagerly adopted were: 1) the new seeds themselves, which involved the creation of new seed farms around the country, the establishment of a National Seeds Corporation to produce, stock and supply "foundation seeds,"[8] and the founding of the Tarai Seed Development Corporation at the Agricultural University in Pantnagar (U.P.); 2) the acceptance of the necessity for chemicalization of Indian agriculture through the production and use of fertilizers, pesticides, weedicides, and other plant protection chemicals; 3) a commitment to national and international cooperative research to develop new and improve existing seed varieties by establishing new research institutes and enlarging the links of older research institutes in India with CIMMYT (International Maize and Wheat Improvement Centre), IRRI (International Rice Research Institute), and other international crop research agencies; 4) the acceptance of the American concept of developing modern scientific agriculture through the creation of a network of land grant colleges in every state in the country where teaching, research, and extension would be integrated and through which the latest results of scientific research in agriculture could be spread to the farmers in the country.

THE EXTENT AND LIMITS OF THE GREEN REVOLUTION

Since the inauguration of the New Agricultural Strategy, there have been considerable increases in aggregate foodgrain production in India, from 95 million tons in 1967–68 to nearly 130 million tons in 1980–81.[9] However, the World Bank's World Development Report for 1984 shows a trend line for foodgrain production for India as a whole between 1950 and 1983 that moves gradually upward in this period and does *not* indicate a sharp upward movement since

[8] *Report of the National Commission on Agriculture, 1976*, Pt. 1: *Review and Progress*, p. 156.
[9] B. H. Farmer, "Perspectives on the 'Green Revolution' in South Asia," *Modern Asian Studies*, xx, No. 1 (February, 1986), p. 176.

1967–68. The average annual growth rate in foodgrains production in this entire period is 2.7 percent, which compares to an annual average growth rate of 2.1 percent in population in the same period.

Moreover, although the trend line goes gradually upward, it is marked by fluctuations up and down, some of them significantly downward. Finally, cereal yields in India overall remain among the very lowest in the world, averaging 1.34 tons per hectare in 1979–81 compared to 4.77 in Korea and 5.27 in Japan.[10] In short, therfore, in terms of aggregate production increases, the Green Revolution has not altered the basic, slightly upward trend line, it has not eliminated major downward fluctuations produced primarily by severe regional droughts, and it has not altered India's standing as one of the least productive agricultural countries in the world today.

Nevertheless, it would be a mistake to infer from these aggregate figures and trend lines for India as a whole that the Green Revolution has had no significant effect on agricultural production and productivity in India. Regionally, the greatest effect has occurred in the wheat-growing areas of Punjab, Haryana, and western U. P.,[11] but the new dwarf wheats have also increasingly spread down the Gangetic plain as far as Bengal (figure 7). Although the Green Revolution has to some extent brought about increases in rice production as well as wheat production, these effects also have been concentrated regionally, principally to the three southern states, of Andhra, Tamil Nadu, and Kerala, on the one hand, and to Punjab, Haryana, and western U. P. as a winter crop, on the other hand.

Moreover, it remains true that the Green Revolution's most spectacular effects have occurred with wheat production. A comparison of yields for rice and wheat in the post-Green Revolution period, that is, from 1969–70 to 1984–85, brings out the difference. The average yield of rice went up by 34.8 percent in this period, whereas it went up by 64.7 percent for wheat, nearly double the rate of growth in yield for rice (table 9.1). Although wheat production has increased enormously in India as a result, both because of

10 World Bank, *World Development Report 1984* (New York: Oxford University Press, 1984), p. 94.
11 Two-thirds of the wheat production in the country comes from Punjab, Haryana, and U. P. and most of the wheat grown in U. P. comes from the western districts of the state adjacent to Punjab and Haryana; Government of India, Ministry of Agriculture, *Indian Agriculture in Brief* (Delhi: Controller of Publications, 1985), p. 332.

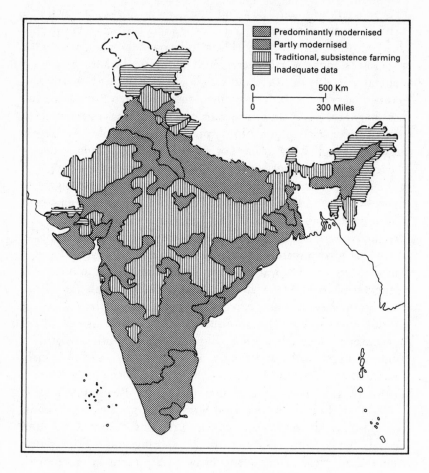

Figure 6   Use of modern techniques to produce rice and wheat under
the high-yielding varieties programe, 1976
Ashok K. Dutt and M. Margaret Geib, *Atlas of South Asia* (Boulder,
CO: Westview Press, 1987).

288

Table 9.1. *Index numbers of agricultural production, area, and yield of principal crops, 1969–70 to 1984–85 (post-Green Revolution), base year 1969–70 = 100*

Crop/Year	Production	Area	Yield
All cereals			
1970–71	114.1	102.0	110.4
1975–76	128.8	104.0	118.8
1980–81	143.1	104.5	129.3
1984–85	161.1	104.0	143.5
Rice			
1970–71	107.4	101.5	105.8
1975–76	124.7	106.7	116.9
1980–81	137.2	108.6	126.3
1984–85	150.0	111.3	134.8
Wheat			
1970–71	132.1	114.9	115.0
1975–76	159.9	128.8	124.1
1980–81	201.1	140.3	143.4
1984–85	244.9	148.7	164.7
Coarse cereals			
1970–71	114.7	98.0	117.2
1975–76	111.8	93.1	118.2
1980–81	106.7	88.8	118.8
1984–85	115.1	83.1	137.0
All pulses			
1970–71	104.4	102.5	102.1
1975–76	115.3	111.2	105.0
1980–81	95.8	103.2	95.6
1984–85	110.2	104.4	107.1
Gram			
1970–71	99.7	101.7	98.0
1975–76	112.9	108.2	104.3
1980–81	83.2	85.6	97.2
1984–85	87.3	89.2	97.9

Source: Government of India, Ministry of Finance, *Economic Survey, 1985–86* (Delhi: Controller of Publications, 1986), pp. 108–110.

increased yields and shifts in sown area from other crops (particularly inferior millets and pulses) to wheat, rice remains the
principal food crop in India in area, production, and consumption,
constituting 23.3 percent of the gross cropped area in 1980–81
compared to half that for wheat (12.8 percent), 31.4 percent of the
total sown area under food crops and 39.4 percent of total foodgrain
production in 1983–84 compared to 18.7 and 29.8 percent,
respectively, for wheat.[12]

The overall results of the Green Revolution, therefore, can be
summarized broadly as follows. There have been only marginal
increases in rice production in contrast to a trebling of wheat
production. Production of most other inferior grains and pulses,
consumed mostly by the poor, has also gone down as wheat
production has increased. The overall per capita availability of food
in India, therefore, has not increased much and continues to
fluctuate very considerably (see table 9.2).

Nevertheless, the Green Revolution, though it does not deserve
the name insofar as India as a whole is concerned, "continues to
increase productivity and production"[13] in various regions in the
subcontinent. Such considerable increases in production, concentrated in particular regions, on particular crops, especially in irri-
gated areas, and in the winter season have, therefore, perpetuated
existing regional imbalances, and created new ones, leading overall
to "increased interregional disparities in agricultural production and
so in prosperity."[14] Moreover, in the less favored areas of the
country, famine conditions are a recurring phenomenon.

The most controversial issues surrounding the Green Revolution
concern its social consequences, that is, whether it has increased,
reduced, or had no effect on social disparities. One radical Marxist
critique of the Green Revolution argues that it has benefited mostly
the big farmers, "rich peasants," *kulaks*, or capitalists. Moreover, so
the argument goes, it has led to an increasing gap between rich and
poor peasants and landless, to "differentiation of the peasantry,"
class polarization, "growing landlessness," and "agrarian revolts".[15]
Most non-Marxist perspectives, however, see greater diffusion

---

[12] Calculated from *Indian Agriculture in Brief*, pp. 44–45, 236.
[13] Farmer, "Perspectives on the 'Green Revolution,'" p. 81.
[14] Farmer, "Perspectives on the 'Green Revolution,'" p. 178.
[15] Farmer, "Perspectives on the 'Green Revolution,'" pp. 187–188.

Table 9.2. *Per capita net availability of cereals and pulses*

Year	Per capita availability per day (in grams)		
	Cereals	Pulses	Total
1956	360.4	70.3	430.7
1961	399.7	69.0	468.7
1962	398.9	62.0	461.9
1963	384.0	59.8	443.8
1964	401.0	51.0	452.0
1965	418.5	61.6	480.1
1966	359.9	48.2	408.1
1967	361.8	39.6	401.4
1968	404.1	56.1	460.2
1969	397.8	47.3	445.1
1970	403.1	51.9	455.0
1971	417.6	51.2	468.8
1972	419.1	47.0	466.1
1973	380.5	41.1	421.6
1974	410.4	40.8	451.2
1975	365.8	39.7	405.5
1976	373.8	50.5	424.3
1977	386.3	43.3	429.6
1978	422.5	45.5	468.0
1979	431.8	44.7	476.5
1980	379.5	30.9	410.4
1981*	416.2	37.5	453.7
1982*	414.8	39.2	455.0
1983*	396.9	39.5	436.4
1984*	436.1	41.8	477.9
1985*	424.4	38.9	463.3

* Provisional.
Source: As for table 9.1, p. 120.

of the gains of the Green Revolution, while recognizing its "differential spread"[16] and while also recognizing that it is not a panacea or a substitute solution for other problems of agrarian order, industrial-agrarian relations, and economic development in India.

[16] Farmer, "Perspectives on the 'Green Revolution,'" p. 189.

In general, it is known that HYVs respond most favorably to good water control, require greater capital inputs for seeds, fertilizer, pesticides, weedicides, are more "labor intensive" also, and do not benefit especially from "economies of scale."[17] Clearly, therefore, bigger farmers are in a better position to take the risks involved in adopting such a technology, especially in the early stages, but it is also accessible to the small and middle peasantry. However, the following qualifications to these general observations need to be made.

The poorest farmers in the least favored rainfed paddy-growing regions simply do not have the resources to purchase and arrange timely supplies of needed inputs. In more favored areas, the small and marginal farmers do benefit from and will adopt technologies that provide substantial increases in yield and profitability with small risks. However, in the rice-growing areas especially, the new technology often offers only marginal improvements that carry high risks. Only the bigger farmers can afford to experiment with and stand to gain from the adoption of such technological changes. These qualifications, however, do not mean that the technology is particularly limited to the rich.[18] It has spread among and benefited "many small farmers,"[19] but not in such a way as to change dramatically their structure of opportunities in life.

Why has the Green Revolution not lived up to its hopes? First, the orientation of the "New Agricultural Strategy," as of the IADP before it, was towards increasing aggregate production in the country as a whole. That orientation, it has already been noted above, led to favoring the already favored areas and relying on the "progressive" farmers. Alternative orientations to solving rural poverty, making small farms viable, and eliminating landlessness were either rejected outright or included as secondary goals. Secondly, the basic capital-intensive industrialization orientation was retained. Agriculture, and especially rice cultivation, continued to be slighted in resource allocations. Third, it was generally believed that the new technology was exogenous and was adequate

[17] Edison Dayal, "Regional Response to High Yield Varieties of Rice in India," *Singapore Journal of Tropical Geography*, IV, No. 2 (1983), 88, 90.
[18] Farmer, "Perspectives on the 'Green Revolution,'" pp. 189–190.
[19] M. Lipton, "The Technology, the System and the Poor: The Case of the New Cereal Varieties," offprint, Hague, Institute of Social Studies, 1977, p. 123.

for the job. It had only to be imposed somehow upon a backward, illiterate, and resistant peasantry. All these assumptions turned out to be wrong or misinformed.

There have been technological factors as well that have limited the spread of the Green Revolution, particularly insofar as rice is concerned. The technological reasons for the failure of a Green Revolution in rice, emulating the authentic one for wheat, are numerous but they all reflect the greater ecological diversity of the rice-growing areas. Therefore, Farmer argues that the search for a single variety or a small number of varieties adaptable "to a wide range of environments" must give way to a search for varieties that are adaptable to local and seasonal variations.[20]

It is not, however, only more research and improved technology that are required but a new set of underlying assumptions, values, and goals. If the Green Revolution is to spread widely in India, values must shift from developing technology to increase the urban food supply as rapidly as possible while maintaining the lowest prices possible for urban consumers to another set of goals which would be oriented towards the needs of the poor and marginal food-producing peasantry. In the latter case, the goals would have to change towards helping the barely viable or nearly viable peasants to develop technologies suited to their local environments, which would enable them regularly to produce enough food to feed themselves and their families and to enter the market as well with a modest surplus or with a crop which provides them with enough cash to obtain the other basic needs of rural life.

The original emphasis on increasing aggregate production in the country as a whole by concentrating resources in favoured areas and providing support to "progressive" farmers was justified by reference to the myth of impending Malthusian catastrophe. Unless food production was increased rapidly and dramatically, starvation loomed for the millions, especially for the poor urban consumers. This myth gained strong support in India especially at the time of the Bihar famine. Like all myths, it contained a partial truth, while ignoring other possibilities and potentials, notably the fact that

[20] B. H. Farmer, "The 'Green Revolution' in South Asian Ricefields: Environment and Production," *Journal of Development Studies*, xv (1979), 317. See also Barrie M. Morrison, "The Persistent Rural Crisis in Asia: A Shift in Conception," *Pacific Affairs*, LII, No. 4 (Winter, 1979–80), 631–646.

agricultural production in India did somehow, even without adequate support and resources, manage to keep somewhat ahead of population increases and that a major diversion of resources to agricultural production activities might move the trend line upward more dramatically. Like all myths also, it hid some harsh realities from public opinion, such as the greater prevalence of rural than urban poverty and the widespread rural malnutrition that would not be solved by policies that focused on aggregate production increases and channeling food supplies to cities and towns.

Among the most serious impediments to the adoption of an agricultural strategy designed to preserve the small farmers and increase their productivity are the implications of such a shift for overall economic development in India and the lack of dramatic results to be anticipated from such a shift. For, a truly agriculture-oriented economic development strategy would require both a reallocation of resources away from urban, industrial development and a willingness to accept a slow, gradual process of change instead of crash programs with dramatic results. It would require an overall policy to promote extensive, continuous, incremental changes designed to preserve the viability of small farmers and promote the viability of marginal farmers.

There is not much evidence, however, to suggest that Indian policy makers are prepared to initiate and sustain such a major shift in priorities. The pressures and prospects for change from the agricultural sector itself, therefore, need to be explored.

THE ABSENCE OF A REVOLUTIONARY TRADITION OR POTENTIAL IN THE INDIAN COUNTRYSIDE

In his work on *Agrarian Radicalism in South India*, Bouton has noted that there is a sharp division of opinion among scholars on the issue of peasant revolt and revolution in South Asia. At one extreme is Barrington Moore, who has argued that peasant revolts in India have been sporadic, ineffective, and, with rare exceptions such as Telangana in 1948, insubstantial. At the other extreme is Kathleen Gough, who has compiled a list of 77 peasant revolts from the end of Moghul rule to the post-Independence period to support her view that there is a vital revolutionary tradition in India and a basis for revolutionary peasant action in the present that has not been properly exploited by contemporary radical parties.[21] Interest in the bases for such action has intensified among both scholars and policy makers in India in recent years out of a concern (or hope) that technological changes in agriculture precipitated by the Green Revolution have intensified social disparities, caused depeasanti-zation/proletarianization and class polarization, and therefore have created a new potential for peasant revolution.

The most significant aspect of Gough's long list is the support it provides for Stokes' argument that the most important peasant revolts have occurred among clan and caste communities.[22] It is especially noteworthy that the very largest proportion of revolts in Gough's list, somewhere between a third and a half, were either exclusively tribal in origin or contained a significant tribal element. Another very large proportion occurred among specific caste groups or religious minorities. Thus, most of the peasant revolts under British rule occurred either among tribals, who are a small minority in the subcontinent as a whole, have suffered from especially severe discrimination and oppression, and are often outside the basic structure of Hindu village agrarian organization, or among ethnic and religious groups whose solidarity could not be explained satisfactorily in class terms alone and did not extend beyond members of their own group.

When we come to the post-Independence period, the case for the existence of a tradition of "peasant uprisings which were primarily class struggles" is based upon seven episodes, all directed by one or another of the several Communist parties in India. Of these, the most famous and important are "the Tebhaga uprising" in north Bengal in 1946, the Telangana insurrection in the former Hyderabad princely state in 1948, "peasant struggles involving land claims and harvest shares in 1966–71" in Andhra, the Naxalbari incidents in a sub-division of Darjeeling district in West Bengal in 1967, and some

[21] Marshall M. Bouton, *Agrarian Radicalism in South Asia* (Princeton, NJ: Princeton University Press, 1985), p. 6, and Kathleen Gough, "Indian Peasant Uprisings," *Bulletin of Concerned Asian Scholars*, VIII, No. 3 (July–September, 1976), 2–18. See also A. R. Desai (ed.), *Peasant Struggles in India* (Delhi: Oxford University Press, 1979) for a comprehensive survey of the major tribal and peasant revolts of the nineteenth and twentieth centuries.

[22] Eric Stokes, *The Peasant and the Raj* (Cambridge: Cambridge University Press, 1978), ch. 12.

other "Naxalite" incidents in small areas in Andhra, Bihar, and elsewhere in India in 1969–70, of which the uprising in Srikakulum district of Andhra was the largest.[23]

Tebhaga

The Tebhaga movement was a movement principally of share-croppers against the *jotedars* or rich peasants in four districts of north Bengal, demanding an increase in their share of the crop from one-half to two-thirds. The Tebhaga movement also drew strong support from tribal groups "who have a long tradition of militant struggle" in this area.[24] Alavi, however, argues that the principal role in this movement was played by middle peasants who also "supplemented their incomes by sharecropping."[25] There was, in addition, a communal element in this movement, though it did not dominate it. The non-tribal peasants were mostly Muslims, the *jotedars* both Hindu and Muslim. The Communist cadres were "mostly Hindu." Although the movement as a whole, therefore, cannot be characterized as a primarily communal uprising, it foundered on the communal issues that led to the creation of Pakistan. Since the peasant rising was in districts most of which went to East Pakistan in 1947, the Hindu Communist organizers left for India "and the movement was virtually decapitated."[26]

Telangana

The most widespread, violent, and long-lived peasant action in India since Independence – it actually began in 1946 – was the famous Telangana movement. In origins, the Telangana movement resembles other less extensive and even non-violent peasant actions that occurred during the nationalist movement and centered around eviction of tenants and "oppressive feudal extortions."[27] It swelled into a widespread, violent insurrectionary movement principally for three reasons. First, the response of the government of the princely

[23] Gough, "Indian Peasant Uprisings," p. 12.
[24] Hamza Alavi, "Peasants and Revolution," in Kathleen Gough and Hari P. Sharma (eds.), *Imperialism and Revolution in South Asia* (New York: Monthly Review Press, 1973), pp. 322–323.
[25] Alavi, "Peasants and Revolution," p. 323.
[26] Alavi, "Peasants and Revolution," p. 325.
[27] Mohan Ram, "The Communist Movement in Andhra," in Paul R. Brass and Marcus Franda (eds.), *Radical Politics in South Asia* (Cambridge, MA: MIT Press, 1973), p. 295.

state of Hyderabad was very harsh and violent. Second, the issue of the peasant movement quickly merged with the broader question of the merger of Hyderabad into the Indian Union and took on both communal and nationalist aspects. Although Muslim peasants also participated in the Telangana movement against the landlords, who in turn were both Hindus and Muslims, the more violent the movement became the more it looked like an action of Muslim armed forces defending the authority of a Muslim ruler and oppressing the rural population, whose vast majority were Hindus. Naturally, therefore, the Telangana movement also drew support from Hindus who favored the destruction of the Hyderabad state and its merger into the Indian Union. A third feature of the Telangana movement was the very fact that the Communists provided the organizational basis for it, which itself was made possible by the abstention of the Indian National Congress from nationalist mobilization in the princely states.

Naxalbari

The most famous incidents of radical agrarian protest in India since Telangana took place in the Naxalbari subdivision of Darjeeling district in West Bengal in 1967.[28] The ingredients which precipitated these incidents comprised the following: the existence of "a tea-plantation economy" with large tea estates, whose owners also controlled extensive paddy lands which were often allowed to lie fallow; a large population of tribal cultivators working on the tea plantations and covetous of these uncultivated lands; a history of tribal uprisings with indigenous leadership; local resentment in the 1960s over the failure to implement land reform legislation; a strong local Communist party organization, factionalized, but containing dedicated local revolutionary cadres. To these ingredients were added in March, 1967, the installation of the first Communist-led government in the state, placed soon after taking office in the uncomfortable position of having to confront a revolt led by members of a splinter group from the CPM itself.

The incidents which precipitated the violence associated with the name of Naxalbari occurred after a decision taken by one of the local

[28] The account here is largely derived from Marcus F. Franda, *Radical Politics in West Bengal* (Cambridge, MA: MIT Press, 1971), pp. 152–168.

Communist party factions to launch agitations against the landlords in possession of large illegal landholdings. Groups of tribal cultivators went round the area confronting the landlords and taking "possession," usually symbolically, of land which was considered to be illegally held. After the killing of a policeman on May 23, 1967, the movement became increasingly violent as the police began to take stronger counter-measures and the movement participants began to threaten terrorist actions after which a number of murders and incidents of arson occurred. The movement ended only after the Communist-led state government decided in July to take decisive action to suppress the revolt with a large police force and to jail its leaders.

Although the movement itself, therefore, was suppressed quickly and failed to achieve significant results, it spawned a new period of revolutionary romanticism in Indian politics in the 1970s. Numerous "Naxalite" incidents occurred, characterized principally by the tactics of terrorist violence against large landholders, in pockets in several areas of the country, notably in Bihar and Andhra. Some larger revolts also occurred which borrowed consciously from the Naxalite experience and sought the advice of the leaders of the original revolt in Naxalbari.

Srikakulam

A second major Naxalite movement, actually more violent and long-lived than the one in Naxalbari itself,[29] occurred in Srikakulam district of Andhra Pradesh in the late 1960s. The movement was centered in the forest areas of Srikakulam among the tribal population known as *girijans*. During British rule, many persons of the tribal population of Srikakulam had progressively lost land to non-tribals, had become indebted to moneylenders and reduced to debt bondage, had become proletarianized, and had become a largely impoverished population among whom "chronic hunger" was endemic.[30] Although the Andhra government passed new legislation after independence to prevent alienation of tribal land to non-tribals and to reduce tribal debt and eliminate debt bondage,

[29] Leslie J. Calman, *Protest in Democratic India: Authority's Response to Challenge* (Boulder, CO: Westview, 1985), p. 19.
[30] Calman, *Protest in Democratic India*, pp. 21–23.

the laws were not implemented. Moreover, other post-Independence legislation to "protect" and develop forest lands led to "the steady loss of tribal access to forest land" and further "harassment and exploitation" of the tribal population "by private contractors, moneylenders, and government officials."[31]

The CPM had been involved in organizing the *girijans* in Srikakulam and neighbouring districts of Andhra since the late 1950s. Incidents of violence between the Communist-led Girijan Sangam workers and the police began in 1968.[32] In late 1968 and early 1969, the local Communist cadres adopted a "Maoist" line and affiliated with the All India Coordination Committee of Communist Revolutionaries, which "converted itself into the Communist Party of India (Marxist-Leninist) (CPML) on 22 April 1969."[33]

During 1969 and 1970, the revolutionaries pursued a line of "annihilation of the class enemy," which "in practice," according to Mohan Ram, "turned out to be nothing more than the murder of landlords through conspiratorial squad actions, unrelated to mass movements or mass struggle."[34] The annihilation movement predictably was met with a massive police response from the Andhra government, whose forces succeeded in suppressing the movement and killing or arresting "all of the frontline leaders of the CPML" by mid-1970.[35]

The Andhra movement, 1969–1971

The fourth post-Independence peasant uprising that has found a place in radical lore in India was the movement led by a Maoist formation, the Andhra Pradesh Revolutionary Coordination Committee (APRCC), among tribal people in three districts of Andhra between 1969 and 1971. The movement began in April, 1969, with forcible occupation by tribals of "government wasteland, forest land, and landlords' farms."[36] Repression "by police and paramilitary forces" followed which, however, precipitated a broader

---

[31] Calman, *Protest in Democratic India*, p. 31.
[32] Ram, "The Communist Movement in Andhra," p. 313.
[33] Ram, "The Communist Movement in Andhra," p. 314.
[34] Ram, "The Communist Movement in Andhra," p. 315.
[35] Ram, "The Communist Movement in Andhra," p. 316.
[36] Mohan Ram, "The Communist Movement in India," in Gough, *Imperialism and Revolution in South Asia*, p. 354.

movement that ultimately required intervention by the Indian Army in March, 1971.

Summary

The following features of the major post-Independence peasant uprisings are especially noteworthy. First, all involved tribal peoples. Second, the two most impressive movements, Tebhaga and Telangana, occurred at the time of Independence and became enmeshed in broader communal and nationalist trends which initially gave added force to them, but ultimately doomed them. Third, all the movements were localized to parts of districts within a single linguistic region. Fourth, Communist cadres took the lead in organizing these movements. Fifth, all the major movements precede the Green Revolution. There has been no major movement anywhere in India since the Green Revolution for which even a *prima facie* case can be made that it arose as a consequence of technological changes in agriculture.

Post-Green Revolution incidents

There have, however, been numerous instances of highly localized confrontations, involving considerable violence and repression, which radical observers have attributed to changes brought about by the Green Revolution. Probably the most famous was the Kilvenmani incident in Thanjavur district in December, 1968, when 43 women and children, families of striking Scheduled Caste farm laborers, were burned alive in their huts. The incident came at the end of "a chain of events" involving strikes for higher wages by local laborers at paddy harvest time, followed by the importation by the local landlords of outside laborers, which in turn precipitated clashes between local and imported laborers and the hiring by the landlords of *goondas* (hooligans) to rough up the laborers and their families. Rather than providing "evidence of a burgeoning revolutionary situation,"[37] the Kilvenmani incident demonstrates the ultimate power of the landlord groups even in a district which has a long history of mass, Communist-led, class action by the rural

[37] Terrence J. Byres, "The Political Economy of Technological Innovation in Indian Agriculture," in Robert S. Anderson *et al.*, *Science, Politics, and the Agricultural Revolution in Asia* (Boulder, CO: Westview Press, 1982), p. 57.

proletariat. Finally, although it occurred in an IADP district, neither the events that preceded it nor the incident itself can be easily used to demonstrate the precipitation of class warfare produced by Green Revolution technological changes. The incident in fact preceded the Green Revolution proper, which only came to Thanjavur in the years after 1968.

The strongest evidence against the argument that the Green Revolution has had a radicalizing effect is the relative absence of major peasant movements in the one area in India where there is no dispute that a Green Revolution has taken place that has altered significantly the older agrarian structure, namely, Punjab and Haryana. Indeed, in his review of the consequences for peasant and laborer class action in Punjab and Haryana up to 1977, Byres could find only one major incident of class confrontation between rich peasants and laborers in a single village in Ludhiana.[38]

In contrast to the situation in Punjab and Haryana, reports from Bihar, one of the regions in India least affected by the Green Revolution, have indicated a considerable increase in rural class confrontations and repressive violence by landlords and other dominant land controlling castes. Most of the violent incidents that have occurred in Bihar and the non-violent movements as well have special features that do not suggest either the beginnings of a broad revolutionary situation or a close connection with technological changes in agriculture.

In the late 1960s and early 1970s, there was a series of violent actions led by Naxalites as well as some non-violent movements among the peasantry in several places in Bihar. The Naxalite revolutionary activites were limited to a few pockets in scattered

[38] Byres, "The Political Economy of Technological Innovation," p. 53. There is an argument that the Punjab movement of the 1980s, including the rise of Bhindranwale, is itself to be attributed to the inequalities produced by the Green Revolution, and particularly the dissatisfaction of "the ones left behind by it"; Iqbal Singh, *Punjab under Siege: A Critical Analysis* (New York: Allen, McMillan and Enderson, 1986), p. 130 and ch. 6. See also Sucha Singh Gill and K. C. Singhal, "The Punjab Problem: Its Historical Roots," *EPW*, xix, No. 14 (7 April, 1984), pp. 603–608, and Prakash Tandon, "Another Angle," *Seminar*, 294 (February, 1984), pp. 35–37 for analyses that include aspects of the Green Revolution in broader socio-economic explanations. My own view is that such explanations are at best remote causes for a movement which is better understood in terms of political and sectarian conflicts, as indicated above, ch. 6, and in Paul R. Brass, "The Punjab Crisis and the Unity of India," in Atul Kohli (ed.), *India's Democracy: An Analysis of Changing State–Society Relations* (Princeton, NJ: Princeton University Press, 1988).

areas of the state and to isolated acts of terrorism in a number of places. Nor do the major incidents themselves provide support either for the view that there is a latent revolutionary movement in the Bihar countryside or that the incidents were a response to technological changes in agriculture. Rather, the following features seem more prominent in them: 1) heavy involvement of tribal populations; 2) situations of dispossession or other kinds of exploitation of peasants, sharecroppers, and laborers by large land-lords and commercial farmers from outside the local area holding massive illegal farms; 3) location of several incidents in border and forest areas outside the centers of traditional, settled village agri-culture; 4) a strong connection with unimplemented land reforms or outright violations of land reforms laws.

There is one apparent exception to this pattern in Bihar. Throughout the 1970s up to the present, Bhojpur district, located in the most agriculturally advanced region of Bihar, served since the late nineteenth century by the Son Canal system and by the IADP and HYVP since the Green Revolution, has been a recurrent scene of agrarian violence. There is some evidence that agarian violence in this district has been connected to attempts by landowners to increase their gains from the Green Revolution through reneging on or reducing traditional payments to attached laborers in the form of land and grain and through labor-displacing tractorization.

Like Thanjavur, Bhojpur has had a long history of agrarian struggles, going back to the Mutiny. A second feature in common with Thanjavur district is the simultaneous existence of both a relatively high degree of concentration of landownership among rich peasants and former landlords with a high proportion of landless laborers in the total workforce.

Mobilization of the poor and landless was launched after 1967 by outside Naxalite elements working with local Scheduled Caste leaders. As in Thanjavur, landlords and the local police hit back and beat and murdered Scheduled Caste and backward caste laborers in several villages. However, whereas laborers in Thanjavur, despite the Kilvenmani incident, have had powerful support from Com-munist party organizers and have benefited from ameliorative reforms introduced by the Tamil Nadu state government, it is the landlords who have emerged more powerfully in Bhojpur. With the complicity of the Congress state government and the local police, the local landlords are now generally armed, well organized, and ready to let loose their "musclemen" upon landless laborers who cause trouble in any part of the district.

Insofar as the question of the relationship between technological change in agriculture and agrarian unrest is concerned, there are two principal similarities between Bhojpur and Thanjavur. First, Bhojpur district, when it was part of the district of Shahabad, was close to the top in growth rates of agricultural productivity between 1963–64 and 1971–72,[39] that is, in the years just before and just after the Green Revolution, which suggests an association between post-Green Revolution changes in Bhojpur and recent agrarian tensions. Second, however, the current phase of unrest began with the Naxalites in 1967 *before* any significant Green Revolution changes occurred in Bhojpur.

Conclusion

The above review of major peasant movements in India since Independence suggests the following general conclusions concerning their extent, the conditions for their occurrence, and the reasons why they have not been more common, more sustained, and more widespread.

1. There has been no peasant revolt in India since 1948 that has been as prolonged and widespread as the one in Telangana. The Telangana revolt itself was regionally confined.

2. There have been only two periods of sustained revolutionary activity in India since Independence. The first was the time of Independence itself when there were two major movements in progress in different parts of the country at approximately the same time: Tebhaga in Bengal and Telengana in Andhra.[40] The second was the post-Naxalbari period from 1967 to the early 1970s when a

---

[39] Calculated from Government of India, Ministry of Agriculture, Directorate of Economics and Statistics, *Bulletin on Rice Statistics in India (District-Wise)* (Delhi: Controller of Publications, 1974).

[40] A third movement, in part of the former princely state of Travancore, also was in progress at this time, in which urban and rural wage demands were merged with a movement led by the CPI to thwart efforts of the prince to establish Travancore as an independent state; see Sumit Sarkar, *Modern India: 1885–1947* (Madras: Macmillan, 1983), pp. 441–442.

number of separate movements and incidents occurred in different parts of the country, notably in Naxalbari itself, in Srikakulam, in other Andhra districts, and in pockets in Bihar.

3. The existence of an organized Communist movement in a locality has been one of the more important factors in sustaining peasant and tribal uprisings. The uneven distribution of the organizational strength of the Communist and other radical parties in India is, therefore, another factor, along with their internal divisions on strategy and tactics, that have limited the extent of the peasant movements that have been guided by them.

4. However, it is clear that an even more significant limitation on peasant rebellions in India has been the fact that the predominant leaderships of both leading Communist parties in most of the post-Independence period have been reformist, oriented to parliamentary and electoral politics rather than towards revolutionary action.

5. It is evident that the majority of the cases of peasant unrest since Independence – and a very large proportion of all instances of such unrest in modern Indian history – have either been nearly exclusively tribal-based or have "involved a large component of tribal people."[41] It is clear why tribals are so prone to revolt. They are among the most unfairly treated groups in India. They have suffered loss of land, loss of access to forest resources, and increasing indebtedness leading to debt bondage. The miseries they have suffered affect most members of their groups. The tribal groups themselves are in any case more internally cohesive and less internally differentiated than village societies in predominantly Hindu India. Most important, their victimizers are invariably aliens, usually Hindus originally from the plains. Finally, the tribals find no recourse from government, which adds to their frustrations by passing laws to aid them that are not implemented. Indeed, government officers at the local level tend rather to be seen and to behave as their oppressors, harassing them, extracting corrupt income from them, and cooperating and socializing with their exploiters, the landlords and moneylenders to whom they are indebted.

6. Aside from predominantly tribal revolts, the other principal source of violent agrarian unrest is the discontent of landless

[41] Gough, "Indian Peasant Uprisings," p. 12.

laborers in some areas of India. However, such discontent has led to revolts or violent confrontations only under special circumstances.

7. The power of the Indian state and its armed police forces also needs to be noted. Even if the basis existed for the spread of violent agrarian movements from one district to another in India, it would not be permitted by the authorities, who have never hesitated to meet local violent uprisings with overwhelming force. There is no "vacuum of power"[42] in the Indian countryside such as existed in China in the 1930s and 1940s or in Vietnam with the withdrawal of French colonial administration.

8. It is clear that agrarian unrest in India is very much the exception rather than the norm and that it is the extraordinary stability of agrarian society in the face of caste divisions, considerable inequalities, and pervasive poverty that requires explanation.

CASTE AND CLASS IN THE INDIAN COUNTRYSIDE

Since Independence, debate has raged, particularly among Marxist economists, concerning whether or not there is now a fairly uniform hegemonic class of rich farmers who are the new "lords of the land" virtually everywhere in India.

The rise of this new class has been associated particularly with three sets of events. The first is the land reforms adopted in nearly all parts of the country, which abolished the tax-farming system, but did not involve effective land ceilings with land redistribution, thus enhancing the position of the groups with land below the big ex-landlords. The second set of events were various government policies adopted by the state governments, which themselves came to be largely controlled by persons from the dominant peasant castes, such as price supports, easy credit, and subsidized inputs of all sorts, which favored the peasantry. The third was the technological changes associated with the Green Revolution which, it is argued, benefited principally the members of this new class and increased substantially the profitability of their farm operations.

This new class of rich farmers is generally characterized not only as capitalist, but as a politically dominant class as well. Its dominance is evidenced and expressed in numerous forms: through its

[42] Calman, *Protest in Democratic India*, p. 10.

control of local institutions of government and administration, such as the district boards, the *panchayats*, the cane unions or cooperatives, the managing boards of educational institutions, and the like, all of which assure its members of continued preferential access to economic resources and to education; through its organization into caste *senas* or armies which suppress or repress any signs of revolt or even unwillingness on the part of laborers to work at the desired low wages for the *kisans* (peasant cultivators) and *maliks* (owners); through its brutality in such notorious places as Kilvenmani in Tamil Nadu and several places in Bihar, where rebellious or recalcitrant laborers and their families were murdered by irate and vengeful land owners; and through their continued control of most state governments in India.

This widespread attempt to identify a universal hegemonic rural capitalist, exploiting class in India, which has become virtually an accepted orthodoxy among both Indian and foreign political economists, suffers from several deficiences. These include oversimplification, elevation of the exceptional to the general, and a distorted view of the benefits which the peasants are said to receive from their alleged partial control of the Indian state.

Oversimplification occurs in the identification of the rich farmer or *kulak* class itself. While there are certainly many big peasants in India now who fit the description of capitalist farmer, if not *kulak*, most peasants from the dominant castes are not for the most part either labor-exploiting or capitalist in the sense of treating their land and its produce *primarily* as commodities for exchange and investment. Most continue to depend on family and animal power for the bulk of their labor requirements and operate farms whose produce satisfies both considerable subsistence requirements as well as being sold in the market. Only a minority have sufficient landholdings in relation to the number of dependents who must be fed from the produce of their lands to enable them to orient their production primarily for sale in the market.

Elevation of the exceptional to the general includes extending the range of the Green Revolution and its consequences far beyond the limited regions, crops, and groups in the country who have benefited from it to the country as a whole, which allows one to argue that there is a rural hegemonic capitalist class all over the country which has benefited from it. While the Green Revolution has led to the development of programs, such as input subsidies, which apply throughout the country and benefit the larger farmers everywhere, their impact is much more substantial in the Green Revolution areas proper. Moreover, in those areas where the Green Revolution has had *less* effect, the consequences of the extension of benefits such as input subsidies, are more likely to divide the landed castes in struggles for differential access to these benefits than to create a rural hegemonic class united against the lower clases.

Finally, the benefits which peasants have received from the Indian state are exaggerated. As large-scale irrigation projects and other development benefits in the countryside became available, as the Green Revolution in some parts of the country made agricultural operations more profitable, and as the state extended credit and subsidies to the farmers, planners and urban intellectuals in New Delhi argued that the landowning cultivators, especially the rich peasants, were gaining vast benefits for which they paid virtually nothing in taxes. These observers chose to ignore the facts that most inputs remained scarce, that the supplies of water, electricity, credit, diesel, and fertilizers were highly irregular, and that the peasants generally had to pay bribes to the operators of canals and tubewells, to the bankers for credit, and to the officers for every service provided by government, all of which constitute a very considerable financial burden on the farmers. The advantages to the peasantry even of institutional credit as opposed to resort to traditional moneylenders also may be exaggerated.[43]

What then are the realities of caste, class, and power in the Indian countryside? The first is that there are, indeed, sets of landed castes in every region of India who control most of the land and other economic resources and who are also politically powerful. The

[43] See, for example, the argument of Subrata Ghatak in *Rural Money Markets in India* (Delhi: Macmillan, 1976), p. 102, that interest rates charged by moneylenders are not as high as has commonly been assumed. When one weighs the ease of getting loans from the moneylender against the difficulties of gaining access to institutional credit, the difference between the effective rate of interest charged by the moneylenders, on the one hand, and the banks and cooperatives, on the other, appears less significant. As with most government policies for agriculture, the rich farmers get around these difficulties more easily than the ordinary peasants, but both are too often lumped by critics of the Green Revolution and its consequences as "rich peasants" benefiting from easy credit at low interest rates.

POLITICAL ECONOMY

second is that these caste groups constitute politically solidary groups in relation to other castes, whether of elite, lower, or untouchable status. The third is that where there is a diversity of land-controlling castes, these relatively solidary caste groups are in strong competition with each other for favored access to scarce resources and political power. The fourth is that the landless and wage laborers at the bottom of the caste Hindu hierarchy are relatively powerless. The untouchable castes who form the largest numbers of the landless laborers live in separated hamlets where they and their families are vulnerable to attack by the landed caste men and their *goondas*.

In routine politics, the low castes who form the bulk of the landless are coopted by the factional and party leaders of the dominant castes in village, district, and state politics. When they attempt to mobilize for political agitations for higher wages against the landed castes, however, they generally meet strong resistance and their movements usually fail, except in states such as Kerala and West Bengal at times when the ruling Communist parties there support their demands. Since low caste movements tend to be local, it is usually sufficient for the members of one of the dominant castes immediately threatened by such movements to take action against the low castes without seeking any broader unity.

One strong element in the Marxist argument is that the various forces of change that have been in operation in India since Independence, particularly land reforms which benefited the so-called *kulaks* and the Green Revolution, have created class contradictions in the form of increasing inequalities between the rich farmers and the poorest, "depeasantization" and proletarianization of the marginal farmers, fundamental conflicts of interest between them and the rich farmers, and enhanced class consciousness on both sides tending towards class polarization which is preparing the ground for a major class struggle over land.[44] In fact, this scenario is far-fetched. The conflicts are greatest not in the Green Revolution areas, but in the more backward areas and the struggles are over wages not over land.

Since there is no real class struggle over land in the Indian countryside, therefore, there is no need for the landed castes to form

[44] Byres, "The Political Economy of Technological Innovation," pp. 39–46.

a united front, to become a class-for-itself. The dominant castes constitute collectively a class-in-itself, whose components agree upon what is best for the land-controlling communities and who can be mobilized by political movements to make demands for better prices, more subsidies, and cheaper inputs, but they are not mobilized for class action against the landless and the poor.

It is here that one must make the sharpest departure from the Marxist perspective, for the landless and the poor are pawns both in the power struggles of the landed castes and in the intellectual exercises of the Marxist elites. Rather than seeing the bulk of the land-controlling castes as themselves in need of support through an agriculture-oriented plan with an emphasis on research, extension, and improved technology, they are all portrayed as *kulaks* or dominated by *kulaks* repressing and brutalizing the poor and landless below them. The lumping together of all the landed castes in India into a united body under the hegemony of its leading segments, the so-called *kulak*, reflects a deep anti-peasant bias rather than the realities of the Indian countryside.

In most states, particularly in north India, the Congress has adopted the political strategy of aligning with the big farmers, the elite proprietary castes, and the poor, squeezing the bulk of the peasantry in the middle and denying them access to party nominations and local positions of power. The Communist parties – unlike many Marxist theoreticians – recognizing in fact the absence of class polarization in the countryside and the dangers of antagonizing the bulk of the peasantry, have attempted to counter the Congress strategy by mobilizing the poor and the middle segments of the peasantry together in pursuit of reformist goals of ameliorating the living conditions and wages of the landless and gaining secure rights for tenants and sharecroppers, without attacking fundamentally the control of the landed castes over their land. In practice, the Communist parties seek the support even of the bigger peasants.

Thus, the existence of similar structures of local power in most parts of India, based upon the predominance of the traditional land-controlling castes of elite and middle status, has consequences quite different from those that might be expected to flow from the Marxist notions of rich peasant hegemony and class polarization.

On the contrary, one consequence has been the organization of political conflicts primarily along the lines of competition *among* land-controlling castes more than between the latter and the poor and landless. Second, political organization of the poor against the landed castes is, therefore, a risky enterprise even for the radical left parties because no stable power base can be built upon the poor and landless. Finally, it follows also that fundamental change in the agrarian order is not likely to come in the form of mass revolutionary action from below.

CHAPTER 10

CONCLUSION: PROBLEMS AND PROSPECTS

THE PROBLEM OF THE PERSISTENCE OF THE PRESENT PARLIAMENTARY SYSTEM

India is virtually unique among contemporary post-colonial countries in having functioned since Independence, with the exception of the Emergency, with a parliamentary system modeled on the British form of government. India's parliamentary system has evolved from one in which the Cabinet and the Prime Minister were dominant and the President was a figurehead – though potentially important – into a form of prime ministerial government, in which both the Parliament and the Cabinet play a secondary role. The specific role of each Prime Minister and the relationship between the Prime Minister and other central government institutions and forces has varied somewhat, but one can also see an evolution over the past forty years. Nehru's period was one of prime ministerial government in which the Cabinet played an important role as well and Parliament was a place where opinions were expressed but little real power was exercised. Under Shastri, the influence of the Cabinet declined and that of the Prime Minister's Secretariat increased, a trend which continued under Mrs. Gandhi. However, there was a further shift under Mrs. Gandhi's leadership away from reliance upon any of the formal channels of authority in the system to dependency upon a narrow clique of personal advisers accountable only to the Prime Minister herself. Rajiv Gandhi continued his mother's pattern so that, in effect, prime ministerial government moved a further step towards a form of personal authority in which succession was dynastic and rulership was conducted with the counsel of a virtual princely court, and in which both Cabinet and senior bureaucrats were reduced in importance. During the Janata period, an entirely different pattern, based on a form of coalition politics, developed in which the Prime Minister was only *primus inter pares* in a divided government, which ultimately fell in a Parliament that came to

311

reflect the divisions within the Cabinet and for a brief period exercised indirectly its ultimate power of granting or withholding confidence in the government of the day.

Behind the adopted form of British prime ministerial government, therefore, there lie two indigenous adaptations: the predominant patrimonial system of the Nehru family and the politics of personal ambition, personal conflict, and political opportunism of the Janata coalition. Each of these indigenous adaptations is inherently unstable for the one depends upon the fate of a family and on the fragilities of personal leadership in general, while the second offers the prospect of the disintegration of any central authority in the system.

India's federal parliamentary system also presents some peculiarities and adaptations of a well-known form of government. Although politics in India are more regionalized than in any other federal polity in the world, reflecting the unrivaled cultural diversity of the country, the system has more unitary features than most federal systems including especially that of the United States. Residuary powers in the system rest with the Center, not with the states and the people. Virtually unique to India's federal system, moreover, has been the institution of President's Rule which allows the Center, either with or without the simultaneous exercise of constitutionally sanctioned emergency powers, to impose a unitary form of government upon a single state, a number of states, or the entire country.

Structurally, as in most federal systems, the institutions of the central government have been replicated in each state, with the governor playing the role of head of state and the chief minister the head of government, with a cabinet responsible to a popularly elected legislative assembly. In practice, however, state politics and government have functioned entirely differently from the Center and have evolved in different directions. The governors have become pliable instruments of central intervention in state politics, the state legislatures have been generally fragmented, unstable, and so opportunistically motivated that few governments can stay in power if a state legislature is allowed to remain in session for more than a few weeks. Consequently, once a chief minister has been appointed, he sees to it for the sake of maintaining himself in power that the legislature meets as infrequently as possible. Much, often most, state legislation is in fact passed by ordinance rather than by the state legislative assemblies.

Though their positions are often unstable, the post of chief minister or any ministerial position in a state government is highly coveted, partly for conventional reasons of prestige and power, but increasingly because of the opportunities provided for the distribution of patronage and the acquisition of corrupt income. It is hardly surprising, therefore, that the performance of state governments, though it varies from state to state and from time to time within each state, has generally been poor.

In the Nehru period, there were some states which developed a sort of chief ministerial form of government comparable to the prime ministerial pattern at the Center, while other states developed more in the direction of an unstable factional and coalition politics of personal ambition, patronage, and corruption. During Mrs. Gandhi's period, most of the states in which the Congress ruled lost their autonomy and came directly under the control of the central leadership even without the use of President's Rule. However, underlying the overall pattern of Congress dominance in the states and increasing central control over the state governments was an alternative type of politics, involving the assertion of regional political and social forces and identities. Those tendencies have become increasingly powerful during the past decade. Where the central government has become directly involved in an effort to maintain Congress control and prevent the regionalization of politics, there has been instability and violence, most notably in the Punjab, in Assam, and at times in Kashmir. Where it has allowed or been unable to prevent the assertion of regional political forces and identities, the Congress has been displaced as the ruling party, as in West Bengal and Kerala by the CPM, in Tamil Nadu by the AIADMK and the DMK, in Andhra by the Telugu Desam, in Karnataka by the Janata party, among other cases.

While the struggles for power at the Center and between regionalizing and centralizing forces have produced singular adaptations of both parliamentarism and federalism in India, they have also created tensions that have from time to time aroused a desire among some of the participants to change the system to ensure continuity and authority at the Center and the primacy of the central government in relation to the states. Indeed, a general feeling has developed during the past two decades that the present system of parliamentary government is not working well. The apparent stability of leadership in the Nehru family at the head of the system has not prevented a widespread loss of authority in the country, manifested in its most extreme forms in increased disorder and violence in the countryside and new secessionist threats in the Punjab and in the northeastern region of the country. Widespread corruption has undermined the legitimacy of all institutions, including the legislatures, whose members are often bought and sold in struggles for the votes necessary to sustain or bring down a government, the cabinets, whose ministers use their positions to aggrandize themselves, and the bureaucracy, whose members enrich themselves at the cost of the public and the health of the economy.

Although India has made considerable progress in economic development, particularly in the indigenous production of goods and services that were completely lacking at Independence, there is also a perception among many leaders of the country that the pace of economic development has been too slow to satisfy their desires for the rapid emergence of India as a modern, industrialized military power. Many leaders in politics, in the universities, and in business also feel that the pace of socio-economic change has been too slow, that India remains too agrarian, its population too illiterate, its social customs too backward. All these tendencies and ideas have converged in a current of opinion which favors the adoption of a new form of government of a presidential type which would enhance still further the authority of the central leaders and the Union government to restore order in troubled areas of the country, to eliminate corruption, and to increase the pace of economic and social change.

The presidential system most widely favored is not the American type, but the French system as it functioned in the Gaullist period, with its strong executive and unitary pattern of government. Although members of Mrs. Gandhi's government from time to time attempted to precipitate some public discussion of a shift towards a presidential regime – notably during the Emergency and again in 1984 – no sustained discussion of such an alternative has as yet taken place nor has a broad consensus developed in the country. The very problems which have produced a desire for stronger central authority have also produced a counter-tendency in the form of demands for greater regional autonomy from several states and in somewhat more feeble, but recurrent proposals from politicians who continue to draw inspiration from the Gandhian tradition for greater decentralization of institutions in India down to the district and village level as well. In these recurring debates concerning the desirability of retaining or modifying the parliamentary system, there is a tacit recognition of the persistence of some structural problems in governing the country, in maintaining its unity, and in averting a descent into anomie, violence, and disintegration.

THE PROBLEM OF ESTABLISHING A STABLE STRUCTURE OF NATIONAL POWER: PARTIES, POLITICS AND ELECTIONS

The Congress was the dominant, ruling party at the Center from Independence until 1977. However, its dominance was always somewhat deceptive, less secure than it often appeared. Even during the Nehru period, the Congress faced persistent problems in maintaining its dominance in and control over the several states. Moreover, in 1969, the Congress itself split nationwide, leading to speculation and fear on the part of its leaders that its power at the Center would soon be lost as well. Although Mrs. Gandhi succeeded on the face of things in reestablishing the overwhelming dominance of the Congress in the country and in virtually all the states by 1972, she knew very well that that dominance was not secure in the states and that Congress power at the Center was always threatened by the potential disintegration of the party in important states in the Union.

Within two years of her overwhelming victories in 1971–72 in the parliamentary and legislative assembly elections, Mrs. Gandhi was confronted with widespread mass demonstrations against her party leaders in the states of Gujarat and Bihar, which caused her and other Congress leaders to fear loss of power in the country as a whole. When her own election was overturned by the judgment of the Allahabad High Court in 1975, Mrs. Gandhi was faced with the imminent prospect of loss of power, which she met with the imposition of the Emergency regime in 1975. Although the imposition of the Emergency preserved her in power temporarily, the public reaction to various excesses committed by her government caused an unprecedented revulsion against Congress rule in north India that brought the Congress down and out of power in Delhi for the first time since Independence.

The Janata party, which displaced the Congress from power in 1977, itself proved unable to govern effectively and its disintegration in 1979 prepared the way for the return of Mrs. Gandhi and the Congress to power in the 1980 elections. By 1984, an accumulation of discontents with the ruling party, particularly focusing on the events in the Punjab, once again had threatened the power of the Congress to such an extent that Mrs. Gandhi delayed until virtually the eleventh hour the calling of the parliamentary elections, which she had not yet done when she was herself assassinated in November, 1984. The assassination and the Punjab crisis now converged in a new way to build support behind the new leader, Rajiv Gandhi, and the Congress won an unprecedented 80 percent majority in the parliamentary elections held in December, 1984.

Rajiv Gandhi's victory notwithstanding, it is now evident that the political system has become more competitive at the national level with the central leadership of the Congress aware that power can be lost at the Center under certain conditions. Those conditions include the disintegration of the Congress and the rise of opposition forces within particular states, the occurrence of an incident or incidents that arouse widespread discontent in north India, such as the sterilization campaign during the Emergency and the Punjab crisis in the early 1980s, and the development of unity among the important non-Congress parties.

Congress dominance has always been less secure in the states than at the Center, though the Congress under Nehru succeeded – after some intitial problems in a few states – after Independence in establishing its preeminence in every state in the Union except Kerala until 1967. Between 1967 and 1972, however, when the Congress lost power in half the Indian states, a period of instability and coalition politics ensued in many states. Moreover, the Congress never regained ground lost during that period in some states such as West Bengal and Tamil Nadu. The delinking by Mrs. Gandhi of parliamentary and state legislative assembly elections in

1971 was designed both to free her from dependence on state party bosses for success in the parliamentary elections and to separate the parliamentary elections in general from the unstable conditions prevailing in many states. With the success of that strategy in 1971, the further pattern was developed of holding state assembly elections after the parliamentary elections to reinforce and stabilize a victory at the Center.

The new pattern introduced initially by Mrs. Gandhi has had three major results. The first was the destruction of the power of state party bosses in the Congress and the increased dependence of the Congress in the states upon the central leadership of the party and its ability to win national elections. The second has been the isolation of regional political forces within the states, in some cases including specific alliances between the Congress and a regional party such as the AIADMK in which the Congress agrees to give up power in the state for the sake of the regional party's support in the parliamentary elections. The third consequence has been a general nationalization of politics and political issues with a corresponding increased focus on power at the Center.

Since the delinking of parliamentary and legislative assembly elections in 1971, a new cycle of consolidation and disintegration of national power has come into being, which reproduces itself in a series of five steps. Each cycle begins with the call for parliamentary elections either by the ruling party or, as in 1979, as a consequence of the disintegration of the governing coalition. So far, every parliamentary election since 1971 has led to a decisive result in favor of one party or another, that is, in favor either of the Congress or the Janata coalition in 1977. If the Congress wins, it is clear who will be the new Prime Minister, for the party has gone to the country in each election with no doubts about its leadership. In the Janata case, however, the electoral victory was followed by a factional struggle over the selection of the Prime Minister. The installation of a Prime Minister by either of these methods concludes the second stage of the cycle. The new Prime Minister then introduces the third step, which is the dismissal of most state governments controlled by the opposition and the holding of fresh state legislative assembly elections, which invariably lead to the victory of the ruling party or its allies in the several states. Step four involves the selection, with or

317

without some struggle, of the chief ministers of the states in which elections have just been held. At this very point, when power is consolidated in Delhi and in nearly all the states, the fifth step in the cycle occurs, namely, the beginning of a new cycle as a consequence of the disintegration of power in state after state either through factionalism in the Congress or through inter-party struggles in the non-Congress coalitions.

Herein lies the great political dilemma at the heart of Indian politics, which has often caused national political leaders to long for the stability of a presidential system with fixed terms in office in a more centralized state. That dilemma is simply that it is impossible in such a diverse country within the framework of a federal parliamentary system to maintain a stable structure of national power for long. It is an extremely difficult, prolonged, and absorbing task to build national power in the country and it begins to disintegrate at the very point when it appears to have been consolidated. The task is so absorbing that, even with the best will in the world, it is impossible for the national leaders to focus their attentions on the goals of economic development and the fulfillment of the basic needs of the people. Indeed, those goals themselves must be subordinated to the imperative need of maintaining the power so laboriously constructed.

At this fifth stage, therefore, the central leadership of the country faces an agonizing choice: either permit the disintegration of the power so painstakingly built up and face the possible loss of power in the next elections or even earlier, or impose an Emergency regime or use President's Rule and other extreme constitutional but politically ruthless measures to remain in power. At this point also, the third alternative must enter the minds of the leaders, namely, to try to change the system altogether to a presidential type. Thus, authoritarian solutions or alternative regimes as a possible resolution to the central political dilemma of Indian politics remain always lurking in the background and make it impossible to say, even 40 years after Independence, that a stable parliamentary regime of the Westminster type has been established in India.

This dilemma at the heart of Indian politics, surrounding the problems of building and maintaining a stable structure of national power, had to be faced by both Nehru and his successors, though they handled it differently. Under Nehru's leadership, the Government of India adopted a system of centralized economic planning which required centralized decision-making and uniform national policies for optimal implementation. Nehru, however, was unwilling or unable to impose a centralized system of political control and preferred instead to attempt to bring along with him the powerful but independent-minded chief ministers who, he hoped, would support his policies for economic development if he supported them politically, or left them alone in their home states.

Under Mrs. Gandhi's leadership, quite in contrast, the struggle for political power at the Center became primary and centralized economic development planning, increasingly subordinated to political goals, has been disintegrating.[1] Plans and schemes such as the anti-poverty programs, however noble their intentions, have been integrated more into designs for centralized political control than into a design for a new national economic order.

THE PROBLEM OF MAINTAINING THE UNITY OF THE COUNTRY

Among the strongest reasons for the predominant consensus among the top leaders of the country in favor of a strong centralized state has been not only the fear of losing power in Delhi but of the disintegration of all authority in Delhi and, therefore, of the unity of the country itself. Although a sense of the fragility of Indian unity has always been present among Indian political leaders in modern times, it was strongly reinforced by the bitter experience of partition of the country in 1947. For that reason, the national leaders have always moved cautiously and reluctantly in handling regional, linguistic, communal, and other ethnic conflicts which have developed in the post-Independence period.

Since Independence, the central leadership has, nevertheless, confronted several major challenges to the unity of the country with skill and success. These have included the integration of some 562 semi-autonomous princely states into the Indian Union in the years immediately after Independence, the linguistic reorganization of

[1] The formulation of the argument in the previous two paragraphs was stimulated by the comments of an anonymous reader.

319

states, the resolution of the official language controversy, and the granting of partial official status in many states to minority languages, including Urdu among others. The resolution of most of these conflicts by the Center has been pluralist in form. Most of the major languages of India now have a federal unit – or units in the case of Hindi – in which their language is dominant and is the official language of the state or states. Bilingualism has become entrenched at the Center, with some multilingual features in some respects as well.

On the other hand, none of the resolutions has resolved all relevant problems. The integration of the princely states left Kashmir divided and three wars with Pakistan have been fought in which the unresolved international status of Kashmir figured. Within the linguistically reorganized states, minorities and minority language speakers sometimes experience varying degrees of discrimination. Demands for greater regional autonomy, at times bordering on secessionism, have emerged from time to time in many states. Hindu–Muslim relations have remained tense and suspicion-ridden since Independence. Communal riots have been persistent, especially in north India, and have become an institutionalized feature in some towns in the north. In recent years, there has been an increasing polarization of communal hostilities and feelings and a great deepening of distrust between members of the two communities.

Migrant problems also have intensified and added a new dimension to ethnic hostilities in some parts of the country, particularly in major cities such as Bombay and in several regions of the country where migrants have taken jobs desired by local residents. The problems in Assam have been the most serious in this regard, where migrants from neighboring states and from Bangladesh have come in large numbers and threatened both the dominance of the Assamese people in the region they consider their own and the displacement of tribal peoples from their land. Agitations and violent incidents were widespread in the 1980s on these issues, although the demands of Assamese leaders for the removal of large numbers of foreign migrants from the electoral rolls were partly conceded by Rajiv Gandhi's government in an accord with the Asom Gana Parishad, which restored peace and parliamentary politics to that state in 1985.

The most bitter, violent and prolonged unresolved struggle facing the government of Indian in 1989, however, was the Punjab crisis. In 1989, the accord between Rajiv Gandhi and the Akali Dal, reached in August, 1985, had not been implemented. A moderate Akali Dal government, which won the September, 1985, elections in that state and was supported in power by the Congress until May, 1987, was removed by the central government, which placed the state under President's Rule and strengthened further the army and paramilitary forces. The persistence of terrorist acts of individual and mass violence, however, provided the central government with a pretext for passage of a constitutional amendment in 1988, the 59th, which imposed a state of emergency upon Punjab, removing all the civil liberties of the people and effectively placing the province under military control.

Despite numerous successes, therefore, in resolving some of the major problems threatening the unity of the Indian state since Independence, some of the problems that remain are so severe as to cast doubts on the ability of the central government under a centralized parliamentary system to maintain the unity of the country. Moreover, the remaining problems cannot be considered to be merely the unresolved remnants of old conflicts but reflect a fundamental structural tension in the Indian political system between forces seeking to strengthen further and centralize more decisively the Indian state and regional and other forces demanding further decentralization. The predominant tendencies since Independence have been towards pluralism, regionalism, decentralization, and interdependence between the Center and the states. The counter-tendencies, however, became quite strong during the period of Mrs. Gandhi's dominance of Indian politics and her efforts to centralize power and nationalize issues.

The centralizing and nationalizing measures taken by Mrs. Gandhi included the political destruction of the state political bosses, the selection of the chief ministers of the Congress-dominated states by Mrs. Gandhi herself in consultation with her small clique of advisers, the increased use of President's Rule in the states, the increased use of central police and intelligence forces to monitor and control regional opposition, populist, demagogic appeals to national categories of voters, such as the poor, the landless, and the minorities, and some manipulation of xenophobic and paranoiac nationalism against Pakistan and the American CIA. Since coming to power on a wave of sympathy and Hindu nationalism, Rajiv Gandhi has alternated between the policies and tactics of his grandfather and his mother. He came to power in an election campaign which went beyond even his mother's tactics in manipulating xenophobic nationalism and arousing Hindu nationalism. He then changed his stance to the non-confrontational, mediating posture of his father and sought peaceful and pluralist accommodations to resolve the unresolved problems of Punjab, Assam, and other regions of the country as well as those of India's neighbor, Sri Lanka. Although the Assam accord has so far remained effective in 1989, none of Rajiv Gandhi's other efforts have borne fruit and he has begun to revert to the more confrontational and xenophobic style of his mother, seeking to blame the problems of the country upon foreign forces, notably the U.S.A. and Pakistan.

The primary dangers in Mrs. Gandhi's strategy and its revival by Rajiv Gandhi lie in the collisions that inevitably result between these centralizing, nationalizing, and militantly nationalist tendencies and the predominant tendencies towards regionalism, pluralism, and decentralization. There are two possible strategies that the central government might use to avert these collisions which have become increasingly frequent and violent: reversion to the pluralist policies of the period of Nehru's dominance or a further drastic strengthening of the powers of the central government in an attempt to impose order upon India's diversity. The latter strategy, however, is more likely to lead to the transformation of regional forces into increasingly hostile, potentially secessionist elements threatening the disintegration of the country than to a true resolution of the underlying structural problems.

THE PROBLEMS OF ORDER, DISORDER, AND VIOLENCE

The previous two decades have been marked by a decline of authoritative institutions in Indian politics, of which the most threatening to the future stability and peace of the country have been the disintegration of the Congress organization, the ever-declining effectiveness of and the ever-increasing corruption of the bureaucracy, and the demoralization of the police and its direct involvement in the perpetration rather than control of violence.

The disintegration of the Congress is manifested particularly in four respects. First, the Congress was turned into a Nehru family patrimony by Mrs. Gandhi, dominated by her and a narrow personal and family clique. That patrimony was transmitted by what amounted to a form of dynastic succession to her son, Rajiv, whose style of rulership has increasingly come to resemble his mother's. Second, the old state party bosses were effectively destroyed by Mrs. Gandhi and no new generation of independent state leadership within the Congress has come up to replace them. There are primarily now dependents, sycophants, or corrupt politicans vying for the favor of the central leadership to maintain themselves in power rather than building political support bases in their states. Third, the Congress has disintegrated as a functioning organization. The party's formal institutions either do not exist any longer at the state and district level or they function only sporadically or at the call of the central leadership. Party organization elections are no longer held. Finally, despite the ability of Mrs. Gandhi and Rajiv to win parliamentary elections for the Congress through the force of their popular image, there have been major erosions of electoral support for the Congress in whole states and regions and among social groups within other states. The Congress is no longer the dominant party in the south, in West Bengal, Kashmir, Punjab, and Assam, though a recovery of its position cannot be ruled out in a few of these states.

The second great authoritative institution in the Indian political order at Independence was the bureaucracy, with the efficient and largely incorruptible ICS officers at its head. Since Independence, corruption in the bureaucracy has reached the highest levels of the IAS. Although many IAS officers remain honest and effective and present a facade of efficiency, intelligence, and honesty at the top of the administrative hierarchies in Delhi, the state capital, and the districts, there is a sharp break in the quality of personnel below the elite senior officers. Moreover, corruption below the elite levels has been institutionalized and affects virtually all departments such that no service can be expected as a right and virtually nothing can be done without payment.

The spread of police violence also has eroded public confidence in the legitimacy of state institutions and in the ability of the Indian state to fulfill the elemental function assigned to it by Hobbes of ensuring the basic security of the people from the fear of violent death. As with the IAS, the senior IPS officers in the district head-quarters and in the state capitals are often highly educated, efficient, and honest. At the local level, however, the police constables and station officers are uneducated and underpaid. For many, if not most, of them a police job is a way to make illegal income. Investigations and other police "work" are undertaken upon payment of money by private citizens. The victim of a crime has to pay to get his grievance attended to. "Suspects," often selected without serious evidence against them, have to pay to get released. The guilty also can pay to get released irrespective of the evidence against them.

Since everybody knows very well the methods of police work, people increasingly have taken the law into their own hands. This latter tendency is manifested in the increased display of guns by locally powerful persons, especially politicians, the increased use of violence against one's opponents in politics or otherwise, and the increased incidence of confrontations between police and people.

INDUSTRIALIZATION IN A PEASANT SOCIETY

Development policy changes

At Independence, though it was by no means a classical tropical economy, the Indian market economy was, nevertheless, oriented primarily to external markets, was weak in the capital goods industries, and agriculturally stagnant. Since Independence, there have been significant changes in the Indian economy in these and other respects. The dependence of Indian industry and agriculture on foreign trade has declined and both sectors have been oriented increasingly to the home market and towards inter-sectoral exchange between town and country. Foreign investment has declined as a proportion of total GNP. Indian agriculture has become a dynamic growth sector of the economy, with an average annual rate of growth of output of 3.5 percent.[2]

[2] Aditya Mukherjee and Mridula Mukherjee, "Imperialism and Growth of Indian Capitalism in Twentieth Century," *EPW*, xxiii, No. 11 (March 12, 1988), 536–538.

The major achievement of the early decades of planning has been the development of "a diversified capital goods sector."[3] However, in a high technology century, many of the machines installed in the industries in this sector in the 1960s are already obsolete. The central emphasis of the Government of India's economic development planning is now upon technological modernization of the Indian economy and the capital goods sector. Import restrictions have been reduced significantly in relation to items of technological importance to the modernization of Indian industry. The policy rubric under which these changes have been taking place is "liberalization" of the import and export control regime, which represents the most consistent set of policies of any sort followed by Rajiv Gandhi since his assumption of power in 1985.

A further force antagonistic to the Mahalanobis model of planning with its emphasis on the development of the capital goods industries in the public sector has been the enormous growth in the urban middle class, now estimated to comprise approximately 80 million people with the resources and desire to have a life style comparable to the middle class in the West, with its orientation towards consumer goods, including luxury consumer goods such as air conditioners, color television and video sets, and stereo systems.[4] It is now being argued, therefore, that the demand for consumer goods should be allowed to lead the rest of the economy and that restrictions on the development of the consumer goods industries, including luxury goods, should be reduced or eliminated.[5]

The changes in Indian economic development planning are being made without a comprehensive statement from the government, which has been introducing them bit by bit, through the announcement of measures to liberalize imports, through new emphases in the annual budget statements presented to Parliament, and through the inauguration of new "centrally-sponsored schemes." The Planning Commission as such, however, has ceased to provide a coherent, integrated statement of the goals and directions for the Indian economy, with detailed guidelines for their

[3] Ranjit Sau, "The Green Revolution and Industrial Growth in India: A Tale of Two Paradoxes and a Half," *EPW*, xxiii, No. 16 (April 16, 1988), 793.

[4] Bhabani Sen Gupta, "Crisis of the Indian State," *EPW*, xxiii, No. 16 (April 16, 1988), 765.

[5] Sau, "The Green Revolution and Industrial Growth in India," p. 791.

implementation. With the new measures for liberalization of the economy, "market forces" are playing an increasing role in "determining investment priorities, production and consumption patterns and income distribution."[6]

The second great success often claimed for the Indian economy since Independence is the "green revolution" in agriculture. However, it needs to be reiterated in the face of the tall claims often made for it that while the "green revolution" has transformed agriculture in a small region of the country and has had considerable effects on the cropping patterns and productivity in other parts of the country as well, it has merely kept pace with the food consumption needs of an ever-expanding population.[7]

There is talk now of introducing another "new agricultural strategy" to produce a "second green revolution."[8] The new strategy is being designed to extend the green revolution to other crops, particularly rice, maize, gram, and arhar, and other regions of the country, especially the eastern rice-producing states.[9]

The potential for a "second green revolution" in India is quite high. Even in the areas most affected by the first green revolution, there remains considerable potential for further increases in agricultural output through increased fertilizer applications and other means.[10] The potential of many of the so-called "backward districts" in eastern U. P. and Bihar and elsewhere, which were half a century ago ahead of the Western green revolution districts, has hardly been explored.

Neither the old nor the new mixture of primary development goals, however, promise solutions to the persisting problems of poverty, hunger, and malnutrition in the foreseeable future for "the mass of the poor" population of the country, urban and rural, who have become not only a burden but a stigma and an eyesore.[11] It is increasingly the policy of the government to project an international image in which India's poor have no place and to keep them away from foreign eyes by restricting the access of foreign scholars to the

[6] B.M., "Privatisation, Indian Style," *EPW*, xxii, No. 32 (August 8, 1987), 1,326.
[7] Sau, "The Green Revolution and Industrial Growth in India," p. 789.
[8] *EPW*, xiii, No. 12 (March 19, 1988), 560.
[9] Nilakantha Rath, "A Budget for Farmers!" *EPW*, xxiii, Nos. 14 & 15 (April 2–9, 1988), 739.
[10] Kirit S. Parikh, "A Development Strategy for the 1990s," *EPW*, xxiii, No. 12 (March 19, 1988), 598.
[11] Sen Gupta, "Crisis of the Indian State," p. 765.

countryside. Since, however, the rural population, including the poor, continue to comprise the bulk of the population and the votes in India's representative system, their problems and needs continue to obtrude into public view.

Not only do the rural population and the poor continue to comprise a majority of India's population, their numbers also continue to increase. The rate of growth of the Indian population has been between approximately 2.00 and 2.25 percent.[12] The majority of this ever-increasing population, whose numbers will reach a billion by the turn of the century, remains poor, illiterate, and without modern health care, and a substantial minority are malnourished as well.

The politicization of the peasantry

One of the arguments of this book is that the main responsibility for the development within India of an economy based on rural–urban disparities and gross inequalities in income and resource control has been the insistent drives of the Indian political leadership for equality with the advanced industrial countries, but an equality of the Indian state measured in terms of the output of iron and steel, the size of the GDP, possession of modern weaponry, and the assertion of regional hegemony. Since, however, the main intellectual critics and self-appointed watchdogs of the planning process in India have come primarily from the Marxist Left, who retain an unshakable faith in centrally-directed planning, huge public investments, and heavy industrialization, the failures of Indian economic development planning have been attributed to inequalities in society rather than to the inherent deficiencies of the approach itself. Despite the dominance of Nehru and of socialist thinking during this era of leadership and despite the Mahalanobis plans themselves, it is contended that the Indian bourgeoisie has established and extended its "ideological hegemony" in Indian society and that the recent changes in Indian development goals reflect their influence rather than the failures of the previous policies.

The second great enemy of the critics of Indian development

[12] Arun Ghosh, "The Plan versus Departmental Prerogatives," *EPW*, XXIII, Nos. 14 & 15 (April 2–9, 1988), 677, and V. M. Dandekar, "Population Front of India's Economic Development," *EPW*, XXIII, No. 17 (April 23, 1988), 837.

planning are the rich and middle peasant castes and classes. They are variously categorized as "kulaks" or "big peasants" or new "provincial rich." Evidence is marshalled to show the pervasive influence of this class as one member of either a triple (bourgeoisie-bureaucrats-rich farmers) or dual alliance (bourgeoisie-rich farmers).

Such evidence includes especially the setting of support prices for the procurement of foodgrains by the government, which the left critics invariably consider too high. It is noted that the state governments are generally dominated by the rich farmer lobbies and that their power is evidenced in such widespread state practices as the raising of procurement prices above the prices set by the central Agricultural Prices and Costs Commission (APCC)[13] or in practices such as that of Lok Dal chief minister Devi Lal in Haryana of writing off farmers' loans. Further evidence of the increasing power of the rich farmers is provided by the fact that the central government and Congress leaders have taken to vying with opposition state governments and even with rival Congress factions in adopting pro-farmer stances.[14]

The supporters of the old planning process use such evidences as these to identify this class even more than the capitalists as the chief "enemy of the masses." Some left critics even argue that the leaders of this rural class are not peasants at all, but a class of capitalist farmers or "provincial rich" leading even the rich peasantry, using caste to link them in turn with the "better-off sections of the peasantry" and recruiting "an army of foot soldiers from out of the middle peasantry to put down the poor."[15]

This left critique greatly exaggerates the influence of the rich and/or middle peasants in the Indian political order and misinterprets and maligns genuinely popular mass peasant movements. Despite the alleged inordinate influence of the rich peasants over policy, agriculture continues to be neglected in the plans.[16] The continuing neglect of agriculture in the plans, efforts to introduce

[13] B.M., "Government Helping Rich Farmers Profit from Drought," *EPW*, xxii, No. 44 (October 31, 1987), 1,848.
[14] *India Today*, March 15, 1988, p. 32 and April 15, 1988, p. 15.
[15] K. Balagopal, "An Ideology for the Provincial Propertied Class," *EPW*, xxii, No. 50 (December 12, 1987), 2,178.
[16] Rath, "A Budget for Farmers!", p. 739.

new agricultural strategies without providing adequate resources for the widespread and equitable dissemination of the new technologies associated with them, the inefficiencies and corruption associated with the distribution of new agricultural inputs and credit, and the like have contributed to a rising tide of disaffection among the most dynamic middle sectors of the peasantry and to their increasing politicization.

The strongest counter-argument to the Marxist attack on the undue influence of the "better-off" peasantry comes from the middle peasant farmers' movements themselves, which have acquired increasing prominence in recent years, notably in Maharashtra and western U. P. The very rise of such mass movements directed against state policies and which identify "urban capitalists and the state" as "the main exploiters" of the peasantry must lead one to wonder how its participants, even the "better-off" segments among them, can be members of a dominant class or of a dual alliance with the urban capitalists they are attacking. It also stretches the imagination to believe that hundreds of thousands of peasants can be mobilized to agitate for an increase in farm prices if the prices are already pegged high enough to provide secure and reasonable profits for them.

The most impressive peasant movement in 1988 in India was that led by Tikait, an ordinary Jat middle peasant from western U. P. who was clearly drawing upon the ideas and building upon the work of Chaudhury Charan Singh, who died in 1987. Tikait's demand was not simply for an arbitrary increase in farm prices but for "fair prices" for farm produce, measured in part at least in terms of a balance between the cost of inputs and the price of the produce. He also called for policy changes which would make available to the ordinary peasantry some of the opportunities and amenities of urban life, such as "improved educational facilities and more jobs for children of farmers" and for "narrowing the . . . gap between the standard of living in towns and villages" generally.[17]

The ruling Congress has adjusted to peasant discontent in several different ways in the different regional contexts of Indian politics. One adjustment has been to coopt through caste appeals segments of the rich and middle peasantry into the ruling coalition and to give

[17] *India Today*, February 29, 1988, pp. 5, 9, 36 and March 15, 1988, pp. 44–46.

them preferential access to the scarce resources made available in the countryside. A second strategy used especially in the north has been to squeeze the middle peasantry politically between the old landed elites and the rural poor, providing political access and differential economic benefits to the former and ameliorative economic benefits to the poor while ignoring the needs and demands of the middle peasantry of middle caste status. A third approach has been to build a ruling political coalition from below, based on the non-dominant backward castes, Scheduled Castes, minorities, and tribals, notably in Gujarat.

There is also a tradition of more radical and even violent insurrectionary movements among the poor peasants and agricultural laborers in modern India, but it has been argued above that such movements have been local, sporadic, and heavily concentrated among tribal peoples. Moreover, since the *garibi hatao* campaign of 1971, organization of the poor by opposition parties and radical movements has been partly preempted by government patronage measures. The latest efforts in this respect have been the loan *melas* (fairs), in which tens of millions of rupees in "loan" money are distributed in public places to persons from poor and disadvantaged groups.[18]

It remains true that such power and wealth as exists in the Indian countryside belongs to the land controlling castes. In some districts and localities in the country, particularly in north India, ex-landlords with extensive illegal holdings remain powerful and have even extended their sway politically over large segments of a district or even over an entire district. Where they are descendants of former princes or local rajas and especially where they maintain some of the traditions of local kingship by acting as the benefactors and protectors of the local populations, they draw upon traditional loyalties which cross both class and caste boundaries to a considerable extent.

The new "provincial rich," in contrast, are primarily interested in making money rather than in exercising a form of princely or semi-princely power. However, the opportunities available to the new rich class in the countryside with surplus profits to be invested are limited. Much of it, therefore, goes into politics and does provide a basis for the "provincial rich" to enter politics and to aggrandize

[18] *India Today*, January 15, 1988, p. 41 and April 15, 1988, p. 13.

themselves still further. Such politicians, however, are mostly in the Congress and are not the persons who lead the peasant movements condemned by the left.

The contradictory interests of the urban middle classes and the urban and rural poor

Policies which favor urban industrial development also tend to bring ever-increasing numbers of the poor and landless to the cities, who crowd into urban slums more degraded than any the world has ever before seen. These vast populations entering the cities intrude into their centers seeking any kind of living as domestic servants, rickshaw pullers, messengers, peddlers, and the like. They also "squat" in village-like settlements or on the pavements sleeping or selling or begging.

During the Emergency, an attempt was made by Sanjay Gandhi to break up the ugliest and most intrusive of such settlements and squatter's stalls. The inevitable violence which accompanied these efforts caused a considerable backlash, however, which contributed to the rising tide of resentment against the Emergency regime and the displacement of the Congress from power at the Center by an opposition coalition in 1977. A major effort to prevent further urban degradation by removing the poor is, therefore, unlikely to be made in the future as long as the electoral and competitive party system is retained.

The long-term political danger of a policy which caters increasingly to the urban consuming middle classes is that it may threaten the persistence of the parliamentary system itself in which the votes of the rural peasantry and the rural and urban poor continue to far outweigh those of the urban middle classes. It is necessary, therefore, to revise the traditional view of the urban middle classes as the main supporters of systems of political democracy. In developing countries, their expanding consumption demands can be met only by ignoring or repressing the needs of the majority.[19]

---

[19] The general argument here comes from Albert O. Hirshman, "The Turn to Authoritarianism in Latin America and the Search for its Economic Determinants," in D. Collier (ed.), *The New Authoritarianism in Latin America* (Princeton, NJ: Princeton University Press, 1979), p. 80. It is applied to India in Ranjit Sau, "The Green Revolution and Industrial Growth in India: A Tale of Two Paradoxes and a Half," *EPW*, XXIII, No. 16 (April 16, 1988), 792.

Centralized economic development and center–state relations

A further danger to the maintenance of a competitive parliamentary system is the potential strain on center–state relations and on the maintenance of local institutions of self-government which arises from the continued emphasis on centralized distribution of economic resources and centralized political control of the entire country. For example, despite the fact that one of the major long-term goals of centralized economic development planning has been to rectify regional economic imbalances, the latter have persisted and even become greater in some respects.

A further potential danger to center–state relations arises from the increasing use of the resources available to the Center for purposes of political patronage. Those resources include the distribution of food from the buffer stocks to food-deficit states, the siting of major centrally-sponsored schemes for agricultural development, and the location of public sector enterprises, among others.

The persistence of centralized economic control over the most dynamic segments of the economy and the ability of the central government to intervene in individual states or to deny them resources is an irritant in center–state relations, particularly in those which have been dominated for some time by non-Congress parties such as West Bengal or Andhra, among other states. Central projects may be granted to particular states when the Congress rather than the opposition is in power or may be sited even in districts within particular states to reward loyal local leaders who have produced Congress victories. The figures on resource distribution, therefore, may not show systematic discrimination for or against particular states, but their timing and precise location often has much to do with state and local political alignments.

As the state governments have come increasingly under central control and direction and the local Congress organizations have disintegrated, the Congress-controlled state governments have themselves become perpetual election machines, distributing patronage primarily with a view to consolidating the control of a political faction in the state government, whose performance is in turn judged by the central government solely by its leader's ability to influence the results of the next election and especially to prevent any major outbreaks such as caste wars in Gujarat, which would cause the Congress to lose political control over a state. As for local institutions of self government, the Congress-dominated state and central governments have deliberately dismantled these institutions or superseded them virtually everywhere because it is too difficult to control them and because they tend to fall into the hands of opposition leaders or even local Congress politicians or non-party persons who then use whatever patronage is available as *they* choose rather than as the central and state government leaders choose.

The Indian state and the armies of the discontented

The armies of the discontented continue to increase throughout the subcontinent. They include especially the middle peasants in the rural areas, to whom emphasis has been given in this volume. They also include especially students in urban areas seeking employment, who are concerned about their life chances, who express their fears and resentments in a variety of ethnic movements, and who play a considerable role in the initiation of violent agitations everywhere in South Asia. They include the urban poor crowded in slums whose numbers are increasing every year as municipal services continue to deteriorate.[20] They include also tribal groups and others in remote areas of the country who continue to be dispossessed of their lands without adequate compensation in the name of economic development.[21]

These groups are disparate, dispersed, and often unorganized. They will not coalesce into a movement which will overthrow the regime. Rather, it is more likely that regime leaders will find the endless task of appeasing them too distracting, will take further measures to restrict the functioning of what is left of the democratic political process, and will use increasingly the instruments of state oppression and violence against them in order to get on with the transcendent goal of building the Indian state.

PROSPECTS

Most scholarly observers of contemporary Indian politics agree that since Independence there has been a considerable decay in the

[20] *India Today*, January 31, 1988, p. 66.
[21] Satinath Sarangi and Ramesh Billorey, "The Nightmare Begins: Oustees of Indira Sagar Project," *EPW*, XXIII, No. 17 (April 23, 1988), 830.

functioning of political institutions and in their public legitimacy. From a comparative perspective, however, India's political institutions appear quite differently. Despite the evident decay over time within India, the performance of India's political institutions compare favorably in many respects with those of her neighbors or with most other post-colonial societies. Indeed, the Indian political regime is one of the most democratic in the world, by most conventional measures of political participation, electoral and party competition, and persistence of parliamentary institutions. It is also among the least repressive regimes in the world. With some exceptions such as the annihilation of Naxalites, terrorists, and those suspected or wrongly accused of being in those two categories, opposition politicians and students and others who engage in public demonstrations against the regime or the dominant party are not normally harassed or imprisoned without cause and are certainly not tortured. There is a free press and ordinary people are free to speak their minds in public and private.

It is sometimes argued that many of the deviations from accepted standards of parliamentary performance, bureaucratic probity, and police honesty which developing countries such as India have been undergoing are stages that every developing or modernizing country, including the United States and Great Britain, have undergone. This kind of argument, however, is a form of intellectual distortion. If conditions improve in a given society, one may say that the bad periods were a "stage," even a necessary stage in its development. However, conditions often do not improve in developing countries or take a long time in doing so and they can also get worse. One may equally speculate that India's recent political difficulties are a pre-fascist stage as a stage on the road to institutionalized democracy or republicanism. The point is that India's political system is unique and has to be described in its own terms and its future is uncertain.

Although the Indian political system shows signs of disintegration, it is unlikely that it will do so, at least not through secessionist movements. The Center and the army remain strong enough to resist any such attempts. Nor are there any foreign powers who are in a position to support secessionism in India or who stand to benefit from its disintegration. Pakistan or China might be happy to see such a disintegration but are in no position to support secessionist movements in India effectively. The United States and the Soviet Union clearly have no wish to do so and would most likely ignore such movements or would support the Government of India against such a threat supported by any other power.

The more immediate danger for India is the further spread of violence, lawlessness, and disorder at the local level. If such a spread continues, the Center may feel the necessity of a further assertion of its power and authority, possibly including another venture into authoritarian practices, which will have its own costs. Those costs, if the evidence from neighboring countries is any guide, would include a long-term threat of major violence from discontented segments of society, more insistent demands from the states for regional autonomy, and even the spread of terrorist movements to other groups in society and other states in the Union.

Alternative solutions, however, are available within India's traditions and political philosophies. They would include a move, which would be sanctioned by Gandhian ideas, towards greater decentralization of power to the states, districts, and villages of India, a return to the pluralist policies of the Nehru period, and major reforms of the bureaucracy and the police. Reform of the civil and police bureaucracies would require a complete transformation in patterns of recruitment, pay, and promotion to foster career orientations, work satisfaction, and incentives to resist corruption. The overall size of the civil bureaucracy might also be reduced for it is overstaffed, inefficient, and a great drain on the resources of the country.

It is possible that decentralization and a return to the pluralist policies of the Nehru period would slow down overall rates of economic growth and make even more difficult the formulation and implementation of desirable programs to accelerate industrial growth, increase agricultural productivity, and introduce further measures of social justice. However, the performance of India's public sector industries, the minimal direct public investment in agricultural research and extension, and the failures to promote social equality through efforts at economic and political centralization all argue for a dramatic change in both respects, rather than for a return to centralized planning or to heavy investment in public sector enterprises.

If decisive moves towards either further centralization and authoritarianism or decentralization and pluralism are not initiated, the future is likely to bring persisting social disorder and alternating periods of reassertion and decline of authority. It would be folly, however, to be sanguine about the future of India, to consider that the country is only going through a "stage" in its development, and to fail to recognize that a grave systemic crisis is in progress.

BIBLIOGRAPHY

INDIAN PUBLIC DOCUMENTS

Ministry of Agriculture. *Indian Agriculture in Brief*. Delhi: Controller of Publications, 1985.

Ministry of Agriculture. Directorate of Economics and Statistics. *Bulletin on Rice Statistics in India (District-Wise)*. Delhi: Controller of Publications, 1974.

Ministry of Agriculture and Irrigation. *Report of the National Commission on Agriculture, 1976*, Pt. 1: *Review and Progress*. Delhi: Controller of Publications, 1976.

Census of India, 1981, Series 1: *India*, Pt. 11-B (iii), *Primary Census Abstract: Scheduled Tribes*, by P. Padmanabha. Delhi: Controller of Publications, 1983.

Census of India, 1981, Series 1: *India*, Paper 3 of 1984: *Household Population by Religion of Head of Household*, by V. S. Verma. Delhi: Controller of Publications, 1985.

Census of India, 1971, Series 3: *Assam*, Pt. 1-A: *General Population*, by K. S. Dey. Delhi: Controller of Publications, 1979.

Census of India, 1971, Series 3: *Assam*, Pt. 11-C (ii): *Social and Cultural Tables*. Delhi: Controller of Publications, 1981.

Communal Riots and Minorities, unpublished, undated, mimeo report.

Economic Survey of Indian Agriculture, 1966–67.

Election Commission of India. *Report on the General Elections to the Legislative Assemblies of Andhra Pradesh, Assam, Haryana, Himachal Pradesh, Jammu & Kashmir, Karnataka, Kerala, Meghalaya, Nagaland, Tripura, West Bengal and Delhi (Metropolitican Council) 1982–83*, vol. 11: *Statistical*. Delhi: Controller of Publications, 1983.

Third Annual Report, 1985. Delhi: Controller of Publications, 1985.

Ministry of Finance (Economic Division). *Economic Survey, 1985–86*. Delhi: Controller of Publications, 1986.

Report of the Finance Commission, 1973. Delhi: Controller of Publications, 1973.

Ministry of Home Affairs. *Report, 1966–67*. New Delhi: Government of India Press, 1967.

Report, 1967–68. New Delhi: Government of India Press, 1968.

Report, 1982–83. New Delhi: Government of India Press, 1983.

Seventeenth Report of the Commissioner for Linguistic Minorities in India (For the period July 1974 to June 1975). Delhi: Controller of Publications, 1977.

BIBLIOGRAPHY

The Twenty-Third Report by the Deputy Commissioner for Linguistic Minorities in India, for the Period July 1982 to June 1983. Delhi: Controller of Publications, 1985.

Home Department. *Report of the States Reorganisation Commission, 1955.* New Delhi: Government of India Press, 1955.

Ministry of Information and Broadcasting. *Annual Report of the Registrar of Newspapers for India 1961,* I. Delhi: Manager of Publications, 1961.

Press in India, 1971, I. Delhi: Manager of Publications, 1971.

Press in India, 1981, I. Delhi: Controller of Publications, 1981.

Press in India, 1984. Delhi: Controller of Publications, 1986.

Planning Commission. *Report of Joint Study Team, Uttar Pradesh (Eastern Districts): Ghazipur, Azamgarh, Deoria, Jaunpur.* Delhi: Government of India Press, 1964.

The Seventh Five-Year Plan, 1985–90, Vol. I: *Perspectives, Objectives, Resources.* Delhi: Controller of Publications, 1985.

Planning Commission, *The Seventh Five-Year Plan, 1985–90,* Vol. II: *Sectoral Programmes of Development.* Delhi: Controller of Publications, 1985.

BOOKS, ARTICLES, AND DISSERTATIONS

A Correspondent. "The MGR Myth: An Appreciation," *EPW,* XXIII, Nos. 1 & 2 (January 2–9, 1988), 23–24.

Ahluwalia, Isher Judge. *Industrial Growth in India: Stagnation Since the Mid-Sixties.* Delhi: Oxford University Press, 1985.

Ahluwalia, Montek S. "Rural Poverty, Agricultural Production, and Prices: A Reexamination," in John W. Mellor and Gunvant M. Desai (eds.), *Agricultural Change and Rural Poverty: Variations on a Theme by Dharm Narain.* Delhi: Oxford University Press, 1986, pp. 59–75.

"Rural Poverty in India: 1956/57 to 1973/74," in Montek S. Ahluwalia *et al.,* *India: Occasional Papers,* World Bank Staff Working Paper No. 279. Washington, D.C.: World Bank, 1978.

Alavi, Hamza. "Peasants and Revolution," in Kathleen Gough and Hari P. Sharma (eds.), *Imperialism and Revolution in South Asia.* New York: Monthly Review Press, 1973, pp. 291–337.

Almond, Gabriel and G. Bingham Powell, Jr., *Comparative Politics: System, Process, and Policy.* 2nd edn. Boston: Little, Brown, 1978.

Amin, Shahid. "Gandhi as Mahatma: Gorakhpur District, Eastern UP, 1921–2," in Ranajit Guha (ed.), *Subaltern Studies III: Writings on South Asian History and Society.* Delhi: Oxford University Press, 1984, pp. 1–61.

Anderson, Robert and Walter Huber, *The Hour of the Fox: Tropical Forests, the World Bank, and Indigenous People in Central India.* Seattle: University of Washington Press, 1988.

Anonymous. "The Problem," in The Punjab Tangle, *Seminar,* 294 (February, 1984), 12–14.

Ansari, M. M. "Financing of the States' Plans: A Perspective for Regional Development," *EPW*, xviii, No. 49 (December 3, 1983), 2,077–2,082.

Antulay, A. R. "The Constitution, the Supreme Court and the Basic Structure," transcript of a talk broadcast in the Spotlight programme of All India Radio on October 28, 1976 by Shri A. R. Antulay, Member of Parliament.

Austin, Granville. *The Indian Constitution: Cornerstone of a Nation*. Oxford: Clarendon Press, 1966.

Azeem, Anwar. "Urdu – A Victim of Cultural Genocide?" in Zafar Imam (ed.), *Muslims in India*. New Delhi: Orient Longman, 1975, pp. 256–272.

B. M. "Sixth Plan in Limbo," *EPW*, xviii, No. 24 (June 11, 1983), 1,041–1,042.

"Catch-words for Seventh Plan," *EPW*, xix, No. 26 (June 30, 1984), 974–975.

"Selling the Seventh Plan," *EPW*, xix, No. 35 (September 1, 1984), 1,507–1,509.

"Policy-Frame for Seventh Plan," *EPW*, xx, No. 28 (July 13, 1985), 1,165–1,167.

"Making the Plan Irrelevant," *EPW*, xxi, No. 2 (January 11, 1986), 60–61.

"Privatisation, Indian Style," *EPW*, xxii, No. 32 (August 8, 1987), 1,325–1,327.

"Government Helping Rich Farmers Profit from Drought," *EPW*, xxii, No. 44 (October 31, 1987), 1,325–1,848.

Bailey, F. G. *Politics and Social Change: Orissa in 1959*. Berkeley: University of California Press, 1963.

Balagopal, K. "Congress (I) *vs* Telugu Desam Party: At Last a Lawful Means for Overthrowing a Lawfully Constituted Government," *EPW*, xxii, No. 41 (October 10, 1987), 1,736–1,738.

"An Ideology for the Provincial Propertied Class," *EPW*, xxii, No. 50 (December 12, 1987), 2,177–2,178.

"Meerut 1987: Reflections on an Inquiry," *EPW*, xxiii, No. 16 (April 16, 1988), 768–771.

Balasubramanyam, V. N. *The Economy of India*. London: Weidenfeld and Nicolson, 1984.

Bardhan, Pranab. "On Class Relations in Indian Agriculture: A Comment," *EPW*, xiv, No. 19 (May 12, 1979), 857–860.

The Political Economy of Development in India. Delhi: Oxford University Press, 1984.

"Dominant Proprietary Classes and India's Democracy," in Atul Kohli (ed.), *India's Democracy: An Analysis of Changing State–Society Relations*. Princeton, NJ: Princeton University Press, 1988.

Baruah, Sanjib. "Immigration, Ethnic Conflict, and Political Turmoil – Assam, 1979–1985," *Asian Survey*, xxvi, No. 11 (November, 1986), 1,184–1,206.

Bayley, David H. *The Police and Political Development in India*. Princeton, NJ: Princeton University Press, 1969.

"The Police and Political Order in India," *Asian Survey*, xxiii, No. 4 (April, 1983), 484–496.

Beller, Gerald E. "Benevolent Illusions in a Developing Society: The Assertion of Supreme Court Authority in Democratic India," *The Western Political Quarterly*, xxxvi, No. 4 (December, 1983), 513–532.

Bernard, Jean Alphonse. "A Maturation Crisis in India: The V. P. Singh Experiment," *Asian Survey*, xxvii, No. 4 (April, 1987), 408–426.

Bhasin, Prem. *Riding the Wave: The First Authentic Account of the Recent Struggle for Power in India*. New Delhi: Ashajanak Publications, 1972.

Bhat, L. S. *et al. Regional Inequalities in India: An Inter-State and Intra-State Analysis*. Papers presented at an all-India conference on Centre–State Relations and Regional Disparities in India at New Delhi in August, 1980. New Delhi: Society for the Study of Regional Disparities,1982.

Bhowmik, Sharit Kumar. "Tripura Elections and After," *EPW*, xxiii, No. 16 (April 16, 1988), 776–777.

"Development Perspectives for Tribals," *EPW*, xxiii, No. 20 (May 14, 1988), 1,005–1,007.

Bjorkman, James. "Public Law 480 and the Policies of Self-Help and Short-Tether: Indo-American Relations, 1965–68," in Lloyd I. Rudolph and Susanne H. Rudolph *et al.*, *The Regional Imperative*. Atlantic Highlands, NJ: Humanities Press, 1980, pp. 201–262.

Bouton, Marshall M. *Agrarian Radicalism in South India*. Princeton, NJ: Princeton University Press, 1985.

Brass, Paul R. *Factional Politics in an Indian State: The Congress Party in Uttar Pradesh*. Berkeley: University of California Press, 1965.

"The Politics of Ayurvedic Education: A Case Study of Revivalism and Modernization in India," in Susanne H. and Lloyd I. Rudolph, *Education and Politics in India*. Cambridge, MA: Harvard University Press, 1972.

"The Punjab Crisis and the Unity of India," in Atul Kohli (ed.), *India's Democracy: An Analysis of Changing State-Society Relations*. Princeton, NJ: Princeton University Press, 1988.

Language, Religion, and Politics in North India. London: Cambridge University Press, 1974.

"Class, Ethnic Group, and Party in Indian Politics," *World Politics*, xxxiii, No. 3 (April, 1981), 449–467.

"Pluralism, Regionalism, and Decentralizing Tendencies in Contemporary Indian Politics," in A. J. Wilson and Dennis Dalton (eds.) *The States of South Asia: Problems of National Integration*. London: C. Hurst, 1982, pp. 223–264.

Caste, Faction and Party in Indian Politics, Vol. i: *Faction and Party*. Delhi: Chanakya Publications, 1983.

"National Power and Local Politics in India: A Twenty-Year Perspective," *Modern Asian Studies*, xviii, No. 1 (February, 1984), 89–118.

Caste, Faction and Party in Indian Politics, Vol. ii: *Election Studies*. Delhi: Chanakya Publications, 1985.

Brass, Paul R. and Marcus F. Franda. *Radical Politics in South Asia*. Cambridge, MA: MIT Press, 1973.

Brecher, Michael, "Succession in India 1967: The Routinization of Political Change," *Asian Survey*, VII, No. 7 (July, 1967), 423–443.
Succession in India: A Study in Decision-Making. London: Oxford University Press, 1966.
Bryce, James. "Preface," in M. Ostrogorski, *Democracy and the Organization of Political Parties*, trans. by Frederick Clarke, Vol. 1. New York: Macmillan, 1922.
Byres, T. J. "The Dialectic of India's Green Revolution," *South Asian Review*, V, No. 2 (January 1972), 99–116.
"The Political Economy of Technological Innovation in Indian Agriculture," in Robert S. Anderson *et al.*, *Science, Politics, and the Agricultural Revolution in Asia*. Boulder, CO: Westview Press, 1982, pp. 19–75.
Calman, Leslie J. *Protest in Democratic India: Authority's Response to Challenge*. Boulder, CO: Westview, 1985.
Centre for Research in Rural and Industrial Development. Communal Violence and Its Impact on Development and National Inegration. Chandigarh: Mimeo, n.d.
Chatterjee, Partha. "Gandhi and the Critique of Civil Society," in Ranajit Guha (ed.), *Subaltern Studies III: Writings on South Asian History and Society*. Delhi: Oxford University Press, 1984, pp. 153–195.
Chatterji, Rakhahari. "Democracy and the Opposition in India," *EPW*, XXIII, No. 17 (April 23, 1988), 843–847.
Chaube, S. K. *Electoral Politics in Northeast India*. Madras: Universities Press, 1985.
Chopra, R. N. *Evolution of Food Policy in India*. Delhi: Macmillan, 1981.
Cohen, Stephen P. *The Indian Army: Its Contribution to the Development of a Nation*. Berkeley: University of California Press, 1971.
"The Military," in Henry C. Hart (ed.), *Indira Gandhi's India: A Political System Reappraised*. Boulder, CO: Westview Press, 1976, pp. 207–240.
"The Military and Indian Democracy," in Atul Kohli (ed.), *India's Democracy: An Analysis of Changing State–Society Relations*. Princeton, NJ: Princeton University Press, 1987, pp. 99–143.
Dandekar, V. M. "Unitary Elements in a Federal Constitution," *EPW*, XXII, No. 44 (October 31, 1987), 1,865–1,870.
"Indian Economy Since Independence," *EPW*, XXIII, Nos. 1 & 2 (January 2–9, 1988), 41–50.
"Population Front of India's Economic Development," *EPW*, XXIII, No. 17 (April 23, 1988), 837–842.
Dandekar, V. M. and N. Rath. "Poverty in India: Dimensions and Trends," *EPW*, VI, No. 1 (January 2, 1971), 25–48, and No. 2 (January 9, 1971), 106–146.
Das Gupta, Jyotirindra. "The Janata Phase: Reorganization and Redirection in Indian Politics," *Asian Survey*, XIX, No. 4 (April, 1979), 390–403.
Das, Arvind N. *Agrarian Unrest and Socio-Economic Change in Bihar, 1900–1980*. New Delhi: Manohar, 1983.

"Bihar: Landowners' Armies Take Over 'Law and Order'," *EPW*, xxi, No. 1 (January 4, 1986), 15–18.

Dasgupta, Biplab. *Agrarian Change and the New Technology in India.* Geneva: United Nations Research Institute for Social Development, 1977.

Dayal, Edison, "Regional Response to High Yield Varieties of Rice in India," *Singapore Journal of Tropical Geography*, iv, No. 2 (1983), 87–98.

Deka, K. N. "Assam: The Challenge of Political Integration and Congress Leadership," in Iqbal Narain (ed.), *State Politics in India.* Meerut: Meenakshi Prakashan, 1976, pp. 30–50.

Desai, A. R. (ed.). *Peasant Struggles in India.* Delhi: Oxford University Press, 1979.

Dhanagare, D. N. "Agrarian Reforms and Rural Development in India: Some Observations," offprint from *Research in Social Movements, Conflict and Change*, Vol. 7 (JAI Press, 1984), pp. 177–201.

Dua, Bhagwan D. "A Study in Executive–Judicial Conflict: The Indian Case," *Asian Survey*, xxiii, No. 4 (April, 1983), 463–483.

"Federalism or Patrimonialism: The Making and Unmaking of Chief Ministers in India," *Asian Survey*, xxv, No. 8 (August, 1985), 793–804.

Dutt, V. P. "The Emergency in India: Background and Rationale," *Asian Survey*, xvi, No. 12 (December, 1976), 1,124–1,138.

Engineer, Asghar Ali. "The Causes of Communal Riots in the Post-Partition Period in India," in Ashgar Ali Engineer (ed.), *Communal Riots in Post-Independence India.* Hyderabad: Sangam Books, 1984, pp. 33–41.

"Old Delhi in Grip of Communal Frenzy," *EPW*, xxii, No. 26 (June 27, 1987), 1,020–1,021.

Farmer, B. H. "The 'Green Revolution' in South Asian Ricefields: Environment and Production," *Journal of Development Studies*, xv (1979), 304–319.

"Perspectives on the 'Green Revolution' in South Asia," *Modern Asian Studies*, xx, No. 1 (February, 1986), 175–199.

Franda, Marcus F. *West Bengal and the Federalizing Process in India.* Princeton, NJ: Princeton University Press, 1968.

Radical Politics in West Bengal. Cambridge, MA: MIT Press, 1971.

Small is Politics: Organizational Alternatives in India's Rural Development. New Delhi: Wiley Eastern, 1979.

Frankel, Francine R. *India's Green Revolution: Economic Gains and Political Costs.* Princeton, NJ: Princeton University Press, 1971.

India's Political Economy, 1947–1977: The Gradual Revolution. Princeton, NJ: Princeton University Press, 1978.

Friedmann, Yohanan. "The Attitude of the *JAM'IYYAT-'ULAMA' – HIND* to the Indian National Movement and the Establishment of Pakistan," *Asian and African Studies*, vii (1971), 157–180.

Frykenberg, Robert Eric. "The Emergence of Modern 'Hinduism' as a Concept and as an Institution: A Reappraisal with Special Reference to South India," in Gunther Sontheimer and Herman Kulke (eds.), *Hinduism Reconsidered.* Heidelberg: South Asia Institute, 1988, pp. 1–29.

Gangal, S. C. *Prime Minister and the Cabinet in India*. New Delhi: Navachetna Prakashan, 1972.

Ghatak, Subrata. *Rural Money Markets in India*. Delhi: Macmillan, 1976.

Ghosh, Anjan. "Caste Idiom for Class Conflict: Case of Khanjawala," *EPW*, xiv, Nos. 5 and 6 (February 3–10, 1979), 184–186.

Ghosh, Arun. "The Plan versus Departmental Prerogatives," *EPW*, xxiii, Nos. 14 & 15 (April 2–9, 1988), 675–678.

Gill, Sucha Singh and K. C. Singhal. "The Punjab Problem: Its Historical Roots," *EPW*, xix, No. 14 (April 7, 1984), 603–608.

Goswami, Atul and Jayanta K. Gogoi. "Migration and Demographic Transformation of Assam: 1901–1971," in B. L. Abbi (ed.), *Northeast Region: Problems and Prospects of Development*. Chandigarh: Centre for Research in Rural and Industrial Development, 1984, pp. 60–80.

Gough, Kathleen. "Indian Peasant Uprisings," *Bulletin of Concerned Asian Scholars*, viii, No. 3 (July-September, 1976), 2–18.

Gould, Harold A. "A Sociological Perspective on the Eighth General Election in India," *Asian Survey*, xxvi, No. 6 (June, 1986), 630–652.

Graff, Violette. "La Jamaat-i-Islami en Inde," in Olivier Carré and Paul Dumont (eds.), *Radicalismes Islamiques*. Vol. ii. Paris: L'Harmattan, 1986, pp. 59–72.

"The Muslim Vote in the Indian General Election of December,1984," in Paul R. Brass and Francis Robinson (eds.), *The Indian National Congress and Indian Society, 1885–1985: Ideology, Social Structure and Political Dominance*. Delhi: Chanakya Publications, 1987.

Grewal, B. S. *Centre–State Financial Relations in India*. Patiala: Punjabi University, 1975.

Grierson, G. A. (ed.). Linguistic Survey of India, vol. i, pt. i: *Introductory*; vol. v, *Indo-Aryan Family, Eastern Group*, pt. ii: *Specimens of the Bihari and Oriya Languages*; vol. ix, *Indo-Aryan Family, Central Group*, pt. i: *Specimens of Western Hindi and Panjabi*. Delhi: Motilal Banarsidass, 1967–68.

Gujral, I. K. "The Sequence," in The Punjab Tangle, *Seminar*, 294 (February, 1984), 14–17.

Gupta, Dipankar. "The Communalising of Punjab, 1980–1985," *EPW*, xx, No. 28 (July 13, 1985), 1,185–1,190.

Hardgrave, Robert L., Jr. "The Congress in India – Crisis and Split," *Asian Survey*, x, No. 3 (March, 1970), 256–262.

"India in 1984: Confrontation, Assassination, and Succession," *Asian Survey*, xxv, No. 2 (February, 1985), 131–144.

Hardgrave, Robert L., Jr. and Stanley A. Kochanek. *India: Government and Politics in a Developing Nation*. 4th edn. San Diego: Harcourt Brace Jovanovich, 1986.

Hart, Henry C. "The Indian Constitution: Political Development and Decay," *Asian Survey*, xx, No. 4 (April, 1980), 428–451.

"Introduction," in Henry C. Hart (ed.), *Indira Gandhi's India: A Political System Reappraised*. Boulder, CO: Westview Press, 1976.

Hauser, Walter and Wendy Singer. "The Democratic Rite: Celebration and Participation in the Indian Elections," *Asian Survey*, xxvi, No. 9 (September, 1986), 941–958.

Heginbotham, Stanley J. *Cultures in Conflict: The Four Faces of Indian Bureaucracy*. New York: Columbia University Press, 1975.

Henderson, Michael. "Setting India's Democratic House in Order: Constitutional Amendments," *Asian Survey*, xix, No. 10 (October, 1979), 946–956.

Hirway, Indira. "Direct Attacks on Rural Poverty," review of *Direct Attack on Rural Poverty: Policy, Programmes and Implementation* by Prabhu Ghate (New Delhi: Concept Publishing Company, 1984), *EPW*, xxi, No. 1 (January 4, 1986), 22–23.

Huntington, Samuel P. *Political Order in Changing Societies*. New Haven: Yale University Press, 1968.

Hussain, Monirul. "Tribal Movement for Autonomous State in Assam," *EPW*, xxii, No. 32 (August 8, 1987), 1,329–1,332.

Jha, Prem Shankar. *India: A Political Economy of Stagnation*. Bombay: Oxford University Press, 1980.

Jones, Kenneth W. *Arya Dharm: Hindu-Consciousness in 19th-Century Punjab*. Berkeley: University of California Press, 1976.

Joshi, P. C. "Land Reform and Agrarian Change in India and Pakistan since 1947: I," *Journal of Peasant Studies*, I, No. 2 (January, 1974), 164–185.

Kamalakar, Jaya. "Ethnic Politics in Municipal Corporations," *EPW*, xxiii, No. 19 (May 7, 1988), 945–946.

Kamath, P. M. "Politics of Defection in India in the 1980s," *Asian Survey*, xxv, No. 10 (October, 1985), 1,039–1,054.

Kaur, Amarjit. "Akali Dal: The Enemy Within," in Amarjit Kaur *et al.*, *The Punjab Story*. New Delhi: Roli Books International, 1984, pp. 14–28.

Kochanek, Stanley A. "Post Nehru India: The Emergence of the New Leadership," *Asian Survey*, vi, No. 5 (May, 1966), 288–299.

The Congress Party of India: The Dynamics of One-Party Democracy. Princeton, NJ: Princeton University Press, 1968.

Business and Politics in India. Berkeley: University of California Press, 1974.

"Mrs. Gandhi's Pyramid: The New Congress," in Henry C. Hart (ed.), *Indira Gandhi's India: A Political System Reappraised*. Boulder, CO: Westview Press, 1976, pp. 93–124.

"The Politics of Regulation: Rajiv's New Mantras," *Journal of Commonwealth & Comparative Politics*, xxiii, No. 3 (November, 1985), 189–211.

"Regulation and Liberalization Theology in India," *Asian Survey*, xxvi, No. 12 (December, 1986), 1,284–1,308.

Kohli, Atul. "Democracy, Economic Growth, and Inequality in India's Development," *World Politics*, xxxii, No. 4 (July, 1980), 623–638.

"Parliamentary Communism and Agrarian Reform: The Evidence from India's Bengal," *Asian Survey*, xxiii, No. 7 (July, 1983), 783–809.

The State and Poverty in India: The Politics of Reform. Cambridge: Cambridge University Press, 1987.

Kothari, Rajni. "India: The Congress System on Trial," *Asian Survey*, VII, No. 2 (February, 1967), 83–96.

Krishna, Raj. "Growth, Investment and Poverty in Mid-Term Appraisal of Sixth Plan," *EPW*, XVII, No. 47 (November 19, 1983), 1,972–1,977.

Kulkarni, Sharad. "Forest Legislation and Tribals: Comments on Forest Policy Resolution," *EPW*, XXII, No. 50 (December 12, 1987), 2,143–2,148.

Kumar, Arun. "Punjab: Wages of Past Sins," *EPW*, XIX, No. 28 (July 14, 1984), 1,076–1,077.

Lakdawala, D. T. "Budget and the Plan," *EPW*, XVIII, No. 12 (March 19, 1983), 449–450.

"Eighth Finance Commission's Recommendations," *EPW*, XIX, No. 35 (September 1, 1984), 1,529–1,534.

LaPalombara, Joseph. "Penetration: A Crisis of Governmental Capacity," in Leonard Binder *et al.*, *Crises and Sequences in Political Development.* Princeton, NJ: Princeton University Press, 1971, pp. 205–232.

Lele, Jayant. *Elite Pluralism and Class Rule: Political Development in Maharashtra.* Bombay: Popular Prakashan, 1982.

Lipton, Michael. "The Technology, the System and the Poor: The Case of the New Cereal Varieties," offprint, Hague, Institute of Social Studies, 1977, pp. 121–135.

Why Poor People Stay Poor: A Study of Urban Bias in World Development. New Delhi: Heritage, 1980.

M.T. "The God that Died: The MGR Phenomenon," *EPW*, XXIII, Nos. 1 & 2 (January 2–9, 1988), 21–22.

Mahajan, O. P. "Balanced Regional Development: An Evaluation of Planning Strategy in India," in L. S. Bhat *et al. Regional Inequalities in India*, pp. 35–55.

Mahendra Dev, S. "Direction of Change in Performance of All Crops in Indian Agriculture in Late 1970s: A Look at the Level of Districts and Agro-Climatic Regions," *EPW*, XX, Nos. 51 & 52 (December 21–28, 1985), A-130–136.

Maheshwari, Shriram. *Rural Development in India: A Public Policy Approach.* New Delhi: Sage Publications, 1985.

Majumdar, Grace. "Trends in Inter-State Inequalities in Income and Expenditure in India," in L. S. Bhat *et al. Regional Inequalities in India*, pp. 24–34.

Malik, Harji. "A Punjab Report," *EPW*, XIX, No. 37 (September 15, 1984), 1,607–1,608.

Mehta, Asoka. *A Decade of Indian Politics, 1966–77.* New Delhi: S. Chand & Co., 1979.

Mellor, John W. *The New Economics of Growth: A Strategy for India and the Developing World.* Ithaca: Cornell University Press, 1976.

Mies, Maria. "The Shahada Movement: a Peasant Movement in Maharashtra (India) – its Development and its Perspectives," *Journal of Peasant Studies*, III, No. 4 (July, 1976), 472–482.

Minault, Gail. "Some Reflections on Islamic Revivalism vs. Assimilation Among Muslims in India," *Contributions to Indian Sociology*, XVIII, No. 2 (1984), 301–305.

Misra, B. B. *Government and Bureaucracy in India, 1947–1976.* Delhi: Oxford University Press, 1986.

Mitra, Subrata. "The Perils of Promoting Equality: The Latent Significance of the Anti-Reservation Movement in India," *Journal of Commonwealth and Comparative Politics*, XXV, No. 3 (November, 1987), 292–312.

Morris-Jones, W. H. *The Government and Politics of India.* London: Hutchinson University Library, 1964.

"India: Under New Management, Business as Usual," *Asian Survey*, V, No. 2 (February, 1965), 63–73.

"India: The Trial of Leadership," *Asian Survey*, VI, No. 2 (February, 1966), 67–75.

"India Elects for Change – and Stability," *Asian Survey*, XI, No. 8 (August, 1971), 719–741.

"India – More Questions Than Answers," *Asian Survey*, XXIV, No. 8 (August, 1984), 809–816.

Morrison, Barrie M. "The Persistent Rural Crisis in Asia: A Shift in Conception," *Pacific Affairs*, LII, No. 4 (Winter, 1979–80), 631–646.

Mukherjee, Aditya and Mridula Mukherjee. "Imperialism and Growth of Indian Capitalism in Twentieth Century," *EPW*, XXIII, No. 11 (March 12, 1988), 531–546.

Nambiar, K. V. "Criteria for Federal Resource Transfers," *EPW*, XVIII, No. 22 (May 28, 1983), 965–968. (Book reviews)

Nandy, Ashis. *At the Edge of Psychology: Essays in Politics and Culture.* Delhi: Oxford University Press, 1980.

Narain, Iqbal. "India 1977: From Promise to Disenchantment?" *Asian Survey*, XVIII, No. 2 (February, 1978), 103–116.

"India in 1985: Triumph of Democracy," *Asian Survey*, XXVI, No. 2 (February, 1986), 253–269.

Nayar, Baldev Raj. *The Modernisation Imperative and Indian Planning.* Delhi: Vikas, 1972.

Nicholson, Norman K. *Rural Development Policy in India: Elite Differentiation and the Decision Making Process.* DeKalb, Illinois: Center for Governmental Studies, Northern Illinois University, 1974.

Nishtar. "Time for a Political Initiative in Punjab," *EPW*, XXII, No. 41 (October 10, 1987), 1,731–1,732.

Noorani, A. G. "Amnesty Report in Meerut Killings," *EPW*, XXII, No. 50 (December 12, 1987), 2,139–2,140.

"Civil Liberties: Supreme Court and Punjab Crisis," *EPW*, XIX, No. 38 (September 22, 1984), 1,654.

Oldenburg, Philip. "Middlemen in Third-World Corruption: Implications of an Indian Case," *World Politics*, XXXIX, No. 4 (July, 1987), 508–535.

Omvedt, Gail and Chetna Galla. "Ideology for Provincial Propertied Class?" *EPW*, XXII, No. 45 (November 7, 1987), 1,925–1,926.

Paranjpe, H. K. "Centre–State Relations in Planning," in S. N. Jain *et al.*, *The Union and the States*. Delhi: National, 1972, pp. 207–241.

Parikh, Kirit S. "A Development Strategy for the 1990s," *EPW*, XXIII, No. 12 (March 19, 1988), 597–601.

Park, Richard. "Political Crisis in India, 1975," *Asian Survey*, XV, No. 11 (November, 1975), 996–1,013.

Patel, Sujata. "Legitimacy Crisis and Growing Authoritarianism," *EPW*, XXIII, No. 19 (May 7, 1988), 946–948.

Patel, Surendra J. "India's Regression in the World Economy," *EPW*, XX, No. 39 (September 28, 1985), 1,651–1,659.

Paul, Samuel. "Mid-Term Appraisal of the Sixth Plan: Why Poverty Alleviation Lags Behind," *EPW*, XIX, No. 18 (May 5, 1984), 760–766.

Pettigrew, Joyce. "Take Not Arms Against Thy Sovereign," *South Asia Research*, IX, No. 2 (November,1984), 102–123.

Potter, David C. *India's Political Administrators: 1919–1983*. Oxford: Clarendon Press,1986.

Prakasa, Sri. *State Governors in India*. Meerut: Meenakshi Prakashan, 1966.

Prasad, Pradhan H. "Poverty and Agricultural Development," *EPW*, XX. No. 50 (December 14, 1985), 2,221–2,224.

Presler, Franklin A. "Studying India's Political Culture," *Journal of Commonwealth & Comparative Politics*, XXII, No. 3 (November,1984), 224–234.

Pylee, M. V. *Constitutional Government in India*. New York: Asia Publishing House, 1965.

Ram, Mohan. "The Communist Movement in Andhra," in Paul R. Brass and Marcus Franda (eds.), *Radical Politics in South Asia*. Cambridge, MA: MIT Press, 1973.

"The Communist Movement in India," in Gough, *Imperialism and Revolution in South Asia*. New York: Monthly Review Press, 1973.

Ram Reddy, G. and G. Haragopal. "The Pyraveekar: 'The Fixer' in Rural India," *Asian Survey*, XXV, No. 11 (November, 1985), 1,148–1,162.

Rath, Nilakantha. " 'Garibi Hatao': Can IRDP Do It?" *EPW*, XX, No. 6 (February 9, 1985), 238–246.

"A Budget for Farmers!" *EPW*, XXIII, Nos. 14 & 15 (April 2–9, 1988), 739–744.

Ray, Amal and Jayalakshmi Kumpatla. "Zilla Parishad Presidents in Karnataka: Their Social Background and Implications for Development," *EPW*, XXII, Nos. 42 & 43 (October 17–24, 1987), 1,825–1,830.

Robinson, Francis. "Islam and Muslim Society in South Asia: A Reply to Das and Minault," *Contributions to Indian Sociology*, XX, No. 1 (January–June, 1986), 97–104.

Rosenthal, Donald B. *The Expansive Elite: District Politics and State Policy-Making in India*. Berkeley: University of California Press, 1977.

Roy, Ajit. "Darjeeling: Hopeful Turn and Remaining Obstacles," *EPW*, XXIII, No. 30 (July 23, 1988), 1,511.

Roy, K. C. and A. L. Lougheed. "The Green Revolution in India: Progress and Problems," *World Review*, XVI, No. 2 (July, 1977), 16–27.

Rubin, Barnett R. "The Civil Liberties Movement in India: New Approaches to the State and Social Change," *Asian Survey*, XXVII, No. 3 (March 1987), 371–392.

Rudolph, Lloyd I. and Susanne H. Rudolph. *In Pursuit of Lakshmi: The Political Economy of the Indian State*. Chicago: University of Chicago Press, 1987.

Rudra, Ashok. "Political Economy of Indian Non-Development," review of *The Political Economy of Development in India* by Pranab Bardhan, *EPW*, XX, No. 21 (May 25, 1985), 914–916.

Sarangi, Satinath and Ramesh Billorey. "The Nightmare Begins: Oustees of Indira Sagar Project," *EPW*, XXIII, No. 17 (April 23, 1988), 838.

Sarkar, Sumit. *Modern India: 1885–1947*. Madras: Macmillan, 1983.

Sau, Ranjit. "The Green Revolution and Industrial Growth in India: A Tale of Two Paradoxes and a Half," *EPW*, XXIII, No. 16 (April 16, 1988), 789–796.

Saxena, N. C. "Caste and Zamindari Abolition in U. P.," *Mainstream* (June 15, 1985), 15–19.

Schlesinger, Lee I. "Agriculture and Community in Maharashtra, India," in George Dalton (ed.), *Research in Economic Anthropology*. JAI Press, 1981, IV, pp. 233–274.

Sen, Amartya. "Poverty, Inequality, Unemployment: Some Conceptual Issues in Measurement," *EPW*, VIII, Special Number (August, 1973).

Sen Gupta, Bhabani. "Communism Further Divided," in Henry C. Hart (ed.), *Indira Gandhi's India: A Political System Reappraised*. Boulder, CO: Westview Press, 1976, pp. 153–180.

"The Fourth Year," *EPW*, XXII, No. 50 (December 12, 1987), 2,135–2,136.

"Crisis of the Indian State," *EPW*, XXIII, No. 16 (April 16, 1988), 764–766.

Sengupta, Barun. *Last Days of the Morarji Raj*. Calcutta: Ananda Publishers, 1979.

Sethi, J. D. "Secularism, Communalism and Nationalism," in Amrik Singh (ed.), *Punjab in Indian Politics: Issues and Trends*. Delhi: Ajanta Books, 1985, pp. 434–446.

Shah, Ghanshyam. "Grass-Roots Mobilization in Indian Poliltics," in Atul Kohli (ed.), *India's Democracy: An Analysis of Changing State-Society Relations*. Princeton, NJ: Princeton University Press, 1988, pp. 263–304.

Singh, B. P. "North-East India: Demography, Culture and Identity Crisis," *Modern Asian Studies*, XXI, No. 2 (1987), 257–282.

Singh, Charan. *Joint-Farming X-Rayed: The Problem and its Solution*. Bombay: Bharatiya Vidya Bhavan, 1959.

Economic Nightmare of India: Its Cause and Cure. New Delhi: National, 1981.

Singh, Iqbal. *Punjab under Siege: A Critical Analysis*. New York: Allen, McMillan and Enderson, 1986.

Singh, Pritam. "Punjab: Lessons of Panchayat Elections," *EPW*, XVIII, No. 43 (October 22, 1983), 1,822–1,823.

"Akali Agitation: Growing Separatist Trend," *EPW*, XIX, No. 5 (February 4, 1984), 195–196.

Singh, Rajendra. "Agrarian Social Structure and Peasant Unrest: A Study of Land-Grab Movement in District Basti, East U.P.," *Sociological Bulletin*, XXIII, No. 1 (March, 1974), 44–70.

Singh, V. B. and Shankar Bose. *Elections in India: Data Handbook on Lok Sabha Elections, 1952–85*, 2nd edn. New Delhi: Sage Publications, 1984.

State Elections in India: Data Handbook on Vidhan Sabha Elections, 1952–85, vols. I, II, III, IV – Pt. ii and v. New Delhi: Sage Publications, 1987–88.

Sinha, Arun. "Bihar: Bajitpur: Landlord's Violence," *EPW*, XIII, No. 50 (December 16, 1978), 2,031–2,032.

"Recurrent Pattern of Jharkhand Politics," *EPW*, XXII, No. 45 (November 7, 1987), 1,887–1,889.

Sisson, Richard. "Prime Ministerial Power and the Selection of Ministers in India: Three Decades of Change," *International Political Science Review*, II, No. 2 (1981), 137–157.

Srivastava, Arun. "Landlords' Mafias in Bhojpur," *EPW*, XVI, Nos. 1 and 2 (January 3–10, 1981), 17–18.

Stokes, Eric. *The Peasant and the Raj*. Cambridge: Cambridge University Press, 1978.

Subba Reddy, N. "Depriving Tribals of Land: Andhra Move to Amend Land Transfer Laws," *EPW*, XXIII, No. 29 (July 16, 1988), 1,458–1,461.

Tandon, Prakash. "Another Angle," *Seminar*, 294 (February, 1984), 35–37.

Taub, Richard P. *Bureaucrats Under Stress: Administrators and Administration in an Indian State*. Berkeley: University of California Press, 1969.

Thakur, Ramesh C. "The Fate of India's Parliamentary Democracy," *Pacific Affairs*, XLIX, No. 2 (Summer, 1976), 263–293.

Thimmaiah, G. and Abdul Aziz. "The Political Economy of Land Reforms in Karnataka, a South Indian State," *Asian Survey*, XXIII, No. 7 (July, 1983), 810–829.

Toye, John. *Public Expenditure and Indian Development Policy: 1960–1970*. Cambridge: Cambridge University Press, 1981.

Tummala, Krishna K. "Democracy Triumphant in India: The Case of Andhra Pradesh," *Asian Survey*, XXVI, No. 3 (March 1986), 378–395.

Wade, Robert. "The System of Administrative and Political Corruption: Canal Irrigation in South India," *Journal of Development Studies*, XVIII, No. 3 (April, 1982), 287–328.

"The Market for Public Office: Why the Indian State Is Not Better at Development," *World Development*, XIII, No. 4 (April, 1985), 467–497.

Wariavwalla, Bharat. "India in 1987: Democracy on Trial," *Asian Survey*, XXVIII, No. 2 (February, 1988), 119–125.

Weiner, Myron. "India's Two Political Cultures," in Myron Weiner, *Political Change in South Asia*. Calcutta: Firma K. L. Mukhapadhyay, 1963.

"Political Participation: Crisis of the Political Process," in Leonard Binder *et al.*, *Crises and Sequences in Political Development*. Princeton, NJ: Princeton University Press, 1971, pp. 159–204.

"India's New Political Institutions," *Asian Survey*, XVI, No. 9 (September, 1976), 898–901.

India at the Polls: The Parliamentary Elections of 1977. Washington, DC: American Enterprise Institute, 1978.

Sons of the Soil: Migration and Ethnic Conflict in India. Princeton, NJ: Princeton University Press, 1978.

"Congress Restored: Continuities and Discontinuities in Indian Politics," *Asian Survey*, XXII, No. 4 (April, 1982), 339–355.

India at the Polls, 1980: A Study of the Parliamentary Elections. Washington, DC: American Enterprise Institute, 1983.

"The Political Consequences of Preferential Policies: A Comparative Perspective," *Comparative Politics*, XVI, No. 1 (October, 1983), 35–52.

"Ancient Indian Political Theory and Contemporary Indian Politics," in S. N. Eisenstadt *et. at.*, *Orthodoxy, Heterodoxy and Dissent in India*. Berlin: Mouton, 1984, pp. 111–130.

"The Political Economy of Industrial Growth in India," *World Politics*, XXXVIII, No. 4 (July, 1986), 596–610.

"Rajiv Gandhi: A Mid-Term Assessment," in Marshall M. Bouton (ed.), *India Briefing, 1987*. Boulder, CO: Westview Press, 1987, pp. 1–23.

Weiner, Myron and Mary F. Katzenstein. *India's Preferential Policies: Migrants, the Middle Classes, and Ethnic Equality*. Chicago: University of Chicago Press, 1981.

Wood, John R. "Extra-Parliamentary Opposition in India: An Analysis of Populist Agitations in Gujarat and Bihar," *Pacific Affairs*, XLVIII, No. 3 (Fall, 1975), 313–334.

Wood, John R. (ed.). *State Politics in Contemporary India: Crisis or Continuity?* Boulder, CO: Westview Press, 1984.

World Bank. *World Development Report 1984*. New York: Oxford University Press, 1984.

NEWSPAPERS AND PERIODICALS

Asian Recorder
Congress Bulletin
Economic and Political Weekly (EPW)
India Today
Mainstream
Muslim India
Seminar

UNPUBLISHED PAPERS AND DOCUMENTS

Duncan, Ian. Party Politics and the North Indian Peasantry: The Rise of the

Bharatiya Kranti Dal in Uttar Pradesh. School of African and Asian Studies, University of Sussex, 1987.

Krishna, Gopal. The Problem of Integration in the Indian Political Community – Muslim Minority and the Political Process. No date.

Spodek, Howard. From Gandhi to Violence: Ahmedabad's 1985 Riots in Historical Perspective. 1987.

UCLA Conference on Parties & Elections, June, 1987

Baviskar, B. S. Factional Conflict and the Congress Dilemma in Rural Maharashtra (1952–75).

Blair, Harry W. Electoral Support and Party Institutionalization in Bihar: Congress and the Opposition, 1977–1985.

Bose, Pradip Kumar. The Congress and the Tribal Communities in India.

Dua, Bhagwan D. India: Federal Leadership and the Secessionist Movements on the Periphery.

Mitra, Subrata. Political Integration and Party Competition in Madhya Pradesh: Congress and the Opposition in Parliamentary Elections, 1977–1984.

Shah, Ghanshyam. Strategies of Social Engineering: Reservation and Mobility of Backward Communities in Gujarat.

Singh, Ranbir. Pattern of Support Base of Congress Party in Haryana.

Vakil, F. D. Patterns of Electoral Performance in Andhra Pradesh and Karnataka.

Wood, John R. Reservations in Doubt: The Backlash Against Affirmative Action in Gujarat, India.

INDEX

THE NEW CAMBRIDGE HISTORY OF INDIA